Systematic Theology

VOLUME III

- SOTERIOLOGY -

By

LEWIS SPERRY CHAFER, D.D., Litt.D., Th.D.

President and Professor of Systematic Theology
Dallas Theological Seminary

PUBLISHED BY

DALLAS SEMINARY PRESS

DALLAS, TEXAS

First Printing, March, 1948, 2,500
Second Printing, November, 1948, 2,500
Third Printing, May, 1950, 2,500
Fourth Printing, December, 1953, 2,500
Fifth Printing, October, 1957, 2,500
Sixth Printing, January, 1962, 2,500
Seventh Printing, October, 1964, 2,500
Eighth Printing, October, 1967, 3,000
Ninth Printing, December, 1969, 3,000
Tenth Printing, May, 1971, 3,000
Eleventh Printing, October, 1973, 3,000
Twelfth Printing, August, 1974, 5,000
Thirteenth Printing, June, 1976, 5,000

PRINTED IN THE UNITED STATES OF AMERICA
BY THE VAIL-BALLOU PRESS, INC., BINGHAMTON, N. Y.

TABLE OF CONTENTS

SOTERIOLOGY

THE SAVIOR

DIVINE ELECTION

THE SAVING WORK OF THE TRIUNE GOD

THE ETERNAL SECURITY OF THE BELIEVER

THE TERMS OF SALVATION

SOTERIOLOGY

SOTERIOLOGY

CHAPTER I

INTRODUCTION TO SOTERIOLOGY

SOTERIOLOGY is that portion of Systematic Theology which treats of salvation. The word *salvation* is a translation of the Greek word σωτηρία (cf. σώζω and σωτήριος), and is derived immediately from the word σωτήρ which means *Savior*. Σωτηρία appears forty-five times in the New Testament. Forty times it is translated *salvation,* once it is translated *deliver* (Acts 7:25), once *health* (Acts 27:34), once *saving* (Heb. 11:7), and twice *saved* (Luke 1:71; Rom. 10:1).

In comparison with that which obtains in the New Testament, the Old Testament doctrine of salvation is more involved, largely because of that which enters into all Old Testament revelation, namely, the progress of doctrine. This progression may well be stated in the words of Christ: "First the blade, then the ear, after that the full corn in the ear" (Mark 4:28). It appears that, in the Old Testament, the English word *salvation* presents a latitude of meaning ranging from deliverance from enemies to right relations with God. Deuteronomy 28:1–14 describes the desired estate of an Israelite in the land, and to him salvation consisted largely in deliverance from all that might hinder those blessings. Such, indeed, were the benefits which Jehovah Himself held before His people. A still greater hope was ever before Israel of a spiritual triumph in their yet future covenanted kingdom. In reference to their estate in that kingdom it is written:

"And the LORD thy God will bring thee into the land which thy fathers possessed, and thou shalt possess it; and he will do thee good, and multiply thee above thy fathers. And the LORD thy God will circumcise thine heart, and the heart of thy seed, to love the LORD thy God with all thine heart, and with all thy soul, that thou mayest live" (Deut. 30:5–6); "But this shall be the covenant that I will make with the house of Israel; After those days, saith the LORD, I will put my law in their inward parts, and write it in their hearts; and will be their God, and they shall be my people. And they shall teach no more every man his neighbour, and every man his brother, saying, Know the LORD: for they shall all know me, from the least of them unto the greatest of them,

3

saith the LORD: for I will forgive their iniquity, and I will remember their sin no more" (Jer. 31:33–34); "For I will take you from among the heathen, and gather you out of all countries, and will bring you into your own land. Then will I sprinkle clean water upon you, and ye shall be clean: from all your filthiness, and from all your idols, will I cleanse you. A new heart also will I give you, and a new spirit will I put within you: and I will take away the stony heart out of your flesh, and I will give you an heart of flesh. And I will put my spirit within you, and cause you to walk in my statutes, and ye shall keep my judgments, and do them. And ye shall dwell in the land that I gave to your fathers; and ye shall be my people, and I will be your God" (Ezek. 36:24–28); "And so all Israel shall be saved: as it is written, There shall come out of Sion the Deliverer, and shall turn away ungodliness from Jacob: for this is my covenant unto them, when I shall take away their sins" (Rom. 11:26–27).

These Scriptures, which represent a very large array of similar promises, speak of the nation as a whole, and predict restoration and salvation of that people according to Jehovah's eternal purpose. Over against this national expectation were the issues involved in the relation which the individual sustained to God, which reality was a matter wholly independent of those great promises which secure the salvation of the nation.

Abraham begat seed by Hagar, by Sarah, and by Keturah; but only "in Isaac [Sarah's son] shall thy seed be called" (Rom. 9:7). And, again, the election of God for the nation of promise determines that, of the sons of Israel, "the elder shall serve the younger" (Rom. 9:12; cf. Isa. 60:12), and only through Jacob shall the national covenants be realized. Of the seed of Jacob, though as a nation they are preserved in their solidarity and entity and "though the number of the children of Israel be as the sand of the sea, a remnant shall be saved" (Rom. 9:27); a remnant who as individuals were in right relation to God appeared in every generation. To this group the Apostle refers when he says, "For they are not all Israel, which are of Israel" (Rom. 9:6), and it is of this spiritual Israel that he also speaks when he declares, "And so all Israel shall be saved" (Rom. 11:26). Thus the final outworking of the divine purpose in behalf of the people to whom the earthly covenants belong, and whose destiny is that of the earth (cf. Matt. 5:5), is consummated both with respect to the elect nation and the fulfilling of the hope for each individual Israelite whose life was lived in the particular time when distinctive Jewish promises obtained. The present age must ever be seen in its exceptional character, namely, that there is now no difference between Jew and Gentile either with regard to their lost estate or their need of salvation by grace (Rom. 3:9), and no difference with regard to the terms upon which they may be saved (Rom. 10:12; cf. Acts 15:9). The distinctive doctrines of Judaism must be discerned as such, both with reference to their character and with reference to the dispensation in which they are in force. For want of specific revelation, the salvation of the individual under Judaism—with regard to terms, time, and general character—is obscure to men.

With respect to the meaning of the word *salvation,* the Old and New Testaments are much alike. The word communicates the thought of deliverance, safety, preservation, soundness, restoration, and healing; but though so wide a range of human experience is expressed by the word *salvation,* its specific, major use is to denote a work of God in behalf of man. When thus employed, it represents what is evidently the most comprehensive one doctrine of the Bible. It gathers into one conception at least twelve extensive and vital doctrines, namely, redemption, reconciliation, propitiation, conviction, repentance, faith, regeneration, forgiveness, justification, sanctification, preservation, and glorification.

It may be observed, also, that two fundamental ideas inhere in the meaning of the word *salvation:* on the one hand, to be saved is to be rescued from a lost estate, while, on the other hand, to be saved is to be brought into a saved estate, vitally renewed, and made meet to be a partaker of the inheritance of the saints in light. Gospel preaching may follow either of these conceptions. It may warn the wicked to flee from the wrath to come, or it may woo them by the contemplation of those benefits which God's infinite grace provides. The undesirable estate from which God's salvation would rescue men has been partially defined in previous portions of this work. Under satanology it was pointed out that unregenerate men are under the power of Satan, being energized by him, and that only the deliverance of God which translates out of the power of darkness into the kingdom of the Son of His love (Col. 1:13) can avail. Likewise, in both Anthropology and hamartiology it has been demonstrated that man is born of a fallen race, condemned because of his participation in Adam's sin, doomed because of the fact that he has only a fallen nature, judged as one who is under sin, and guilty before God because of his personal sins. It is also asserted that divine salvation is from the curse of the law (Gal. 3:13), from wrath (1 Thess. 5:9; John 3:36), from death (2 Cor. 7:10), and from destruction (2 Thess. 1:9). On the other hand, divine salvation provides a dismissal and removal of every charge against the sinner and equips him with eternal life in place of death, with the perfect merit of Christ in place of condemnation, and with forgiveness and justification in place of wrath.

In its broadest significance, the doctrine of salvation includes every divine undertaking for the believer from his deliverance out of the lost estate to his final presentation in glory conformed to the image of Christ. Since the divine objective is thus all-inclusive, the theme is divided naturally into three tenses: (a) The Christian *was* saved when he believed (Luke 7:50; Acts 16:30–31; 1 Cor. 1:18; 2 Cor. 2:15; Eph. 2:8, R.V.; 2 Tim. 1:9). This past-tense aspect of it is the essential and unchanging fact of salvation. At the moment of believing, the saved one is completely delivered from his lost estate, cleansed, forgiven, justified, born of God, clothed in the merit of Christ, freed from all condemnation, and safe for evermore. (b) The believer is *being* saved from the dominion of sin (Rom. 6:1–14; 8:2; 2 Cor. 3:18; Gal. 2:20; 4:19; Phil. 1:19; 2:12; 2 Thess. 2:13). In this second tense of salvation the believer is being divinely preserved and sanctified. (c) The believer is *yet* to be saved from the presence of sin when presented faultless in glory (Rom. 13:11; 1 Thess. 5:8; Heb. 1:14; 9:28; 1 Pet. 1:3–5; 1 John 3:1–3). To this may be added other passages which, each in turn, present all three tenses or aspects of salvation—1 Corinthians 1:30; Philippians 1:6; Ephesians 5:25–27; 1 Thessalonians 1:9–10; Titus 2:11–13.

Similarly, no greater fact regarding divine salvation can be declared than is asserted in Jonah 2:9 (R.V.), "Salvation is of Jehovah," and in Psalm 3:8 (R.V.), "Salvation belongeth unto Jehovah." The truth that salvation is of Jehovah is sustained both by revelation and by reason. As for revelation, it is the testimony of the Scriptures, without exception, that every feature of man's salvation from its inception to the final perfection in heaven is a work of God for man and not a work of man for God. As for reason, there need be but a moment's consideration of the supernatural character of every step in this great achievement to discover that man could contribute nothing whatsoever to its realization. That every step is by faith is a necessity since man, having no power to effect a supernatural result, must be cast back in faith upon Another who is able. These obvious truths may be viewed from two different angles: (a) What may be termed the *legal* aspect of the problem of the salvation of a sinful being is one of satisfying those unyielding and infinitely holy demands of divine righteousness and divine government which are outraged by sin in its every form. No man can make an atonement for his soul and thus save himself. The penalty for his sinful condition requires so great a judgment that, in the end, were he to pay it, there would be nothing left to save. Over against this, is the truth that God has wrought in the substitutionary death of His Son to the end that the penalty is paid. This becomes the only hope for man, but the attitude of dependence upon Another, as a principle, is far removed from man's own effort to save himself. (b) What may be termed the *practical* aspect of the problem of the salvation of a sinful being is seen in the character of all that enters into the estate of the saved. No one under any circumstances could forgive his own sin, impart eternal life to himself, clothe himself in the righteousness of God, or write his name in heaven. Thus it is concluded that no more obvious truth will be found on the sacred pages than this, that "salvation is of Jehovah." Not only is all that enters into salvation in its first tense wrought by God instantly, in response to that simple faith which trusts Him for it, on the ground of the confidence that He is able to save righteously only through the death of His Son, but God is revealed to the sinner as One who desires to save with an infinite longing. He that spared not His own Son but delivered Him up for us all, could hardly demonstrate more fully His passion to save the lost.

The greatest of all motives which actuates God in the exercise of His saving grace is the satisfying of His own infinite love for those ruined by sin. In this may be seen the truth that the salvation of a soul means infinitely more to God than it could ever mean to the one who is saved, regardless of the glorious realities which constitute that salvation. But, in addition to the satisfying of infinite love, three other divine motives in the salvation of the lost are disclosed: (a) It is written, "For by grace are ye saved through faith; and that not of yourselves: it is the gift of God: not of works, lest any man should boast. For we are his workmanship, created in Christ Jesus unto good works, which God hath before ordained that we should walk in them" (Eph. 2:8–10). Most emphatic is the truth thus declared, that salvation is a divine undertaking on the basis of pure grace in which no human works or merit may enter. This salvation is *unto* good works, it is never *by* good works; and it is *unto* such good works as are foreordained of God. (b) In like manner, it is declared that God is motivated in His salvation of men by the advantage which their salvation will be to them. John 3:16 states: "For God so loved the world, that he gave his only begotten Son, that whosoever believeth in him should not perish, but have everlasting life." It is clearly asserted in this familiar text that a twofold benefit accrues to all who believe on Christ—they do not perish and they do receive everlasting life. These advantages are immeasurably great both in their intrinsic value and in their endless duration. The question may be asked whether there could be any higher actuating motive on the part of God in man's salvation than the benefit man receives from it. There is an objective in God's exercise of His saving grace which is far more a reality to God than either good works or man's own benefit. It is (c) the fact that man's salvation is by divine grace to the end that the grace of God may have an adequate manifestation. Of this truth it is recorded, "that in the ages to come he might shew the exceeding riches of his grace in his kindness toward us through Christ Jesus" (Eph. 2:7). There was that in God which no angel had ever seen. They had observed His wisdom and power displayed in the creation and upholding of all things. They had beheld His glory, but they had not seen His grace. There could be no manifestation of divine grace until there were sinful creatures who were objects of grace. The importance, in heavenly realms, of the unveiling of infinite grace could not be estimated in this world. There was no complete exhibition of divine love until God gave His Son to die for lost men. The momentousness of that demonstration is also beyond human understanding. In like manner, there could be no complete exhibition of divine grace until sinners were saved through the death of God's Son, and the measure of that grace is also beyond finite understanding. The thought transcends all comprehension, that even one from this fallen sinful race will be so changed by divine power that he will be satisfying to God as an exhibition of His infinite grace, and, though the vast spaces of heaven be thronged with such, the demonstration is not enhanced by multiplied representations, for each individual will be the expression of God's superlative grace.

By the perfect accomplishment of Christ in His death—dying the Just for the unjust—the saving arm of God is no longer shackled on account of those just claims of judgment which His outraged character and government must otherwise impose, and, being thus freed to act, He does all that infinite love dictates. Naught in heaven or on earth—naught within the Godhead or among created beings—could surpass the end which divine salvation achieves for a lost soul as the manifestation of God's grace and the satisfaction of His love. This incomprehensible, illimitable result is assured in the promise that every saved one will be "conformed to the image of his Son" (Rom. 8:29); and the Apostle John also testifies, "When he shall appear, we shall be like him; for we shall see him as he is" (1 John 3:2). This is evidently what is in the mind of the Apostle when he writes, "And as we have borne the image of the earthy, we shall also bear the image of the heavenly" (1 Cor. 15:49). Even now Christ is in the believer as "the hope" of that "glory" (Col. 1:27), and this body itself will be fashioned "like unto his glorious body" (Phil. 3:21). It is no small distinction for a hell-deserving sinner that God should so love him that, having borne his judgments, He should employ him as the agent by whom He will declare eternally to the universe the precise scope and character of His unqualified grace.

The gospel preacher would do well to study, to the end that he may rightly emphasize the two divine perfections in man's salvation, before mentioned, both of which are gained on righteous grounds through the death and resurrection of Christ. One of these is a disposal of that which is evil, while the other is the securing of that which is good. These two divine perfections are (1) that by the death of Christ, all judgment and condemnation are so perfectly borne that they can never again be reckoned against the believer (Rom. 8:1, R.V.). Even in the salvation of a soul, no blow is struck, no criticism or censure is uttered. (2) Likewise, and on the ground of that same death and on the ground of Christ's resurrection, every requirement for eternal association with God in heaven is bestowed—all, indeed, on the principle of uncomplicated grace.

In concluding this introduction to the study of Soteriology, the student is enjoined to give exceptional attention to this great theme, and for two important reasons, which are, (1) God's message includes the whole human family in its outreach, and since the great proportion are unregenerate, and since the gospel of salvation is the only word addressed to the unsaved, it is reasonable to conclude that, in a well-balanced ministry, gospel preaching should account for no less than seventy-five percent of the pulpit testimony. The remainder may be for the edification of those who are saved. It stands to reason that, if so much of the preacher's message should be within the general field of Soteriology, the study of this division of Systematic Theology should be attended with great diligence, sincerity, and prayerful expectation. (2) The preacher is an important link in the chain which connects the heart of God with the souls of lost men. Concerning the other links in this chain, it may be remarked that there is no deficiency in the provisions of redemption through the sacrifice of Christ. There is no flaw in the record of that redemption as revealed in the Oracles of God. There is no weakness or failure on the part of the enabling Spirit. There should be no omissions, defects, or derelictions in the preacher's presentation of redemption to those for whom it is provided. When seriously contemplated, the responsibility of gospel preaching cannot but solemnize the heart and be the cause of an ever increasing dependence upon God. It is not to be wondered at that the Apostle, speaking for the Holy Spirit, declares with that unique emphasis which a twofold repetition imposes, "But though we, or an angel from heaven, preach any other gospel unto you than that which we have preached unto you, let him be accursed. As we said before, so say I now again, If any man preach any other gospel unto you than that ye have received, let him be accursed" (Gal. 1:8–9). This *anathema* has never been revoked, nor could it be so long as the saving grace of God is to be proclaimed to a lost world. From the human point of view, a misrepresentation of the gospel might so misguide a soul that the way of life is missed forever. It behooves the doctor of souls to know the precise remedy he is appointed to administer. A medical doctor may, by an error, terminate what at best is only a brief life on earth. The doctor of souls is dealing with eternal destiny. Having given His Son to die for lost men, God cannot but be exacting about how that great benefit is presented, nor should He be deemed unjust if He pronounces an anathema on those who pervert the one and only way of salvation which was purchased at so great a cost. A sensitive man, when realizing these eternal issues, might shrink from so great a responsibility, but God has not called His messengers to such a failure. He enjoins them to "preach the word" and assures them of His unfailing presence and enabling power. Probably at no point in the whole field of theological truth is the injunction more applicable which says, "Study to shew thyself approved unto God, a workman that needeth not to be ashamed, rightly dividing the word of truth" (2 Tim. 2:15).

The study of Soteriology is to be pursued under the following main divisions: (1) the Savior, (2) divine election, (3) for whom did Christ die? (4) the saving work of the triune God, (5) the eternal security of the believer, (6) deliverance from the reigning power of sin and human limitations, (7) the terms of salvation.

THE SAVIOR

CHAPTER II

THE PERSON OF THE SAVIOR

THERE IS but one Savior and only One who in every respect is qualified to save. The truth thus asserted is the foundation of Soteriology, and, of these two declarations, the first calls for an investigation into the *Person* of Christ—which line of truth has been considered in many pages under trinitarianism, and there properly restricted to contemplation of His Person. The second declaration—that He alone is qualified to save—calls for an investigation into the *work* of Christ on the cross and is the ground of all that enters into Soteriology. Thus, in turn, Soteriology is the cornerstone of Systematic Theology, being, as it is to the fullest degree, that which man may comprehend of God's self-revelation to a fallen race. Volume V in this work on Systematic Theology is assigned to the pursuance of Christology. On those pages a more orderly and comprehensive treatment of that great theme will be undertaken. As stated above, under trinitarianism specific consideration has been given to Christ's Person. Under Soteriology (apart from an introductory word), specific consideration is to be given to Christ's work, while under Christology these two fundamental truths are to be considered together. As before intimated, it is essential, when approaching the study of the work of Christ, to restate or review certain facts relative to His Person to the end that some larger recognition may be secured about who it is that undertakes to provide so great a salvation. Attention is therefore first directed to the Person of the Savior. That man is incapable of a comprehension of Deity is a truism, and it is equally certain that man is incapable of depicting what he cannot comprehend. In the Bible, God has spoken regarding Himself, and this has accomplished much for impotent man in his attempt to know the truth about God; yet this revelation—even when the mind is illuminated by the Spirit—is dimly apprehended. It is under such unavoidable restrictions that a human author may write or a human voice may speak. Unspeakably exalted is the theme of the Person of Christ; but, for the present emergency, this division of the general thesis may be subdivided into four aspects—(a) Christ's seven positions, (b) His offices, (c) His sonships, and (d) the hypostatic union.

I. CHRIST'S SEVEN POSITIONS

The entire field of Christology is well comprehended in the seven positions in which Christ is set forth in the Scriptures. Though these are observed more thoroughly under Christology, there seems to be no more illuminating approach to this vast theme respecting the Person and work of Christ. The purpose in this preparatory treatment is an attempt to comprehend—as far as may be possible—the infinite greatness of the One who has undertaken to save the lost. The spiritual progress of the Christian may be measured by the growth he makes in "the knowledge of our Lord and Saviour Jesus Christ" (2 Pet. 3:18). It is stated by Christ Himself that the work of the Spirit in the heart of the believer will be to "glorify me" (John 16:14). By these Scriptures it is indicated that the believer's conception of Christ who saves him should not only be extended to supernatural proportions, but should be increasing with every passing day. That He may have pre-eminence, these seven positions are introduced here.

1. THE PREINCARNATE CHRIST. It is doubtless true that, in view of the truth that He took upon Himself the human form and nature, the mind of man is disposed to think of Christ in terms of finite inability and incompetency. A certain cure for this misleading practice is meditation and reflection on His preincarnate existence. Such consideration always tends to an apprehension of the incarnate Christ which is free from human misconceptions. Having received and welcomed something of His eternal Godhood, it will be natural to give His Deity its proper place when pursuing the truth respecting His incarnate mode of existence.

It is hoped that the student is mindful of the somewhat extended investigation, under Theology Proper, of the major passages (Isa. 7:14; 9:6–7; Micah 5:2; Luke 1:30–35; John 1:1–2, 14; Phil. 2:6–8; Col. 1:13–17; 1 Tim. 3:16) bearing on Christ's preincarnate existence as one in the triune Godhead. But one passage will be reconsidered in this connection, namely,

John 1:1–2, 14. Though, so far as the record goes, the Son of God did not apply the specific term *Logos* to Himself, it is applied to Him by the Holy Spirit in the passage under consideration. This appellation might with the best of reason be used more than it is to identify the preincarnate Son of God. A distinctive name which relates Him to eternity is not only needed, but is thus supplied by the Holy Spirit, whose use of this title in this connection is complete authority for its employment, for the same purpose, under all circumstances. By its very meaning, the designation *Logos* bears a far-reaching revelation, not only of His Deity, but of His essential and eternal relation to the First Person. Of this name *Logos,* A. B. D. Alexander writes:

The doctrine of the Logos has exerted a decisive and far-reaching influence upon speculative and Christian thought. The word has a long history, and the evolution of the idea it embodies is really the unfolding of man's conception of God. To comprehend the relation of the Deity to the world has been the aim of all religious philosophy. While widely divergent views as to the Divine manifestation have been conceived, from the dawn of Western speculation, the Greek word *logos* has been employed with a certain degree of uniformity by a series of thinkers to express and define the nature and mode of God's revelation. *Logos* signifies in classical Greek both "reason" and "word." Though in Biblical Greek the term is mostly employed in the sense of "word," we cannot properly dissociate the two significations. Every word implies a thought. It is impossible to imagine a time when God was without thought. Hence thought must be eternal as the Deity. The translation "thought" is probably the best equivalent for the Greek term, since it denotes, on the one hand, the faculty of reason, or the thought inwardly conceived in the mind; and, on the other hand, the thought outwardly expressed through the vehicle of language. The two ideas, thought and speech, are indubitably blended in the term *logos;* and in every employment of the word, in philosophy and Scripture, both notions of thought and its outward expression are intimately connected.—*The International Standard Bible Encyclopaedia,* III, 1911–12

The Second Person, fulfilling the significant meaning of the title *Logos,* is, and always has been, as He ever will be, the manifestation of God. This is implied in the term *Logos;* for He who bears that name within the Godhead, is to the Godhead what speech is to thought—the expression of it. Dr. W. Lindsay Alexander writes clearly of this:

This word carries its own meaning with it; in other words, that the simple idea presented to the mind by this word is so truly descriptive of Jesus Christ that it may be used without any qualification as a designation of Him, just as the words life, light, manna, passover, peace, etc., elsewhere are used. But this throws us upon the inquiry, In what sense is Jesus Christ the Word? for it must be allowed that the term does not so immediately yield up its meaning as do some of those other terms with which we have compared it. Now, in reply to this I think the oldest answer is still the best. "The Son," says Origen, "may be the Word because He announces the hidden things of His Father;" or, as another of the Fathers gives it, because He is the interpreter of the will of

God. The idea here is, that as a word is the interpreter of the hidden invisible spirit of man, so Jesus, coming forth from the bosom of the Father, of Him whom no man hath seen at any time, has revealed Him to us. Words bridge over the chasm between spirit and spirit, and form a medium of communication between mind and mind. They are winged messengers that come from that which sense cannot descry, and through the medium of sense convey to others knowledge of that hidden power that sent them forth. They are thus emphatically revealers of the invisible, palpable exponents to us of what, but for them, must ever have remained hidden from us, being supersensible. In like manner has Jesus Christ made known and expounded God to us. In Himself God is utterly beyond our knowledge; we cannot by searching find Him out; and it is only as He reveals Himself to us that we can have any just thought of Him at all. But of all the revelations of Himself which He has given to men, none is so full, so clear, so impressive, as that which He has given in the Person of His Son. Here all the other rays of light which God has sent forth to illuminate our darkness are concentrated in one blaze of glory. Here all the other words which God hath spoken to men are gathered up and condensed into one grand and all-embracing utterance, which therefore becomes emphatically *The Word*—the living personal manifestation of God to men. . . .

The attentive reader of the O. T. cannot have failed to observe how there runs through the writings which it contains a distinction between God as He is in Himself,—hidden, invisible, unsearchable, incomprehensible; and God as He is in relation to His creatures,—revealed, manifested, declared. Sometimes this is conveyed very distinctly and unmistakably, as by the appearances of the Angel of Jehovah, who is both Himself Jehovah and yet distinct from Jehovah —a representation which can be rendered intelligible only on the supposition of a distinction between God as revealed and God as concealed. In other cases the same idea is presented by certain forms of expression which presuppose it, and are explicable only on the assumption of it. Such, for instance, is the frequently-recurring expression, the "Name of God"—an expression which indicates something distinct from God as God, but to which, nevertheless, personal and divine qualities are ascribed; for men are commanded to put their trust in God's name, God serves men by His name, God puts His name in a person or place, the result of which is that God is in that person or place; and many other similar usages, which can be explained satisfactorily only on the supposition that the name of God is God, not as He is in Himself, but as He is revealed to men. Such also is the distinction made between the "face of God," which no man can behold, and His "back," which Moses was permitted, in compliance with his earnest request, to see. As the countenance is the index of the soul, the spiritual part, so to speak, of the body, the face of God is His inner essential glory, His essence as a Spirit; and as the back part of a man is purely material, and subject to the scrutiny of the senses, so this is used by God to denote what of Him may be revealed, and by being revealed may be known by His creatures. What that is He Himself expressly declares when, in the same connection, in answer to the prayer of Moses, "Show me Thy glory," God says, "I will make all my goodness [properly, *beauty, majesty*] to pass before thee, and will proclaim the name of the Lord before thee." This was what Moses could see, and this—the divine name or revelation of God, the beauty, the manifested perfection of God—He would make to pass before him; and it is of this that God speaks as His back, because it could be made known to men in contradistinction to His face, His essential being, which no man could see and live. These instances may suffice to show that the idea of a distinction between God as He is in Himself and God as revealed to His creatures could not but be familiar to an attentive reader of the ancient Jewish Scriptures; so that St. John, in representing the great Revealer of God as with God and as God, would not overstep the limits of enlightened Jewish thought and intelligence.—*System of Biblical Theology*, I, 360–63

There are three determining truths set forth by John in his Gospel concerning the Logos: (a) He, as one with God and as God, is from all eternity (1:1–2), (b) He becomes flesh (1:14), and (c) He ever manifests the First Person (1:18). With this comprehensive revelation all the Bible is in accord, and such is the adorable, almighty, all-wise, eternal Person who came into the world to be the Savior of men.

2. THE INCARNATE CHRIST. In a reasonable effort to attain to a worthy appraisement of the Redeemer, this fundamental truth must be fixed in mind as the ground for all other realities which enter into His marvelous, exalted Being, namely, that, since He combines in Himself undiminished Deity and perfect humanity, there is none other comparable to Him, either within the Godhead, among angels, or among men. This theanthropic Person is as much God as is the Father or the Holy Spirit; but neither the Father nor the Spirit has come into union with that which is human. Similarly, this theanthropic Person is in every respect the embodiment of every feature of a true human being; but no other human being has ever been so united to the Godhead. There is no implication here that this theanthropic Person is superior to the Father or the Spirit; it is only pointed out that He differs from all others in heaven or on earth in that the breadth of the sphere of His Being has been expanded to a point to which none other has ever attained or will ever attain. He functions perfectly and finally in the service for which a theanthropic Person was indicated. No need of another could ever arise. In view of the later consideration of the whole field of mediation, pursuance of this theme is discontinued for the present. However, most urgently the truth is stressed that, apart from an interminable investigation into, and meditation on, the peculiar features of this unique theanthropic Person, there can be no commendable growth "in the knowledge of our Lord and Saviour Jesus Christ."

3. CHRIST IN HIS DEATH. Again, extended discussion awaits a later contemplation of the sufferings of Christ; yet the right evaluation of the

Savior is bound up, to a large degree, with His work upon the cross. Such an evaluation had come to the Apostle when, in personal adoration, he said of Christ, "who loved me, and gave himself for me." Vast indeed are the triumphs of Christ through the cross—reaching on to the transformation of things on earth and in heaven. A right understanding of these will result in a richer and fuller knowledge of the One who is mighty to save.

4. THE RESURRECTED CHRIST. The incarnation accomplished the union of two natures in one theanthropic Person, in which union His Deity was veiled and His humanity, though sinless, was such as might mingle in the common experiences with other men; but the resurrection accomplished the unveiling of His Deity and the glorification of His humanity. Through the resurrection, He became what He ever will be and that which none other had ever been before—a glorified man in heaven. Of Him it is said, "Who only hath immortality, dwelling in the light which no man can approach unto; whom no man hath seen, nor can see: to whom be honour and power everlasting" (1 Tim. 6:16). Because of His sufferings and death, God hath, in resurrection, highly exalted Him and given Him a name which is above every name. In any recognition of all the Savior is, there must be a contemplation of His present estate—that which He ever will be in heaven.

5. CHRIST ASCENDED AND SEATED IN HEAVEN. The omnipresent Savior, though indwelling every believer, though present where two or three are met unto His name, and though accompanying every messenger to the end of the age, is, nevertheless, locally present in heaven, seated on His Father's throne and there administering as Savior of lost men, as Head over all things to the Church; and is preparing a place for the sons whom He is bringing into glory. When on earth, none knew Him more intimately than John, the beloved disciple. He saw Him as a child, in His public service, in transfiguration, in death, and in resurrection; yet, when he saw Him in glory—as described in Revelation 1:13–18—it was then that John fell at the glorified Savior's feet as one dead, and was able to arise only as he was lifted up and strengthened by his glorified Lord. It is with that same glorified Savior that Christians will be confronted as they enter heaven, and it is of this Savior the believer must now be aware if he would know who it is that saves his soul.

6. CHRIST RETURNING. The utmost capacity of language to express limitless glory is strained in those passages wherein the second advent of Christ is described (cf. Isa. 63:1–6; Dan. 7:13–14; Matt. 24:27–31; Acts 15:16–18; 2 Thess. 1:7–10; Rev. 19:11–16), and that conception

of this glorious Person must be added to the sum total of all that the Savior is, by whom the lost are saved and by whom they are presented faultless before the presence of His glory.

7. CHRIST REIGNING FOREVER. By the authority of the Father, the Son, to whom all authority is given, must reign upon the throne of David until all enemies are put under His feet. Then, by the same authority He will reign forever and ever, that God may be all in all (1 Cor. 15:24–28). It is predicted that His reign shall be everlasting—on the throne of His father David (cf. Isa. 9:6–7; Ezek. 37:21–25; Dan. 7:13–14; Luke 1:31–33; Rev. 11:15). Such is He in whom the sinner trusts and such is He whom all Christians are admonished to know. The call to know "our Lord and Saviour Jesus Christ" is a call to enter an immeasurable realm of reality—even all that the Savior is.

II. CHRIST'S OFFICES

It has been the belief, based on the Scriptures, of the Bible interpreters living in the Old Testament dispensation as well as of those living in the New Testament dispensation, that the title *Messiah* of the Old Covenant and the title *Christ* of the New Covenant imply a three-fold official responsibility—that of Prophet, Priest, and King. There is every reason to retain this general division of truth, and these offices are to be considered separately.

1. PROPHET. The underlying conception of a prophet is that he is a channel or means of communication through whom God's message may be delivered to man. In this respect the prophet's service is the opposite of that of the priest, whose responsibility is to represent man to God. Both ministries belong equally to Christ and together constitute two major aspects of His mediatorial work. He, as Mediator, stands between God and man and represents each in turn to the other.

Distinction must be made between the prophet of the Old Testament and the prophet of the New Testament. In either instance the field of service is twofold—*foretelling* and *forthtelling*. The ministry of the Old Testament prophet was largely that of a reformer or patriot. He sought the restoration to covenant blessings of the people who were under the covenants. No better illustration of this will be found than John the Baptist—the last prophet of the old order and the herald of the Messiah. Of him Christ said, "A prophet? yea, I say unto you, and more than a prophet" (Matt. 11:9); and no greater prediction was uttered by John than that couched in the words, "Behold, the Lamb of God, that taketh away the sin of the world!" (John 1:29, R.V.). Having the attitude of a reformer and revivalist, the Old Testament prophet was appointed of God to give warnings about the chastisement of God that was impending upon His erring people, and, with the predictions, to give the witness from Jehovah that the purpose and faithfulness of Jehovah with respect to Israel's ultimate blessings could never fail. Because of their sins, the people would suffer trials, but, in the end, God's covenant blessings would be experienced since God could not change. With respect to Israel, "The gifts and calling of God are without repentance" (Rom. 11:29). Concerning the Old Testament prophet, an order of development is to be observed. He was first styled *the man of God,* later he was known as *the seer,* and finally he was identified as *the prophet.* The order of development is easily traced. The man of God could, on the basis of the unvarying principle that the pure in heart see God, see, and therefore became known as the seer. For those who have spiritual sight, it is but a short step to the ability to declare both by foretelling and by forthtelling.

In Volume I of this work, under Bibliology and in Chapter V devoted to canonicity, it has been pointed out that certain responsibilities on the part of Jewish authorities with respect to the Scriptures were assigned. The responsibility of the people is declared in Deuteronomy 4:2, "Ye shall not add unto the word which I command you, neither shall ye diminish ought from it, that ye may keep the commandments of the LORD your God which I command you." The instruction to the king upon the throne—though no king would rule in Israel for five hundred years to come—was disclosed in Deuteronomy 17:18–19, "And it shall be, when he sitteth upon the throne of his kingdom, that he shall write him a copy of this law in a book out of that which is before the priests the Levites: and it shall be with him, and he shall read therein all the days of his life: that he may learn to fear the LORD his God, to keep all the words of this law and these statutes, to do them." The judges interpreted the law contained in the Scriptures; but should a matter arise which the judges could not determine, it was referred to the priests who served as a supreme court, and the offender who would not abide by the ruling of the priests was put to death. This important provision is recorded in Deuteronomy 17:8–10, "If there arise a matter too hard for thee in judgment, between blood and blood, between plea and plea, and between stroke and stroke, being matters of controversy within thy gates: then shalt thou arise, and get thee up into the place which the LORD thy God shall choose; and thou shalt come unto the priests the Levites, and unto the judge that shall be in those days, and enquire; and they shall shew thee the sentence of judgment: and thou shalt do according to the sentence, which they of that place which the LORD shall choose shall shew thee; and thou shalt observe to do according to all that they inform thee." To the Levites was given the custody of the Scriptures. It is written, "Take this book of the law, and put it in the side of the ark of the covenant of the LORD your God, that it may be there for a witness against thee" (Deut. 31:26). But to the prophet was given the high responsibility of receiving and delivering the Word of God. The commission of the prophet to speak for God and the requirement of the people to hear is set forth in the midst of Israel's constituted law. No doubt, the passage, as many another, has its final fulfillment in the prophetic ministry of Christ. Christ is the final Prophet of all prophets, the final Priest of all priests, and the final King of all kings. This instruction is an immediate authorization of the prophets who under God were to succeed Moses. The passage reads: "The LORD thy God will raise up unto thee a Prophet from the midst of thee, of thy brethren, like unto me; unto him ye shall hearken. . . . I will raise them up a Prophet from among their brethren, like unto thee, and will put my words in his mouth; and he shall speak unto them all that I shall command him. And it shall come to pass, that whosoever will not hearken unto my words which he shall speak in my name, I will require it of him" (Deut. 18:15, 18–19). The true prophet's message had to be received and heeded by the whole house of Israel from the king on the throne to the least in the kingdom. Of these messages, however, only such portions as the Spirit of God determined became canonical. The true prophet attested his own message and demonstrated its authority by supernatural evidence. This did not preclude one prophet attesting the message another prophet had received and delivered with authority. Such corroboration is observable, especially in regard to writings which have their place in the New Testament Canon.

On the other hand, the New Testament prophets—aside from the specific writing of the New Testament—are appointed more to a ministry of forthtelling than to the ministry of foretelling. The prophetic word is completed in the Bible with the record of all that will be to the end of God's program. There is therefore no further need of the prophet who foretells. The general classification of the New Testament ministries is found in Ephesians 4:11, where it is written concerning the ascended Lord: "He gave some, apostles; and some, prophets; and some, evangelists; and some, pastors and teachers." The apostle, whose right to the title depended upon his immediate relation to Christ while Christ was here in the world, is not, naturally, continued beyond the first generation of the Church on earth. The evangelist is the pioneer missionary, rather than the modern revivalist who bears the name, and who has little recognition in the New Testament. The pastor and teacher —apparently two activities on the part of one person—ministers to the edification of the saints in their work of the ministry. The New Testament prophet's service is well defined in one passage: "But he that prophesieth speaketh unto men to edification, and exhortation, and comfort" (1 Cor. 14:3). Other Scriptures are of equal significance. Writing of the revelation of the mystery, the Apostle declares: "Which in other ages was not made known unto the sons of men, as it is now revealed unto his holy apostles and prophets by the Spirit" (Eph. 3:5). Similarly, the benefaction of gifted men to the Church is again cited by the same Apostle in 1 Corinthians 12:10, where prophecy is treated as one of the gifts to be exercised: "To another the working of miracles; to another prophecy; to another discerning of spirits; to another divers kinds of tongues; to another the interpretation of tongues." In like manner verses 28–29 are revealing: "And God hath set some in the church, first apostles, secondarily prophets, thirdly teachers, after that miracles, then gifts of healings, helps, governments, diversities of tongues. Are all apostles? are all prophets? are all workers of miracles?" The Church is being built upon the apostles and New Testament prophets—not the Old Testament prophets (Eph. 2:19–20).

All that enters into the peculiar ministry of the prophet—both Old Testament and New Testament—serves only to clarify the important truth that Christ is a Prophet, and as such is supreme and final in that office. He fulfills all that ever entered into the divine conception peculiar to the prophet. The earliest and most important anticipation of Christ's prophetic ministry, as noted above, is recorded in Deuteronomy 18:15, 18–19. This preview is distinguished by the fact that it is several times quoted in the New Testament (cf. Acts 3:22–23; 7:37). It is asserted in this Scripture that the anticipated prophet would speak only the words divinely given Him. Every statement by Christ which asserts that His message was given Him by His Father (cf. John 7:16; 8:28; 12:49–50; 14:10, 24; 17:8) is a confirmation of the truth that He is that prophet. This great prediction in Deuteronomy 18:15–19, carries a secondary meaning applicable to all Old Testament prophets who spoke for God. The exceedingly pragmatic test to distinguish between the true and false prophet is set forth in verses 21–22: "And if thou say in thine heart, How shall we know the word which the LORD hath not spoken? When a prophet speaketh in the name of the LORD, if the thing follow not, nor come to pass, that is the thing which the LORD hath not spoken, but the prophet hath spoken it presumptuously: thou shall not be afraid of him." The deeper significance of this test is that, since Christ is a true Prophet, every word He has spoken will assuredly come to pass.

It is also indicated that Christ applied the title of *prophet* to Himself. Speaking thus He said, "A prophet is not without honour, save in his own country, and in his own house" (Matt. 13:57). Likewise, "Nevertheless I must walk to day, and to morrow, and the day following: for it cannot be that a prophet perish out of Jerusalem" (Luke 13:33). It should be observed, also, that Christ was recognized by others as being a prophet. "Then those men, when they had seen the miracle that Jesus did, said, This is of a truth that prophet that should come into the world" (John 6:14). From this it may be seen that an Old Testament prophet is identified by mighty works. In this feature Christ surpassed all others, as He surpassed in the added qualifications of teacher and predictor.

The whole prophetic ministry of Christ may be divided into three time periods, which are:

a. THE PREINCARNATE MINISTRY. As *Logos,* the Second Person has always been the self-revelation of God. This specific method of manifestation is perhaps best set forth in John 1:18: "No man hath seen God at any time; the only begotten Son, which is in the bosom of the Father, he hath declared him." Whenever truth about the Person of God or His message is to be disclosed—whether it be by the Angel of Jehovah or the Incarnate Son—the Second Person as *Logos* is the One who reveals.

b. THE INCARNATE MINISTRY. Quite apart from His teachings, the *Logos* was God manifest in the flesh.

(1) *Six Features of Christ's Incarnate Ministry.* Of Christ the Scriptures declare: "And without controversy great is the mystery of godliness: God was manifest in the flesh, justified in the Spirit, seen of angels, preached unto the Gentiles, believed on in the world, received up into glory" (1 Tim. 3:16). These six great assertions are divinely distinguished subdivisions of the entire scope of the incarnate manifestation.

(a) *"God Was Manifest in the Flesh."* In the Person of Christ the *Logos,* the incomprehensible actuality of God has been translated into terms which the human creature may comprehend. His presence among men was the presence of God. Whatever He did was an act of God and should be recognized as such. It was God who took little children in His arms and blessed them, that healed the sick, that raised the dead, and through death reconciled the world unto Himself. Of this truth Christ thus spoke: "Verily, verily, I say unto you, The Son can do nothing of himself, but what he seeth the Father do: for what things soever he doeth, these also doeth the Son likewise" (John 5:19). Moreover, what Christ said was none other than the word of God. He asserted that He not only did the will of His Father, but the words He spoke were the words of God. It is written: "It is the spirit that quickeneth; the flesh profiteth nothing: the words that I speak unto you, they are spirit, and they are life" (John 6:63). Not only has the kingdom of God drawn nigh to men by the incarnation (Luke 10:9), but God Himself has drawn nigh. As men are estimated and known by their words and deeds, so God may be estimated and known—so far as human capacity, enabled by the Spirit, may serve—by the words and deeds of Christ.

(b) *"Justified in the Spirit."* This declaration indicates that all that Christ undertook was wrought in that perfection which justified it—both in heaven and on earth—being achieved through the eternal Spirit. He was led of the Spirit (Luke 4:1), He wrought in the power of the Spirit (Matt. 12:28), and in His death He offered Himself to God by the eternal Spirit (Heb. 9:14). It is significant, in this connection, that to Him the Spirit was given *without measure* (John 3:34).

(c) *"Seen of Angels."* In this expression, it is indicated that in His incarnate life on earth the whole of the angelic hosts were concerned. From their viewpoint, having known Him from the time of their creation as their Creator and the Object of their ceaseless adoration, His descent from realms of infinite glory to the dark sphere and confines of human existence was the occasion of the deepest interest to the angels.

(d) *"Preached unto the Gentiles."* Beyond the range of all former covenants, Christ became the way of salvation to every member of the race. The assertion is not restricted to an elect few. The term "the Gentiles" could not be more inclusive. The importance of this movement from the confines of an elect nation—to whom He had bound Himself by immutable testaments—to a redemption as limitless as the human race, cannot be estimated.

(e) *"Believed on in the World."* While Christ was here in the world a very few sustained this relationship to Him, but they were the beginning of an unnumbered host from every kindred, tribe, and nation who have believed to the saving of their souls. What that means in heavenly realms cannot be known in this world.

(f) *"Received up into Glory."* Christ removed His abode from this *cosmos* world and ascended into heaven where His redeeming work was accepted by His Father who had sent Him into the *cosmos* world. His reception into glory was a public acknowledgment of the work He had accomplished.

Though coming late in point of time, but perhaps with reference to its actual beginning, the prophetic ministry of Christ was attested on the Mount of Transfiguration by a voice from heaven, as was His priestly office at His baptism, and as His kingly office will be attested when He comes again (Ps. 2:7). It is of special import that in each of the three reports of the transfiguration the voice not only declares "This is my beloved Son [Matthew adds here, 'in whom I am well pleased']," but adds the words—indicative of the prophetic office—"Hear ye him," or "Hear him."

(2) *Christ Forthtelling and Foretelling.* In the most integral sense, Christ fulfilled the prophetic ministry of forthtelling and foretelling.

(a) *Christ Forthtelling.* As for Christ's preaching and teaching, a vast amount was delivered in three and a half years to those who heard Him. Only the merest fragment of this ministry has been preserved in the Gospels. However, under the guidance of the Spirit, precisely that is preserved which is needed for a permanent representation of the message which He gave. Here the claim of Rome to the possession of truth from Christ not contained in the Gospels is proved to be spurious, for no item of truth not found in the Gospels has been demonstrated to be of equal importance with the body of truth found in the Bible. An analysis of all that fell from the lips of Christ belongs to another line of theological discipline. Suffice it to say that, above and beyond the many brief conversations or averments of truth which are recorded—such as John, chapters 5 to 9, which portion is so strongly apologetical in its nature—there are three major discourses, and these should be attended most faithfully by all who would know the surpassing import of Christ's prophetic ministry.

Matthew 5:1—7:29. This discourse, identified as *The Sermon on the Mount,* was delivered by Christ in His early ministry and at a time in that ministry when He was offering Himself to Israel as their anticipated Messiah. This discourse was given at the time when it was being proclaimed that "the kingdom of heaven is at hand," and when Christ was sending forth His disciples with explicit instructions that they were not to go to the Gentiles, or to the Samaritans, but only to the lost sheep of the house of Israel (Matt. 10:5–7). The most casual reader must be impressed with the change in these directions as later directions are declared by Him (cf. Matt. 13:38; 28:19; Acts 1:8). This discourse presents the King's own pronouncement on the terms of admission into the yet future earthly kingdom and prescribes the required manner of life in that kingdom. That the yet future earthly kingdom, which is covenanted to Israel, was first offered to them, then rejected by them, and on that ground postponed until the second advent will be more fully examined under Eschatology. The offer of the kingdom and its rejection by Israel, which was signified by the crucifixion of the King, was God's predetermined (Acts 2:23) way of accomplishing the sacrifice of His Lamb, and in no sense a jeopardizing of the redemptive purpose which has been in view from all eternity (Rev. 13:8). Nevertheless, by the crucifixion, not only was the redemption wrought out, but the sin of rejecting the King, which was latent in the hearts of men, became a concrete, overt act, and, therefore, subject to judgment as such. A reigning monarch with a rule over all the earth is the assured prediction in connection with His second advent. However, if the setting up of the kingdom was by divine intention postponed until the return of the King, the application of that which this discourse enjoins is deferred until the kingdom is established on the earth. The Sermon on the Mount is characterized—among other features—by the absence of those elements which are distinctly Christian—redemption by the blood of Christ, faith, regeneration, deliverance from judgment, the Person and work of the Holy Spirit. The absence of these vital elements cannot but arrest the attention of those who are awake to, and jealous for, the faith once delivered to the saints. Nevertheless, this great discourse presents, as divinely intended, the future kingdom relationships with the perfection which characterizes all Scripture.

Matthew 24:1—25:46. The Olivet Discourse, delivered by Christ on the Mount of Olives but a very few days before His death, concerns Israel primarily and assumes the form of a farewell message to that nation. Like the Sermon on the Mount, this discourse is partially recorded by both Mark and Luke, and its extended record is found in Matthew's Gospel. The dominant themes in this discourse are the great tribulation and Israel's warnings concerning it (Matt. 24:9–28); the glorious appearing of Messiah in relation to Israel (24:29—25:30), including exhortations to "watch" (24:36—25:13), judgments upon Israel (24:45—25:30), and judgments upon the nations because of their treatment of Israel (25:31–46). No reference is made in this discourse to the Church—her beginning, her course, her ministries, her departure from this *cosmos* world. Similarly, no reference is made to salvation by grace or the security of those thus saved (cf. 24:50–51; 25:30). In like manner, no reference is made to the Person and work of the Holy Spirit.

John 13:1—17:26. These sublime teachings, not intimated in the Synoptic Gospels, are identified as *The Upper Room Discourse,* and usually include the High Priestly Prayer, chapter 17. This message is spoken to the eleven after the dismissal of Judas, for the most part, and they are no longer reckoned to be Jews under the Law (cf. 15:25), but are those who are "clean" through the Word spoken unto them (cf. 13:10; 15:3). As for its application, it is dated by Christ beyond His death, beyond His resurrection, beyond His ascension, and beyond the Day of Pentecost. The discourse embodies, in germ form, every essential of that system of doctrine which is distinctively Christian. Being addressed to Christians, it does not present truth which is peculiar to Israel, and being addressed to those who are saved, it does not present any feature of salvation by grace which is made possible through the death and resurrection of Christ, which truth is implied. This portion is like a seed plot in which all is found that is later developed in the epistles of the New Testament. It serves as Christ's farewell address to believers—those whom the Father has given Him out of the *cosmos* world (17:6).

When these three major discourses are diligently compared, it is discovered that they present the widest differences in objectives, subjects, and terminology. The recognition of these variations is, naturally, the inception of the discernment of much vital doctrine. However, the same discriminating study should be given to every word which Christ in His forthtelling prophetic ministry has declared.

(b) *Christ Foretelling.* In this field of truth, Christ excelled all other prophets that ever have spoken. It cannot but stimulate awe and wonder when specific attention is given to the character and extent of Christ's predictive ministry. With reference to His own message He stated that the Holy Spirit would not only bring His words to the disciples' remembrance, but that He would show them things to come (John 14:26; 16:13). The foretelling ministry of Christ included the immediate future actions of individuals; His own death, resurrection, and ascension; the advent of the Spirit; the work of the Spirit in this age; the fact and character of the new age; the Church; the removal of the Church from the world; His second coming, preceded by the great tribulation; the presence of the abomination of desolation spoken of by Daniel the prophet; the judgments of Israel and her kingdom glory; the judgment of the nations and their destiny; and the future state of both the saved and the unsaved.

c. THE MINISTRY FROM HEAVEN. In this classification may be included the forty-day postresurrection predictions and teachings of Christ. In this He spoke primarily of the kingdom of God (Acts 1:3) and, evidently, of its future aspects; so, also, of Israel's "times and seasons" which the Father has kept in His own power (Acts 1:7). He then anticipated the world-wide proclamation of the gospel (Acts 1:8). From heaven He spoke to the seven churches which were in Asia (Rev., chapters 2–3), which portion of Scripture bears a prophetic forecast of the course of church history throughout this age. Much of direct utterance from the glorified Christ is recorded in the Revelation, which book closes with His words of assurance, "Surely I come quickly." There is a sense, also, in which Christ as Prophet is forthtelling throughout all this age in and through His messengers. This is implied in Acts 1:1, where His earthly proclamation is seen to be but the beginning of that which is now in progress. He, too, is speaking through the Holy Spirit, for it is to His voice that the Spirit listens with a view to reproducing the same (John 16:12–13).

2. PRIEST. No fact concerning Christ is more established than that of His priesthood. It is seen in various Old Testament types, and is the essential truth set forth in the Epistle to the Hebrews. The Messiah, it is declared, is to be a Priest after the order of Melchizedec (Ps. 110:4). Aside from this specific declaration, Israel could have had no recognition of a priesthood which did not come by Levi and the Aaronic line. Public consecration at the age of thirty was prescribed by the Law of Moses (Num. 4:3) and the precise manner in which it was to be accomplished was indicated (Num. 8:7 ff.). By His consecration, Christ fulfilled all righteousness and, as on the Mount of Transfiguration when His prophetic office was attested and as it will be when He takes the Davidic throne that His kingly office will be attested, so at His baptism His priestly office was attested by the voice from heaven. Added confirmation was given His priestly consecration by the descent of the Spirit, in the appearance of a dove upon Him, and by the recognition of John, "Behold the Lamb of God, which taketh away the sin of the world" (John 1:29). But Christ was of the tribe of Judah, and no high priest would be willing to consecrate as priest one from any other tribe

than Levi. The mission of John the Baptist was twofold: He was to make ready a people prepared for the Lord (Luke 1:17), and to manifest the Messiah. Of the latter he said: "But that he [Christ] should be made manifest to Israel, therefore am I come baptizing with water" (John 1:31). John identified the Messiah by pointing to Him as the "Lamb of God, that taketh away the sin of the world" (John 1:29, R.V.), and by inducting Him into His public ministry by baptism. It is significant that no question was raised relative to John's baptizing of the people, or of his baptism of Christ. Objection would have been raised had it been outside the demands of the Mosaic system. It is certain that Christ is a Priest and as such He must be consecrated. John was the son of a priest and himself eligible to consecration. That John served in a specific way in the baptism of Christ is most evident. The baptism of Christ by John is to be distinguished from "John's baptism." The latter was unto repentance and remission of sin, all of which was wholly foreign to Christ. The former was a compliance with prescribed ritual, and therefore a fulfilling of the Law.

It is obvious that the Melchizedec priesthood expectation was free from all tribal issues. Christ is a priest after the order of Melchizedec (Heb. 7:17). In but one respect did He conform as antitype to the Aaronic pattern, namely, He made an offering unto God. It is true that the offering was Himself and thus He became both the sacrificer and the sacrifice. He was both the officiating priest—after the pattern of Aaron —and the sacrificed lamb. He "offered himself without spot to God" (Eph. 5:2; Titus 2:14; Heb. 9:14; 10:12). In one notable feature, Christ did not follow the Aaronic pattern. Of Aaron, as of all subsequent high priests, it was required on the Day of Atonement that he offer a sacrifice for his own sins (cf. Lev. 16:6; Heb. 9:7). That Christ offered Himself to God does not contradict the added truth that He was offered by the Father (John 3:16; Rom. 8:32; 2 Cor. 9:15; Isa. 53:10), or that He was offered by the eternal Spirit (Heb. 9:14).

In respect to the Melchizedec priesthood, Christ followed that pattern in three particulars:

a. IN HIS PERSON. Whatever may be the identification of Melchizedec —whether he be a Gentile priest to whom typical significance is accorded, or whether he be recognized as one of the theophanies of the Old Testament—it still remains true that the type is declared to be a king-priest, which type finds its antitype only in the Lord Jesus Christ—the final Priest of the most high God, and the King of Peace. So marked is this twofold distinction, that it is said of those who are *in Him* that they are a "kingdom of priests," or, more accurately, kings and priests (Rev. 5:10). By this designation, the closest possible union to Christ and partnership with Him is asserted. It is by this designation, also, that the Church will be identified in all ages to come. Of Israel it may be said that she had a priesthood; but of the Church it may be said that she *is* a priesthood, and that she is appointed to reign with Christ (Rev. 20:4, 6). Similarly, as there was a high priest over Israel's priesthood, so, in like manner, Christ is High Priest over the Church. He is Priest over those who are themselves priests. It is said, "Seeing then that we have a great high priest, that is passed into the heavens, Jesus the Son of God, let us hold fast our profession. For we have not an high priest which cannot be touched with the feeling of our infirmities; but was in all points tempted like as we are, yet without sin. Let us therefore come boldly unto the throne of grace, that we may obtain mercy, and find grace to help in time of need" (Heb. 4:14–16). A summarization of the doctrine of New Testament priesthood is given by Dr. C. I. Scofield thus:

(1) Until the law was given the head of each family was the family priest (Gen. 8:20; 26:25; 31:54). (2) When the law was proposed, the promise to perfect obedience was that Israel should be unto God "a kingdom of priests" (Ex. 19:6); but Israel violated the law, and God shut up the priestly office to the Aaronic family, appointing the tribe of Levi to minister to them, thus constituting the typical priesthood (Ex. 28:1). (3) In the dispensation of grace, all believers are unconditionally constituted a "kingdom of priests" (1 Pet. 2:9; Rev. 1:6), the distinction which Israel failed to achieve by works. The priesthood of the believer is, therefore, a birthright; just as every descendant of Aaron was born to the priesthood (Heb. 5:1). (4) The chief privilege of a priest is access to God. Under law the high priest only could enter "the holiest of all," and that but once a year (Heb. 9:7). But when Christ died, the veil, type of Christ's human body (Heb. 10:20), was rent, so that now the believer-priests, equally with Christ the High Priest, have access to God in the holiest (Heb. 10:19–22). The High Priest is corporeally there (4:14–16; Heb. 9:24; 10:19–22). (5) In the exercise of his office the New Testament believer-priest is (1) a *sacrificer* who offers a threefold sacrifice: (*a*) his own living body (Rom. 12:1; Phil. 2:17; 2 Tim. 4:6; 1 John 3:16; Jas. 1:27); (*b*) praise to God, "the fruit of the lips that make mention of His name" (R.V.), to be offered "continually" (Heb. 13:15; Ex. 25:22; "I will commune with thee from above the mercy seat"); (*c*) his substance (Heb. 13:16; Rom. 12:13; Gal. 6:6; 3 John 5–8; Heb. 13:2; Gal. 6:10; Tit. 3:14). (2) The N.T. priest is also an *intercessor* (1 Tim. 2:1; Col. 4:12).—*Scofield Reference Bible*, pp. 1313–14

The essential truth remains that, in every conceivable particular, Christ in His Person is a King-Priest, and that believers, though constituted kings and priests unto God, are such by virtue of their union with Him.

b. BY APPOINTMENT. The Priesthood of Christ is not self-assumed, but is rather the appointment of His Father. It is written: "So also Christ glorified not himself to be made an high priest; but he that said unto him, Thou art my Son, to day have I begotten thee. As he saith also in another place, Thou art a priest for ever after the order of Melchisedec. . . . Called of God an high priest after the order of Melchisedec" (Heb. 5:5–6, 10). Thus, also, it is written of Christ in heaven: "Whither the forerunner is for us entered, even Jesus, made an high priest for ever after the order of Melchisedec" (Heb. 6:20).

c. ETERNAL DURATION. In contrast to the crisis ministry of Christ as Priest after the Aaronic pattern, it is declared of His priesthood which was after the Melchizedec order, that it is eternal and is sealed as such by the oath of Jehovah. This is the assertion of both Testaments:

"The LORD hath sworn, and will not repent, Thou art a priest for ever after the order of Melchizedek" (Ps. 110:4); "And inasmuch as not without an oath he was made priest: (for those priests were made without an oath; but this with an oath by him that said unto him, The Lord sware and will not repent, Thou art a priest for ever after the order of Melchisedec:) by so much was Jesus made a surety of a better testament. And they truly were many priests, because they were not suffered to continue by reason of death: but this man, because he continueth ever, hath an unchangeable priesthood. Wherefore he is able also to save them to the uttermost that come unto God by him, seeing he ever liveth to make intercession for them. For such an high priest became us, who is holy, harmless, undefiled, separate from sinners, and made higher than the heavens; who needeth not daily, as those high priests, to offer up sacrifice, first for his own sins, and then for the people's: for this he did once, when he offered up himself. For the law maketh men high priests which have infirmity; but the word of the oath, which was since the law, maketh the Son, who is consecrated for evermore" (Heb. 7:20–28).

Thus it is seen that, in its duration and its unchanging value, Christ's priesthood follows that of Melchizedec who was the God-designed type of Christ's priesthood—being king of peace, without recorded father or mother, and without recorded beginning or ending of days. The inspired record declares: "For this Melchisedec, king of Salem, priest of the most high God, who met Abraham returning from the slaughter of the kings, and blessed him; to whom also Abraham gave a tenth part of all; first being by interpretation King of righteousness, and after that also King of Salem, which is, King of peace; without father, without mother, without descent, having neither beginning of days, nor end of life; but made like unto the Son of God; abideth a priest continually" (Heb. 7:1–3).

3. KING. A partial recognition of Christ's office as King has been included above. A greater body of Scripture relates Him to the Davidic throne, and asserts that He will yet reign on that throne forever. An extended treatment of the doctrine of Christ's kingship is deferred at this point, to be resumed under Eschatology. Citation, however, of two passages which record the divine purpose in His birth respecting the throne of David, follows: "For unto us a child is born, unto us a son is given: and the government shall be upon his shoulder: and his name shall be called Wonderful, Counsellor, The mighty God, The ever-lasting Father, The Prince of Peace. Of the increase of his government and peace there shall be no end, upon the throne of David, and upon his kingdom, to order it, and to establish it with judgment and with justice from henceforth even for ever. The zeal of the LORD of hosts will perform this" (Isa. 9:6–7); "And, behold, thou shalt conceive in thy womb, and bring forth a son, and shalt call his name JESUS. He shall be great, and shall be called the Son of the Highest: and the Lord God shall give unto him the throne of his father David: and he shall reign over the house of Jacob for ever; and of his kingdom there shall be no end" (Luke 1:31–33). The extent of Christ's kingship is seen in His birth—"born King of the Jews" (Matt. 2:2), as rightful Heir to David's throne, and so recognized by the people (John 12:13); He claimed to be a king (Matt. 27:11); He died under that accusation (Matt. 27:37); and He comes again as "King of kings, and Lord of lords" (Rev. 19:16).

III. THE SONSHIPS OF CHRIST

As a further step in the general investigation into who the Savior is, consideration should be given to the sonships which He sustained while here on earth. There are four.

1. THE SON OF GOD. Various theories which contend that Christ was: (a) Son of God by virtue of His incarnation—a Being comprising in Himself both Deity and humanity and who could not have merited the title either as God alone or as man alone; (b) that He was Son of God by virtue of His resurrection; or (c) that He was Son of God by mere title or official position, break down before the volume of Biblical testimony which asserts that He was Son of God from all eternity. It is not a question of the eternal existence of the Second Person, but rather of whether the sonship feature was a reality in all eternity past. Not all

that enters into the human conception of father and son relationship is represented between the First and Second Persons of the Godhead. In no sense is the Second Person inferior to the First Person. They are One with respect to eternal existence, and every attribute and capacity. It is almost wholly in the sphere of manifestation—the *Logos* character— that the sonship of the Second Person is exercised. It is true that He, for purposes of incarnation and redemption, assumed while here on earth a place of subjection to the First Person, and that He was pleased to work in the power of the Third Person; but this subordination enters in no way into the truth of His sonship. The theological term *eternal generation* implies that without beginning or ending, the Second Person is the manifestation of the Godhead. It is thus that the "only begotten Son" hath declared God to man (John 1:18). The Son said, "I have manifested thy name unto the men which thou gavest me out of the world" (*cosmos*—John 17:6; cf. 1 John 1:2; 4:9). He was Only Begotten in the uniqueness of His begetting. In like manner, He was First Begotten, being first in point of time, as well as in His essential Being, above all others begotten. God gave to the world for its salvation Him who ever was His Son. The One who was given did not become a son by the process of being given, but was a son before and when He was given. Isaiah declares, "For unto us a child is born," which relates to His humanity; and "Unto us a son is given," which not only relates to His Deity, but implies that, though a child born, He is a son, and as such not born, but given. After the same manner it is announced that "God so loved the world, that he gave his only begotten Son." As He was and what He was, such indeed, was that Gift which was given, namely, the Son of God.

2. THE SON OF MAN. This aspect of Christ's sonship, with due sanction, also terms Him *the Son of Adam*, or *the Son of Mary*. The *Son of man* title, used about eighty times in the New Testament, was Christ's own almost universal designation for Himself, and its primary significance is of His humanity. In several notable instances, the appellation *Son of man* is used in association with divine undertakings, as, in like manner, the appellation *the Son of God* is used a few times in association with human features. An interesting question arises at this point, asking why Christ placed a striking emphasis upon that name for Himself which so clearly designates His humanity. Could it be that, from the divine viewpoint—and quite outside the range of human appraisals—the element which was *new,* and therefore to be made impressive, was His humanity? The statement, "The Word was made flesh,

and dwelt among us" (John 1:14), indicates the beginning of an eternal reality in Christ. What is true about His incarnation is equally true of His association with His people, since they, being in Him, can never be separated from Him. The two facts, then, of His humanity and of His identification with His people cannot but demand a supreme recognition both on earth and in heaven. To the same end it will be seen that the redemption which Christ supplies is made possible through His humanity, and, though there is no redemption apart from both His Deity and His humanity, the Deity, being from everlasting, is not the immediate theme for public proclamation. It is *the Son of man* that has come to seek and to save that which was lost (Luke 19:10).

Of the title *the Son of man*, Dr. C. I. Scofield writes thus:

Our Lord thus designates Himself about eighty times. It is His racial name as the representative Man, in the sense of 1 Cor. 15:45–47; as Son of David is distinctively His Jewish name, and Son of God His divine name. Our Lord constantly uses this term as implying that His mission (e.g. Matt. 11:19; Luke 19:10), His death and resurrection (e.g. Matt. 12:40; 20:18; 26:2), and His second coming (e.g. Matt. 24:37–44; Luke 12:40), transcended in scope and result all merely Jewish limitations. When Nathanael confesses Him as "King of Israel," our Lord's answer is, "Thou shalt see greater things . . . the angels of God ascending and descending upon the Son of man." When His messengers are cast out by the Jews, His thought leaps forward to the time when the Son of man shall come, not then to Israel only but to the race (Matt. 10:5, 6 with v.23). It is in this name, also, that universal judgment is committed to Him (John 5:22, 27). It is also a name indicating that in Him is fulfilled the O. T. foreview of blessing through a coming man (Gen. 1:26, *note;* 3:15; 12:3; Psa. 8:4; 80:17; Isa. 7:14; 9:6, 7; 32:2; Zech. 13:7).—*Ibid.,* p. 1006

In another context, Dr. Scofield states:

"Son of man," used by our Lord of Himself seventy-nine times, is used by Jehovah ninety-one times when addressing Ezekiel. (1) In the case of our Lord the meaning is clear: it is His racial name as the representative Man in the sense of 1 Cor. 15:45–47. The same thought, implying transcendence of mere Judaism, is involved in the phrase when applied to Ezekiel. Israel had forgotten her mission (Gen. 11:10, *note;* Ezek. 5:5–8). Now, in her captivity, Jehovah will not forsake His people, but He will remind them that they are but a small part of the race for whom He also cares. Hence the emphasis upon the word "man." The Cherubim "had the likeness of a *man*" (Ezek. 1:5); and when the prophet beheld the throne of God, he saw "the likeness as the appearance of a *man* above upon it" (Ezek. 1:26). See Matt. 8:20, *note;* Rev. 1:12, 13. (2) As used of Ezekiel, the expression indicates, not what the prophet is in himself, but what he is to God: a son of man (*a*) chosen, (*b*) endued with the Spirit, and (*c*) sent of God. All this is true also of Christ who was, furthermore, the representative man—the head of regenerate humanity.—*Ibid.,* pp. 841–42

3. THE SON OF DAVID. The theme of Christ's kingship has received previous, though partial, consideration. Extended investigation into the Davidic covenant, with all that the name *Son of David* connotes, must await a fuller treatment under Eschatology. Like the term *Messiah*, the designation *Son of David* is wholly Jewish in its import. As Christ is Lord and Head over the Church, so He is King and Messiah over Israel. Later, indeed, He will be King of kings, but that supreme authority will be exercised from the Davidic throne and in connection with His immediate relation to Israel.

4. THE SON OF ABRAHAM. Though the Davidic sonship is restricted to David's house and David's people, the Abrahamic sonship extends to "all families of the earth," in whose redemption they are blessed (Gen. 12:3). It is significant that the order of truth in the Gospel by Matthew is indicated in the opening verse, "The book of the generation of Jesus Christ, the son of David, the son of Abraham." This gospel of the King is primarily of His relation to Israel (Matt. 10:5–7; 15:24, 26); but, following His rejection, He turns to that redemptive work described in the closing chapters of this Gospel, and in this redemptive service Christ —the Son of Abraham—procures blessings for all the families of the earth (Matt. 28:18–20).

IV. THE HYPOSTATIC UNION

The uniqueness of the incomparable Person who is the Savior, as has been indicated, is exhibited in His union in His one Person of two natures. He is Deity in the full and absolute sense. In this He is comparable to the Father and to the Spirit. Notwithstanding, He took upon Himself a perfect and complete human nature, and in this respect He was comparable to unfallen Adam, and to other men—except for the injury which sin imposes. That, then, which isolates the God-man from all other beings—whether it be in the Godhead Three, or in the realm of created beings—is this union of two natures in one Person. None other of such character has ever existed, and none other will exist; for no need for such could ever arise. He is the eternal satisfaction of all that requires such a union.

In coming to know Christ as enjoined by the Apostle Peter (2 Pet. 3:18) and thus to be gaining conviction about who it is that undertakes the salvation of men, the mind must ever be alert to recognize both His Deity and His humanity. All thought of this theanthropic Person must be adjusted to the presence in Him of that latitude of Being which completes an uncomplicated participation on His part in two spheres—Deity and humanity. Both of these natures were present in every moment of His existence, beginning with His birth of the Virgin Mary; but it is evident that, when considering any particular act or utterance of Christ's, such will be found to arise either from His divine nature or from His human nature, but in no instance will such action or utterance arise from a combined action of these two natures. It is recognized that theologians differ widely with regard to their beliefs on this particular point. Probably there are situations presented which defy any final analysis by finite minds; yet much light may be gained by any thoughtful reader of the Gospels, and this investigation will take the student far along in the never ending procedure of coming to know the Savior. Since the two natures which together constitute the one and only theanthropic Person are distinct, the Spirit of God, in bringing to the believer's attention the things of Christ (John 16:14), is pleased to make the Savior more real to those who preserve with utmost care the recognition of these two natures which are, in themselves, as dissimilar as are things infinite and things finite.

CONCLUSION

Having reached the termination of this somewhat extended investigation into who the Savior is, this thesis may now proceed to the contemplation of the next theme under the first major division of Soteriology, namely, *The sufferings of Christ.*

CHAPTER III

INTRODUCTION TO THE SUFFERINGS OF CHRIST

As MOSES, in the presence of the burning bush, was commanded to remove the shoes from off his feet since he stood on holy ground, thus an approach should be made, with such a degree of holy awe and reverence as may be possible to those who are subject to human limitations, to the mysterious, sublime, and solemn revelation concerning the sufferings and death of Christ. On the plea that they transcend the range of human understanding, it would be easy to relinquish all attempts to penetrate into these inscrutable and unfathomable verities, were it not for the fact that the theme is so extended as set forth in the Bible—first by type and later by antitype. It is necessary to conclude, since it is thus set forth, that it is the divine purpose that these aspects of truth shall be pursued with intent and zeal, and be as much comprehended as it shall please the Spirit of God to reveal them to the waiting, attentive heart. The theme sweeps the broadest field of reality. On the one hand, the theme of the sufferings and death of Christ reaches out to the solution of the greatest problem of the universe itself, whereas, on the other hand, it reaches down to the level of the lowliest among men. It is also asserted that He who suffered and died learned, or entered experimentally into, obedience through the things which He suffered (Heb. 5:8; Phil. 2:8). Thus, also—and strangely indeed—He was perfected as an efficient Savior (Heb. 2:10), and, having been thus tested, He is able to succor them that are tested (Heb. 2:18). The individual heart may rejoice with eternal joy over the truth that its own needs are answered in the sufferings and death of Christ, but it is well to remember that the solution of the problem of the universe is in itself an achievement as much greater in extent than the issues related to the individual as the universe exceeds the interests of a single person. There are features in each case which relate themselves to infinity, but one exceeds the other by knowledge–surpassing magnitude; and what may be said of all that lies in between these extremes of mass benefits such as redemption of Israel, the purchase of the Church by His precious blood, the judgment of principalities and powers, and that marvelous achievement by which the eternal and holy God is free to satisfy the compassion of His own heart toward a lost world! The challenge of this inexhaustible thesis is yet further extended when it is remembered that the theanthropic Person who suffered and died is none other than "God manifest in the flesh." It was God who suffered and it was the blood of God that was shed (Acts 20:28).

The fact that the sufferings and death of Christ reach out to the universe and into the restricted sphere of the immediate need of one human life in but one of its testings, impels the devout mind to the query why so great a need could have ever arisen. The need is apparent and its answer in Christ's sacrifice is perfect, but why should such a need arise in a universe which God has created as holy as Himself and as holy as are all the works of His hands—a universe over which He is supreme and ever must be? In this connection, it is equally as perplexing to note the truth that the intrusion of sin into the universe was, as He foreknew, to cost Him the greatest of all sacrifices that even God could make—the death of His Son. The evangel that "Christ died for our sins according to the Scriptures" (1 Cor. 15:3) is indeed wonderful, but the Bible does not limit the purpose of Christ's death to the need of a human soul. There are larger issues in the Word of God, and to these consideration must be given. That evil would become a reality and need to be judged was clearly anticipated in the mind of God from all eternity, for, in the divine purpose, Christ was a Lamb slain from the foundation of the world (Rev. 13:8). Sin was in anticipation and is in reality of such a nature that only the sufferings and death of Christ could answer its claims. If God could have saved a sinner from one sin by a mere release, discharge, or leniency, then He might have temporized with the problem of the universe and spared Himself the immeasurable sacrifice of His Son; but neither the problem of one sin in one life nor the problem of a universe could be answered apart from that sacrifice. When entering upon the contemplation of the sufferings and death of Christ, it is important that this truth respecting its necessity should be emphasized.

Though there is immeasurable inequality in their importance, the general theme of the sufferings and death of Christ is divided into (a) His sufferings in life and (b) His sufferings in death. In that order these themes are to be considered.

I. SUFFERINGS IN LIFE

Far beyond the mere fact of Christ's suffering in various ways during His ministry of three and a half years is the theological importance of those sufferings, first, because of the typical significance of those sufferings, and, second, because they have been overstressed in a number of respects, being supposed to achieve what is plainly not designed for them.

In type, the paschal lamb was proved to be without blemish by being confined—a symbol of suffering—from the tenth day of the month to the fourteenth (Ex. 12:3, 6). Thus, also, the life sufferings of Christ served to give full proof of His sinless character, even in the midst of manifold testings, for He was "in all points tested like as we are"—apart from the sin nature (Heb. 4:15). Though unrelated to this immediate theme, it is also to be observed that the four days of confinement of the paschal lamb typified the truth that Christ was "foreordained before the foundation of the world" and was "manifest in these last times for you" (1 Pet. 1:20).

The life sufferings of Christ—too often misrepresented—are well classified as (a) sufferings due to His *character,* (b) sufferings due to His *compassion,* and (c) sufferings due to His *anticipation* of the supreme ordeal of His sacrificial death. However, before these three aspects of life sufferings are taken up separately, it should be noted that in none of them, nor in any other feature of Christ's life, did He undertake any aspect of that work upon which the salvation of a soul depends. Only dire confusion of doctrine results when it is not conceded that, whatever His life-ministry under divine appointment may have been, the *finished work* did not begin until He came to the cross and that work was consummated when He died. The distinctive, efficacious character of the doctrinal aspect of the sufferings of Christ in death cannot be preserved from confusion unless this division of truth is observed.

1. SUFFERINGS DUE TO HIS HOLY CHARACTER. If Lot's righteous soul was vexed by seeing and hearing the unlawful deeds of the dwellers in Sodom (2 Pet. 2:7–8), how much more distressed was the spotless Son of God in the midst of the moral darkness and corruption of fallen men! Such suffering could be estimated only by one who is infinite purity and holiness; yet there is no saving value in these sufferings. What He suffered because of His holiness finds no parallel with His sufferings in death. In the one instance, the unique purity of His holy nature was offended, yet preserved in the midst of surrounding evil. In the other instance, He took the sinner's place and was Himself "made sin," even He who knew no sin (2 Cor. 5:21). All that evil men or Satan might inflict upon Him in His lifetime was suffered because of His own holy character. Had He been one with fallen humanity and in league

with the enemy of God, there would have been no occasion for Him to suffer in this respect. This truth is the basis of His warning to His own who, as He was, are now in this *cosmos* world. He said to them, "If the world hate you, ye know that it hated me before it hated you. If ye were of the world, the world would love his own: but because ye are not of the world, but I have chosen you out of the world, therefore the world hateth you. Remember the word that I said unto you, The servant is not greater than his lord. If they have persecuted me, they will also persecute you; if they have kept my saying, they will keep your's also" (John 15:18–20). At no time in Christ's earth ministry could it be implied that He was forsaken of His Father. But once, and only once, did He cry, "My God, my God, why hast thou forsaken me?" Only inattention will assume that Christ was bearing sin as a substitute at any other time than those darkest hours of Calvary. On the contrary, the voice from heaven, both at His baptism and on the Mount of Transfiguration, declared that in Him—the Son—there was infinite pleasure. Though Christ always did His Father's will—even in death—He was not always making His soul "an offering for sin" (Isa. 53:10). The precise line of division between the life sufferings and the death sufferings is not easy to determine. In Isaiah 53, all that enters into His death as the immediate preparation for it, is included. He is there said to be *wounded, bruised, chastised,* and subject to *stripes* by which there is healing.[1] In the minds of those who inflicted the death sufferings of Christ, it is probable that the scourging, the buffeting, the spitting, and the crown of thorns, like the nails and the spear, were but parts of the whole project. If this be true, the stripes are included in the death sufferings and it would be without controversy that "with his stripes we are healed."

2. SUFFERINGS DUE TO CHRIST'S COMPASSION. Christ was in every respect the manifestation of the Father (John 1:18). The Psalmist declares, "Like as a father pitieth his children, so the LORD pitieth them

---

[1] There is no reference here to physical healing. According to the Old Testament, healing might be either physical or spiritual. Reference is evidently made in Ps. 103:3 to physical healing and in Ps. 147:3 to spiritual healing. In Isa. 53:5 and its parallel in the New Testament—1 Pet. 2:24—the accompanying words employed are all related to things spiritual, namely, *trangression, iniquity, peace, death to sins,* and *healing.* The last, to be in harmony with the context, must relate to healing of the soul. Christ did not bear disease as He bore sin; nor was He *made* disease as He was *made* sin. He was made poor that others might be made rich (2 Cor. 8:9); but none would assert that, because of that truth, men have temporal riches provided for them in the death of Christ, which riches only await the faith that claims them. Reference to riches contemplates spiritual riches which do wait on faith to claim them. In the same manner, healing by the stripes which Christ received is spiritual, or that of the soul, and not physical, or that of the body.

that fear him" (103:13), and in this the Lord Jesus Christ was a perfect representation of the Father's heart. All His miracles of healing and restoration were prompted by His compassion. In Matthew 8:16–17 it is written: "When the even was come, they brought unto him many that were possessed with devils: and he cast out the spirits with his word, and healed all that were sick: that it might be fulfilled which was spoken by Esaias the prophet, saying, Himself took our infirmities, and bare our sicknesses." Much error is abroad because of a form of teaching which avers that Christ when healing was bearing as a substitute the diseases of those whom He healed. It is true that Matthew relates the physical healing described in this text to Isaiah, chapter 53, but a careful examination of this chapter will disclose that Isaiah refers to both the life sufferings of Christ (vss. 1–4a), and the death sufferings (vss. 4b–12). The turning point is in verse 4 and is marked by the word *yet,* which verse reads: "Surely he hath borne our griefs, and carried our sorrows: yet we did esteem him stricken, smitten of God, and afflicted." If this division be accepted, the bearing of disease and sickness, reported in Matthew 8:16–17, which is there based on Isaiah 53:4, belongs to His life sufferings and is wholly in the realm of His compassion, which compassion, due to His infinite perfection, was beyond human measurement. Isaiah 53:4a was fulfilled by Christ when He, moved by this boundless compassion, healed those who came before Him. Not all the sufferers in that land or in the world were healed by Him, and no such offer is ever extended to them. Compassion naturally is drawn out toward those immediately observed. None could deny the reality of physical healing on the part of God today, but it is properly based on His compassion for His own and not on the death sufferings of Christ.

3. SUFFERINGS DUE TO ANTICIPATION. The anticipation of the cross was constantly before Christ. The words, "For this cause came I unto this hour" (John 12:27), are but one of His recorded forward looks into the dark shadow which was before Him. His predictions concerning His own death (Matt. 16:21; 17:12, 22–23; Mark 9:30–32; Luke 9:31, 44, etc.), the inauguration of the Lord's Supper, the cup to be emptied, and the sufferings of Gethsemane, all belong to His sufferings in anticipation. On this aspect of Christ's sufferings, C. H. Mackintosh in his *Notes on Leviticus* states:

We find the dark shadow of the cross casting itself athwart His path, and producing a very keen order of suffering, which, however, must be as clearly distinguished from His atoning suffering as either His suffering for righteousness or His suffering by sympathy. Let us take a passage, in proof—"And He came out, and went, as He was wont, to the mount of Olives; and His disciples also followed Him. And when He was at the place, He said unto them, 'Pray that ye enter not into temptation.' And He was withdrawn from them about a stone's cast, and kneeled down, and prayed, saying, 'Father, if Thou be willing, remove this cup from Me: nevertheless not My will, but Thine, be done.' And there appeared an angel unto Him from heaven, strengthening Him. And being in an agony, He prayed more earnestly: and His sweat was as it were great drops of blood falling down to the ground" (Luke xxii. 39–44). Again, we read, "And He took with Him Peter and the two sons of Zebedee, and began to be sorrowful and very heavy. Then saith He unto them, 'My soul is exceeding sorrowful, even unto death: tarry ye here, and watch with me.' . . . He went away again the second time, and prayed, saying, 'O My Father, if this cup may not pass from Me, except I drink it, Thy will be done' " (Matt. xxvi. 37–42). From these verses, it is evident there was a something in prospect which the blessed Lord had never encountered before,—there was a "cup" being filled out for Him of which He had not yet drunk. If He had been a sin-bearer all His life, then why this intense "agony" at the thought of coming in contact with sin and enduring the wrath of God on account of sin? What was the difference between Christ in Gethsemane and Christ at Calvary if He were a sin-bearer all His life? There was a material difference; but it is because He was not a sin-bearer all His life. What is the difference? In Gethsemane, He was *anticipating* the cross; at Calvary, He was actually *enduring* it. In Gethsemane, "there appeared an angel unto Him from heaven, strengthening Him"; at Calvary, He was forsaken of all. There was no angelic ministry there. In Gethsemane, He addresses God as *"Father,"* thus enjoying the full communion of that ineffable relationship; but at Calvary, He cries, "My *God,* my *God,* why hast Thou forsaken me?" Here the Sin-bearer looks up and beholds the throne of Eternal Justice enveloped in dark clouds, and the countenance of inflexible Holiness averted from Him, because He was being "made sin for us."—2nd ed., pp. 64–65

At this point, occasion demands that a return be made to the subject of Christ's baptism because of the fact that His baptism is too often deemed to be an act of Christ's which identified Him as Sin-Bearer with those He came to save. This conclusion is based on the conception of water baptism, that it signifies the death of Christ rather than the all-transforming baptizing work of the Spirit, and that, by His baptism, Christ anticipated His death sufferings and was in the act of baptism taking His place with sinners. In harmony with this, it is believed that Christ received "John's baptism." It is true He was baptized by John, but it is not true that He received what is identified in the New Testament as *John's baptism,* which was a well-defined, specific baptism unto repentance and unto the remission of sin. The following from George Smeaton (*The Doctrine of the Atonement,* p. 99) serves to illustrate the manner in which this theory is usually set forth: "Impurity of His own He had none. But He had truly entered into humanity, and come within the bonds of the human family; and, according to the law, the person who had but touched an unclean person, or had been in contact with him, was unclean. Hence, in submitting Himself to baptism as Mediator in an official capacity, the Lord Jesus virtually said, 'Though sinless in a world of sinners, and without having contracted any personal taint, I come for baptism; because, in my public or official capacity, I am a debtor in the room of many, and bring with Me the sin of the whole world, for which I am the propitiation.' He was already atoning for sin, and had been bearing it on His body since He took the flesh; and in this mediatorial capacity promises had been made to Him as the basis of His faith, and as the ground upon which His confidence was exercised at every step." Over against this, the words of Dr. James W. Dale (*Christic and Patristic Baptism,* pp. 27–28) serve to discover the weakness and error of the contention that Christ was baptized by "John's baptism":

It is one thing to be baptized by John and quite another thing to receive the "baptism of John." Therefore, while the Scriptures teach us that Jesus came to the Jordan to be baptized by John, they do not teach us that he came to receive John's baptism. Indeed it is impossible, in any just aspect of the case, that he could have received it. Whatever involves an absurdity must be impossible and untrue. That an absurdity is involved in such a supposition is thus shown: "The baptism of John" was for sinners; demanding "repentance," "fruits meet for repentance," and promising "the remission of sins." But the Lord Jesus Christ was not a sinner, could not repent of sin, could not bring forth fruit meet for repentance on account of sin, could not receive the remission of sin. Therefore the reception of "the baptism of John" by Jesus is impossible, untrue, and absurd. Again: The baptism of John was "to prepare a people for the Lord." But to address such a baptism to the Lord (preparing the Lord for himself) is absurd. Therefore the reception of John's baptism by the Lord Jesus is impossible, untrue, and absurd. It is just as absurd to suppose that he received this baptism formally but not substantially. A baptism exists only while its essence exists. The essence of John's ritual baptism is found in its symbolization of purification in the soul through repentance and remission of sin. But in the Lord Jesus there was no basis for such symbolization, and consequently there was no basis for the baptism of John. The idea that John's baptism could be received representatively is just as impossible. To the glory of God in the highest, the Lord Jesus did "bear our iniquities," was "made sin for us"; but he was not hereby the more qualified to receive John's baptism. The Lord Jesus did not represent penitent sinners, nor sinners whose iniquities were remitted. He came as the Friend of publicans and sinners, to call sinners to repentance, to give repentance to Israel; there was no adaptation in the baptism of John to such Sin-Bearer. He must accomplish a baptism for himself; it must be of blood and not of water; "without the shedding of blood there is no remission of sin" such as Jesus bore. In his character as Bearer of the sins of others, he neither had nor could have anything to do with John's baptism.

Reference is made at this point to Christ's baptism only because of the fact that His baptism is the event which, as often interpreted, serves more than any other to confuse the issues of Christ's life and ministry with the issues of His death. It must be recognized that He anticipated His death from the beginning of His public service—as did the Baptist (John 1:29); but no contribution was made to His redeeming, reconciling, and propitiatory work by His baptism. The efficacious work which His Father gave Him to do was inaugurated at the cross; there it was prosecuted, and there it was consummated. If the distinction between that which Christ wrought in His life and that which He wrought in His death—and many are apparently not awake to it—is not observed, only confusion of doctrine will result.

Yet another consideration arises, namely, a distinction which devout men have made between what is termed the *active* obedience of Christ and His *passive* obedience. By the word *active* they refer to that obedience in which the Savior maintained a perfect rectitude of life, keeping every divine requirement in infinite perfection. By the word *passive* they refer to that obedience which endured suffering both in life and in death. He not only did not do wrong, but He fulfilled perfectly every right action belonging to man. Later it will be demonstrated that, in His substitution, Christ not only bore the penalty of sin, but also presented His own infinitely perfect character to God. This offering included His earth life in which He fulfilled all the will of God in the sense that His own character would have been incomplete without it. Similarly, it is asserted by some that His *passive* obedience entered into every privation which He endured while in this *cosmos* world, and by this aspect of His obedience as much as by the death sufferings, souls are saved. Jonathan Edwards declared that the blood of Christ's circumcision when He was eight days old was as efficacious as that which flowed from the thrust of the spear. The weakness of such a claim is exposed in the fact that the Word of God does not assign saving value to any obedience of the sufferings of Christ other than that connected with His death. The declaration that He became obedient unto death, even the death of the cross (Phil. 2:8), intimates that a particular obedience was exhibited, or one peculiar to its own purpose, in the cross. It is true that salvation for sinners depends upon Christ's passive obedience in His death sufferings and the offering of Himself without spot to God. Salvation is based on the blood of the cross and not on the blood of circumcision or even the blood which He sweat in the garden. He provided no redemption, reconciliation, or propitiation when circumcised or when baptized.

II. SUFFERINGS IN DEATH

The centrality of the cross has been acknowledged by all devout minds from its day to the present hour. The unregenerate see in it little more than a "stumblingblock"—which it is to the Jew—and "foolishness"—which it is to the Gentile; but to those who are the called, both Jews and Gentiles, it is the power of God—since by it His saving power is released—and the wisdom of God—since by it the greatest problem is solved which ever confronted Him, namely, How can God remain *just* and yet justify the ungodly who do no more than to believe in Jesus (1 Cor. 1:23–24; Rom. 3:26; 4:5)? When it is asserted that the cross is to the Gentiles *foolishness,* it is not implied that they are ridiculing it, but rather it is indicated that the interpretations they give to Christ's death are foolish in that those interpretations are not worthy of the Son of God; and such is every interpretation save the one assigned in the Word of God, which is that of a blood sacrifice for sin offered by a substitute who dies in the room and stead of sinners. To the Apostle Paul, the cross became the supreme theme of his boasting. He said, "But God forbid that I should glory, save in the cross of our Lord Jesus Christ, by whom the world is crucified unto me, and I unto the world" (Gal. 6:14).

In the opening paragraph of his book *The Atonement and the Modern Mind,* Dr. James Denney asserts: "It will be admitted by most Christians that if the Atonement, quite apart from precise definitions of it, is anything to the mind, it is everything. It is the most profound of all truths, and the most recreative. It determines more than anything else our conceptions of God, of man, of history, and even of nature; it determines them, for we must bring them all in some way into accord with it. It is the inspiration of all thought, the impulse and the law of all action, the key, in the last resort, to all suffering. Whether we call it a fact or a truth, a power or a doctrine, it is that in which the *differentia* of Christianity, its peculiar and exclusive character, is specifically shown; it is the focus of revelation, the point at which we see deepest into the truth of God, and come most completely under its power. For those who recognise it at all it is Christianity in brief; it concentrates in itself, as in a germ of infinite potency, all that the wisdom, power and love of God mean in relation to sinful men." A like emphasis was given by the great Calvinistic theologian, Francis Turretin (1623–1687), when he wrote regarding the importance of that death, that it was "the chief part of our salvation, the anchor of Faith, the refuge of Hope, the rule of Charity, the true foundation of the Christian religion, and the richest treasure of the Christian Church. So long as this doctrine is main-- tained in its integrity, Christianity itself and the peace and blessedness of all who believe in Christ are beyond the reach of danger; but if it is rejected, or in any way impaired, the whole structure of the Christian faith must sink into decay and ruin" (cited by R. W. Dale, *The Atone-ment*, 4th ed., p. 3). Not only does the theme of Christ's sufferings and death exceed all others, as these witnesses testify, and not only is it central in Biblical truth, but it is eternal with respect to its past— Christ a slain Lamb before the foundation of the world (Rev. 13:8)— and eternal with respect to its future, being as it is the theme of coming glory, "And they sung a new song, saying, Thou art worthy to take the book, and to open the seals thereof: for thou wast slain, and hast re- deemed us to God by thy blood out of every kindred, and tongue, and people, and nation; and hast made us unto our God kings and priests: and we shall reign on the earth. And I beheld, and I heard the voice of many angels round about the throne and the beasts and the elders: and the number of them was ten thousand times ten thousand, and thousands of thousands; saying with a loud voice, Worthy is the Lamb that was slain to receive power, and riches, and wisdom, and strength, and honour, and glory, and blessing" (Rev. 5:9–12).

In approaching the theme of Christ's sufferings and death, certain truths of general import about which there has been much misunder- standing, should be considered.

1. CONTRAST BETWEEN THE CRUCIFIXION AND THE CROSS. There is the distinction to be drawn between the crucifixion—the greatest of all crimes—and the cross—contemplated as the sign of God's redeem- ing grace: that which Dr. R. W. Dale describes as "the sublimest mo- ment in the moral history of God" (cited by Henry C. Mabie, *The Meaning and Message of the Cross*, p. 23). Could a greater contrast be conceived? It is possible to think of the death sufferings of Christ only as that which originated with men and was executed by men. Such a re-

stricted conception may result in strange reasoning. Dr. Henry C. Mabie cites the following statement illustrating this impression:

In the correspondence column of Rev. R. J. Campbell of London in *The British Weekly,* an enquirer recently put this question: "I have a Bible class, some of the members of which are fine, thoughtful young fellows. We are studying the life of Christ, and will shortly reach the crucifixion. How can I make clear that the act of crucifying Christ was a *crime,* while at the same time it is *the hope* on which the Christian builds?" And Mr. Campbell, before proceeding to answer, remarks: "This difficulty occurs far more generally than I should have thought." Lord Beaconsfield is said once to have caricatured the Atonement in the following terms: "If the Jews had not prevailed upon the Romans to crucify our Lord, what would have become of the Atonement? The immolators were preordained like the victim; and the holy race supplied both. Could that be a crime which secured for all mankind, eternal joy?" A leading Unitarian minister in New York City, in a sermon preached in his own church a few years since, touching this subject, used these words: "What does atonement mean to the world? It means that the Eternal Father either will not, or cannot receive back to His heart His own erring, mistaken, wandering children, unless the only begotten Son of God is *slaughtered,* and we, as the old, awful hymn has it, 'are plunged beneath this ocean of blood.' " A supposedly evangelical American minister in his recoil from certain misconceptions of evangelicalism against which he was protesting, once went so far as to say,— "Strictly speaking, the death of Christ was not necessary to human salvation . . . He was not a suicide; He was *murdered.* To say that His death was an indispensable condition to human salvation is to say that God's grace had to call in the aid of murderers in order that it might find a way to human hearts. I am not willing to acknowledge any indebtedness to Judas Iscariot for the forgiveness of my sins."—*Ibid.,* pp. 21–22

It would seem probable that the Satan-imposed blindness of the unregenerate respecting the gospel (2 Cor. 4:3–4), and the illumination which the regenerate receive, center at this crucial point, on the meaning of Christ's death. In the one instance, men see only a brutal murder, and, since the victim was innocent—a lovable, admirable character— there is a field for meditation on certain lessons which may be drawn from that tragic death. By so much and with sincerity the cross is made *foolishness.* In the other instance, the regenerate by illumination granted them are able to see in the cross the whole scope and plan of redeeming grace. It is declared—and how many passages might be cited—that Christ was "set forth" (which is evidently a reference to His position as a victim on the cross) to declare the righteousness of God, that "he might be just, and the justifier of him which believeth in Jesus" (Rom. 3:25–26).

Since the sufferings and death of Christ are central in all revealed truth and since these may be estimated so differently—on the one hand as the major crime, and on the other hand, as "the sublimest moment in the moral history of God"—His sufferings and death demand a careful and prayerful consideration above all the facts of the universe. Probably no writer has more faithfully set up this great contrast with all it involves than Dr. Henry C. Mabie. Though somewhat extended, the following quotation (*Ibid.*, pp. 25–30) is a contribution needed at this point in this discussion:

In this study I start then by pointing out that the tragedy of Christ's crucifixion in its awful criminality, and the cross of the divine reconciliation in its unique moral majesty, are in character wholly distinct. The crucifixion on the human side was incipient in the sin of the race; and the reconciliation on the divine side, since God is what He is in His long-suffering holiness, was ever eternally in the heart of God waiting to be enacted. It is true that in those last hours upon the cross, the deep, spiritual work of the reconciliation was being consummated *simultaneously* with the crime which Christ's crucifiers were perpetrating upon Him: in spirit, however, and in moral character, the two enactments were at the farthest possible remove from each other. . . . A concrete picture drawn from the New Testament account of the crucifixion may make clearer the distinction treated in this chapter. In observing the record of the execution of Jesus, a careful reader will notice the varied mental attitudes of the several types of people who stood before the cross. There are at least five classes of people whose attitudes were fundamentally the same; the common crowd, that "passed by wagging their heads"; the Jewish rulers who had connived at the crucifixion; the railing malefactor who rejected Christ; the Roman soldiers, who knew no king but Caesar; and the half-superstitious beholders, who in the cry of "Eli, Eli," supposed Jesus to be calling for Elias. Each of these five classes appealed alike to Christ to demonstrate that He was really the Messiah, by coming down from the cross and saving His life. The crowd said, "Ha, Thou that destroyest the temple and buildest it in three days, save Thyself and come down from the cross" (Mark 15:29). The rulers said, "He saved others, Himself He cannot save; let the Christ, the King of Israel, now come down from the cross, that we may see and believe" (Mark 15:31–32). The malefactor said, "Art not Thou the Christ? Save Thyself and us" (Luke 23:39). The soldiers said, "If Thou art the king of the Jews, save Thyself" (Luke 23:37). The superstitious said, "Let be; let us see whether Elijah cometh to take Him down" (Mark 15:36). Each of these, observe, in effect said to Jesus, *"Save Thyself."* These all saw chiefly the tragedy of the crucifixion, they supposed the cross in that sense to be finality in the life of Jesus. Unless Jesus should use His miraculous power to take Himself off the scaffold,—supernaturally keep Himself alive,—they would have no faith in Him; the demonstration to their minds would be complete that He was not what He claimed to be, the Son of God, the Messiah of Israel, the Saviour of the world. Now, over against these five classes, there is a single shining exception, of one whose position radically differed from that of these types just noted, and he expresses himself differently: The dying penitent was the first and only one among all that spoke out at the execution of Jesus, who did not say, "*Save Thyself.*" He did cry, "*Save me.*" And he said "Jesus"; that is, he used the saving name, with discernment of who and what He really was. He and he alone saw there was something deeper transpiring than the cruci-fiers recognized; that Jesus really was allowing the sanctuary of His body to be taken down, in order that it might be rebuilt. He discerned that if Jesus would save others from the spiritual necessities of the case, He could not "save Himself"; He must endure what sin would impose on Saviourhood; he saw that Jesus really was "the King of Israel," "the chosen of God," "the good shepherd," laying down His life for the sheep, so laying it down that He "might take it again." This penitent was the first and only one at the crucifixion that saw a whole new kingdom lying beyond the impending death of Jesus, of which he might become a member. That kingdom, however, was to be built upon the divine side of what was going on. He saw at least in principle the coming resurrection, and the glorious possibilities involved in it . . . Doubtless he was spiritually, preternaturally endued with the insight of one on the border-land of the celestial world; and thus saw both sides of the crucifixion event, the basely human and the nobly divine. But he especially saw with great vivid-ness the reality of the reconciliation, saw it from the heaven-side, as God sees it—as we all should learn to see it;—and he exclaimed in that model prayer, marked with its peculiar illumination, "Jesus, remember me when Thou comest into Thy kingdom" (Luke 23:42);—a kingdom conditioned on what was now being borne by Christ. This man and this one only, so far as we know, of all that stood about the Christ on Calvary, apprehended the reconciliation, God's act,—an act as both deliberate and permissive,—the reconciliation as distinguished from man's criminality in the crucifixion. There was probably not a disciple that stood there, not one of the women, not even the Saviour's own mother Mary, that would not, if possible, in their sheer inability to perceive what God was achieving, have prevented the completion of Christ's purpose on the cross. As yet, none of these disciples understood as they did afterwards in the light of Pentecost—the cross of the redemption. This dying man so unfortunately stigmatized in the common epithet, as "the dying thief," is really the ideal penitent. He and he only, had the vision of the cross of recon-ciliation. He alone looked beyond the tragic horrors of the crucifying deed. He was absorbed with the larger reality, that Christ, despite man's treatment of Him, was really bearing away the sin of the world, preparatory to a spiritual kingdom which lay beyond the climacteric of His dying hour. The penitent sought membership in that kingdom, a privilege of grace instantly assured by the reply of Jesus, "Verily I say unto thee, to-day shalt thou be with me in Paradise" (Luke 23:43).

As before intimated, the unenlightened, unregenerate people can dis-cern nothing in Christ's death beyond the human tragedy that it was, and in vain do they with sincerity attempt to invest it with some spirit-ual significance. It is dramatized, crucifixes are multiplied, pictures are painted, preachers and poets dwell upon the physical aspects of that death and, too often, discover nothing beyond the bodily anguish which was His. However, none have wrought more confusion than has the Church of Rome by her asserted transubstantiation and the approach to idolatry which her use of images provides. Rome is the supreme example of a religion based on the *crime* of the crucifixion, which, at the same time, is void of any conception of the glory of the cross. There was a tragedy in the crucifixion which none should minimize, but it is not the ground of redemption. God is not basing His immeasurable love-gift on the supreme crime of all crimes. He bases it upon the sublime truth that He so loved the world that He gave His only begotten Son to be His own, provided sacrificial Lamb. Christ was God's Lamb—not Pilate's. God provided the redeeming blood—not Caiaphas.

As is to be expected, there is no point in human history where the divine sovereignty and human responsibility, or free will, come into more vivid juxtaposition than they do in the crucifixion of Christ. On the divine side, Christ's death was predetermined in such a way that God assumes all responsibility for it, nor could He share its achievement with another. It was His purpose from all eternity. It was foreshadowed in God-wrought types. All its details were predicted by Spirit-empowered prophets. In Psalm 22 there is recorded the cry of suffering: "My God, my God, why hast thou forsaken me? why art thou so far from helping me, and from the words of my roaring?" (vs. 1); the precise words the tormentors would utter: "He trusted on the LORD that he would deliver him: let him deliver him, seeing he delighted in him" (vs. 8); the acknowledgment of the divine responsibility: "And thou hast brought me into the dust of death" (vs. 15); the piercing of the hands and feet: "They pierced my hands and my feet" (vs. 16); and the parting of the garments and casting lots for His vesture: "They part my garments among them, and cast lots upon my vesture" (vs. 18). To the same end, there is in Isaiah, chapter 53, the recital of the truth that it was Jehovah who bruised Him, who put Him to grief, who made His soul an offering for sin (vs. 10). Likewise, the sovereignty of God is reflected in the more than forty times the word *fulfilled* occurs in the New Testament and in reference to the realization of the purpose of God in the death of His Son. On the human side, men were doing and saying precisely what was predicted of them, yet in such a way as that the responsibility fell alone upon them. Christ was rejected by the Jews, betrayed by Judas, condemned by Herod, and crucified under Pontius Pilate. Beyond all this human action it is declared that it was God who was in Christ reconciling the world unto Himself (2 Cor. 5:19). It is written that Christ was *made* sin (by the Father—certainly not by Judas Iscariot), that lost souls might be made (by the Father—certainly not by Pontius Pilate) the righteousness of God in Him (2 Cor. 5:21). Two immeasurable facts—as far removed from each other as the east is from the west—were spoken by Peter in his Pentecostal sermon, "Him, being delivered by the determinate counsel and foreknowledge of God, ye have taken, and by wicked hands have crucified and slain" (Acts 2:23). In precisely the same manner in which there is no gratitude due Judas, Herod, or Pontius Pilate, there is no doctrine based on what they did. The transforming power of Christ's death is not in the human tragedy; it is in the divine reconciliation. The death and resurrection of Christ are counterparts of one divine undertaking. None will predicate of man that he had any part in the resurrection; yet the divine accomplishment in the cross is as void of human cooperation as is the resurrection.

2. WHO PUT CHRIST TO DEATH? Closely related to the contrast between the divine and human sides of Christ's death, is the question: Who put Christ to death? As already indicated, the Scriptures assign both a human and a divine responsibility for Christ's death—not a cooperation or partnership, for each is treated, in its own sphere, as wholly answerable. In all, eight individuals or groups are held accountable. Four of these are named in Acts 4:27–28: "For of a truth against thy holy child Jesus, whom thou hast anointed, both Herod, and Pontius Pilate, with the Gentiles, and the people of Israel, were gathered together, for to do whatsoever thy hand and thy counsel determined before to be done." Here, again, the Holy Spirit safeguards the all-important truth that these individuals and groups were doing precisely what the hand and counsel of Jehovah determined. The fifth responsible individual is Satan—though he may have been aided by uncounted cohorts of evil spirits. In the great protevangelium of Genesis 3:15, it is stated that not only would Christ bruise the serpent's head, but that the serpent would bruise His heel. Thus it is implied that Satan did what he could in the exercise of his power—directly, or indirectly, through human agents—against the Savior. There is much Scripture which reveals that a mighty conflict was waged between Christ and the powers of darkness. It is written: "Now is the judgment of this world: now shall the prince of this world be cast out" (John 12:31); "Hereafter I will not talk much with you: for the prince of this world cometh, and hath nothing in me" (John 14:30); "Of judgment, because the prince of this world

is judged" (John 16:11); "Blotting out the handwriting of ordinances that was against us, which was contrary to us, and took it out of the way, nailing it to his cross; and having spoiled principalities and powers, he made a shew of them openly, triumphing over them in it" (Col. 2:14–15). What transpired between the Son of God and Satan at the cross is related to heavenly spheres and cannot be comprehended by men.

The remaining three who are said to be accountable for Christ's death are the Father, the Son, and the Holy Spirit. The action of the Father is presented in types, in prophecies, and in direct declarations. It is written: "God will provide himself a lamb" (Gen. 22:8); "Thou hast brought me into the dust of death" (Ps. 22:15); "My God, my God, why hast thou forsaken me?" (Ps. 22:1); "Reproach hath broken my heart" (Ps. 69:20); "Yet it pleased the LORD to bruise him; he hath put him to grief: when thou shalt make his soul an offering for sin" (Isa. 53:10); "Behold the Lamb of God" (John 1:29); "Him, being delivered by the determinate counsel and foreknowledge of God" (Acts 2:23); "For to do whatsoever thy hand and thy counsel determined before to be done" (Acts 4:28); "He that spared not his own Son" (Rom. 8:32); and "God so loved the world, that he gave his only begotten Son" (John 3:16).

The action of the Son is typified in the nonresistance of Isaac on Mount Moriah; also in prophecy by the words "But thou art holy" (Ps. 22:3), and "Yet he opened not his mouth" (Isa. 53:7); and in direct statement: "No man taketh it from me, but I lay it down of myself. I have power to lay it down, and I have power to take it again. This commandment have I received of my Father" (John 10:18); "And when Jesus had cried with a loud voice, he said, Father, into thy hands I commend my spirit: and having said thus, he gave up the ghost" (Luke 23:46); "Christ also loved the church, and gave himself for it" (Eph. 5:25); "Who loved me, and gave himself for me" (Gal. 2:20); "Who gave himself for us, that he might redeem us from all iniquity, and purify unto himself a peculiar people, zealous of good works" (Titus 2:14); "Even as the Son of man came not to be ministered unto, but to minister, and to give his life a ransom for many" (Matt. 20:28); "Hereby perceive we the love of God, because he laid down his life for us: and we ought to lay down our lives for the brethren" (1 John 3:16). The willingness of the Son in the Father's hand is the answer to the contention that it is immoral for God to offer His Son. Such an act on the part of God, it is freely admitted, might be the most terrible crime or the most glorious consummation of divine grace. All depends on the one issue of whether the sacrifice is imposed upon the Son against His will or whether He is in agreement and cooperation with His Father. That He was in agreement is assured in the above Scriptures, which indicated that He offered Himself, and in every passage in which He is seen to be subject to His Father's will, notably, "Then said I, Lo, I come (in the volume of the book it is written of me,) to do thy will, O God" (Heb. 10:7).

The action of the Holy Spirit in the sufferings and death of Christ is revealed in one passage in particular: "How much more shall the blood of Christ, who through the eternal Spirit offered himself without spot to God, purge your conscience from dead works to serve the living God?" (Heb. 9:14).

3. WHAT CHRIST SUFFERED AT THE HANDS OF MEN AND WHAT HE SUFFERED AT THE HANDS OF HIS FATHER. Still more closely related to the major distinction between the crucifixion as a crime and the cross as the supreme manifestation of divine compassion, is the difference to be seen between that which Christ suffered at the hands of men and that which He suffered at the hand of His Father. Human hands might inflict physical suffering and death as any victim would die, but only the hand of God could make Christ a sin offering, or could lay on Him the iniquity of others (2 Cor. 5:21; Isa. 53:6). No more impossible notion has been formed into verse than the line of a hymn which reads, "I lay my sins on Jesus, the spotless Lamb of God." It is not in the power of any man to lay his sins on Jesus, or to lay anyone's sins on Jesus. Had Pontius Pilate been moved with superhuman compassion for lost souls and had he crucified the Savior with that in view, he could have done no more than to crucify Him. God alone might provide a sin-bearer and God alone could impute sin to the One He provided.

4. THE VALUE OF CHRIST'S SUFFERINGS TO THE FATHER. Yet another vital distinction—essential, indeed, to a clear understanding of the nature of the sufferings and death of Christ—is that which may be seen when the value of Christ's sufferings and death, as pertaining to the Father, is compared with that value as it pertains to those who are saved by it. An exact computation of those values is not possible by any human being. That the one who is saved will not perish, but is in present possession of eternal life, that he is united to Christ to share His peace and glory, and that he shall, when he sees his Savior, be like Him, could never be accurately appraised by men. Over against this is the truth that, regardless of His infinite love which would bless the creatures of His hand, the moral restraint on God which sin imposes could not be removed even by a sovereign decree; it was necessary, in the light of His holy

character and government, that the price of redemption should be required at the hand of the offender or at the hand of a substitute who would die in the offender's place. By the death of Christ for sinners, the moral restraint is removed and the love of God is free to act in behalf of those who will receive His grace and blessing. No measurement may be placed on the meaning of this freedom which the cross has secured for God. It is revealed, however, that, when thus untrammelled, God, in the satisfaction of His love, accomplishes the greatest thing that God can do, which is, so to transform the sinner who trusts Him that the sinner will appear in eternal glory conformed to the image of Christ. There is nothing conceivable that would be a greater achievement than this; but it is wrought, primarily, to satisfy the love of God for the sinner. Those who trust Him will not perish, but have everlasting life. However, all this was made possible because of the fact that God so *loved* that He gave His only begotten Son. What the freedom to exercise such love, which is secured by the death of Christ, means to God is as incomprehensible as the divine love itself.

To the same end, it may be added that, as the salvation of a soul demonstrates the exceeding grace of God, which grace could not be exhibited by any other means, the death of Christ has secured and made possible that exalted experience on God's part of the exercise of His superabounding grace. Again, all human estimations are incapable of any adequate knowledge of the value to God of Christ's death.

5. THE WISDOM, POWER, AND SACRIFICE OF GOD. A reasonable approach to the contemplation of the sufferings and death of Christ requires that due thought be given to the wisdom, power, and sacrifice which God has exercised in devising and achieving the plan by which the lost may be saved. As before observed, the cross is to the Jew a stumbling block and to the Gentile foolishness, but to those who are called—whether Jew or Gentile—Christ is the power of God and the wisdom of God (1 Cor. 1:23–24). Thus it is asserted that God's power is set free to act in behalf of the lost, and His wisdom is demonstrated in the plan of salvation—all through the cross of Christ. As for His power, it is noticeable that, according to Psalm 8:3—"When I consider thy heavens, the work of thy fingers"—creation is said to be but the finger-play of God; but, when He would save the lost, according to Isaiah 53:1—"to whom is the arm of the LORD revealed?"—the great right arm of Jehovah, the symbol of all His strength, is made bare and called into action. As for His wisdom, it is disclosed that, by the death of His Son, He has solved His greatest problem, namely, how He might

be just and yet justify the ungodly (Rom. 3:26; 4:5). As for His sacrifice, no greater immolation could be designed than is indicated by the words, "He that spared not his own Son, but delivered him up for us all" (Rom. 8:32). It would be folly indeed for men to suppose that it is within their capacity to comprehend the *power* of God, the *wisdom* of God, or the *sacrifice* of God as revealed in the salvation of a soul.

6. THE UNIFIED ACTION OF THE THREE PERSONS. Still another introductory word concerns the unified action of the three Persons of the Godhead in saving the lost. The three Persons are seen achieving the creation of the universe. To each this vast work is accredited separately and with the implication that each acted alone and when so acting was wholly sufficient and responsible. In the greater work of redemption—specifically the sufferings and death of Christ—it is the Son who suffers and dies, but the Father gives the Son and the Son is offered by the Eternal Spirit. Here is revealed the deepest unified action and cooperation. The Son cries, "My God, my God, why hast thou forsaken me?" (Ps. 22:1; Matt. 27:46), yet it is affirmed that it was the very God to whom He cried that was, at that precise moment, "in Christ, reconciling the world unto himself" (2 Cor. 5:19). To finite minds all this is paradoxical, yet it serves to emphasize anew the deeper truth that, though there are three Persons in the Godhead, there is but one essence. Neither the Father nor the Spirit became incarnate. The action of the Son was always according to the will of the Father and never more so than in His death (Phil. 2:8). All the Son wrought was in the power of the Spirit and never more perfectly than in His death. Objectively, not only did the Father *give* the Son (John 3:16), but He *sent* the Son (John 3:17), He *loved* the Son (John 3:35), He is *glorified* in the Son (John 14:13), and He *glorified* the Son (Acts 3:13); yet wholly consonant is this truth with a deeper reality, namely, that the Father and the Son are one (John 10:30; 14:9–11; 17:21). Thus in the larger revelation, which men may not comprehend, the triune God is the Savior of the world. Neglect of this aspect of truth has always resulted in notions respecting God which are injurious. When specific attributes are assigned to one Person over the other Two, a theology arises which conceives of the Father as the arbiter of justice, the defender of holiness, while the Son is the manifester of that divine love which would rescue the sinner from the judgments which the Father requires. The Son does not save from the Father, He saves from righteous judgments against sin; and of the Savior it is said that into His hands all judgment has been committed (John 5:27; Acts 10:42; 17:31). The Father is not

the condemner of the world. He it was who sent His Son into the world, that the world through Him might be saved (John 3:17). It still remains true that the Father gave the Son, the Son died, and the Spirit applies the value of that death to those who believe.

7. TWO MAJOR FEATURES OF SOTERIOLOGY. And finally, by way of words of introduction, there are two major features of Soteriology—(a) the finished work of the Savior on the cross, and (b) the application of that work to those who believe. Each of these factors is declared to have been determined divinely from a dateless past. Of the Savior's work it is written that He was a Lamb slain from the foundation of the world (Rev. 13:8). Of the saved one it is said that he was "chosen in him before the foundation of the world" (Eph. 1:4). To this will be added under Ecclesiology a third aspect of the eternal purpose, namely, that the good works of the saved one are foreordained that he should walk in them (Eph. 2:10). These three—a foreordained Savior, a foreordained salvation, and a foreordained service—constitute the essential elements in the eternal counsels of God respecting the Church which is His body. Confusion too often characterizes the treatment men give to the first two of these eternal purposes. The Savior has finished the work and it only remains for the sinner to *believe* and be saved. What Christ has done on the cross and what He will do now for the one who believes are widely different aspects of truth. On the one hand, there are those who teach that it is equivalent to the salvation of a soul if Christ dies for that soul. On the other hand, there are those who direct the unsaved to plead with God for their salvation. Certainly the unsaved are not called upon to ask Christ to die for them; and as certainly they are not called upon to urge the Savior to apply His salvation. The promise is not to those who ask, but to those who *believe*. Since, through the death of Christ, God is propitious, saints may be restored and sinners saved without reproof or punishment from God—no blow is struck and no condemnation is uttered. The Savior has died. That may be believed, and such belief leads to the salvation of the soul; but what He did for the sinner two millenniums ago should not be confused with that salvation which is wrought now when the sinner believes. Hypothetically considered, the Savior might have died, thus providing every ground for a perfect salvation, and no one have believed; for the cross compels no one to believe. It is the sovereign election of God, that which made choice of men for salvation before the foundation of the world, which insures the salvation. In the execution of that sovereign election, the Spirit calls, illuminates, engenders faith, and applies all the value of Christ's death to the one who thus believes.

CHAPTER IV

THINGS ACCOMPLISHED BY CHRIST IN
HIS SUFFERINGS AND DEATH

WHEN ANTICIPATING His cross Christ said, "For this cause came I into the world" (John 18:37), and, again, "For the Son of man is come to seek and to save that which was lost" (Luke 19:10). In the light of these sayings, it may be concluded that, as before asserted, the theme of the sufferings of Christ in death is the ground of all right doctrine and the central fact in this cosmic universe. It exceeds the importance of the material universe—in so far as the universe provides a sphere wherein evil may be tested, judged, and banished forever. Of all that the cross of Christ achieved in angelic realms and toward the final judgment of evil as a principle, somewhat has been said previously under hamartiology; yet it is clear that unaided finite minds cannot follow far in this vast domain of reality. Some revelation is recorded with respect to these immeasurable issues, and to this attention will be directed in due time. The general theme of that which Christ accomplished in His death sufferings and in His death may, in an attempt at clarity, be divided into the following fourteen divisions: (1) a substitution for sinners, (2) Christ the end of the law principle in behalf of those who are saved, (3) a redemption toward sin, (4) a reconciliation toward man, (5) a propitiation toward God, (6) the judgment of the sin nature, (7) the ground of the believer's forgiveness and cleansing, (8) the ground for the deferring of righteous divine judgments, (9) the taking away of precross sins once covered by sacrifice, (10) the national salvation of Israel, (11) millennial and eternal blessings upon Gentiles, (12) the spoiling of principalities and powers, (13) the ground of peace, (14) the purification of things in heaven. To the end that the student may be encouraged to pursue these limitless themes more exhaustively, an introductory outline or condensed survey of each is here undertaken.

I. A SUBSTITUTION FOR SINNERS

Though it underlies much of all that Christ accomplished, His vicarious sufferings and death, being the foundation of all truth respecting

55

the divinely provided cure for sin, will first be treated separately and recognizing five particulars, namely, (1) the words which imply substitution, (2) vicarious suffering in general, (3) mediation, (4) substitution with respect to the judgment of sin, and (5) substitution in the realms of divine perfection.

1. The Words Which Imply Substitution. Two prepositions are involved in this aspect of this theme—ἀντί and ὑπέρ. On the meaning and force of these words, Archbishop R. C. Trench, in his *New Testament Synonyms* (9th ed., pp. 290–91), writes thus:

It has been often claimed, and in the interests of an all-important truth, namely the *vicarious* character of the sacrifice of the death of Christ, that in such passages as Heb. ii.9; Tit. ii.14; 1 Tim. ii.6; Gal. iii.13; Luke xxii.19, 20; 1 Pet. ii.21; iii.18; iv.1; Rom. v.8; John x.15, in all of which Christ is said to have died ὑπὲρ πάντων, ὑπὲρ ἡμῶν, ὑπὲρ τῶν προβάτων, and the like, ὑπέρ shall be accepted as equipollent with ἀντί. And then, it is further urged that, as ἀντί is the preposition first of equivalence (Homer, Il.ix.116,117) and then of exchange (1 Cor. xi.15; Heb. xii.2, 16; Matt. v.38), ὑπέρ must in all those passages be regarded as having the same force. Each of these, it is evident, would thus become a *dictum probans* for a truth, in itself most vital, namely that Christ suffered, not merely *on our behalf* and *for our good*, but also *in our stead*, and bearing that penalty of our sins which we otherwise must ourselves have borne. Now, though some have denied, we must yet accept as certain that ὑπέρ has sometimes this meaning . . . but it is not less certain that in passages far more numerous ὑπέρ means no more than, on behalf of, for the good of; thus Matt. v.44; John xiii.37; 1 Tim. ii.1, and continually. It must be admitted to follow from this, that had we in the Scripture only statements to the effect that Christ died ὑπὲρ ἡμῶν, that He tasted death ὑπὲρ παντός, it would be impossible to draw from these any irrefragable proof that his death was vicarious, He dying in our stead, and Himself bearing on His Cross our sins and the penalty of our sins; however we might find it, as no doubt we do, elsewhere (Isa. liii.4–6). It is only as having other declarations, to the effect that Christ died ἀντὶ πολλῶν (Matt. xx.28), gave Himself as an ἀντίλυτρον (1 Tim. ii.6), and bringing those other to the interpretation of these, that we obtain a perfect right to claim such declarations of Christ's death *for us* as also declarations of his death *in our stead*. And in them beyond doubt the preposition ὑπέρ is the rather employed, that it may embrace both these meanings, and express how Christ died at once *for our sakes* (here it touches more nearly on the meaning of περί, Matt. xxvi.28; Mark xiv.24; 1 Pet. iii.18; διά also once occurring in this connexion, 1 Cor. viii.11), and *in our stead;* while ἀντί would only have expressed the last of these.

As intimated by Archbishop Trench, there is no problem connected with the word ἀντί. In as definite a manner as language may be made to serve, this word means *substitution*—one taking the place of another. The word ὑπέρ, however, is broader and does mean in some instances no more than a benefit provided and received; yet, in other instances, it as certainly becomes the equivalent of ἀντί. The way is therefore open to some extent for those who would belittle the doctrine of *substitution* to stress the more general use of ὑπέρ, while those who heartily defend this doctrine stress its vicarious meaning. The reasonable attitude is to allow ὑπέρ its full latitude to the extent that when, according to the context, it seems to express actual substitution, to give it the same force as ἀντί. If, by the restriction of ὑπέρ to the idea of mere *benefit,* the doctrine would be eliminated, the case would be different; but as long as ἀντί serves its specific purpose and cannot be modified, the truth is only clarified and strengthened by the more specific and wholly legitimate use of ὑπέρ as implying an actual *substitution*. Philemon 1:13— "Whom I would have retained with me, that in thy stead he might have ministered unto me in the bonds of the gospel"—and 2 Corinthians 5:14 —"For the love of Christ constraineth us; because we thus judge, that if one died for all, then were all dead"—may serve to demonstrate the truth that ὑπέρ does convey, when the context sustains it, the thought of actual substitution. This twofold meaning of ὑπέρ serves a real advantage, for Christ died in the sinner's place and as a benefit to the sinner. The word ἀντί appears in such a declaration as, "The Son of man came . . . to give his life a ransom for many" (Matt. 20:28), and the absolute character of *substitution* is seen in such Scriptures as Matthew 2:22; 5:38; Luke 11:11. However, in a much larger body of Scripture the word ὑπέρ occurs and in these the deeper meaning should be read: "This cup is the new testament in my blood, which is shed for you" (Luke 22:19–20); "The bread that I will give is my flesh, which I will give for the life of the world" (John 6:51); "Greater love hath no man than this, that a man lay down his life for his friends" (John 15:13); "Christ died for the ungodly . . . while we were yet sinners, Christ died for us" (Rom. 5:6–8); "He . . . delivered him up for us all" (Rom. 8:32); "If one died for all, then all died" (2 Cor. 5:14–15, lit.); "He hath made him to be sin for us" (2 Cor. 5:21); "Being made a curse for us" (Gal. 3:13); "Christ . . . gave himself up for us, an offering and a sacrifice to God" (Eph. 5:2, 25, R.V.); "The man Christ Jesus . . . gave himself a ransom for all" (1 Tim. 2:5–6); Christ did "taste death for every man" (Heb. 2:9); Christ "suffered . . . the just for the unjust" (1 Pet. 3:18).

2. Vicarious Suffering in General. As the term *vicar* refers to a deputy or agent who acts in the place of another, thus the word *vicarious* means that one takes the place of another, serving or acting as a substi-

tute. In the case of an obligation between man and man, the law permits
the debt to be discharged by a third party, provided no injustice to
others is wrought. However, the divine permission for a substitute to
act for man in his relation to God is one of the most fundamental provisions of saving grace. As fallen man stands obligated to God as an
offender—both in his federal head and in himself—against his Creator
and against the divine government, he owes an obligation which he could
never pay in time or eternity. Unless a vicar shall intervene there is no
hope for any member of this fallen race. No sin-laden human being could
be vicar for a fellow being. The vicar must be sinless as well as prepared
to bear those immeasurable judgments which divine holiness must ever
impose upon sin. In God there are two attributes which are at once involved when a creature sins. These are justice and mercy. Justice imposes, and continues to impose, the undiminished judgment which sin
entails. Not for one instant is justice softened or curtailed in the interests of mercy. Because of His holy character, God cannot look upon
sin with the least degree of allowance. The truth abides, that the soul
that sinneth, it shall die. No greater misrepresentation could be formed
against the holy character of God and the government of God than the
implication that His justice is ever softened or modified in the interests
of mercy. To contend that God could save one sinner from the judgment
of one sin by the exercise of mercy, is to accuse God of the greatest folly
that could be known in the universe; for if one sin could be cured by
mercy alone the principle would be established by which all sin could be
cured and the sacrificial, vicarious death of Christ would be rendered
wholly unnecessary. When Christ died at the hand of His Father as
an offering for sin, it is evident—except God be deemed the example of
infinite foolishness, if not infinite wickedness—that there was no other
way by which sinners could be saved. The Bible teaches without devia-
tion that Christ by His death met the demands of justice in behalf of the
sinner—in the sinner's room and stead—and those who will come unto
God by Him are saved without the slightest infringement upon divine
holiness. If it be inquired relative to where divine mercy appears, the
answer is that it is manifested in the provision of a Savior to meet the
demands of infinite justice.

Theologians are wont to distinguish between *personal* and *vicarious*
satisfaction to God for sin. When the sinner bears his own penalty, he is
lost forever and his achievement, though a failure, is a thing which originates in him and which he offers to God. This is *personal* satisfaction to
God. On the other hand, when a sinner accepts the vicarious Sin-Bearer,

he is saved forever and the achievement originates with the Savior and is offered to the sinner. This is *vicarious* satisfaction to God. These two principles—personal and vicarious satisfaction to God—are better known by the terms *works* and *faith*. The principle of works represents all that man can do for himself; the principle of faith represents all that God can do for man. The one is void of mercy; the other is the greatest possible display of mercy. The one has no promise of blessing in it; the other secures every spiritual blessing in Christ Jesus. None have stated the value of Christ's sacrifice more clearly than Augustine. He states: "The same one and true Mediator reconciles us *to* God by the atoning sacrifice, remains one *with* God to whom he offers it, makes those one in himself *for* whom he offers it, and is himself both the offerer and the offering" (*Trinity*, IV. xiv. 19, cited by Shedd, *Theology*, II, 400). The doctrine of the Bible is that God saves His own people—those who trust Him—from His own wrath (cf. Ps. 38:1; Isa. 60:10; Hos. 6:1; Job 42:7–8). Unconfused and without counteraction the one against the other, God experiences both wrath and love at the same time and each to the extent of His infinite Being. Ezekiel portrays Jehovah as beating His breast in lamentation over the fall of Lucifer who became Satan (Ezek. 28:12); yet there is no redemption for that angel and the lake of fire forever awaits him (Rev. 20:10). How great is Jehovah's wrath and indignation against Israel as seen in the chastisements which fall upon them! Yet He loves them with an everlasting love. The Christian, likewise, discovers that the grace by which he is saved is exercised toward him by the very tribunal which condemned him. A throne of awful judgment has become a throne of grace. Upon these two characteristics in God—wrath and love—Dr. Henry C. Mabie writes thus:

The whole Deity is behind the atonement, within it, and at the root of it. Grace is after all God's grace. When our sin arose, it created an antinomy, a self-opposition, so to speak, in God. God, as holy, must oppose and condemn sin, otherwise He could not be God. That side or polarity of the divine nature must judge and punish sin. But there is another side, or polarity to God's being called love. And as such it just as eagerly and spontaneously yearns to pardon and save. How then could these opposite polarities which even the anticipation of sin as well as its actual occurrence called into exercise in one and the same Trinity, be reconciled, and so reconciled as to save the guilty? We answer at once, God Himself, reconciled them by His own voluntary vicarious suffering, whatever it was. This was the essential reconciliation—the cosmic reality —the divinely satisfying thing to God Himself. But He could not so manifest it as to give the needed assurance and help that man needed, except as it came to concrete and visual and God-human disclosure of its reality, in Christ on the Cross. Nor could the historic fact of sin without it be met and demonstrated upon the same earth where the sin had occurred but by an adequate answering historical event. . . . Thus only evidently could God be *exhibited* as "just and the justifier of him which believeth in Jesus" (Rom. iii.26). Hence, the atonement conceived in any way that separates the Father from the fullest participation in it is but a partial view. Grace in the nature of the case, is something that must be construed as an expression of *government* —it is a governmental function—and also has reference to a unified divine government. The source of grace can never be divided. Yet the Trinity is not excluded thereby, and the Trinity is not tri-Theism. Dual relations, *rapports* arise in God as the expression of two moral poles of His being; and the reconciliation made necessary by the incoming of sin is conceived as immanent in God, in His very unity. So God on one side of His nature *provides* what on another side of His nature He *exacts*. That is, God may do one thing in order to another.—*Under the Redeeming Aegis*, pp. 89–92

As certainly as God foresees and predetermines, the event of Calvary was ever as real to Him as it was in the hour of its enactment—the hour of the greatest of all achievements, the answering of all that an offended God demanded to the end that He might be free to exercise His love unhindered in behalf of the objects of His affection. These opposites in God were ever reconciled in His anticipation of the cross; yet there was the necessity—the thing He anticipated—that the cross should become historical, an actual doing of that which could not be avoided. In truth, if the heart of God could be seen as it is now, and always has been, not only would infinite hatred for evil be discovered, but the same willingness to give His Son to die for the ungodly and His enemies would be discerned. Calvary was, then, the necessary working out in time of that which was eternally in the heart of God. It is the fact that within God a reconciliation was anticipated from all eternity, made real in time, and to be recognized by Him in all eternity to come, that forms the basis of His grace. Grace and love are not the same. Love may long to save, but, because of the immutable demands of justice, be powerless to do so. On the other hand, grace in God is that which love accomplishes on the ground of the truth that Christ has met the demands of justice. The self-reconciliation in God, which the cross provides, opens a field for divine achievement in the salvation of the lost which otherwise must be impossible. Doubtless God was free to act toward sinners in grace in past ages on the ground of His anticipation of the cross; but with great assurance it may be believed that He is free so to act since the cross. By its very character, grace is related to divine government. It is a way of getting things done. Whatever God does in grace He is free to do because of the cross. In ages to come He will display His grace by means of that salvation of sinners which He will have achieved (Eph. 2:7). To those thus saved He says: "For by grace are ye saved through faith; and that not of yourselves: it is the gift of God: not of works, lest any man should boast" (Eph. 2:8–9). This incomparable grace is not only wrought out *by* God, but is wrought out *in* God. He is "the God of all grace." Peace is sealed by the Holy Spirit in the heart of those who believe and because of the fact that they are right with God and God is right with them.

3. MEDIATION. In the broadest significance of the term, *mediation* implies at least two parties between whom it functions. The lament of Job reflects the need of a mediator as that need existed in the world before the advent of Christ. Job said: "For he is not a man, as I am, that I should answer him, and we should come together in judgment. Neither is there any daysman betwixt us, that might lay his hand upon us both" (Job 9:32–33). The separation between the righteous God and sinful Job is recognized when Job said, "For he is not a man, as I am, that I should answer him, and we should come together in judgment"; and the case was even more hopeless since no "daysman" existed "that might lay his hand upon us both." The English term *daysman* means 'arbitrator' or 'umpire.' The thought in Job's mind is of an established and accepted mediator between God and man. Job's conception, which pictures this intermediate agent as having the right to lay his hand on each party, is exceedingly clear, reaching, as it does, far beyond the range of conditions which might arise between men. The laying on of the hand, which Job visualizes, speaks of inherent equality between the daysman and the one on whom the hand is placed. Since Job has indicated that the estranged parties are God and himself, the placing of the daysman's hand upon God requires that the daysman shall be equal with God, and the placing of the daysman's hand on Job requires that the daysman shall stand, also, on the same level with Job, having the inherent right which belongs to a fellow man—a representative of actual kin. Thus, in terms which breathe more of the wisdom and purpose of God than is common to man, Job has declared the fundamental features which of necessity are found in the theanthropic Mediator. Sin caused an estrangement between God and man, and since all have sinned, the need is universal. That God is offended by sin need not be argued. It is less recognized, however, that sin has hardened the heart of man, befogged his mind, and caused him to be full of unreason and prejudice. When Adam and Eve sinned, they hid, not from each other, but from God.

There is a *public* or general sense in which Christ's reign as King will be mediatorial in that, standing between God and man, He will put down authority and every enemy of God, thus restoring peace in a universe torn and distressed by sin (1 Cor. 15:25–28); but His *personal* mediation is the combined functioning of His work as Prophet and Priest. In the one He represents God to man, while in the other He represents man to God. In the priestly office He offers a sacrifice which answers the demands of divine justice and the uttermost need of the doomed sinner. He thus puts His hand upon God and upon man. He is the true Daysman. In its relation to the sinner, the work of the Mediator is none other than the substitutionary work of Christ, and, to avoid repetition, the theme need not be pursued separately at this point.

4. SUBSTITUTION WITH RESPECT TO THE JUDGMENT OF SIN. A previous paragraph has lent itself to the consideration of the force of the doctrine of substitution as expressed by the words ἀντί and ὑπέρ. This doctrine is not only clearly taught in the Bible, but its truth has done more to engender trust in God for the pardon of sin than all the ethical teachings of Christ, as such, and His life-example combined. It is well to note, also, that it is not the doctrine of Christ's death for sin but rather the death itself that provides relief to the burdened heart. The study of theories becomes the student of theology, but that which the burdened sinner needs is the truth that Christ actually died in his room and stead.

Perhaps more has been written on the theme of Christ's death than any other subject in the Bible. Passages have been classified and analyzed with utmost care. The Biblical assertions are convincing and confirming, that "Christ died for our sins"; "He bare our sins"; "He was made to be sin for us"; "He was made a curse for us." Remission of sin and deliverance from wrath are said to be wholly through His death for sin: "He gave his life a ransom for many." His death was a redemption, a reconciliation, and a propitiation. Every objection that human learning could devise has been hurled against these declarations, but to no avail. The truth is self-justifying, and it is difficult indeed to argue against that which always produces the blessing it proffers. In this connection a statement from William Ellery Channing (1780–1842), "the apostle of Unitarianism," is of interest. He declared:

We have no desire to conceal the fact, that a difference of opinion exists among us (Unitarians) in respect to an interesting part of Christ's mediation; I mean in regard to the precise influence of his death on our forgiveness. Many suppose that this event contributes to our pardon, as it was a principal means of confirming his religion, and of giving it a power over the mind; in other words, that it procures forgiveness by leading to that repentance and virtue which is the great and only condition on which forgiveness is bestowed. Many of us are dissatisfied with this explanation, and think that the Scriptures ascribe the remission of sins to Christ's death, *with an emphasis so peculiar that we ought to consider this event as having a special influence in removing punishment,* though the Scriptures may not reveal the way in which it contributes to this end. Whilst, however, we differ in explaining the connection between Christ's death and human forgiveness, *a connection which we all gratefully acknowledge,* we agree in rejecting many sentiments which prevail in regard to his mediation.—*Complete Works,* cited by John Stock, *Revealed Theology,* pp. 149–50

The fact that One who demonstrated His Deity, in ways which candid minds cannot reject, came into this world and died a sacrificial death— asserting with unimpeachable truthfulness that it was to the end that men might be saved from their sins, that satisfaction might be made to God, that man might be pardoned and justified on the ground of His death, that in no other way might God's moral government be upheld— has imposed a body of truth upon the thought of the world which is calculated to become the most dominant factor in their philosophy of life. If it fails to become this, the reason must be sought in the sphere of inattention, or incapacity, or wanton insincerity. It is near dishonesty for men to say, as they have done, that there is not a word in the Bible about the punishment due for our sins having been inflicted by a just God upon His own Son. Nor does it answer the demands of the revealed truth to assert that Christ shared human sin only in sympathy for the sinner, or that He offered some kind of a vicarious confession for the sinner, or that, as a man, He virtually took His share of the consequences of sin as it is in the world. All this suggests the foolishness of 1 Corinthians 1:23.

An extended classification of the passages which bear on that which is accomplished by Christ in His death was prepared in 1871 by T. J. Crawford in the volume *The Doctrine of Holy Scripture Respecting the Atonement.* This analysis (as edited by R. W. Dale, *Atonement,* 4th ed., 443–58) is appended herewith:

I. PASSAGES WHICH SPEAK OF CHRIST
(1) As *dying for sinners.*
Matthew 20:28; Luke 22:19a; 22:19b, 20; John 6:51; 10:11, 15, 18; 15:12, 13; Romans 5:6–8; 8:32; 2 Corinthians 5:14, 15; 5:21; Galatians 2:20; 3:13; Ephesians 5:2, 25; 1 Thessalonians 5:9, 10; 1 Timothy 2:5, 6; Titus 2:13, 14; Hebrews 2:9; 1 Peter 3:18; 1 John 3:16.
(2) As *suffering for sins.*
Romans 4:25; 8:3; 1 Corinthians 15:3; Galatians 1:4; Hebrews 10:12; 1 Peter 3:18; Isaiah 53:5, 8.

(3) As *bearing our sins.*
Hebrews 9:28; 1 Peter 2:24; Isaiah 53:6, 11, 12.
(4) As *being "made sin" and "made a curse for us."*
2 Corinthians 5:21; Galatians 3:13.

II. PASSAGES WHICH ASCRIBE TO THE DEATH OF CHRIST
(1) The *removal and remission of sins, and deliverance from their penal consequences.*
John 1:29; Hebrews 9:26; Matthew 26:28; 1 John 1:7; Luke 24:46, 47; Acts 10:43; 13:38, 39; Ephesians 1:6, 7; Colossians 1:13, 14; Revelation 1:5, 6; John 3:14–17; 1 Thessalonians 5:9, 10.
(2) *Justification.*
Isaiah 53:11; Romans 5:8, 9; 3:24–26.
(3) *Redemption.*
Matthew 20:28; Acts 20:28; Romans 3:23, 24; 1 Corinthians 6:19; Ephesians 1:7; Colossians 1:14; Hebrews 9:12; 1 Peter 1:18, 19; Revelation 5:9.
(4) *Reconciliation to God.*
Romans 5:10, 11; 2 Corinthians 5:18, 19; Ephesians 2:16; Colossians 1:21, 22.

III. PASSAGES IN WHICH THE LORD JESUS CHRIST IS REPRESENTED
(1) As *a Propitiation for sin.*
1 John 2:2; 1 John 4:10; Hebrews 2:17; Romans 3:25.
(2) As *a Priest.*
Psalm 110:4; Hebrews 3:1; 2:17; 10:21; 4:14; 7:26.
(3) As *a Representative.*
Hebrews 5:1; 7:22; Romans 5:12, 18, 19; 1 Corinthians 15:20–22, 45–49.

IV. PASSAGES WHICH REPRESENT THE SUFFERINGS OF CHRIST
(1) As *"sacrificial."*
Under this head, "Behold the Lamb of God," etc., should reappear. To these may be added: 1 Corinthians 5:7; Ephesians 5:2; Revelation 7:14, 15; Hebrews 9:22–28; 10:11–14.

V. PASSAGES WHICH CONNECT OUR LORD'S SUFFERINGS WITH HIS INTERCESSION.
1 Timothy 2:5, 6; 1 John 2:1, 2; Revelation 5:6; already quoted, reappear, and Philippians 2:8, 9, 10.

VI. PASSAGES WHICH REPRESENT THE MEDIATION OF CHRIST
(1) As *procuring the gracious influence of the Holy Spirit.*
John 7:39; 16:7; 14:16, 17; 15:26; 14:26; Acts 2:33; Galatians 3:13, 14; Titus 3:5, 6.
(2) As *conferring all Christian graces which are fruits of the Spirit.*
John 1:16; 15:4, 5; 1 Corinthians 1:4–7; 1:30; Ephesians 1:3, 4; 2:10; 4:7; Colossians 2:9, 10.
(3) As *delivering us from the dominion of Satan.*
1 John 3:8; John 12:31, 32; Hebrews 2:14, 15; Colossians 2:15.
(4) As *obtaining for us eternal life.*
John 3:14, 15; 5:24; 6:40, 47, 51; 10:27, 28; 14:2, 3; 17:1, 2; Romans

5:20, 21; 6:23; 2 Timothy 2:10; Hebrews 5:9; 9:15; 1 Peter 5:10; 1 John 5:11; Jude 21.

VII. Passages Which Indicate the State of the Saviour's Mind in the Prospect and in the Endurance of His Sufferings.

John 10:17, 18; Luke 12:50; John 12:27; Matthew 26:36–44; 27:46.

VIII. Passages Which Speak of the Mediation of Christ in Relation

(1) To *the free calls and offers of the gospel.*

John 14:6; 1 Corinthians 3:11; 1 Timothy 2:5; Acts 4:12.

(2) To *the necessity of faith in order to obtain the blessings of the gospel.*

John 1:12; 3:18, 36; 6:35; Acts 13:38, 39; 16:31; Romans 1:16; 3:28; 5:12; 10:4; Galatians 5:6; Ephesians 2:8, 9.

IX. Passages Which Speak of the Mediatorial Work and Sufferings of Christ in Relation

(1) To *His covenant with the Father.*

John 6:38–40, 51.

(2) To *His union with believers.*

John 15:4; Romans 6:5; 2 Corinthians 4:10; Galatians 2:20; Ephesians 2:5, 6; Philippians 3:10; Colossians 2:12; 3:3.

X. Passages Which Speak of the Death of Christ

(1) As *a manifestation of the love of God.*

John 3:16; Romans 5:8; 8:32; 1 John 4:9, 10.

(2) As *furnishing an example of patience and resignation.*

Hebrews 12:1–3; 1 Peter 2:20, 21; Luke 9:23, 24.

(3) As *designed to promote our sanctification.*

John 17:19; Hebrews 10:10; 13:12; 2 Corinthians 5:15; Galatians 1:4; Ephesians 5:25–27; Titus 2:14; 1 Peter 2:24.

It is natural that much that has been written regarding Christ's first advent should assume that His objective in coming is exhausted in the one purpose that He was to be a sacrifice for sinners. It is thus claimed by not a few that all His sacrifice, even His leaving heaven, and every privation and rejection, was vicarious in character, that is, it was wrought in behalf of others. No doubt others were benefited; but such sacrifice was not in any sense a substitution, since no other was ever appointed to the path which He pursued. All His life was a sacrifice, but by universal Biblical usage only that sacrifice by which He gave His life on the cross is vicarious and substitutionary. It will be remembered, also, that there was much accomplished in Christ's first advent in manifesting God, in bringing the nation Israel to trial, and in satisfying the love of God. The sinner gained a benefit, but God gained a benefit of infinite proportions. Similarly, the death of Christ reaches out in its effect to angelic spheres and to heaven itself. Therefore, it is not sufficient to assume that the substitutionary death of Christ for sinners contemplates all that His sufferings and death accomplished. Certain titles suggest the wide scope of Christ's interests and gracious undertakings. He is the Last Adam, Head, High Priest, Husband, Advocate, Propitiation, Intercessor; but in none of these is He taking the place of another as vicar or substitute.

In the midst of so great and complex a disclosure respecting the relationships and achievements of Christ, none is so constantly emphasized as that of His substitution in suffering and in death for sinners. If this great transaction—the Father offering His Son as the Lamb of God to take away the sin of the world—were supremely immoral, as some declare (which it is not), it would yet stand on the pages of the Bible more sustained by repeated assertion than almost any other one subject. In other words, the doctrine of substitution is not only revealed to man by God as His gracious solution of the problem of sin, but is real, leaving but one obligation upon those for whom the Savior died, which is that they *believe*. It would be difficult indeed to explain the Savior's agony in the garden and on the cross—an agony far exceeding physical torture —if it is contended that sin was not laid on Him. On this aspect of truth Henry Rogers, in his third letter on the atonement, wrote: "And remember, that if you insist on the injustice of God's inflicting suffering on Christ, for the sins of others, you cannot escape similar difficulty, and greater in degree, on your own system; for, can it be less unjust to inflict such sufferings on Christ *for no sins at all?* If it be unjust to accept Him as sacrifice for the guilty, how much *more* unjust must it be to insist on the sacrifice for nothing, and when the victim thrice implored in agony, that, *if it were possible, the cup might pass from Him*" (cited by Stock, *op. cit.*, p. 156). The difficulty in accounting for the sufferings and death of Christ is greatly increased when it is considered that He was Himself the holy, undefiled, and spotless Lamb of God. In this there is no receding from the essential truth that Christ became a legal substitute, which undertaking demanded of Him that He meet the judgment due for the failure of those whom He represented. He became the voluntary Bondsman, their Surety (Heb. 7:22), meeting their liabilities and providing the required ransom. This is the precise import of the language employed in the Sacred Text. If it be inquired to whom the ransom was paid and whose demands are met by the payment, it is answered that the obligation is to God in respect to His holiness. There is a distinction to be seen between *pecuniary* and *moral* obligations; yet the Bible implies that an actual parallel exists between these when it speaks of the sacrifice and blood of Christ as a ransom and a redemption. A debt of obligation to a broken law or offended authority may be as real as a financial debt which is contracted with a fellow being. A criminal in prison, or when executed, is paying the debt he owes to out-raged law and government. The basis of all obligation is the duty of the creature to fulfill the purpose and will of the Creator. In this, all have sinned and come short of the glory of God. A sinless Substitute *pur-chased* the deliverance of sinners (Acts 20:28), He paid the required *price* (1 Cor. 7:23), a *ransom* (Matt. 20:28), and *redemption* (Eph. 1:7). The legal aspect of this revelation is that God required the sinner's obligation to be met. There could be no receding from this holy demand. The love of God is seen in the fact that Christ *voluntarily* consented to pay the debt, and in the fact that the Father accepts the payment at the hand of the Substitute. Thus the way of salvation for sinners on the ground of the sufferings and death of the Substitute is established; and, in addition to the indisputable reality which this revelation sets forth, the same truth is vindicated by the unfailing efficacy of it in the experi-ence of those who believe. It is possible to disbelieve and reject God's provisions for the sinner in the Substitute, but it is puerile to assert that the Bible does not teach the doctrine of substitution. God is "of purer eyes than to behold evil, and cannot look on iniquity" (Hab. 1:13). He rather magnifies the law and makes it honorable (Isa. 42:21), and no more perfect upholding of the law of His holy Being could be conceived than is exemplified in the voluntary assumption of a qualified substitute taking on himself the discharge of the sinner's obligation. The Apostle Paul states: "For the love of Christ constraineth us; because we thus judge, that if one died for all, then were all dead: . . . to wit, that God was in Christ, reconciling the world unto himself, not imputing their trespasses unto them; and hath committed unto us the word of reconciliation. . . . For he hath made him to be sin for us, who knew no sin; that we might be made the righteousness of God in him" (2 Cor. 5:14, 19, 21).

The import of these and other Scriptures is not that Christ, in a com-mercial sense, bore the sin of the world. This would mean that had there been one more sinner His sufferings would have been increased by so much, or had there been one less sinner His sufferings would have been decreased by so much. In a *forensic* sense Christ made a legal sacrifice for sin the value of which is available for all who believe. Had it pleased God to terminate human sin immediately after the first human sin, it would have required precisely the same sufferings and death on the part of the Savior to save that one sinner from his one sin. On the other hand, the invitation is extended to a lost world of humanity, since Christ has borne the judicial penalty of sin, to receive these provided benefits. On this vital truth, Dr. Augustus H. Strong writes: "Just as much sun and rain would be needed, if only one farmer on earth were to be benefited. Christ would not need to suffer more, if all were to be saved. His sufferings, as we have seen, were not the payment of a pecuniary debt. Having endured the penalty of the sinner, justice permits the sinner's discharge, but does not require it, except as the fulfillment of a promise to his substitute, and then only upon the appointed condition of repentance and faith. The *atonement* is unlimited,—the whole human race might be saved through it; the *application* of the atonement is limited,—only those who repent and believe are actually saved by it" (*Systematic Theology*, p. 422). The Biblical illustration of forensic suffering and death is presented in type. A lamb might serve for an individual, as in the case of Abel; a lamb might serve for a family, as was true of the Passover; or a ram might serve for a nation, as on the day of atonement.

The value of the sacrifice is not to be discovered in the intensity of the Savior's anguish but rather in the dignity and infinite worth of the One who suffers. He did not give more or less; He gave *Himself*, He offered Himself, but this self was none other than the Second Person of the Godhead in whom measureless dignity and glory reside.

Closely related to the above aspect of the substitutionary death of Christ is that held by earlier theologians, namely, that Christ actually became *sin*, rather than that He bore its penalty; that is, the actual estate of the Second Person ceased to be holy and became that which a fallen sinner is. What Christ bore or became cannot be measured by man, simply because of the fact that no man is able to contemplate these issues from the vantage point of the spotless lamb of God. Nevertheless, God not only invites men to be saved by faith in His Lamb but as faithfully declares that the salvation He offers is based on the substitution which Christ undertook—the Just for the unjust. Sin was *laid* on Him, He was *made* sin, He *bore* our sins, His soul was made an *offering* for sin, and He *gave* Himself for us (cf. Isa. 53:6, 10–12; Rom. 8:3; 2 Cor. 5:21; Gal. 3:13; Heb. 9:28; 1 Pet. 2:24); thus it becomes man to seek to know *all* that God has spoken, believing that He means man to understand it and has greatly honored man by such a revelation. Dr. W. Lindsay Alexander, in his *System of Biblical Theology* (II, 102–6), discusses this feature of Soteriology in a manner well suited to this thesis. He writes:

Beginning with those who look upon the atonement of Christ in the light of a legal satisfaction or judicial expiation, I remark that all agree in thinking that the work of Christ derives its worth from the union of the divine and the human natures in His person, and all admit that worth to be not only supreme, but infinite. There is a difference, however, between certain schools or classes of them as to the nature of the compensation rendered to the divine government and law on our behalf by Christ, His special purpose and intention in offering it, and the consequent extent to which His work was designed to be sufficient. Of these varying shades of opinion we notice the following: (1) *That of the Hyper-Calvinists,*—a name which has been given, not because those to whom it is attached are regarded as having gone beyond Calvin in their doctrine, but because they carry the views of Calvin on this head to their utmost extent, and hold them with unbending rigidity. *a.* According to them, the work of Christ was of the nature of a price paid for the release of man from penalties which he had incurred,—a price which bore a fixed and exact relation to the amount of debt which man had incurred by his sins. According to this view, what He rendered was strictly a *quid pro quo;* there was as much on the one side as on the other; the suffering obedience of the Saviour being an exact equivalent for the sins of the saved, and that not by a *solutio tantadem,* but by a *solutio ejusdem, i.e.* not by paying something of equal value of the same kind, but by paying the very thing that was due. This opinion cannot be ascribed to Calvin, who expresses himself in a very general manner as to the satisfaction made for man by Christ. "When we say," he remarks, "that favour was procured for us by the merit of Christ we mean this, that by His blood we have been cleansed, and that His death was an expiation for our sins." "This I take for granted, that if Christ satisfied for our sins, if He suffered the punishment due to us, if by His obedience He propitiated God, if, in fine, He, the just, suffered for the unjust, then salvation was procured by His righteousness for us, which is equivalent to our having merited it" (*Instit.,* ii.17.4, 3). These statements are so general that they might be advanced by any one holding the Satisfaction theory. Among Calvin's followers, however, both on the Continent and in this country, there were found some by whom the doctrine as above stated was asserted in all its rigidity. Not only was it maintained that Christ became "sponsor for those alone who by eternal election had been given to Him, . . . and them alone did He reconcile unto God" (*Form. Cons. Helvet.,* art. 13),—that He did not make satisfaction or in any way die save for all and only those whom the Father had given Him, and who are actually saved (Witsius, *Oecon. Foed.,* ii. c.9, Par. 6); but the opinion was broadly avowed that there was a transference of the sin of the elect to Christ, and that He actually suffered the same as they should have suffered, and thereby paid for their redemption exactly what the law demanded as the due penalty of their offences. Thus, Owen says of the satisfaction made by Christ: "It was a full, valuable compensation made to the justice of God for all the sins of all those for whom He made satisfaction by undergoing that same punishment which, by reason of the obligation that was upon them, they themselves were bound to undergo. When I say *the same,*" he goes on to explain, "I mean essentially the same in weight and pressure, though not in all accidents of duration and the like; for it was impossible that He should be detained by death" (*Death of Christ, Works,* vol. x. p. 269). Farther on, in the same treatise (*ibid.,* p. 285), he says, in reference to the laying of sins upon Christ, God "charged on Him and imputed to Him all the sins of all the elect, and proceeded against Him accordingly. He stood as our Surety, really charged with the whole debt, and was to pay the utmost farthing, as a surety is to do if it be required of him; though he borrow not the money, nor have one penny of that which is in the obligation, yet if he be sued to an execution, he must pay all. The Lord Christ (if I may so say) was sued by His Father's justice unto an execution, in answer whereunto He underwent all that was due to sin." In another treatise the same great theologian gives the following as the expression of his view concerning the satisfaction rendered by Christ: "Christ paid the same thing that was in the obligation; as if in things real a friend should pay twenty pounds for him that owed so much and not anything in another kind." . . . "I affirm that He paid *idem,* that is, the same thing that was in the obligation, and not *tantundem,* something equivalent thereunto in another kind" (*Death of Christ, Works,* vol. x. c. ii. p. 438). And farther on he says, "The assertion I seek to maintain is this: That the punishment which our Saviour underwent was the same that the law required of us, God relaxing His law as to the person suffering, but not as to the penalty suffered" (*ibid.,* p. 447). These statements of Owen may be regarded as presenting clearly and in few words what were the views entertained by the English Puritans and early Nonconformists regarding the nature and extent of the atonement made for sin by Christ. They believed that to be in itself of infinite value; but they regarded it as limited both in design and in effect to the elect, and as being of the nature of a paying to the law of a *quid pro quo,* an enduring by Christ of the very penalty which they as sinners had deserved in order to secure their deliverance. By some the commercial character ascribed to the atonement was carried out still farther, and the idea of an actual and exact commutation of man's sins on the one hand, and Christ's righteousness on the other, was entertained and advocated. The principal representative of this school was Dr. Crisp, minister of Brinkworth in Wiltshire, about the middle of the 17th century; and it numbers the names of Chauncy, Saltmarsh, and Gill among its adherents. The republication of Dr. Crisp's works by his son at the close of the century led to his peculiar views on the subject of the atonement being commented upon by Dr. Daniel Williams, an English Presbyterian minister, in a work entitled, *Gospel-Truth Stated and Vindicated* (Lond. 1692), which passed through several editions, and gave rise to a somewhat violent controversy. Of the views advanced by Dr. Crisp a correct idea will be obtained from his own words, which I quote from the work of Dr. Williams. Writing of the laying of our sins on Christ, he says: "It is the iniquity itself that the Lord hath laid upon Christ; not only our punishment, but our very sin. . . . This transaction of our sins to Christ is a real act; our sins so became Christ's that He stood the sinner in our stead. . . . To speak more plainly: Hast thou been an idolater, hast thou been a blasphemer, hast thou been a murtherer, an adulterer, a thief, a liar, a drunkard? If thou hast part in the Lord, all these transgressions of thine become actually the transgressions of Christ."

In another place he thus insists on the transfer of our sin to Christ and His righteousness to us: "Mark it well: Christ Himself is not so completely righteous, but we are as righteous as He; nor we so completely sinful, but Christ became, being made sin, as completely sinful as we. Nay more, we are the same righteousness, for we are made the righteousness of God; that very sinfulness that we were, Christ is made that very sinfulness before God. So that here is a direct change—Christ takes our person and condition and stands in our stead, we take Christ's person and condition and stand in His stead." These passages may serve to convey a clear view of the doctrines held by this school—a school which, though numbering among its adherents some of the best and holiest of men, has been the main support and promoter of antinomianism in this country. By the great body of the English Nonconformists these views have been and continue to be repudiated. Bates, Howe, Alsop, along with many other very decided Calvinists, joined at the time in denouncing them as unscriptural and dangerous; and in later times the vigorous pen of Andrew Fuller—not to mention less famous names—was employed in exposing them and advocating Calvinistic views apart from them. Even Dr. Owen raised his voice against them, for in one of his greatest treatises, that on the *Doctrine of Justification by Faith,* he expressly says: "Nothing is more absolutely true, nothing is more sacredly or assuredly believed by us, than that nothing which Christ did or suffered, nothing that He undertook or underwent, did, or could, constitute Him subjectively, inherently, and thereon personally, a sinner or guilty of any sin of His own. To bear the guilt or blame of other men's faults—to be *alienae culpae reus*—makes no man a sinner, unless he did unwisely or irregularly undertake it" (p. 201); and again: "Our sin was imputed to Christ only as He was our Surety for a time—to this end, that He might take it away, destroy it, and abolish it. It never was imputed unto Him so as to make any alteration absolutely in His personal state and condition" (p. 203). And, on the other hand, he strenuously maintains that "notwithstanding this full, plenary satisfaction once made for the sins of the world that shall be saved, yet all men continue equally to be born by nature 'children of wrath,' and whilst they believe not the wrath of God abideth on them, that is, they are obnoxious unto and under the curse of the law" (p. 216); and again: "The righteousness of Christ is not transfused into us so as to be made inherently and subjectively ours, as it was in Him" (p. 218). From these passages it is evident that Owen was far from holding the extreme views of Dr. Crisp and his school. The views of Owen were accepted and advocated by the great American theologian Jonathan Edwards, who, is his *Essay concerning the Necessity and Reasonableness of the Christian Doctrine of Satisfaction for Sin,* uses such language as the following: "Christ suffered the full punishment of the sin that was imputed to Him, or offered that to God that was fully and completely equivalent to what we owed to God's justice for our sins" (p. 384). "The satisfaction of Christ by suffering the punishment of sin is properly to be distinguished as being in its own nature different from the merit of Christ. For merit is only some excellency or worth. But when we consider Christ's sufferings merely as the satisfaction for the guilt of another, the excellency of Christ's act in suffering does not at all come into considera-

tion; but only these two things, viz. their equality or equivalence to the punishment that the sinner deserved; and secondly, the union between Him and
them, or the propriety of His being accepted in suffering as the representative
of the sinner" (p. 389).

In conclusion it may be observed that, in His sufferings and death,
Christ bore more than the mere penalty—though it is clear that He bore
the penalty, for the wages of sin is death, and the curse and condemnation fell upon Him. Other Scriptures indicate an identification on Christ's
part with the sinner and suggest that both sin and its penalty were laid
on Him, but never to the injury of His own character or to the end that
it could be said that He needed to be saved or forgiven. In fact, it was
at this hour of His sacrificial death, as will presently be seen, that He
was offering perfect merit to the Father in which the meritless sinner
might be accepted forever. There is no ground for surprise that an inscrutable mystery is confronted when the infinite God is accomplishing
His greatest undertaking, and in a way which is consonant with things
eternal and celestial.

5. SUBSTITUTION IN THE REALMS OF DIVINE PERFECTION. The words
which make up this heading serve to introduce a much neglected feature
of the gospel of God's grace. It is assuredly true that righteous forgiveness of the sinner is secured by the substitution of Christ as Sin-Bearer;
but the salvation of a soul involves much more than that removal or
subtraction of sin from the sinner which forgiveness achieves. A sinner
minus his sins could hardly be counted a fully constituted Christian. In
the saving of a soul much is *added*—eternal life is the gift of God, and
the righteousness of God is imputed to those who believe (Rom. 5:17).
Though eternal life is a sovereign gift, God no more legalizes a fiction
when He imputes righteousness than when He forgives sin. It is conceded that there is no moral issue involved in the gift of eternal life and
the imputation of righteousness as is involved in the forgiveness of sin;
but a righteous ground for such blessings is imperative.

The two features of salvation—the gift of eternal life and the gift of
righteousness—are counterparts of the one great fact of union with
Christ. In the simplest of words—so far as the English translation is
concerned—Christ referred to these two major facts of relationship
when He said, "Ye in me, and I in you" (John 14:20). Of the first relation—*ye in me*—it is asserted that all spiritual blessing is secured by
the Christian's position in Christ. It is written, "Blessed be the God and
Father of our Lord Jesus Christ, who hath blessed us with all spiritual
blessings in heavenly places in Christ" (Eph. 1:3). And of the second

relation—*I in you*—it is written, "He that believeth on the Son hath everlasting life: and he that believeth not the Son shall not see life; but the wrath of God abideth on him" (John 3:36); "And this is the record, that God hath given to us eternal life, and this life is in his Son. He that hath the Son hath life; and he that hath not the Son of God hath not life" (1 John 5:11–12).

Of the gift of God which is eternal life it may be said that it is one of two closely related benefactions—that Christ is thus given to the believer, and that the believer is given by the Father to Christ (John 17:2, 6, 9, 11–12, 24). Both of these gifts are the expression of the Father's love and are sovereignly bestowed when, through the work of Christ, the way is clear for the exercise of that love.

On the other hand, the believer's position in Christ is secured on a righteous ground through the substitution wrought by Christ on the cross. Much has been presented in Volume II, Chapter XVIII, on the doctrine of imputed righteousness and its divine declaration when God pronounces the righteous one to be justified eternally. It has been stated on these pages that justification, grounded upon imputed righteousness, is not the legalizing of a fiction; it is the recognition of a fact, the fact being secured by infinite provisions to that end. In general, this provision is twofold: first, by the Spirit's baptism into Christ's body.

It is notable that the word βαπτίζω is used for both the ritual (water) and the real (Spirit) baptism, and, without reference to whatever convictions may be entertained respecting the mode of water baptism and what it signifies, the essential truth remains that the same word is used for both ritual and real baptism, the only variation being in respect to its primary and secondary meanings. The primary meaning is to *submerge*—not to *dip*, which verb implies two actions, that of putting in and taking out. Βαπτίζω means only to *put in*, and, when used to describe the Spirit's ministry of uniting the believer to Christ, the one thing desired is that there shall be no taking out again. The primary meaning of this word suggests a physical envelopment—an *intusposition*. The secondary meaning—evidently derived from the primary meaning—is that a thing is baptized if joined closely to that which exercises a determining influence over it. Such, indeed, is the baptism into repentance; into the remission of sins; into the Father, the Son, and the Holy Spirit; into Moses; and into Christ. In the case of none of these is there a physical intusposition; yet these are baptisms that are vital beyond measure. By bestowing the Spirit, Christ baptized with the Spirit (ἐν πνεύματι—Matt. 3:11. Cf. Mark 1:8; Luke 3:16; John 1:33;

Acts 1:5). Similarly, of Christ it was promised that He would baptize also with fire (Luke 3:16). In both the baptism with the Spirit, and that with fire, the secondary meaning obtains. Believers are by the Spirit baptized into Christ's body (1 Cor. 12:13; Rom. 6:3; Gal. 3:27), and, as has been stated, in this baptism there is no intusposition, though a vital union is secured which is defined as being *joined to the Lord,* and *becoming a member of His body.* This union determines that which qualifies life itself. To be placed *in Christ* is to have been taken out of the first Adam and his ruin and placed in the Last Adam and thus made partaker of all that He is. No change could be more real, nor could any be more transforming. It is the federal disobedience of the first Adam that has constituted men sinners, and it is the federal obedience of the Last Adam that constitutes those who "receive abundance of grace and of the gift of righteousness" righteous in the sight of God, by an imputation which is based on their new relation to the New Creation head—the resurrected Christ (Rom. 5:15–21). Christ is the righteousness of God and all that are in Him are, by the most arbitrary necessity, constituted what He is.

Though surgery has never yet joined members to the human body, that idea is employed in the New Testament as an illustration (Eph. 4:13–16; 1 Cor. 12:18). A most honorable man—even the president of the country or its king—having lost one of his hands, might be thought of as having acquired by surgery a hand amputated from the most notorious criminal, whose hand was stained with murder and whose fingerprints are recorded by the police. However, after being joined to the new organism, that hand, as a member not only loses its former evil association and dishonor, but is invested at once with all the virtue of the new organism to which it is joined. No member could be joined to Christ without partaking of that which Christ is—the righteousness of God. If difficulty arises when contemplating this marvelous truth, it will be from the inability to recognize the absolute union to Christ which the baptism with the Spirit accomplishes. Yet such an imputation of merit is not a matter of sovereign authority apart from the legal right thus to act. The legal view of this divine action is to be found in, second, that aspect of Christ's death which is typified by the sweet savor offerings.

Reference has been made earlier in this discussion to the legal ground which the non-sweet savor offering aspect of Christ's death provides for the forgiveness of sin, and it was observed that this one feature is too often deemed the sum and substance of the gospel of divine grace.

However, no justification can be advanced for the biased discrimination which discovers so much in that which the two non-sweet savor offerings represent in Christ's death, and yet almost wholly ignores that which the three sweet savor offerings represent. It will be found that the sweet savor aspect of Christ's death secures the same sufficient legal ground for the bestowment of merit as is provided in the non-sweet savor offering aspect for the removal of demerit. In the one case, there is a displacing of sin through the Substitute bearing it for the sinner; in the other case, there is the placing of righteousness through the Substitute releasing it, or making it available, through His death.

The three sweet savor offerings represent the truth that Christ offered Himself without spot to God (Heb. 9:14). Such an offering is wholly free from the thought of sin being borne; it is a sweet savor to the Father since He ever delights in His Son and in all that His Son is. In the non-sweet savor offering the Father's face is turned away and the Son is pleading, "My God, my God, why hast thou forsaken me?" In the sweet savor offerings the worthiness of the Son is presented to the Father and in this He takes delight. Of these three sweet savor offerings, Dr. C. I. Scofield has written in brief and clarifying words in *The Scofield Reference Bible*:

(a) The burnt-offering (1) typifies Christ offering Himself without spot to God in delight to do His Father's will even in death. (2) It is *atoning* because the believer has *not* had this delight in the will of God; and (3) *substitutionary* (Lev. 1.4) because Christ did it in the sinner's stead. But the thought of *penalty* is not prominent (Heb. 9.11–14; 10.5–7; Psa. 40.6–8; Phil. 2.8). The emphatic words (Lev. 1.3–5) are "burnt-sacrifice," "voluntary," "it shall be accepted for him," and "atonement."—P. 126

(b) The meal-offering. The *fine flour* speaks of the evenness and balance of the character of Christ; of that perfection in which no quality was in excess, none lacking; *the fire*, of His testing by suffering, even unto death; *frankincense*, the fragrance of His life Godward (see Ex. 30.34); *absence of leaven*, His character as "the Truth" (see Ex. 12.8, *refs.*); *absence of honey*;—His was not that mere natural sweetness which may exist quite apart from grace; *oil mingled*, Christ as born of the Spirit (Mt. 1.18–23); *oil upon*, Christ as baptized with the Spirit (John 1.32; 6.27); *the oven*, the unseen sufferings of Christ—His inner agonies (Heb. 2.18; Mt. 27.45, 46); *the pan*, His more evident sufferings (e.g. Mt. 27.27–31); *salt*, the pungency of the truth of God—that which arrests the action of leaven.—P. 127

(c) The peace-offering. The whole work of Christ in relation to the believer's *peace* is here in type. He *made* peace, Col. 1.20; *proclaimed* peace, Eph. 2.17; and *is* our peace, Eph. 2.14. In Christ God and the sinner meet in peace; God is propitiated, the sinner reconciled—both alike satisfied with what Christ has done. But all this at the cost of blood and fire. The details speak of fellowship. This brings in prominently the thought of *fellowship* with God through Christ. Hence the peace-offering is set forth as affording food for the priests (Lev. 7.31–34). Observe that it is the breast (affections) and shoulders (strength) upon which we as priests (1 Pet. 2.9) feed in fellowship with the Father. This it is which makes the peace-offering especially a *thank-offering* (Lev. 7.11, 12).—P. 128

If the question be asked why the Second Person is on a cross with the First Person's face turned away, the answer is that He is bearing sin and that God cannot look upon sin with any degree of allowance. If the question be asked why the Second Person is on a cross offering Himself with all His perfections to the First Person, the answer is not that He had some surprise-revelation to make of Himself to the Father, but it is that He was releasing, or making available, His own infinite worthiness. This is substitution in the sphere of that which the most excellent of a fallen race could never present. Thus, when the Father would impute to the believer that righteousness of God which the Son is, and all His worthiness, He finds all this available and legally provided through that aspect of substitutionary death that is typified by the sweet savor offerings.

It is not commendable to ignore the sweet savor aspect of Christ's death, nor necessary to assume that imputed righteousness is an arbitrary sovereign act which rests on no defendable ground. No more assuring word could be spoken than that recorded in Romans 3:26, which is that God is Himself *just* when He justifies those among the ungodly who do no more than to *believe* in Jesus (cf. Rom. 4:5). The glorious achievement of all sin forgiven and the even greater achievement of a perfect standing before God—as perfect as Christ—being imputed, does not involve or jeopardize the character of God. He remains just when He justifies, not, indeed, on the ground of anything He ever finds in man, but on the ground of that which Christ has provided for those who believe. Such is the scope and reality of Christ's substitution for sinners on Calvary's cross.

II. CHRIST THE ENDING OF THE LAW PRINCIPLE IN BEHALF OF THOSE WHO ARE SAVED

The more extended discussion of the law with reference to its inception, its purpose, its reign, and its termination, yet to be undertaken under Ecclesiology, is not in order here. The immediate issue is the truth that, by the death of Christ and for those who believe, the legal, meritorious system of works comes to an end. In its larger aspects, the law exists as two widely different realities, namely, the Law of Moses and inherent law.

The Law of Moses is that rule for conduct which God gave to Israel at Mount Sinai, which law ran its course for 1500 years and was then superseded by "grace and truth" (John 1:17). It is that covenant which God made with Israel (Ex. 19:5) when He "took them by the hand to bring them out of the land of Egypt; which my covenant they brake" (Jer. 31:32). The law covenant was strictly a conditional agreement which conditioned divine blessings upon human faithfulness. The official and final statement of this covenant is recorded in Deuteronomy 28. In the light of new blessings and relationships which were to follow in the present age of grace and in the yet future kingdom age, the Mosaic Law was an *ad interim* divine dealing until the Seed—Christ—should come. It was a παιδαγωγός, a child governor or disciplinarian, to lead to Christ. But after Christ, the object of faith, is come, "we are no longer under a schoolmaster [παιδαγωγός]" (Gal. 3:19–25). Nevertheless, though the legal principle is now done away—and of necessity, because of its incompatibility with the rule for conduct which grace provides—it will, when Israel returns to the land under Messiah's reign, be re-established. Of those requirements and concerning the return of Israel to the land, Moses said, "And thou shalt return and obey the voice of the LORD, and do all his commandments which I command thee this day" (Deut. 30:8). Though it is the very law which Moses commanded that Israel will do, their situation will be altered. Christ will be on the throne of David reigning over Israel and the whole earth; Satan will be in the abyss; and this law, rather than being merely addressed to Israel, will be written on their hearts (Jer. 31:33); but its legal character is not changed. It is that law which Moses commanded them. In passing, it is important to observe that this Mosaic rule, or governing code, did not exist before it was proclaimed by Moses at Mount Sinai; it was never under any circumstances addressed to Gentiles; and as certainly it is never addressed to Christians, though Christians and unsaved Gentiles may, because of ignorance of God's will for them, assume the obligations of the law system. These are reminded that, when thus assuming any portion of the Law of Moses, they are under self-committal to do the whole law. Being *ad interim* in its character, the law which Moses commanded came to its termination at the time and under the circumstances divinely decreed. An exposition of this great body of truth, which will justify these dogmatic assertions, will be undertaken in its proper place.

Inherent law is perhaps best defined as the Creator's right over the creature and, therefore, the creature's responsibility to the Creator. In his wicked assumption of independence of God, man has lost the sense of the Creator's rights and looks upon the authority of God as unjustifiable intrusion into the sphere of human autonomy. However, the philosophy of self-rule, which Satan persuaded Adam to adopt, though so indispensable to fallen man that he can think in no other terms, has never nullified the inherent obligation of the creature to the Creator. "Be ye holy; for I am holy" is a reasonable, though drastic, requirement, being that which a holy God alone can require. Israel was condemned for having failed to keep the commandments of Moses —"which my covenant they brake"—but of man in general and as under inherent law it is said, "There is none righteous, no, not one: there is none that understandeth, there is none that seeketh after God. They are all gone out of the way, they are together become unprofitable; there is none that doeth good, no, not one" (Rom. 3:10–12). During a period of at least 2,500 years between Adam and Moses, only inherent law obtained; but that law was sufficiently definite that God judged men as offenders and purified the earth with a flood. More was known in that period of the demands of inherent law than is now recorded. God's Word respecting Abraham's obedience chronicled in Genesis 26:5 is most suggestive: "because that Abraham obeyed my voice, and kept my charge, my commandments, my statutes, and my laws" (cf. Gen. 18:19; Rom. 5:13). The requirement upon man that he be pleasing to his Creator is an obligation from which none may escape.

These two legal requirements—the Mosaic system and inherent law —are alike in one particular: they each aim at the establishing of human merit as the ground of divine blessing. Alike, these legal obligations impose upon man that only which a holy God might accept and which fallen man has never wrought—even as much as a semblance of them. The failure of Israel under the Mosaic system was such that the law, which in itself was "holy, and just, and good," became a ministration of condemnation and of death (Rom. 7:12; 2 Cor. 3:7, 9), while the failure under inherent law is such that only retribution awaits those who are not saved from it.

These extended introductory words have been penned as a preparation for a right understanding of an extended body of Scripture bearing on this theme—Christ the end of the law for those who believe. The central passage will be first in order and this will be followed by a series of texts which disclose the precise nature of this aspect of Christ's achievement in His death.

Romans 10:4. "For Christ is the end of the law for righteousness to every one that believeth."

The context, disregarding the intrusion of a chapter division, begins with Romans 9:30 and presents a strange paradox, which is, that the believing Gentiles who followed not after righteousness have attained unto righteousness, while Israel, who followed after righteousness, hath not attained to righteousness. There is thus introduced two methods of gaining righteousness. Israel, by self-effort, which the law prescribed, and by ignoring faith, hath not reached the goal of righteousness. Their law-works were, as always, a miserable failure. Over against this, Gentiles who attended not on the law, since it was never their portion, but who did exercise faith, reached the goal of perfect righteousness. A deep truth respecting the divine purpose in the giving of the law to Israel is here disclosed. God is said to have given the law as "a stumbling-stone and rock of offence" to the end that He might accentuate this very truth under discussion, namely, "Whosoever believeth on him shall not be ashamed." The example of Abraham who *believed* Jehovah and it (his faith) was counted unto him for righteousness (Gen. 15:6) was ever before Israel, and David had described the blessedness of the man unto whom God imputeth righteousness without works (Rom. 4:6); nevertheless, Israel stumbled over the stumbling stone of human merit, as humanity is ever prone to do—even many who through faith are already in possession of infinite righteousness. The Apostle at once points out that Israel's difficulty was not a lack of zeal; for, he asserts, they had a great "zeal for God." Their trouble was *ignorance*. They did not know the truth that faith in God would, as witnessed by Abraham, David, and the prophets, bring about, through divine grace, an adjustment all-satisfying to God—even a righteousness as perfect as Himself. The student is reminded of the previous discussion concerning the equitable ground established by the sweet savor aspect of Christ's death whereon God is free to impute all that Christ is—even the righteousness of God—unto those who *believe*, and Himself to be *just* when He justifies the ungodly. Unfortunately, this devastating ignorance respecting imputed righteousness, which so injured Israel, has characterized the church of Christ also. Great multitudes of those who belong to the church as its members have never conceived of any relation to God beyond "the law of works." Their reprehensibleness is far greater than that of Israel; for, while Israel had the witness of Abraham and David, the church has the example of Israel's failure and, in addition, the great body of New Testament Scripture. The Arminian notion that people will not live righteous lives unless placed upon a works basis of relationship to God has permeated the church to a large degree. This ignorance is manifested in the church by the fact that the greatest incentive to holy living that the human heart can know is ignored, which is, to "walk worthy of the vocation wherewith ye are called" (Eph. 4:1). The individual who comprehends that he has attained by faith through grace to the perfect righteousness of God, will be incited by so great an honor and trust to walk more faithfully in the path of God's own choosing than will the individual who hopes—against hope, for it is recognized as an impossible task—to satisfy a holy God by his ever-failing works.

But *is* the perfect righteousness of God secured as a standing, as a wedding garment, by those who do no more than to believe in Jesus? It certainly is, but the ignorance of Israel and of so many in the church does not make any place for so glorious a truth. Naturally, objection is not raised to the requirement that the individual should believe in Jesus. It would dishonor Him not to do so; but repentance, confession, consecration, good works, etc., must be added, it is claimed, to complete what is deemed to be reasonable, not understanding that the addition of one feature of human merit introduces a principle which, of necessity, is to misunderstand the entire character of that grace by which alone the soul is saved. Let the Scripture itself testify of this truth: "For I am not ashamed of the gospel of Christ: for it is the power of God unto salvation to every one that believeth; to the Jew first, and also to the Greek. For therein is the righteousness of God revealed from faith to faith: as it is written, The just shall live by faith" (Rom. 1:16–17); "Even the righteousness of God which is by faith of Jesus Christ unto all and upon all them that believe: for there is no difference . . . to declare, I say, at this time his righteousness: that he might be just, and the justifier of him which believeth in Jesus" (Rom. 3:22, 26); "But to him that worketh not, but believeth on him that justifieth the ungodly, his faith is counted for righteousness" (Rom. 4:5); "For if by one man's offence death reigned by one; much more they which receive abundance of grace and of the gift of righteousness shall reign in life by one, Jesus Christ" (Rom. 5:17); "But the scripture hath concluded all under sin, that the promise by faith of Jesus Christ might be given to them that believe" (Gal. 3:22); "For Christ is the end of the law for righteousness to every one that believeth" (Rom. 10:4).

Returning to the central passage—Romans 10:4, just quoted—it will be seen that some difference of opinion obtains with respect to the sense in which Christ is said to be *the end of the law*. Some see only that He, by His sufferings and death, paid the penalty the law imposed and thus discharged the indictment against the sinner, which is comprehended in forgiveness. Others see that Christ fulfills the law by supplying the merit which the holy Creator demands, which is comprehended in justification. Doubtless both of these conceptions inhere in this passage; but it will be observed that whatever is done is done for those who believe—with no other requirement added—and that belief results in the bestowing of the righteousness of God. As has been observed, the context of the passage under consideration contrasts two widely different principles of procedure, i.e., (1) an attempt to establish righteousness by zealous works, and (2) the securing of perfect righteousness by faith. One is a system of merit—the deadly enemy of grace—which offers self-righteousness to God with the hope that He will accept it by overlooking in generosity its imperfections; the other is a system based wholly on expectation toward God which receives in Christ Jesus the perfect righteousness of God, and, though works are wholly excluded from the ground upon which this righteousness is received, this plan secures the most serious concern on the part of the one who receives that righteousness that the daily life may be in harmony with the position and standing which has been attained by faith alone. Whether this superior incentive for a holy life is valued or not, it remains the unquestionable plan of God for those who are saved by grace through faith. The merit system has no termination, while the faith system seals its objective the moment the individual believes. The merit system represents the best that man can do, while the faith system represents the best that God can do. The merit system has never been, nor could it ever be, anything but ignominious failure, ending in eternal perdition, while the faith system never has been, nor could it ever be, anything but infinite perfection, ending in eternal glory.

How earnestly the great Apostle labors to make clear the truth that these two systems—law, works, and merit, on the one hand, and grace, faith, and promise, on the other hand—cannot coexist! He declares, "And if by grace, then is it no more of works: otherwise grace is no more grace. But if it be of works, then is it no more grace: otherwise work is no more work" (Rom. 11:6); "I do not frustrate the grace of God: for if righteousness come by the law, then Christ is dead in vain" (Gal. 2:21); "For if the inheritance be of the law, it is no more of promise: but God gave it to Abraham by promise. . . . And if ye be Christ's, then are ye Abraham's seed, and heirs according to the promise" (Gal. 3:18, 29).

It is in connection with the last passage quoted—Galatians 3:29—that the Apostle declares, "For as many of you as have been baptized into Christ have put on Christ" (vs. 27). The Spirit's baptism into Christ results in the "putting on" of Christ, and, as the most absolute necessity dictates, being thus in Christ, the blessing of Abrahamic *faith* and the position of an heir according to *promise* are gained on the most righteous ground. No doctrinal ground is set up in Genesis 15:6 in defense of the divine act of imputing righteousness to Abraham, but the imputation of righteousness to the believer, as has been observed, rests upon the absolute provision secured through the substitutionary death of Christ. The word to believers regarding the extending to them of Abraham's blessing on the ground of Abrahamic faith is assuring: "Now it was not written for his sake alone, that it was imputed to him; but for us also, to whom it shall be imputed, if we believe on him that raised up Jesus our Lord from the dead" (Rom. 4:23–24).

Certain other passages which bear on the same contrast with law, works, or merit, should also be considered. These are:

Acts 15:10. "Now therefore why tempt ye God, to put a yoke upon the neck of the disciples, which neither our fathers nor we were able to bear?"

This entire chapter forms the context of this one verse. The question before the first council of the church is that of the relation of the Mosaic system to those from among the Gentiles who are saved. The council determined that Gentile Christians were neither to be circumcised nor to keep the law (cf. vs. 24); and it was asserted by these Jews who were in authority in the church that the keeping of the law as a system of merit had been to those under its rule as "a yoke upon the neck" from which believers are free (cf. Gal. 5:1).

Romans 1:16–17. "For I am not ashamed of the gospel of Christ: for it is the power of God unto salvation to every one that believeth; to the Jew first, and also to the Greek. For therein is the righteousness of God revealed from faith to faith: as it is written, The just shall live by faith."

The notable contribution which this Scripture makes to this great theme is that the availability of the righteousness of God is a vital—so far as this text goes, *the* vital—feature of the gospel of divine grace.

Romans 3:21–22. "But now the righteousness of God without the law is manifested, being witnessed by the law and the prophets; even the righteousness of God which is by faith of Jesus Christ unto all and upon all them that believe: for there is no difference."

No greater human failure could be described than that recounted in Romans 1:18—3:20. From that dark background the Apostle turns abruptly, on the words "But now" (3:21), to the most glorious provision, which is, that perfect righteousness is available through simple faith in Christ. This blessing is secured wholly apart from and independent of any help the merit system of the law might contribute. This divinely provided righteousness is revealed unto all and comes upon all who believe. Twice this uncomplicated condition appears. It is through faith in Jesus Christ and extends to all who believe. Language could not more clearly assert that this is distinctly a righteousness *from* God and received by faith apart from anything or everything belonging to human merit.

Romans 3:31. "Do we then make void the law through faith? God forbid: yea, we establish the law."

Two interpretations of this crucial passage have been advanced: (1) that, through the enabling power of the Spirit, the righteousness which the law demands may be fulfilled by the believer; and (2) that the unsaved may establish the law by standing in that fulfillment of it which Christ has accomplished. All that the law could ever require is satisfied in the one who is perfected in Christ. The former interpretation is only an exalted form of human works which are fulfilled in the believer and never by the believer; yet these works are credited to the believer, since for them he will receive a reward. The latter interpretation is in harmony with all revealed truth, but will be accepted only by those who have apprehended the doctrine of imputed righteousness.

Romans 4:5. "But to him that worketh not, but believeth on him that justifieth the ungodly, his faith is counted for righteousness."

The phrase "worketh not" does not imply carelessness in the believer's daily life; it rather refers to the truth that he does not depend on works of merit. The passage reveals the important truth that believing is the opposite of works of merit. Believing is not doing a meritorious work; it is trusting the finished work of Another. Even the ungodly may be counted righteous on the ground of faith in Christ.

Romans 4:11. "And he received the sign of circumcision, a seal of the righteousness of the faith which he had yet being uncircumcised:

that he might be the father of all them that believe, though they be not circumcised; that righteousness might be imputed unto them also."

What Abraham received before being circumcised and centuries before the law was given cannot be said to have been a divine recognition of works of merit. Abraham is the pattern and, therefore, the father of all who receive imputed righteousness by faith.

Romans 4:13–16. "For the promise, that he should be the heir of the world, was not to Abraham, or to his seed, through the law, but through the righteousness of faith. For if they which are of the law be heirs, faith is made void, and the promise made of none effect: because the law worketh wrath: for where no law is, there is no transgression. Therefore it is of faith, that it might be by grace; to the end the promise might be sure to all the seed; not to that only which is of the law, but to that also which is of the faith of Abraham; who is the father of us all."

In Abraham's case, as is the case of all who exercise Abrahamic faith, the promise of imputed righteousness is (1) by *faith* (nothing on man's part—cf. vs. 5), that it might be by grace (everything on God's part), to the end that the promise might be *sure*. Nothing could be so insecure as a righteousness based on human merit.

Romans 4:23–24. "Now it was not written for his sake alone, that it was imputed to him; but for us also, to whom it shall be imputed, if we believe on him that raised up Jesus our Lord from the dead."

Let it be restated that Abraham is the pattern of a Christian under grace and not of a Jew under law. The character of his faith, as defined in verses 17–22, is worthy of most careful consideration. But righteousness received by faith is not alone the heritage of Abraham; it is "for us also." This blessed truth is well expressed by the Apostle in Galatians 3:7, 9: "Know ye therefore that they which are of faith, the same are the children of Abraham. . . . So then they which be of faith are blessed with faithful Abraham" (cf. John 8:37, 39).

Romans 5:19. "For as by one man's disobedience many were made sinners, so by the obedience of one shall many be made righteous."

Here again, but in a different setting, is presented the truth before emphasized, that it is through the obedient, sweet savor offering of Christ that the many are counted righteous. This, it should be observed, is far removed from the notion that true righteousness is by human works and merit.

2 Corinthians 5:21. "For he hath made him to be sin for us, who knew no sin; that we might be made the righteousness of God in him "

Associated closely with this passage is Romans 3:22. In both there is clear reference to the fact that there is a righteousness from God which is *made* the portion of those who do no more than believe in Jesus.

Galatians 3:8. "And the scripture, foreseeing that God would justify the heathen through faith, preached before the gospel unto Abraham, saying, In thee shall all nations be blessed."

Thus, again, the great benefit of imputed righteousness which came to Abraham in response to his faith is declared to be but a first-fruits, as it were, of that which God in the day of His favor is imputing to all who believe.

Galatians 4:19–31. "My little children, of whom I travail in birth again until Christ be formed in you, I desire to be present with you now, and to change my voice; for I stand in doubt of you. Tell me, ye that desire to be under the law, do ye not hear the law? For it is written, that Abraham had two sons, the one by a bondmaid, the other by a freewoman. But he who was of the bondwoman was born after the flesh; but he of the freewoman was by promise. Which things are an allegory: for these are the two covenants; the one from the mount Sinai, which gendereth to bondage, which is Agar. For this Agar is mount Sinai in Arabia, and answereth to Jerusalem which now is, and is in bondage with her children. But Jerusalem which is above is free, which is the mother of us all. For it is written, Rejoice, thou barren that bearest not; break forth and cry, thou that travailest not: for the desolate hath many more children than she which hath an husband. Now we, brethren, as Isaac was, are the children of promise. But as then he that was born after the flesh persecuted him that was born after the Spirit, even so it is now. Nevertheless what saith the scripture? Cast out the bondwoman and her son: for the son of the bondwoman shall not be heir with the son of the freewoman. So then, brethren, we are not children of the bondwoman, but of the free."

This extended allegory teaches what the Apostle asserts in Romans 11:6, namely, that the two systems—that of works and that of faith—cannot coexist. The bondwoman, Hagar, who typifies the principle of human works, must be dismissed, for the freewoman, Sarah, who typifies promise and faith, and the bondwoman cannot share the inheritance.

Galatians 5:1. "Stand fast therefore in the liberty wherewith Christ hath made us free, and be not entangled again with the yoke of bondage."

The priceless liberty of the Christian, which he is here enjoined to defend at any cost, is the deliverance he has experienced from the merit system, the law, and human works. If, after being thus delivered, he shall lapse into any form of law observance with a view to establishing his own righteousness, he has *fallen from grace* (vs. 4). To that extent, Christ, the bestower of a perfect righteousness in which he stands, has become of no effect. Thus the Apostle declares, "For if I build again the things which I destroyed, I make myself a transgressor" (2:18). This constitutes a most serious warning.

In conclusion it may be restated that, by His death in its sweet savor aspect, Christ secured the righteous ground upon which God is just when He justifies even the ungodly who do no more than to believe in Jesus. They are equally established before God by their union to Christ through the baptism of the Spirit. In these respects, Christ is the *end of the law*—the principle of law, works, and merit—for all those who believe. The entire merit system is, of necessity, dismissed, whether it be the Mosaic system or inherent law. No ground is left for an appeal for works of merit in the life of the one who through riches of grace is constituted as perfect in his standing before God as Christ is perfect. The injunctions of the grace portion of the New Testament are free from any appeal to the believer on the basis of merit. There is abundant ground for an appeal that such a glorious reality as imputed righteousness shall be adorned by a holy life. Such an appeal is indeed far removed from the practice of the ignorant Israelites who went about seeking to establish their own righteousness, not knowing—in spite of much revelation—that there is a righteousness available from God. No more imperious feature is embedded in this great body of Scripture than that this marvel of divine grace—imputed righteousness—is received on the one and only condition of believing on Christ.

III. A REDEMPTION TOWARD SIN

This is closely related to divisions IV on reconciliation and V on propitiation, which follow. These are the three doctrines in each of which the value of the death of Christ is recognized as reaching out to the unsaved. Other doctrines related to the value to men of Christ's death —forgiveness, regeneration, justification, sanctification—are restricted in that they contemplate that death only in its relation to those who believe. However, the trilogy—redemption, reconciliation, and propitiation—is unique in that these parts by which it is constituted extend benefits to both saved and unsaved. The essential benefits which accrue to the Christian from these realities will be considered as the doctrines are contemplated separately. On the other hand, when the truth in each of these three doctrines as related to the unsaved is examined and segregated, and these three segregated portions are combined into one interrelated body of truth, the result is a declaration of all that enters into that which is termed *the finished work of Christ*. This term is derived from the words of Christ on the cross, namely, "It is finished" (John 19:30). There was no reference on Christ's part by these words to the truth that His own life, service, or sufferings were coming to an end. It is rather that a specific undertaking committed to Him by His Father, which could not have begun until He was on the cross, was consummated. It is true that the Father had given Him a work to do in His three and a half years of service. To this reference is made in the words, "Jesus saith unto them, My meat is to do the will of him that sent me, and to finish his work" (John 4:34); "But I have greater witness than that of John: for the works which the Father hath given me to finish, the same works that I do, bear witness of me, that the Father hath sent me" (John 5:36). In contradistinction to this, a specific work was committed to the Savior which began with His cross sufferings and ended with His death. It is to this that His words "It is finished" refer. Of this same saving work of the cross the Savior in His priestly prayer spoke when He said, "I have finished the work which thou gavest me to do" (John 17:4). That He could speak thus of a work which had not at that time even begun is explained by the fact that the whole of the Upper Room Discourse, including the priestly prayer, was dated by Christ in relation to the cross, the resurrection, the ascension, and the advent of the Spirit as though these momentous events were accomplished. What was wrought on the cross and finished when He died will be discovered only through an investigation into that which was included in His redemption, His reconciliation, and His propitiation.

Redemption is the sinward aspect of Christ's work on the cross and as such is restricted in its meaning. In this thesis, redemption will be treated in this Biblical and specific meaning and not as modern theology has employed the term as a representation of all that Christ wrought in His sufferings and death. The work of Christ on the cross is far too extensive to be contemplated in any single phase of it. This work in its totality could as well be represented by either the term *reconciliation* or *propitiation,* as by *redemption.* Not one of these ideas, or all three together, could serve to indicate in its fulness so vast a theme. Perhaps the free use of the word *redemption* to represent the entire saving work of Christ is due, too often, to a failure to comprehend all that He wrought. Such a restriction is manifest when men speak of a *limited redemption,* as though Christ's work on the cross was restricted to, and so exhausted with regard to its value, His death for the elect who comprise the Church. Not only is the value of His death not limited to the Church or even to humanity, since it reaches to angelic spheres, but it would be as reasonable to speak of His work as a *limited reconciliation,* or a *limited propitiation,* as to style it a *limited redemption.* The student is cautioned against any assumption of limitation relative to the value of Christ's death. It will be seen that, while Christ died for the elect who comprise the Church—and at least five aspects of the value of His death are related to that body—He is as definitely said to have died for Israel as a distinct and unrelated people, for a judgment upon fallen angels, for a purification of heaven, and for the whole *cosmos* world. The fallacy of a so-called limited redemption is yet to be examined in a later division of this general theme.

Redemption is an act of God by which He Himself pays as a ransom the price of human sin which the outraged holiness and government of God requires. Redemption undertakes the solution of the problem of sin, as reconciliation undertakes the solution of the problem of the sinner, and propitiation undertakes the problem of an offended God. All are infinitely important and all are requisite to the analysis of the whole doctrine of Christ's finished work—a work finished, indeed, to the point of divine perfection. Though parts of one complete whole, these great themes should never be treated as synonymous. The specific character of each is obvious.

The redemption provided for and offered to the sinner is a redemption from sin, which estate, according to the Bible, is one of bondservitude concerning which both a liberating price must be paid and power be exercised in the deliverance of the slave. Divine redemption is by blood—the ransom price—and by power. Such was the release of Israel from Egyptian bondage—a type of bondslavery to sin. Israel was redeemed by the blood of the sacrificial lamb, and by almighty power was taken out from bondage into freedom. This order is never reversed either in the type or the antitype.

The Old Testament doctrine of redemption concerns, in the main, a redeemed nation, and, therefore, the theme is implied throughout the Jewish Scriptures. Exodus is the book of redemption and Ruth is a type-picture of the Kinsman-Redeemer. The word *gā'al* serves to express the thought of redemption—the act of setting free by payment of a ransom price. The thing redeemed might be a person or an estate (cf. Lev. 25:25, 47–48). Certain requirements, which were highly typical, were imposed upon the one who would redeem: (a) He must be a kinsman. This aspect of truth leads to the meaning of the title *Kinsman-Redeemer,* and is the basic requirement which brought the Son of God from heaven to earth and necessitated the incarnation that He might be a perfect Kinsman-Redeemer. (b) The *gā'al* individual must also be able to redeem. The price, whatever it might be in any case, was paid by the one who redeemed. This requirement was imperative in the type as it is in the antitype. Christ alone could pay the price of redemption— the blood of a holy, undefiled, and spotless Lamb. The blood of a man, especially of a fallen race, would not suffice. It must be the blood of God (cf. Acts 20:28). (c) The *gā'al* individual had to be free from the calamity which had fallen on the one who was to be redeemed. In this particular, Christ the Antitype was free from both the sin nature and the practice of sin. (d) The one who would redeem had to be willing to redeem. This feature Christ fulfilled perfectly. Boaz in the book of Ruth is thus a *gā'al* individual and the divinely provided type of Christ in redemption.[1]

In the New Testament, three different Greek words are used to translate *redeem* or *redemption,* and the distinctions which they set forth are naturally lost to the reader of the English text. These words are: (1) ἀγοράζω which means *to purchase in the market.* Here the essential truth appears that the unsaved are bondslaves to sin—"sold under sin" (Rom. 7:14), dominated by Satan (Eph. 2:2; 1 Cor. 12:2), condemned (John 3:18; Rom. 3:19; Gal. 3:10). Whoever would redeem them must take the slave's place, be made a curse for him, and shed his blood as a ransom-price of redemption (Matt. 20:28). (2) ἐξαγοράζω, meaning to purchase *out* of the market. This is a distinct advance over ἀγοράζω, which implies no more than the payment of the requisite price. The addition of ἐξ supplies the added thought of *removing* or *taking out.* One thus taken out will never again be returned to the place of bondage and exposed to the lot of a slave. (3) λυτρόω, which indicates that the redeemed one is loosened and set free. Redemption, in its fullest meaning, as represented by this word, is assurance

---

[1] Other words than *gā'al* which are found in the Old Testament and which convey the thought of redemption are: *pādhāh* (cf. Lev. 19:20; 27:29; Num. 3:46, 48–49, 51; 18:16; Deut. 7:8; 13:5 [English]; Ps. 49:7–8, 15 [English]; 111:9; 130:7; Mic. 6:4); *kānāh* (cf. Neh. 5:8); *pāraḳ* (cf. Ps. 136:24); *ge'ullāh* (cf. Lev. 25:26, 29, 32; Ruth 4:7; Jer. 32:7–8).

that Christ has not merely transferred the sinner's bondage from one master to another; He has purchased with the object in view that the ransomed one may be free. Christ will not hold unwilling slaves in bondage. All this is typically anticipated in Exodus 21:1–6 (cf. Deut. 15:16–17). A slave set free by his master was wholly free; but he could voluntarily remain as the slave of the master whom he loved. The new voluntary relationship was sealed by the master piercing the ear of the slave with an awl. Thus, according to type, the Christian is set free, but is privileged to yield himself wholly to the One who redeemed him. Of this, the Apostle said, "I beseech you therefore, brethren, by the mercies of God, that ye present your bodies a living sacrifice, holy, acceptable unto God, which is your reasonable service. And be not conformed to this world: but be ye transformed by the renewing of your mind, that ye may prove what is that good, and acceptable, and perfect, will of God" (Rom. 12:1–2). In like manner, Christ, on His human side, was the perfect example of voluntary yielding to the will of another. According to Psalm 40, quoted in Hebrews 10:5–7 and contemplating the sealing of the voluntary slave, Christ said, "Sacrifice and offering thou didst not desire; mine ears hast thou opened: burnt-offering and sin-offering hast thou not required. Then said I, Lo, I come: in the volume of the book it is written of me, I delight to do thy will, O my God: yea, thy law is within my heart" (40:6–8). The phrase "Mine ears hast thou opened" may as well be rendered, "Mine ears hast thou bored," and reference is evidently made to the provision recorded in Exodus 21:1–6. He is in every respect—type and antitype—the yielded servant.

It is therefore to be observed that the doctrine of redemption as set forth by the terms used in the New Testament is a complete fulfillment of the truth foreshadowed in the Old Testament, that there is a sense in which the price is paid but the slave is not necessarily released— which is the estate of all for whom Christ died who are yet not saved— and that, by a deeper and more abundant realization of redemption, the slave may be released and set free—which is the estate of all who are saved. The relation of the unsaved to the truth that by His death Christ paid the ransom price, is to believe what is declared to be true and is true. The relation of the saved to the truth that by His death Christ set them free is to recognize that marvelous freedom and then by self-surrender to become the voluntary slaves of the Redeemer.

IV. A RECONCILIATION TOWARD MAN

The manward aspect of Christ's work on the cross is termed *reconciliation* and is strictly a New Testament doctrine, or, more specifically, a reality made possible by the death of Christ. The words *reconcile* and *reconciliation* occur as such twice in the English A.V. of the Old Testament—1 Samuel 29:4, where it is merely that one would make himself pleasing to another, and 2 Chronicles 29:24, where it refers to the making of an offering. The other Old Testament passages rendered thus— Leviticus 6:30; 8:15; 16:20; Ezekiel 45:15, 17, 20; Daniel 9:24—to be consistent with the original, should be translated *atonement*. Similarly, Hebrews 2:17 should be rendered *propitiation*, as Romans 5:11 should be rendered *reconciliation*. The New Testament doctrine is, however, of major importance. The one Greek root καταλλάσσω has but one meaning, namely, *to change completely*. Should these two pointed words be substituted in the New Testament text wherever the English words *reconcile* or *reconciliation* occur (excepting Hebrews 2:17), the true force of the passage would be preserved. It is written: "For if, when we were enemies, we were reconciled [changed completely] to God by the death of his Son, much more, being reconciled [changed completely], we shall be saved by his life" (Rom. 5:10); "For if the casting away of them be the reconciling [changing completely] of the world, what shall the receiving of them be, but life from the dead?" (Rom. 11:15); "But and if she depart, let her remain unmarried, or be reconciled [changed completely] to her husband: and let not the husband put away his wife" (1 Cor. 7:11); "And all things are of God, who hath reconciled [changed completely] us to himself by Jesus Christ, and hath given to us the ministry of reconciliation [changing completely]" (2 Cor. 5:18); "And that he might reconcile [change completely] both unto God in one body by the cross, having slain the enmity thereby" (Eph. 2:16); "And, having made peace through the blood of his cross, by him to reconcile [change completely] all things unto himself; by him, I say, whether they be things in earth, or things in heaven. And you, that were sometime alienated and enemies in your mind by wicked works, yet now hath he reconciled [changed completely]" (Col. 1:20–21).

The two aspects of reconciliation are best disclosed in 2 Corinthians 5:19–20. In verse 19 it is declared that the world (κόσμος, which term is never by any stretch of exegesis made to represent the elect who are saved out of it) is reconciled to God. This vital passage presents the truth that, in and through the death of Christ, God was *changing completely* the position of the world in its relation to Himself. The Bible never asserts that God is reconciled. If it be supposed that God is represented as having changed completely His own attitude toward the world because of Christ's death, it will be remembered that it is His righteousness which is involved. Before the death of Christ His righteousness demanded its required judgments; but after the death of Christ that same righteousness is free to save the lost. His righteousness is thus not changed nor does it ever act otherwise than in perfect equity. Thus God who sees the world changed completely in its relation to Himself by the death of Christ, is not Himself reconciled or changed. The same interpretation is required in Romans 11:15. There is no need to be overcritical on this point. There is in the cross an outward appearance of changed attitude on the part of God; but this belongs rather to propitiation than to reconciliation. The latter is no more Godward in its objective accomplishments than redemption. Certainly redemption is not Godward, nor, in the final analysis, is reconciliation Godward; for God is immutable. He is always righteous, just, and good. Propitiation, it will be seen, does not infuse compassion into God; it rather secures the freedom on His part to exercise His unchanging compassion apart from those restraints which penal judgments would otherwise impose. There is a truth to be recognized concerning God, that in His own being and from all eternity His holiness and His love have found adjustment concerning the sinner through the death of His Son; but this is only another approach to the same divine propitiation.

It has been claimed that for God to adjust the world in its relation to Himself, as is accomplished in the reconciliation aspect of Christ's death, is universalism. It is assumed, thus, that general reconciliation is equivalent to general salvation. To avoid such a conclusion, it is asserted that Christ died for only the elect. They alone were changed completely in the sphere of their relation to God. Most convincingly the Apostle goes on in verse 20 to state that Christ's messengers, to whom is committed the word of reconciliation, go forth, in His stead, beseeching the very men who according to verse 19 are already divinely reconciled, to be reconciled to God. The word *beseech* implies that they may or may not be reconciled in response to the messengers. What is it that men are thus implored to do? Simply this: God is satisfied with the solution of the sin question as consummated by Christ in His death, and the sinner is petitioned to be satisfied himself with that which satisfies God. Thus the element of faith is present, and it is never absent when the salvation of men is in view. It is evident, then, that whatever *complete change* is indicated—for the κόσμος, according to verse 19, is not equivalent to the saving of anyone—elect or non-elect—it has made the reconciliation of verse 20, which is equivalent to salvation, possible. The unregenerate are saved when they individually elect to stand adjusted to God through the death of Christ. This, indeed, is a thorough change from unbelief and rejection of Christ to belief and acceptance of Christ. In other words, the value of Christ's reconciling death is not applied to the sinner at the time of that death, but rather *when* he believes.

This twofold reconciliation—that of the world and that which is wrought when the individual believes—is in evidence again in Romans 5:10–11: "For if, when we were enemies, we were reconciled to God by the death of his Son, much more, being reconciled, we shall be saved by his life. And not only so, but we also joy in God through our Lord Jesus Christ, by whom we have now received the atonement." In the first instance, the death of Christ is said to have reconciled "enemies" to God, which truth corresponds with the reconciliation of the world; in the second instance, "being reconciled" by a personal faith as well as by the fact of Christ's death, the saved are to be kept saved by Christ's living presence as Advocate and Intercessor in heaven.

There can be no question raised about the fact that there are two aspects of reconciliation: one wrought for all by God in His love for the world and the other wrought in the individual who believes when he believes.

V. A PROPITIATION TOWARD GOD

The value to God of Christ's death as a vindication of His righteousness and law is indicated by the word *propitiation*. This intricate doctrine is set forth by the various forms and uses of this word. No more clarifying analysis of this doctrine has been found than that written by Dr. C. I. Scofield in his *Bible Correspondence Course,* which is here quoted in part:

The word propitiation occurs in the English Bible, A.V., but three times. In 1 John 2:2, and 4:10, Christ is said to be "the propitiation for our sins." Here the Greek word is *hilasmos,* meaning, "that which propitiates." In Rom. 3:25 it is said of Christ: "Whom God hath set forth to be a propitiation through faith in his blood, to declare his righteousness for the passing over of sins done aforetime, through the forbearance of God." Here the Greek word is *hilastērion,* meaning, "the place of propitiation." But in Heb. 9:5 *hilastērion* is the Greek word used by the Holy Spirit for "mercy seat" in referring to the ancient tabernacle worship of Israel: "And over it the cherubims of glory shadowing the mercy seat" (*hilastērion*). This, therefore, sends us back to the Old Testament. Whatever the mercy seat of the tabernacle was, typically, to the Israelite, *that* Christ is, actually, to the believer and to God. . . . Before turning to the Old Testament, the student will note two other New Testament passages. Heb. 8:12: "I will be merciful [*hileōs*, propitious] to their unrighteousness." Luke 18:13: "God be merciful [*hilaskomai*, propitiated] to me a sinner." (1) The mercy seat was the lid or cover of the ark of the covenant. The ark was an oblong box of acacia wood overlaid with gold, two and one half cubits long, and one and one half cubits high and broad. In this box or ark, were placed, along with a pot of the wilderness manna, and Aaron's rod, the "two tables of testimony, tables of stone, written with the finger of God"— the ten commandments, God's holy Law (Ex. 31:18). The cover, or "mercy seat," was made entirely of gold, the symbol of divine righteousness, and at each end, beaten out of the same piece of gold, was a figure with wings extended over the mercy seat, the cherubim. "And the cherubims shall stretch forth their wings on high, covering the mercy seat with their wings, and their faces shall look one to another; toward the mercy seat shall the faces of the cherubims be" (Ex. 25:20). The cherubims are set forth in the Old Testament as especially connected with the *glory* of God, and the guardians and vindicators of what is due to His glory (Ezek. 1:13, 14, 27, 28; Gen. 3:24). (2) The mercy seat (*hilastērion*) of the tabernacle worship was called in the Hebrew, *kapporeth,* place of covering, and is intimately connected with the Old Testament word atonement (Heb. *kaphar,* to cover sin). The sacrificial blood made atonement . . . for sin; the mercy seat was the "place of covering" for it was there the sacrificial blood was sprinkled. "And he [the high priest] shall take of the blood of the bullock, and sprinkle it with his finger upon the mercy seat eastward, and before the mercy seat shall he sprinkle of the blood with his finger seven times" (Lev. 16:13). (3) Typically, therefore, the golden lid of the ark was a mercy seat because, in divine righteousness (gold), it "covered" from the eyes of the cherubim the broken law, while the sprinkled blood "covered" the worshipper's sins. It became, therefore, the meeting place of a holy God and a sinful man. "There will I *meet with thee,* and will *commune* with thee, from above the mercy seat, from between the two cherubims" (Ex. 25:22). "For *I will appear* in the cloud upon the mercy seat" (Lev. 16:2). "And when Moses was gone into the tabernacle of the congregation to speak with him, then he heard the voice of one speaking unto him from off the mercy seat" (Num. 7:89). (4) It follows that Christ is the propitiation (*hilastērion*, mercy seat, "throne of grace," Heb. 4:16), because He is the meeting place and place of communion between a holy God and a sinful but believing human being. Meeting God in Christ, the believer may boldly say: "Who shall lay anything to the charge of God's elect; it is God that justifieth" (Rom. 8:33). And Christ is the *hilastērion,* or mercy seat, because He is the *hilasmos,* the propitiator, who "put away sin by the sacrifice of himself" (Heb. 9:26); and then, "an high priest of good things to come, by a greater and more perfect tabernacle, not made with hands . . . neither by the blood of goats and calves, but by his own blood, he entered in once into the holy place, having obtained eternal redemption for us" (Heb. 9:11, 12). He is Himself the mercy seat sprinkled with His own precious blood. (5) The question still remains: what or whom did He propitiate by the shedding of His own blood? It is the answer to this question which exposes the infelicity of the English word "propitiation" as a rendering of the Greek *hilastērion*, or the Hebrew *kapporeth*. For "propitiate" means *to appease*, and suggests the wholly false notion that God's wrath was appeased, satiated, by sacrificial blood. But the very fact that God Himself provides the mercy seat, the propitiation, should have banished that notion from human thinking. God is love, and holiness His highest attribute. His law is the expression of His holiness, the cross the expression of His love. And in the cross there is such a doing right by the moral order of the universe, such a meeting, in the sinner's behalf, of the inflexible demand of the law,—"the soul that sinneth it shall die"—that the love of God may flow unhindered to the sinner with no compromise of His holiness. What, else, must have been a judgment seat, becomes, for the believer in Christ, a mercy seat; a "throne of grace." Propitiation, then, relates to the law and what is due to God's holiness.—III, 482–85

The prayer of the publican (Luke 18:13) has been greatly misunderstood and misused. The translation of ἱλάσκομαι by the English word *merciful* rather than by the word *propitious,* which is to be indicated, is responsible for great error in the field of gospel appeal. God cannot be merciful toward the sinner in the sense of being generous or lenient, and the publican did not ask God to do such an impossible thing. He did ask God to be propitious. In this connection, it will be remembered that this record is of the experience of a man who stood on Old Testament ground, before the death of Christ. Having brought his offering— as all did who approached God in prayer for forgiveness—he was justified in asking God to be propitious to him *the* sinner (Greek). The error consists in not recognizing that the death of Christ has changed all relationships to God. For an individual to pray to God now that He be merciful toward a sinner is as impossible as it was in Old Testament days. For an individual to ask now that God be propitious is to reject the death of Christ and to ignore its value. It is to plead for something to be done when everything has been done. Men are not saved by coaxing mercy out of God; they are saved when they dare to believe God has been merciful enough to provide a Savior and that He *is* propitious.

As in the case of redemption and reconciliation, there are two aspects of propitiation. There is a propitiation which affects God in His relation to the κόσμος—with no reference to the elect—and one which affects His relation to the elect. This twofold propitiation is set forth in 1 John 2:2, which reads, "And he is the propitiation for our sins: and not for our's only, but also for the sins of the whole world." No more transforming message could be uttered than the proclamation of the truth that God *is* propitious. On the ground of this gospel the unsaved are free to come by faith, knowing that they will not be punished or reproved, but rather received and saved forever. In like manner, the saved who have sinned, confessing their sin, are free to come to God for the needed forgiveness and cleansing, and are never turned away. The prodigal son, who is an illustration of a son returning to the Father for restoration on the ground of confession rather than faith, was kissed by his father *before* he had made his confession. Thus it is revealed that God *is* propitious, not when faith or confession has made Him so, but because of the death of His Son. Neither sinners nor sinning saints are appointed to the task of propitiating God. Christ has accomplished that perfectly, and the door into the grace of God is open wide.

When redemption, which is toward sin, reconciliation, which is toward man, and propitiation, which is toward God—all wrought by Christ in His death—are considered in their specific relation to the unsaved and these three are combined into one doctrine or body of truth, they together form what is properly termed *the finished work of Christ.*

VI. THE JUDGMENT OF THE SIN NATURE

By His sufferings and death Christ wrought with equal definiteness and effectiveness in solving the problem of personal sins and the problem of the sin nature. He "died for our sins" (1 Cor. 15:3), and "he died unto sin" (Rom. 6:10). In preceding pages which deal with the doctrine of substitution, Christ's death for personal sin, or "our sins," has been traced. At this point the deeper and more complex truth is confronted, namely, that Christ died *unto sin.* Light is thrown on this theme when it is observed that in Romans, chapters 6, 7, and 8, and in 1 John, chapter 1, there is a distinction indicated between sin which is personal failure or transgression, and sin which is a nature. Though the same term, *sin,* is used, the context and character of truth disclosed determines where and when one truth or the other is in view. As an illustration of this important distinction, it may be seen that 1 John 1:8—"If we say that we have no sin, we deceive ourselves, and the truth is not in us"—relates to the sin nature, about which good people may easily be self-deceived; nevertheless the truth is not in the one who asserts that he has no sin nature. Over against this and as a wholly different claim, 1 John 1:10 states: "If we say that we have not sinned, we make him a liar, and his word is not in us." In this sphere of personal sin there can be no self-deception. The grieved Spirit, if not the conscience, in the believer has impressed him with the reality of his sin. He knows, also, that he has failed to comply with the instruction given in the Word of God and that God has plainly declared that none are free from sin in His sight. To declare of one's self that one has not sinned, is to make God a liar and not to be benefited by His Word.

The divine method, therefore, of dealing with the believer's sin nature is first to bring it into judgment. This was done by Christ when He "died unto sin once" (Rom. 6:10); but it can never be made too emphatic that this judgment does not consist in that nature being destroyed, nor is its essential power diminished. As Satan was judged by Christ on the cross (Col. 2:14–15; John 16:11) and is yet active—perhaps, as the god of this age, he is more active than before—in like manner, the sin nature is judged though its power is not, because of that judgment, decreased. The second provision in the divine dealing with the sin nature is that it is to be controlled in the believer by the superior power of the indwelling Spirit. It is a form of rationalism to contend that the sin nature is dismissed or eradicated in any believer, so long as he is in this world. This error, so prevalent in many quarters, will be analyzed at its proper place under Pneumatology. Enough will have been said here if it be observed that, as the Christian's enemies are three, namely, the world, the flesh, and the devil (the sin nature, or the "old man," is but a portion of one of these) and not one of them is ever removed or eradicated, it is highly unscriptural and equally unreasonable to contend that the sin nature is thus deposed. Similarly, there might be a semblance of justification for a theory of eradication if anyone had ever demonstrated such a thing in experience. Over against all suppositions of such rationalism is the truth that the Word of God so clearly teaches that the Spirit of God is given to the Christian as the resource by which he may realize a victory over every foe, including the sin nature, which statement of Scripture, in so far as it concerns the sin nature, were eradication the will of God, would be without point or purpose.

The perfect judgment by Christ in His death of the sin nature, had in view the provision of a righteous basis upon which that nature may be wholly controlled by the Spirit of God. The problem is one that is related to God and His holiness. Being wholly evil, the sin nature can only be judged by God directly, or in a substitute of His choice. The Holy Spirit, being holy, could not deal with that evil nature in any life other than to bring upon it the awful judgment it merits, had it not been already judged. Since it is perfectly judged by Christ, all the power of the Spirit is free from restraint, to accomplish a day-by-day, or moment-by-moment, victory over the sin nature. To deal only with fruit of the tree—personal sins—and not with its root—the sin nature—would be almost a useless procedure. God has plainly declared His purpose and method of dealing with the root—the sin nature—and by giving attention to this the Christian may be intelligent in the steps he takes in the direction of an experimental sanctification of daily life. As unregenerate men may continue unsaved because of their failure to enter by faith into the truth that Christ died for their sins, in like manner regenerate men may remain undelivered from evil in their lives because of their failure to enter by faith into the truth that Christ died unto their sin nature.

Romans 6:1—8:13. The central passage bearing on the judgment of the sin nature, or "old man," by the death of Christ and the explanation of the new basis upon which, in view of that judgment, the believer's life may be lived, is Romans 6:1—8:13. As Romans, chapters 1 to 5, discloses the way of salvation into eternal life and a perfect standing, even eternal justification, for those among the unsaved who believe—and that because of the finished work of Christ as a redemption (3:24), as a reconciliation (5:10), and as a propitiation (3:25), thus Romans 6:1—8:13 discloses the way to a God-honoring manner of life for the one who is saved, and that manner of life through what may well be termed *the finished work of Christ for the Christian.* For, by a judgment —infinitely perfect and complete—of the sin nature, the walk by a new life-principle, by the enabling power of the Holy Spirit (8:4), is made possible for the Christian, who by faith reckons himself to be dead unto the sin nature and alive unto God, and counts on the sufficient power of the Spirit. It is of surpassing importance that the "old man is [was] crucified with him [Christ]" (6:6). On this ground the body of sin, or sin's power to manifest itself, may be *disannulled*—not *destroyed,* as in the A.V. Though this great body of truth is but briefly considered in the present connection in relation to the death of Christ, it will be considered at length under Pneumatology and as related to the enabling work of the Spirit.

Both Christ's death *for* sins and His death *unto* sin are substitutionary to the highest degree, and in no Scripture is substitution so emphasized as in Romans 6:1–10. Four steps in which the believer participates are itemized—crucifixion, death, burial, and resurrection. It is significant that the one most forcible and explicit context which deals with the death of Christ for the unsaved presents the same particulars, but without the crucifixion feature. This Scripture declares: "Moreover, brethren, I declare unto you the gospel which I preached unto you, which also ye have received, and wherein ye stand; by which also ye are saved, if ye keep in memory what I preached unto you, unless ye have believed in vain. For I delivered unto you first of all that which I also received, how that Christ died for our sins according to the scriptures; and that he was buried, and that he rose again the third day according to the scriptures" (1 Cor. 15:1-4). In Romans 6:1-4, which presents the ground of the believer's experimental sanctification, or daily walk, in the enabling power of the Spirit, it is written, "What shall we say then? Shall we continue in sin, that grace may abound? God forbid. How shall we that are dead to sin, live any longer therein? Know ye not, that so many of us as were baptized into Jesus Christ were baptized into his death? Therefore we are buried with him by baptism into death: that like as Christ was raised up from the dead by the glory of the Father, even so we also should walk in newness of life." And to this is added in verse 6, "Knowing this, that our old man is crucified with him, that the body of sin might be destroyed, that henceforth we should not serve sin." The whole context, Romans 6:1-10, is so sustained in its thought of substitution that a partnership—cocrucifixion, codeath, coburial, and coresurrection—is indicated. Since there could be no necessity for any one of these features to be enacted for Christ's own sake, it is altogether wrought in behalf of those whose sin nature He thus judges. This so vital passage on which the whole doctrine of the judgment of the Adamic nature rests, is but an enlarging on the one question with which the context opens, namely, "How shall we that are dead [who died] to sin, live any longer therein?" That is, the manner of His death *unto sin* involved a fourfold participation—cocrucifixion, codeath, coburial, and coresurrection. Such, indeed, is the divinely wrought judgment of the "old man" (cf. vs. 6), which forms the basis of a perfect emancipation by the Spirit from the reigning power of the "old man"—the sin nature.

Considering the clear statement that this is a death for the believer in the sense that he partakes of that which Christ wrought in His death unto sin, it is to be deplored that some have interpreted this passage as enjoining self-crucifixion. Similarly, it should be remembered that if this passage is accepted as a directing in the matter of ritual, or water, baptism, as some have considered it, the vital truth respecting Christ's death as a judgment of the sin nature is dismissed, since the passage could not represent both ideas; and if the passage is a directing in the matter of ritual baptism, the one central truth which provides the ground of a possible freedom from the "old man" is sacrificed. The most ardent contender for the claim that ritual baptism is a representation of the death of Christ would hardly wish to relate that ordinance to sanctification or the victorious life by the Spirit, but would require that the ordinance be related to the salvation of the sinner, or Christ's death for sins. In this respect the passage—1 Corinthians 15:1–4—is a more reasonable basis for the ordinance, for Romans 6:1–10 is without question a setting forth of the death of Christ as the ground of experimental sanctification and not of the salvation of the lost. No ritual baptism ever so joins a person to Christ as that he is made to share vitally and perfectly in all that Christ is and all that He has done, but this is precisely what the baptism with the Spirit accomplishes. Thus by being baptized into Christ by the Spirit, an actual participation in crucifixion, death, burial, and resurrection is secured.

In its major aspects, the development of the argument of Romans 6:1—8:13 is: (1) Christ died unto sin to the end that the believer should not continue in sin. It is written, "Let not sin [the nature] therefore reign in your mortal body, that ye should obey it in the lusts thereof" (6:12). The implication cannot be avoided that, if unhindered, the sin nature, though judged, will assert its power in the mortal body. It is also implied that its reigning is not a necessity which it would be if it were unjudged, and likewise that the responsibility is now belonging to the Christian to "let not," employing for this, of course, the divine means and resources available through the Spirit of God. (2) The whole merit system with its appeal to human works and effort as represented in law relationships has passed for the Christian, and those who employ this principle of walking in self-strength are defeated because of their inability to control the sin nature (7:1–25). (3) There is triumphant victory in which the whole will of God is fulfilled *in*, but never *by*, the believer (8:1–13). In this, the final division of this context, it is restated that the deliverance is by the power, or law, of the Spirit of life in Christ Jesus (8:2) and on the basis of the truth that a new principle of achievement is secured which is as much more effective as the power of God is greater than the power of impotent flesh. The whole truth is summarized in two verses (8:3–4) in which both the judgment death of Christ in respect to the old nature and the immediate energy of the Spirit are presented: "For what the law could not do, in that it was weak through the flesh, God sending his own Son in the likeness of sinful flesh, and for sin, condemned [judged] sin in the flesh: that the righteousness of the law might be fulfilled in us, who walk not after the flesh, but after the Spirit."

It may be concluded, then, that, in His death, and as a major objective, Christ secured a judgment against the sin nature on the basis of which the Holy Spirit can righteously deliver from the power of that nature, and will deliver, all those "who walk not after the flesh, but after the Spirit" (8:4). To walk after the Spirit is to walk in conscious dependence upon the Spirit. It is to walk by means of the Spirit (cf. Gal. 5:16).

VII. THE GROUND OF THE BELIEVER'S FORGIVENESS AND CLEANSING

In the second volume and under the general division of hamartiology the specific and unique doctrine respecting the Christian's sin has been considered at length. There it was observed that sin is always equally sinful by whomsoever committed, that it can be cured only by the blood of Christ, and its cure, in the case of a Christian, is by *family* forgiveness and cleansing which is secured by confession of the sin to God. It remains to indicate, as is germane to this theme, that the Christian's forgiveness and cleansing are made righteously possible only through the blood of Christ which He shed in a specific sense for the Christian's sin.

1 John 1:1—2:2. There is much in the New Testament bearing on the forgiveness of the sin of the unsaved as a vital feature of their salvation. That forgiveness, it is assured, is accomplished when the sinner *believes.* The central passage related to the sin of the Christian, which forgiveness is conditioned on *confession,* is 1 John 1:1—2:2. In this context both the effect of the Christian's sin upon himself and the effect of his sin upon God are contemplated. In the first instance, the effect is that of *darkness* and the cure is that of *walking in the light* (1:6–7). To walk in the light is in no sense a matter of attaining to sinless perfection; that would be to *become* the light which God alone is. It is rather to be responsive to the light which God sheds into the heart. It is an attitude of willingness to confess immediately every sin as soon as it is recognized to be sin. Such confession brings the Christian at once into moral agreement with God. He shares God's denunciation of his sin and this becomes the basis of a renewal of fellowship with God. The promise is that, when thus walking in the light and thus adjusted to the light, the blood of Jesus Christ continually cleanses from all sin. This truth is amplified in verse 9 wherein it is said, "If we confess our sins, he is faithful and just to forgive us our sins, and to cleanse us from all unrighteousness." Thus it is revealed that both forgiveness and cleansing for the Christian are based on the blood of Christ. That no punishment is inflicted, that no blow is struck, that no word of condemnation is uttered, and that only perfect forgiveness and cleansing are extended from God on no other terms than confession, is due to the truth that Christ *is* "the propitiation for our [Christians'] sins" (2:2). God, through the death of His Son, *is* propitious.

In the second instance, namely, the effect of the Christian's sin upon God, the cure is said to be through the advocacy of Christ in heaven. As Advocate He appears in behalf of the sinning Christian and pleads, not the weakness of the Christian, but the sufficiency of His own sacrifice. That He bore that sin on the cross, answers all divine judgment against that sin, and, again, God is found to be propitious. No New Testament doctrine—save that of salvation for the lost—is more perfectly grounded on the death of Christ than is the doctrine which sets forth the forgiveness and cleansing of the Christian; and it should not go unobserved that in 1 John 2:2 the sin of the Christian is designated as a specific and major objective in the propitiatory death of Christ on the cross.

VIII. THE GROUND FOR THE DEFERRING OF RIGHTEOUS DIVINE JUDGMENTS

The preceding seven objectives accomplished by Christ in His sufferings and death, though eternal in their character, being foreseen from all eternity and with respect to certain of their features continuing their effect throughout eternity to come, are *personal* and to be valued largely in the light of their present benefit. The seven realities, including the one under consideration, which are yet to be attended are either of limitless application, of other ages, or of other spheres of existence than the earth.

The deferring of righteous judgments, though so obviously in operation throughout all ages, is not a matter of specific revelation. It is disclosed, however, that God, being holy, cannot look upon sin with the least degree of allowance, unless, indeed, that sin be seen by Him as judged in the death of His Son. By the eternal God—He who "calleth those things which be not as though they were" (Rom. 4:17)—every human sin, from the first to the last, is seen in the light of the sacrifice of Christ; and in that sacrifice and upon a plane far more extended than that employed in the saving of individual souls, He is free to defer those holy judgments which otherwise must fall with terrible swiftness upon each sinner. It may be observed, also, that deferred judgments are not abandoned or renounced judgments. The day of divine wrath cannot be escaped unless the offender is sheltered under the redeeming blood of Christ. But the patience of God—based ever upon a righteous ground, else His holy character is compromised with sin—is extended toward sinners in His long-suffering (Rom. 9:22; 1 Pet. 3:20; 2 Pet. 3:9, 15), and His striving (Gen. 6:3). The wise man has written, "Because sentence against an evil work is not executed speedily, therefore the heart of the sons of men is fully set in them to do evil" (Eccl. 8:11). The certainty of judgment for those who despise divine patience is assured (Matt. 24:48–51; Rom. 2:4–5). God is ever holy in character and righteous in action, whether it be in His long-suffering or His judgments.

IX. THE TAKING AWAY OF PRECROSS SIN ONCE COVERED BY SACRIFICE

The divine economy with respect to the disposition of such sins as were represented in animal sacrifices during the extended period between Abel and Christ was one of *covering* as the Hebrew root *kāphar*, translated 'atonement,' indicates. Before the death of Christ, this divine economy based its righteous action with respect to sin upon the anticipation of that death, the animal sacrifice being a symbol or type of the death of God's Lamb. By the presentation of a sacrifice and by the placing of the hand upon the head of the victim, the offender acknowledged his sin before God and entered intelligently into an arrangement in which a substitute died in the sinner's place. Though, as stated in Hebrews 10:4—"it is not possible that the blood of bulls and of goats should take away sins"—God did, nevertheless, provide a release for the offender, but with the expectation on His own part that a righteous ground for such release would eventually be secured by the one sacrificial death of His Son, which death the animal-slaying typified. The Hebrew word *kāphar* expresses with divine accuracy precisely what took place on the Godward side of the transaction. The sin was *covered*, but not "taken away," pending the foreseen death of Christ. To translate *kāphar* by 'atonement,' which etymologically may mean 'at-one-ment,' could truthfully convey no more than that the offender was 'at one' with God by a transaction which rested only on a symbolism. On the human side, the offender was pardoned; but on the divine side the transaction was lacking the one and only act which could make it conform to the requirements of infinite holiness. Two New Testament passages shed light on the restricted divine action respecting those sins which were covered by animal sacrifices. In Romans 3:25 the divine objective in the death of Christ is declared to be, "for the remission of sins that are past, through the forbearance of God." In this text, πάρεσις, translated *remission* and used but once in the New Testament and far removed with respect to the force of its meaning from ἄφεσις (which indicates a full pardon), implies no more than the deferring of judgment and reveals that God pretermitted sin in view of the sacrifices. Likewise, in Acts 17:30 and with reference to the same divine economy, we read, "And the times of this ignorance God winked at; but now commandeth all men every where to repent." The Authorized translation of ὑπερεῖδον by the words 'winked at' today suggests indifference, or a want of gravity, on the part of God toward the righteous judgments which sin must inevitably incur, whereas the real meaning of ὑπερεῖδον in this context is that unavoidable, impending judgments were only temporarily passed over.

A series of vital contrasts between the efficacy of the animal sacrifices of the old order and the efficacy of the final sacrifice of Christ is presented in the letter to the Hebrews. Among these, and as a consummation of the series, it is stated (10:2) that the worshipers of the old order never gained freedom from a "conscience of sins," returning year by year, as they did, with animal sacrifices. This was inevitable, the writer states, "for it is not possible that the blood of bulls and of goats should take away sins" (10:4). Christ, we are told (10:9), took away the old order that He might establish the new. That the old order is done away is again declared (10:26) by the words, "There remaineth no more [the former] sacrifice for sins." This fact is likewise set forth in the following words: "And every priest standeth daily ministering and offering oftentimes the same sacrifices, which can never take away sins: but this man [Christ], after he had offered one sacrifice for sins for ever, sat down [the task being finished] on the right hand of God" (10:11–12). Thus it is seen that the death of Christ was a righteous consummation of the old order as well as the foundation of the new. Since in the old order God had forgiven sins on the ground of a sacrifice that was yet future, that sacrifice, when accomplished, not only *took away* by righteous judgment the sins He had before forgiven, but proved God to have been righteous in deferring His judgments upon those sins.

This is the testimony of Romans 3:25 where in referring to Christ's death it is stated, "Whom God hath set forth to be a propitiation through faith in his blood, to declare his righteousness for the remission [passing over] of sins that are past, through the forbearance of God." Here that divine dealing which pretermitted the sins of the past was based on the forbearance of God, while the present dealing with sin is a completed transaction resulting in absolvence of the sinner and securing his justification upon a basis so righteous that God is said to be just in thus justifying a sinner who does no more than to believe in Jesus (Rom. 3:26). There being no ground provided under the old order for a complete absolvence of the sinner, that transaction is carried forward and becomes a part of the new testament which Christ made in His blood, and by it the elect people of the old order received "the promise of eternal inheritance." We read, "For this cause he is the mediator of the new testament, that by means of death, for the redemption of the transgressions that were under the first testament, they which are called might receive the promise of eternal inheritance" (Heb. 9:15).

The conclusion to be drawn from this extended body of Scripture is that the sins committed in the period between Adam and the death of Christ which were covered by sacrificial offerings were taken away and perfectly judged in righteousness as a major objective in the death of Christ.

X. THE NATIONAL SALVATION OF ISRAEL

The Scriptures bear testimony to the fact that Israel as a nation is to be saved from her sin and delivered from her enemies by the Messiah when He shall return to the earth. It is true that, in this age, the present offers of divine grace are extended to individual Jews as they are to individual Gentiles (Rom. 10:12), and that, without reference to Jehovah's unchangeable covenants with Israel, which covenants are in abeyance (Matt. 23:38–39; Luke 21:24; Acts 15:15–18; Rom. 11:25–27), the individual Jew is now divinely reckoned to be as much in need of salvation as the individual Gentile (Rom. 3:9). These facts, related as they are to the present age-purpose—the calling out of the Church from both Jews and Gentiles alike (Eph. 3:6)—have no bearing upon the divine purpose for the coming kingdom age when, according to covenant promise, Israel will be saved and dwell safely in her own land (Deut. 30:3–6; Jer. 28:5–6; 33:15–17). In the progress of the argument which the Apostle Paul presents in the letter to the Romans, and after having set forth the present fact and plan of individual salvation for Jew and Gentile in chapters 1—8, he proceeds to answer in chapters 9—11 the inevitable question of what, under these new conditions, has become of the irrevocable covenants with Israel (Rom. 11:27–29). The reply to this question could hardly be stated in more definite or understandable terms than the following: ". . . Blindness in part is happened to Israel, until the fulness of the Gentiles be come in. And so all Israel shall be saved [Israel here could not be the Church, since the Church is already saved]: as it is written, There shall come out of Sion the Deliverer, and shall turn away ungodliness from Jacob: for this is my covenant unto them, when I shall take away their sins. As concerning the gospel, they [Israel] are enemies for your [Gentiles'] sakes; but as touching the election, they [Israel] are beloved for the fathers' sakes. For the gifts and calling of God [concerning Israel] are without repentance" (Rom. 11:25–29). It is obvious that Israel as a nation is not now saved, nor are any of the features of Jehovah's eternal covenants with that people now in evidence—the final possession of their land (Gen. 13:15), their national entity (Isa. 66:22; Jer. 31:36), their earthly throne (2 Sam. 7:16), their King (Jer. 33:15, 17, 21), and their kingdom (Dan. 7:14)—but not one of these features could ever fail, since God is faithful who hath promised. The nation, but for certain rebels who are to be "purged out" (Ezek. 20:37–38), will be saved, and that by their own Messiah when He comes out of Zion (cf. Isa. 59:20–21; Matt. 23:37–39; Acts 15:16). "All Israel" of Romans 11:26 is evidently that separated and accepted Israel that will have stood the divine judgments which are yet to fall upon that nation (cf. Matt. 24:37—25:13). The Apostle distinguishes clearly between Israel the nation and a spiritual Israel (cf. Rom. 9:6; 11:1–36).

Out of the facts stated above, the truth which is pertinent to this theme is not the future regathering into their land nor the deliverance of Israel from her enemies—both of which, according to very much prophecy, are yet to be—but rather the fact that Jehovah will, in connection with the second advent of Christ and as a part of Israel's salvation, "take away their sins." This, Jehovah declares, is His covenant with them (Rom. 11:27). It has been observed that, in the age that is past, Jehovah's dealing with Israel's sins—even the sins for which appointed sacrifices were presented—was only a temporary covering of those sins, and that Christ in His death bore the judgment of those sins which Jehovah had before passed over; but the final application of the value of Christ's death in behalf of Israel awaits the moment of her national conversion (cf. Isa. 66:8, a nation born "at once"—*pa'am*—literally, as a time measurement, 'a stroke,' or 'the beat of a foot'). It is then that, according to His covenant, Jehovah will "take away" their sins. In Hebrews 10:4 it is stated that it is impossible that the blood of bulls and goats should "take away" sin, and in Romans 11:27 it is promised that Israel's sins will yet be taken away. The Greek ἀφαιρέω is used in both passages, but, with great significance, the equivalent of the future form of the word appears in the latter passage concerning Israel's national salvation. The induction to be drawn from these and other Scriptures is that Jehovah will yet in the future, in the briefest portion of time, and as a part of Israel's salvation, take away their sins. To no people on the earth has it been more emphatically revealed than to Israel that "without shedding of blood is no remission" (Heb. 9:22), and it is also as clearly stated that no blood could ever avail for any remission of sin other than the blood of Christ. We conclude, therefore, that the nation Israel will yet be saved and her sins removed forever through the blood of Christ. The word of Isaiah is "For the transgression of my people was he stricken" (53:8), and of Caiaphas it is said he gave counsel to the Jews that it was "expedient that one man should die for the people."

The complete regathering of Israel to her own land, which is accomplished at the time of her salvation and in connection with her Messiah's return (Deut. 30:3), is anticipated in prophecy as one of the greatest miracles in the entire history of the earth. In Jeremiah 23:7–8, the regathering of that people is said to surpass, as a divine undertaking, even the crossing of the Red Sea. In like manner, it is stated in Matthew 24:31 that this regathering shall be wrought through the ministration of angels.

Specific terms are employed in the Scriptures to describe the definite character of Israel's salvation, deliverance, and future blessing. None of these, it will be observed, has ever been fulfilled in Israel's history, nor could many of these promises be applied to the Church, composed as she is of both Jews and Gentiles, without employing destructive principles of interpretation. Jehovah promised that He would "turn" their captivity, "circumcise" their hearts (Deut. 30:1–6), write His law in their hearts, and "remember their sin no more" (Jer. 31:33–34). Jehovah also said, "I will be to them a God, and they shall be to me a people," and "All shall know me, from the least to the greatest" (Heb. 8:10–11). Assurance is given unto that nation, when reunited and blessed by Jehovah, that "his rest shall be glorious" (Isa. 11:10). They are to be comforted and their warfare will be accomplished (Isa. 40:1–2). Jehovah shall feed His flock like a shepherd, and gather the lambs with His arm, and carry them in His bosom, and gently lead those that are with young (Isa. 40:11). Again, Jehovah has said to Israel, "Thy Maker is thine husband . . . and thy Redeemer the Holy One of Israel," "With everlasting kindness will I have mercy on thee," "This is the heritage of the servants of Jehovah, and their righteousness which is of me, saith Jehovah" (Isa. 54:5, 8, 17, R.V.). They who were scattered will be gathered (Ezek. 34:11–14); they who were "hated of all nations" will be supreme over all Gentiles (Matt. 24:9 with Isa. 60:12); they who were blind for an age shall see (Rom. 11:25); they who were broken off shall be grafted in (Rom. 11:13–24); and everlasting joy shall be upon their heads, and sorrow and sighing shall flee away (Isa. 35:10). The anticipation of such blessings for Israel is the theme of all the prophets, and such, indeed, is the salvation which awaits that people; but God is righteously free to act in behalf of sinners only on the ground of the fact that the Lamb of God has taken away their sins. A major objective in the death of Christ is, therefore, the national salvation of Israel.

XI. MILLENNIAL AND ETERNAL BLESSINGS UPON GENTILES

The gospel of the grace of God is now being preached to Jews and Gentiles alike and heavenly riches and glories are promised to those who believe its message; however, these heavenly blessings for the Church should not be confused with the millennial earthly blessings which are assured to Israel, and to the Gentiles who share the kingdom with Israel. The presence of certain Gentile nations on the earth during the millennial kingdom is a theme of Old Testament prophecy. The selection of these nations and the basis of that selection is given from the lips of Christ and recorded in Matthew 25:31–46. Their relative position in the kingdom is to abide in the reflected glory of Israel and to serve (Isa. 60:3, 12; 61:9; 62:2). They are to be a people "upon whom my name is called, saith the Lord" (Acts 15:17). In like manner, these same nations are seen as inhabitants of the new earth that is to be and there they are designated as "the nations of them which are saved" (Rev. 21:24). The placing of these nations in the kingdom, the calling of Jehovah's name upon them, and the saving of them, can be accomplished only as God is free through the redeeming blood of Christ to bless sinners. The millennial and eternal blessing of Gentiles is thus seen to be a major objective in the death of Christ.

XII. THE SPOILING OF PRINCIPALITIES AND POWERS

Important, indeed, is the revelation that there are supermundane dignitaries who under divine permission are exercising transcendental authority. These beings are designated as principalities and powers. The title (used twice of earthly rulers—Rom. 13:1; Titus 3:1) does not necessarily imply that these beings are evil, though, according to the context, they are, in the majority of passages wherein this appellation appears, said to be evil. It seems evident that the word *principalities* (ἀρχή) conveys the fact of their dignity, and the word *powers* (ἐξουσία) conveys the fact of their authority. With reference to those angels who "kept not their first estate," Jude, by the use of ἀρχή, declares that they departed from the place of dignity, but no implication is advanced in this passage that they sacrificed any aspect of their power and authority (Jude 1:6). They are created beings (Col. 1:16), and their abode, though above the sphere of humanity (Heb. 2:9), is lower than the throne of God where Christ is now seated (Eph. 1:21; Heb. 10:12). Over these and all supermundane beings Christ Himself is now in supreme authority (Col. 2:10). The Church is now God's instrumentality by which He makes known unto these beings "the manifold wisdom of God" (Eph. 3:10), as in the ages to come He will make known by the Church the "exceeding riches of his grace" (Eph. 2:7). These celestial dignities are now exercising their power in conflict with the saints on earth (Eph. 6:12), and the Apostle Paul states that among all the opposing forces not even the principalities and powers are "able to separate us from the love of God, which is in Christ Jesus our Lord" (Rom. 8:38–39). It is likewise revealed that Satan, who bears the title of *the prince of the power of the air* (Eph. 2:2), is the regnant authority over all fallen angels (Rev. 12:7–9; Matt. 25:41). It is evident that, from the time of his own fall in the dateless past, Satan and his heavenly hosts have been in undisguised rebellion against the will and authority of God, and that it was Satan himself who led the first man into the desire to be independent of God. The godly of all the ages have been given divine exhortations and warnings in view of Satan's opposition to God. Similarly, when offering his temptations to the Son of God in the wilderness, Satan disclosed his own antipathy to the revealed plan and purpose of God. In the end, Satan will be banished forever; but not until he, with his angels, has waged a losing battle against the holy angels (Rev. 12:7), and has been confined to the abyss for a thousand years (Rev. 20:1–3). His final and eternal abode is "the lake of fire" (Rev. 20:10) which is "prepared for the devil and his angels" (Matt. 25:41).

This judgment of Satan, as outlined above, was first predicted, then gained as a legal sentence, and is yet to be executed. The prediction is by Jehovah Himself (Gen. 3:15; cf. Isa. 14:12; Ezek. 28:16–19), and discloses that in the consummation of the enmity between the Seed of the woman—Christ—and Satan, Christ would bruise Satan's head and in so doing Satan would bruise Christ's heel. The conflict was waged at the cross, and, while a legal sentence was there gained against Satan which anticipates its yet future execution or the bruising of Satan's head, the heel of the Son of God was bruised when He died on the cross.

The combat between Christ and Satan which was waged on Calvary's hill, involves issues and powers belonging to higher realms than this earth and things beyond the boundaries of time. The finite mind cannot hope to apprehend the scope and character of this illimitable encounter. It is not only implied that, in this conflict, Satan exercised his utmost power, but that the injury inflicted upon the Son of God, likened to the bruising of His heel, was from Satan. It should be observed, however, that Satan is not the only being who is said to bear responsibility for the death of Christ. Four groups or individual men stand accused (Acts 4:27). It is probable that these were only instruments in Satan's power (Eph. 2:2; Col. 1:13). All this seeming unrestraint is, nevertheless, safeguarded by the assuring declaration that what was done either by Satan or by man was only the outworking of the "counsel determined" of God (Acts 4:28). On the divine side, the death of Christ was at the hand of His Father (John 3:16; Rom. 3:25; 8:32), by Christ Himself as a self-wrought sacrifice (John 10:18; Gal. 2:20), and through the eternal Spirit (Heb. 9:14).

When approaching His death, Christ said: "Now is the judgment of this world: now shall the prince of this world be cast out" (John 12:31); and, "Of judgment, because the prince of this world is judged" (John 16:11). Similarly, the Apostle Paul in referring to the victory Christ gained over principalities and powers by His cross, states: "Blotting out the handwriting of ordinances that was against us, which was contrary to us, and took it out of the way, nailing it to his cross; and having spoiled principalities and powers, he made a shew of them openly, triumphing over them in it" (the cross—Col. 2:14–15). Though the law, which was administered by angels (Gal. 3:19; Heb. 2:2), is not now the rule of life for believers of this age, agreement cannot be accorded to some who assert that it was the law rule which was here "spoiled" by the death of Christ. The *spoiling* is too manifestly of the principalities and powers. In addition to the direct legal sentence which Christ gained at the cross against Satan and his hosts, the issues of which are beyond our understanding, there are at least two factors in this victory which may be apprehended. (a) In their relation to the authority of God, Christ and Satan represent opposing principles. In the past ages Satan uttered five "I will's" against the will of Jehovah (Isa. 14:13–14), and, when coming into the world, Christ said: "Lo, I come . . . to do thy will, O God" (Heb. 10:5–7). This utterance of Christ to His Father, it will be remembered, is made in connection with His anticipated sacrificial death. (b) Of Christ it was prophesied that He would open the door of the prison to them that are bound (Isa. 61:1), but of Satan it is said, "He opened not the house of his prisoners" (Isa. 14:17). The prisoners are Satan's and the release of them by Christ through His death constitutes a far-reaching achievement. Aside from the mere remnant whose sins were covered by animal sacrifices in the long period between Adam and Christ, the vast multitude of human beings stood related to God under the six unalterable indictments recorded in Ephesians 2:11–12. They were without God and without hope, because they were without Christ, in the world. No way of approach either for them to God or for God to them having yet been provided, Satan evidently assumed the rule over them which he could do on the ground of the fact that he had wrested the scepter of authority from Adam. During that extended period, had God approached one of these souls without a righteous provision having been either promised through animal sacrifices or made actual by the blood of His Son, Satan, it is probable, could have challenged the Almighty, charging Him with unrighteousness. Thus on the ground of man's sinfulness Satan held his prisoners bound. But since Christ died for all men, as He certainly did, there remains no barrier between God and man other than a lack of faith on the part of man in the Savior. The prisoners who otherwise would be "without hope" are now confronted with the gospel of divine grace—"Whosoever will may come."

Thus, it may be concluded that one of the major objectives in the death of Christ was the "spoiling of principalities and powers."

XIII. THE GROUND OF PEACE

But a slight conception may be had by finite minds of this boundless theme, which falls naturally into three general divisions. (a) The peace which has been secured for individuals who believe is closely related to both divine reconciliation and propitiation, but is, nevertheless, specified as a major objective in the death of Christ. Since the believer is cleared of every indictment and even justified because of the value of Christ's death—which value is received by faith—there is secured a lasting peace between God and the man of faith. The most illuminating passage related to this personal peace is Romans 5:1, which reads: "Therefore being justified by faith, we have peace with God through our Lord Jesus Christ." Thus, also, the same truth is declared in Ephesians 2:13–14a: "But now in Christ Jesus ye who sometimes were far off are made nigh by the blood of Christ. For he is our peace." And, again, in Colossians 1:20, having declared the broader outreach in securing peace by the blood of the cross, the Apostle continues with the more individual and personal application of that blood and the peace it secures. He writes, "And you, that were sometimes alienated and enemies in your mind by wicked works, yet now hath he reconciled in the body of his flesh through death."

(b) Of great importance, too, is that peace which obtains between Gentile and Jew—in spite of the agelong enmity between them and their disproportionate privilege as declared of the Jew in Romans 9:4–5, and of the Gentile in Ephesians 2:11–12—when these are brought by saving grace into the one Body of Christ. Of this the Apostle writes in Ephesians 2:14–18: "Who hath made both one, and hath broken down the middle wall of partition between us; having abolished in his flesh the enmity, even the law of commandments contained in ordinances; for to make in himself of twain one new man, so making peace; and that he might reconcile both unto God in one body by the cross, having slain the enmity thereby: and came and preached peace to you which were afar off, and to them that were nigh. For through him we both have access by one Spirit unto the Father." This aspect of peace is not alone dependent on a mere experience of grace, one toward another; it is *positional*. Being members of the same body, all distinctions are lost: "Where there is neither Greek nor Jew, circumcision nor uncircumcision, Barbarian, Scythian, bond nor free: but Christ is all, and in all" (Col. 3:11). In the covenants, Israel was already in that place of privilege which is termed *nigh* (Eph. 2:17); but the Gentiles who by relationship were *afar* off are made *nigh* by the blood of Christ (Eph. 2:13).

(c) And, finally, there is a peace to be realized throughout the universe—foreshadowed in the thousand years under the Prince of Peace—which will be established by the judgment of Satan (Col. 2:14-15) and of all the forces of evil. It is written, "And, having made peace through the blood of his cross, by him to reconcile all things unto himself; by him, I say, whether they be things in earth, or things in heaven" (Col. 1:20). The program which Christ will follow is clearly predicted: first, He shall judge the nations (Matt. 25:31-46), having crushed their resistance (Ps. 2:1-3, 8-9; Isa. 63:1-6); second, He shall put down all rule and authority, which will require a millennium of years and involve the subjection of both angelic and human spheres (1 Cor. 15:25-26); and, third, He shall restore to God a universal kingdom of peace in which the Son eternally reigns by the authority of the Father, and God is all in all (1 Cor. 15:27-28).

XIV. THE PURIFICATION OF THINGS IN HEAVEN

Sin has wrought its tragic effects within the angelic hosts as it has within the human race, and the pollution of sin reaches beyond the angels in heaven and beyond men on the earth. Its defilement has extended to inanimate "things" in both spheres. It is stated in Hebrews 9:23 that it was necessary for heavenly "things" to be purified, and in Romans 8:21-23 creation itself, including earth's creatures, has been brought into bondage from which it will not be delivered until the time when the believer's body is redeemed. Because of this bondage, the whole creation now groans and travails in pain. Even the redeemed must "groan within themselves" during the present period in which we await the redemption of our bodies. The fact that defilement has reached to "things" in heaven as well as to "things" upon the earth is an exceedingly important revelation and is, in the Scriptures, considered quite apart from the effect of sin upon angels and men.

Among the contrasts set up in Hebrews, chapters 8—10, between the typical ceremonials which foreshadowed Christ's death and that death itself, it is pointed out (Heb. 9:23) that, as the tabernacle on earth was purified by the blood of animals, so the heavenly "things" were purified on the ground of Christ's blood when He, as High Priest, entered the heavenly realms. We read: "But Christ being come an high priest of good things to come, by a greater and more perfect tabernacle, not made

with hands, that is to say, not of this building [the old tabernacle];
neither by the blood of goats and calves, but by his own blood he entered
in once into the holy place, having obtained eternal redemption for us"
(9:11–12). And, referring to the service of the high priest of old in
the earthly sanctuary, the writer adds: "Moreover he sprinkled with
blood both the tabernacle, and all the vessels of the ministry [things].
And almost all things are by the law purged with blood; and without
shedding of blood is no remission" (9:21–22). Such was the type; but of
Christ's own service in fulfilling the antitype it is stated: "It was therefore necessary that the patterns of things in the heavens [the old taber-
nacle] should be purified with these [the blood of animals]; but the
heavenly things themselves with better sacrifices than these. For Christ
is not entered into the holy places made with hands [the old tabernacle],
which are the figures [ἀντίτυπος] of the true; but into heaven itself"
(9:23–24). The contrasts and parallels thus set up between the type
and the antitype are obvious. The old sanctuary was ceremonially
cleansed by the blood of goats and calves, but by His own blood Christ
entered into the holy place on high and on the ground of that blood the
heavenly "things" were purified and by "better sacrifices" than that of
the animals. The plural *sacrifices* as here used of Christ's one offering
of Himself may be assumed to be categoric—comprehending its many
parts within what is one category.

Various theories have been advanced to explain why the "things" in
heaven, that is, in the sphere of the "holy place" which is heavenly
(Heb. 9:23), should need purification. On this point Dean Alford quotes
F. Delitzsch as follows: "If I see aright, the meaning of the Writer is,
in its ground-thought, this: the supernal holiest place, i.e. as ver. 24
shews, *heaven itself,* the uncreated eternal heaven of God, although in
itself untroubled light, yet needed a *purification* in so far as the light of
Love towards man was, so to speak, outflared and obscured by the fire
of wrath against sinful man; and the heavenly tabernacle, i.e. the place
of God's revealing of His majesty and grace for angels and men, needed
a *purification,* in so far as men had rendered this place, which was
destined for them from the beginning, unapproachable by reason of their
sin, and so it must be changed into an approachable place of manifestation of a God gracious to men" (*New Testament for English Readers,*
new ed., *in loc.*).

This explanation of the problem is not without its difficulties. Not
only has Delitzsch extended the grace of God to the angels which, so far
as has been observed, is never even implied in the Scriptures, but he has

made the purification of "things" to be the removal of the wrath of God against sinners of this earth by the reconciliation of the cross of Christ. It is true that "things in earth and things in heaven" are by the cross reconciled, to the end that peace is made (Col. 1:20)—which fact is far removed from the divine reconciliation of earth dwellers to God. Though the student is by this problem again confronted with supermundane issues too vast for finite apprehension, it may not be amiss to be reminded that sin in its most terrible aspect of lawless rebellion has by the sin of the angels entered heaven, or the abode of those celestial beings divinely designated as "the angels of heaven" (Matt. 24:36). Concerning the "uncreated heaven" to which Delitzsch refers, Scripture seems to be silent.

The revelation that "things in earth and things in heaven" are reconciled by the cross, or that "things" in heaven were purified on the ground of the blood of Christ as the blood of animals served to purify the furnishings of the earthly tabernacle, is no support whatever for the "universal reconciliation" notion. On the contrary, the Scriptures declare in no uncertain terms that all fallen angels and all unregenerate men go on to eternal woe.

Though in its essential features it transcends the range of human understanding, it is clear that the purification of "things" in heaven constituted one of the major objectives in the death of Christ.

CHAPTER V

THE SUFFERINGS AND DEATH OF CHRIST IN TYPES

DR. PATRICK FAIRBAIRN begins his valuable treatise on the types (*The Typology of Scripture*) with the following statement: "The Typology of Scripture has been one of the most neglected departments of theological science." This declaration is significant not only for the recognition of an inestimable loss to the Church of Christ, but for the fact that typology is, by this worthy theologian, given a rightful place in the science of Systematic Theology. Dr. Fairbairn does not assert that no attention has been given to typology in generations past. On the contrary, he goes on to show that from Origen's day to the present hour there have been those who have emphasized this theme, and that some have emphasized it beyond reason. The contention is that theology, as a science, has neglected this great field of revelation. Typology, like prophecy, has often suffered more from its friends than its foes. The fact that extremists have failed to distinguish between that which is typical and that which is merely allegorical, analogous, parallel, happy illustration, or resemblance may have driven conservative theologians from the field. When truth is tortured by faddists and extremists, an added obligation is thereby imposed upon conservative scholarship to declare it in its right proportions. It is obvious that to neglect truth is a greater error than to overemphasize it or to misstate it; and typology, though abused by some, is, nevertheless, conspicuous by its absence from works on Systematic Theology. That typology is neglected is evident from the fact that of upwards of twenty works of Systematic Theology examined, but one lists this subject in its index and this author has made but one slight reference to it in a footnote.

A type is a divinely purposed anticipation which illustrates its antitype. These two parts of one theme are related to each other by the fact that the same truth or principle is embodied in each. It is not the prerogative of the type to establish the truth of a doctrine; it rather enhances the force of the truth as set forth in the antitype. On the other hand, the antitype serves to lift its type out of the commonplace into

that which is inexhaustible and to invest it with riches and treasures
hitherto unrevealed. The Passover-lamb type floods the redeeming grace
of Christ with richness of meaning, while the redemption itself invests
the Passover-lamb type with all its marvelous significance. While it is
true that the type is not the reality, as is the antitype, the elements found
in the type are, in the main, to be observed in the antitype. Thus the type
may, and often does, guide specifically in the right understanding and
structure of the antitype. The type is as much a work of God as is the
antitype. Through the recognition of the relation between the type and
antitype, like that between prophecy and its fulfillment, the supernatural
continuity and plenary inspiration of the whole Bible is established.
The field both in typology and prophecy is vast, there being upwards of
one hundred legitimate types, fully one-half of which concern the Lord
Jesus Christ alone, and there being even a greater field of prophecy
wherein there are upwards of three hundred detailed predictions concerning Christ which were fulfilled by His first advent. There are three
major factors which serve to exhibit the unity between the two Testaments: type and antitype, prophecy and its fulfillment, and continuity in
the progress of narrative and doctrine. These factors, like woven threads
running from one Testament into the other, bind them not only into one
fabric, but serve to trace one design which, by its marvelous character,
glorifies the Designer.

The two Greeks words τύπος and ὑπόδειγμα serve in the New Testament to express the thought of that which is typical. Τύπος means an
imprint which may serve as a mold or pattern, and that which is typical
in the Old Testament is a mold or pattern of that which is antitypical in
the New Testament. Τύπος is translated by eight English words (*form*,
Rom. 6:17; *fashion*, Acts 7:44; *manner*, Acts 23:25; *ensample*, 1 Cor.
10:11; Phil. 3:17; 1 Thess. 1:7; 2 Thess. 3:9; 1 Pet. 5:3; *example*,
1 Cor. 10:6; 1 Tim. 4:12; *figure*, Acts 7:43; Rom. 5:14; *pattern*, Titus
2:7; Heb. 8:5; *print* of the nails, John 20:25). Δεῖγμα means a *speci-
men* or *example*, and when combined with ὑπό indicates that which is
shown plainly under the eyes of men. Ὑπόδειγμα is translated by two
English words (*example* or *ensample*, John 13:15; Heb. 4:11; 8:5;
James 5:10; 2 Pet. 2:6; and *pattern*, Heb. 9:23). Types are generally
to be classified as of *persons* (Rom. 5:14; cf. Adam, Melchizedec,
Abraham, Sarah, Ishmael, Isaac, Moses, Joshua, David, Solomon, etc.);
of *events* (1 Cor. 10:11; cf. the preservation of Noah and his sons in
the Ark, redemption from Egypt, the Passover memorial, the Exodus,
the passing of the Red Sea, the giving of manna, water drawn from the

rock, the serpent lifted up, and all the many sacrifices); a *thing* (Heb. 10:20; cf. the tabernacle, the laver, the sacrificial lamb, Jordan, a city, a nation); an *institution* (Heb. 9:11; cf. the Sabbath, sacrifice, priesthood, kingdom); a *ceremonial* (1 Cor. 5:7; cf. all the Old Testament appointments of service). It is impossible in this space to list the recognized types found in the Old Testament.

In answer to the question how a type can be distinguished from an allegory or analogy, some rules have been advanced. Among these it is declared that nothing is to be deemed typical which is not sustained as such in the New Testament. This statement is subject to two criticisms. (a) In the light of 1 Corinthians 10:11, there is no definiteness to the boundaries of the words "all these things"; yet, whatever is included there is said to be *typical*. (b) There are many easily recognized types which are not directly sanctioned as such by any specific New Testament Scripture. Like the problem of primary and secondary application of the truth, the recognition of a type must be left, in any case, to the discernment of a Spirit-guided judgment.

It is the prerogative of the science of Systematic Theology to discover, classify, exhibit, and defend the doctrines of the Scriptures, and the precise features of typology are yet uncertain largely because of the fact that theologians have given their attention to other things; but who would dare to estimate the restriction imposed on the theological student's own spiritual life and blessing and, through him, upon all to whom he ministers, when the types which are God's great pictures of truth are deleted from every course of study designed to prepare him for a fruitful and worthy ministry of the Word of God! It is not enough to give these themes a passing recognition in the study of evidences; the student should be so saturated with these marvels of God's message that the whole being is set aglow with that spiritual radiance which can never be dimmed.

A true type is a prophecy of its antitype and, being thus designed of God, is not to be rated as so much human speculation, but as a vital part of inspiration itself. Naturally, Christ is the outstanding antitype since the supreme object of both the Old and New Testament is "the testimony of Jesus."

About fifty well-defined types of Christ are to be recognized in the Old Testament and a considerable portion of these are types of His sufferings and death. An exhaustive and conservative treatise on the types of the Old Testament has long been a *desideratum,* but such a work cannot be included here. On the contrary, the briefest survey only of the major types bearing upon Christ's death will be presented.

I. THE GENERAL SACRIFICES OF THE OLD TESTAMENT

1. ABEL'S OFFERING (Gen. 4:4), which not only merits the favor of Jehovah, but indicates the fact that divine instruction on the importance and value of blood sacrifices had been given to the first of the race as they emerged from the Garden of Eden. By his sacrifice, Abel obtained witness that he was righteous. In this connection, attention should be given to Hebrews 11:4; 9:22b, as well as to all Scripture bearing upon the importance of sacrificial blood. The doctrine is not of human origin and as certainly its fulfillment in the death of Christ is alone the plan and purpose of God.

2. NOAH'S ALTAR AND SACRIFICE (Gen. 8:20–22). The necessity of blood sacrifice is the same as in the history of Abel; but the building of an altar is a new responsibility. The altar is one of the most important features of Old Testament doctrine. Man was taught by divine instruction (Ex. 20:24–26) that the altar represents no work of his own hands. It is the sacrifice on the altar which is blessed of God to the benefit of his soul. It is most significant that the divine instruction respecting the building of an altar follows immediately upon the giving of the Decalogue. Of the altar and its significance C. H. Mackintosh writes in his *Notes on Exodus* (3rd ed.):

It is peculiarly interesting to the spiritual mind, after all that has passed before us, to observe the relative position of God and the sinner at the close of this memorable chapter. "And the Lord said unto Moses, 'Thus thou shalt say unto the children of Israel. . . . An altar of earth thou shalt make unto Me, and shalt sacrifice thereon thy burnt-offerings and thy peace-offerings, thy sheep and thine oxen: in all places where I record My name I WILL COME UNTO THEE, AND I WILL BLESS THEE. And if thou wilt make Me an altar of stone, thou shalt not build it of hewn stone; for if thou lift up thy tool upon it, thou hast polluted it. Neither shalt thou go up by steps unto Mine altar, that thy nakedness be not discovered thereon'" (Ver. 22–26). Here we find man not in the position of *a doer,* but of *a worshiper;* and this, too, at the close of Exodus xx. How plainly this teaches us that the atmosphere of Mount Sinai is not that which God would have the sinner breathing,—that it is not the proper meeting-place between God and man! "In all places where I record *My name I will come unto thee, and I will bless thee.*" How unlike the terrors of the fiery mount is that spot where Jehovah records *His name,* whither He "comes" to "bless" His worshiping people! But further, God will meet the sinner at an altar without a hewn stone or a step—a place of worship which requires no human workmanship to erect, or human effort to approach. The former could only pollute, and the latter could only display human "nakedness." Admirable type of the meeting-place where God meets the sinner now, even the Person and work of His Son, Jesus Christ, where all the claims of law, of justice, and of conscience are perfectly answered! Man has, in every age and in every clime, been prone, in one way or another, to "lift up his tool" in the erection of his altar, or to approach thereto by steps of his own making; but the issue of all such attempts has been "pollution" and "nakedness." "We all do fade as a leaf, and all our righteousnesses are as filthy rags." Who will presume to approach God clad in a garment of "filthy rags"? or who will stand to worship with a revealed "nakedness"? What can be more preposterous than to think of approaching God in a way which necessarily involves either pollution or nakedness? And yet thus it is in every case in which human effort is put forth to open the sinner's way to God. Not only is there no need of such effort, but defilement and nakedness are stamped upon it. God has come down so very near to the sinner, even in the very depths of his ruin, that there is no need for his lifting up the tool of legality, or ascending the steps of self-righteousness,—yea, to do so, is but to expose his uncleanness and his nakedness.—Pp. 270–72

Under this general head may be grouped all the sacrifices of the Old Testament, all of which look on to the death of Christ.

II. THE PRESCRIBED SACRIFICES OF THE OLD TESTAMENT

1. THE PASCHAL LAMB. Israel's national and abiding redemption, as well as the safety of the firstborn in each home, was secured by the paschal lamb. So far-reaching is this redemption that Israel was required, in recognition of it, to re-enact the Passover throughout all her generations—not as a renewal of redemption, but as a memorial. The two general aspects of the meaning of the Passover are also well expressed by C. H. Mackintosh:

"And they shall take of the blood, and strike it on the two side-posts and on the upper door-post of the houses, wherein they shall eat it. And they shall eat the flesh in that night, roast with fire, and unleavened bread; and with bitter herbs they shall eat it. Eat not of it raw, nor sodden at all with water, but roast with fire; his head with his legs, and with the purtenance thereof" (Ver. 7–9). We have to contemplate the paschal lamb in two aspects, namely, as the ground of peace, and the centre of unity. The blood on the lintel secured Israel's peace.—"When I see the blood, I will pass over you" (Ver. 13). There was nothing more required in order to enjoy settled peace, in reference to the destroying angel, than the application of the blood of sprinkling. Death had to do its work in every house throughout the land of Egypt. "It is appointed unto men once to die." But God, in His great mercy, found an unblemished substitute for Israel, on which the sentence of death was executed. Thus God's claims and Israel's need were met by one and the same thing, namely, the blood of the lamb. That blood outside proved that *all* was perfectly, because divinely, settled; and therefore perfect peace reigned within. A shade of doubt in the bosom of an Israelite would have been a dishonor offered to the divinely appointed ground of peace—the blood of atonement. . . .

We shall now consider the second aspect of the passover, as the centre round which the assembly was gathered, in peaceful, holy, happy fellowship. Israel saved by the blood was one thing, and Israel feeding on the lamb was quite another. They were saved *only* by the blood; but the object round which they were gathered was, manifestly, the roasted lamb. This is not, by any means, a distinction without a difference. The blood of the lamb forms the foundation both of our connection with God, and our connection with one another. It is as those who are washed in that blood, that we are introduced to God and to one another. Apart from the perfect atonement of Christ, there could obviously be no fellowship either with God or His assembly. Still we must remember that it is to a living Christ in heaven that believers are gathered by the Holy Ghost. It is with a living Head we are connected—to "a living stone" we have come. He is our centre. Having found peace through His blood, we own Him as our grand gathering-point and connecting link.—"Where two or three are gathered together in My name, there am I in the midst of them" (Matt. xviii.20). The Holy Ghost is the only Gatherer; Christ Himself is the only object to which we are gathered; and our assembly, when thus convened, is to be characterized by holiness, so that the Lord our God may dwell among us. The Holy Ghost can only gather to Christ. He cannot gather to a system, a name, a doctrine, or an ordinance. He gathers to a Person, and that Person is a glorified Christ in heaven. This must stamp a peculiar character on God's assembly. Men may associate on any ground, round any centre, or for any object they please; but when the Holy Ghost associates, it is on the ground of accomplished redemption, around the Person of Christ, in order to form a holy dwelling-place for God (1 Cor. iii.16, 17; vi.19; Eph. ii.21, 22; 1 Pet. ii.4, 5).—*Ibid.*, pp. 137–38, 149–50

The six essential requirements to be found in the paschal lamb were: a lamb without blemish; a lamb that was tested; the lamb slain; the blood to be applied; the blood a perfect propitiation against divine judgments; the lamb partaken of as food. That Christ is the antitype in all this could hardly be doubted.

2. THE FIVE OFFERINGS (Lev. 1:1—7:38). The five offerings are: the burnt offering, the meal offering, the peace offering, the sin offering, and the trespass offering. These are properly classed as sweet savor offerings, which grouping includes the first three, and non-sweet savor offerings, which grouping includes the last two. Reference has been previously made to these five offerings, and it will suffice at this point to restate that the sweet savor offerings represent Christ offering Himself

without spot to God (Heb. 9:14), and that this is substitutionary to the extent that, as the sinner is wholly void of merit before God (Rom. 3:9; Gal. 3:22), Christ has released and made available upon grounds of perfect equity His own merit as the basis of the believer's acceptance and standing before God. On the other hand, it should be remembered that the non-sweet savor offerings represent Christ as a sacrifice for sin and as such the Father's face is turned away and the Savior cries, "My God, my God, why hast thou forsaken me?" (Ps. 22:1; Matt. 27:46; Mark 15:34). The ground of a forgiveness both just and complete in the death of Christ is thus foreshadowed in the non-sweet savor offerings.

3. THE TWO BIRDS (Lev. 14:1–7). As on the Day of Atonement when two goats were required to fulfill the entire picture of Christ's death, so two birds are required in the cleansing of leprosy—the type of sin. The first bird slain speaks of Christ "delivered for our offences," while the second bird, dipped in the blood of the first bird and released, speaks of Christ "raised again for our justification" (Rom. 4:25).

4. THE DAY OF ATONEMENT. Again the larger extent and accomplishment of Christ's death is set forth typically in magnificent detail by the events and specific requirements of the Day of Atonement. Of the typical meaning of the offerings prescribed for the Day of Atonement— the bullock for the high priest, and the two goats—Dr. C. I. Scofield states:

The offering of the high priest for himself has no anti-type in Christ (Heb. 7:26, 27). The *typical* interest centres upon the two goats and the high priest. Typically (1) all is done by the high priest (Heb. 1:3, "by Himself"), the people only bring the sacrifice (Mt. 26:47; 27:24, 25). (2) The goat slain (Jehovah's lot) is that aspect of Christ's death which vindicates the holiness and righteousness of God as expressed in the law (Rom. 3:24–26), and is *expiatory*. (3) The living goat typifies that aspect of Christ's work which puts *away* our sins from before God (Heb. 9:26; Rom. 8:33, 34). (4) The high priest entering the holiest, typifies Christ entering "heaven itself" with "His own blood" for us (Heb. 9:11, 12). His blood makes that to be a "throne of grace," and "mercy seat," which else must have been a throne of judgment. (5) For us, the priests of the New Covenant, there is what Israel never had, a rent veil (Mt. 27:51; Heb. 10:19, 20). So that, for worship and blessing, we enter, in virtue of His blood, where He is, into the holiest (Heb. 4:14–16; 10:19–22). The atonement of Christ, as interpreted by the O.T. sacrificial types, has these necessary elements: (1) It is substitutionary—the offering takes the offerer's place in death. (2) The law is not evaded but honored— every sacrificial death was an execution of the sentence of the law. (3) The sinlessness of Him who bore our sins is expressed in every animal sacrifice—it must be without blemish. (4) The *effect* of the atoning work of Christ is typified (*a*) in the promises, "it shall be forgiven him"; and (*b*) in the peace-offering, the expression of fellowship—the highest privilege of the saint.— *The Scofield Reference Bible*, pp. 147–48

The specific features thus required are: the bullock for the high priest, the substitution of the animal for the sinful person, the upholding of the law, the perfect character of the sacrifice, the sin covered by the blood of the first goat, and the guilt taken away by the dismissal of the second goat.

5. THE RED HEIFER (Num. 19:1–22). The New Testament doctrine of cleansing for the believer is stated in 1 John 1:7, 9. Defilement is removed by the blood of Christ upon confession. The type of such cleansing, which also served a grand purpose in the economy of the Mosaic system, is seen in the ordinance of the red heifer. Of this J. N. Darby writes:

The heifer was completely burned without the camp, even its blood, except that which was sprinkled directly before the tabernacle of the congregation, that is, where the *people* were to meet God. There the blood was sprinkled seven times (because it was there that God met with His people), a perfect testimony in the eyes of God to the atonement made for sin. They had access there according to the value of this blood. The priest threw into the fire cedar-wood, hyssop, and scarlet (that is, all that was of man, and his human glory in the world). "From the cedar down to the hyssop," is the expression of nature from her highest elevation to her lowest depth. Scarlet is external glory (the world, if you please). The whole was burned in the fire which consumed Christ, the sacrifice for sin. Then, if anybody contracted defilement, though it were merely through neglect, in whatever way it might be, God took account of the defilement. And this is a solemn and important fact: God provides for cleansing, but in no case can tolerate anything in His presence unsuited to it. It might seem hard in an inevitable case, as one dying suddenly in the tent. But it was to shew that for *His* presence God judges of what is suited to His presence. The man was defiled and he could not go into God's tabernacle. To cleanse the defiled person, they took some running water, into which they put the ashes of the heifer, and the man was sprinkled on the third and on the seventh days; then he was clean.—*Synopsis of the Books of the Bible*, new ed., I, 264–65

The essential features of this ordinance were: an animal without blemish, the slaying of the animal, every part consumed by fire, the retaining of the ashes for cleansing, the mingling of the ashes with water, and the application of the water and ashes for the cleansing of defilement.

III. MISCELLANEOUS TYPES OF CHRIST'S DEATH

1. THE COATS OF SKIN (Gen. 3:21). Jehovah undertook in behalf of the first sinners of the human race. It is declared that He Himself clothed them with skins, the implication being that blood was shed. Reason rather than revelation asserts that animal sacrifice was then introduced by God and that it was from this action on Jehovah's part that Abel knew the truth by which he was guided in presenting an accepted sacrifice to Jehovah. Few types are as complete as this. God undertakes for man, the imputation of sin to a substitute is implied, and the covering of the sinner is revealed.

2. NOAH's ARK (Gen. 6:14—8:19). The history of the flood is replete with suggestions of vital truth. Among these, the safety of those in the ark seems to be a definite preview of the safety of those who are in Christ Jesus. Pitch was used to cover the ark and by it the waters of judgment were resisted. The word translated *pitch* is from the same word everywhere translated *atonement*. The significance of the use of this word has been pointed out by many writers.

3. BREAD AND WINE AT THE HAND OF MELCHIZEDEK (Gen. 14:17–24). Melchizedek bringing forth bread and wine to Abraham suggests two important truths, namely, (a) Abraham throughout the epistles of the New Testament is presented as a pattern of a Christian under grace and not of a Jew under the law. Grace on God's part is made possible only through the death of Christ, who said "Abraham rejoiced to see my day: and he saw it, and was glad" (John 8:56). (b) The partaking of the bread and wine on Abraham's part may have been but dimly understood by either Melchizedek or Abraham—it is but dimly understood by the majority who partake today—but doubtless it all had great significance in the sight of God.

4. THE OFFERING OF ISAAC (Gen. 22:1–14). In this memorable experience, Abraham appears as the type of the Father offering His Son. Abraham was spared the final ordeal, but, according to Romans 8:32, "God spared not his own Son, but delivered him up for us all." Isaac is the type of the Son who is a willing sacrifice and obedient unto death. The ram caught in the thicket is the type of a substitute offered in the place of another.

5. JOSEPH (Gen. 37:2—50:26). Though Joseph as a type of Christ is exceedingly rich in its vital truth, only the placing of Joseph in the pit—a type of death—and the lifting him out—a type of resurrection— are germane to this thesis. However, to this may be added the truths

that, like Christ, Joseph was beloved of his father and was hated by his brethren.

6. Manna in the Wilderness (Ex. 16:14–22). From the use Christ made, as recorded in John 6, of the manna as a type of Himself, none could doubt the typical import of the manna from heaven. Thus Christ as bread come down from heaven has given His life for the world.

7. The Smitten Rock (Ex. 17:5–7; Num. 20:7–13). According to 1 Corinthians 10:4, Christ is that Rock. By His death the water of life is released; but He could be smitten but once. The smiting of the rock the second time is estimated by God to be so great a sin that it precludes Moses from completing his task of taking the people of Israel into the promised land. The death of Christ is infinitely sufficient and admits of no re-enactment. It would be difficult to discover the exceeding sinfulness of Moses' sin apart from the antitype—Christ in His death.

8. The Tabernacle (Ex. 25:1—40:38). In this one structure with its details, the most extensive typology of the Old Testament is presented and there is much that is related to the death of Christ. The tabernacle itself is a type of Christ as the only way to God; the ark of the covenant sprinkled with blood is the place of propitiation; the shewbread is another type of Christ as the Bread of Life given for the world; all references to silver speak of redemption; the brazen altar represents those judgments against sin which Christ bore in His death; the candlestick is a type of Christ the light of the world; the golden altar represents that aspect of Christ's death which was a sweet incense unto God; and the brazen laver foreshadows the cleansing of the believer-priest through the blood of Christ (1 John 1:7, 9).

IV. THE DEATH OF CHRIST ACCORDING TO VARIOUS SCRIPTURES

It will not only be impressive to, but highly advantageous for, the student to observe the place which the death of Christ—both historically and doctrinally considered—occupies in the Bible. No further reference need be made to the typology which characterizes the early portions of God's Word, nor is there important teaching on this theme in the Old Testament historical books; and only major passages will be cited.

1. The Death of Christ according to Genesis. Genesis 3:15 is a preview of the death of Christ. In that Scripture the fact of Christ's

death, its relation to angelic authorities, and its relation to sin and judgment are intimated. It is fitting that a recognition of the cross and its final triumph should appear in those chapters where all beginnings are recorded.

2. The Death of Christ according to Old Testament Prophecy. The Psalms which bear prophetically on the death of Christ are 22:1–21 and 40:6–7. In Isaiah 52:13—53:12 the outstanding prediction occurs.

3. The Death of Christ according to the Gospels. In this portion four extended accounts of Christ's death are found, as well as His own predictions concerning His death.

4. The Death of Christ according to Romans, 1 and 2 Corinthians, and Galatians. Since the theme of salvation is so dominant in these books and since all salvation rests on the death of Christ, the New Testament doctrine is found largely in these four Epistles. Portions to be observed are: Romans 3:22–26; 4:25; 5:7–10; 6:1–15; 14:9, 15; 1 Corinthians 1:18—2:8; 15:3; 2 Corinthians 5:14–21; Galatians 1:4; 2:20; 3:10, 13; 6:14–15.

5. The Death of Christ according to Ephesians, Philippians, and Colossians. The following passages present the most vital truth: Ephesians 5:25–27; Philippians 2:5–8; Colossians 1:14, 20, which passage refers to the reconciliation of *things* and not creatures.

6. The Death of Christ according to the Epistle to the Hebrews. To a large degree, the Epistle to the Hebrews is a treatise on the death of Christ and with special reference to the truth that the old order with its sacrifices has been superseded by the one sacrifice of the cross. The book of Hebrews contributes more on the death of Christ than any other one New Testament book, as Leviticus contributes most of all the books of the Old Testament. Observe: Hebrews 1:3; 2:9; 5:1–10; 7:25–27; 9:12–15, 16–18; 10:1–21; 12:2, 24; 13:10–13.

7. The Death of Christ according to Other Books of the New Testament. In this more general classification certain passages are to be noted: Acts 17:3; 1 Thessalonians 4:14; 5:10; 1 Peter 1:18–21; 2:21; 3:18; 4:1; 1 John 2:2; Revelation 5:6, 9, 12; 13:8.

Chapter VI

BIBLICAL TERMINOLOGY RELATED TO
CHRIST'S SUFFERINGS AND DEATH

In the general field of truth respecting the sufferings and death of Christ there are specific words employed by writers—some of which terms are Biblical and some are not—the meaning of which should be discerned by the student in their precise import. Thirteen of these are here considered:

I. ATONEMENT

Whether it be accurately or inaccurately employed, the student will become aware of the fact that the word *atonement* (Lev. 5:10) is the term upon which men have seized to express the entire work of Christ upon the cross. That such a word is sorely needed cannot be doubted. The almost universal use of *atonement* for this purpose may go far to give it authoritative acceptance regardless of its inaptitude for the immense service thus thrust upon it. Objection to the use of the term as employed generally, arises from the fact that the word is not a New Testament term, and when used in the Old Testament some seventy-seven times it is a translator's attempt at interpretation and poorly represents the meaning of *kāphar*, which it purports to translate, which word originally meant *to cover*. Though etymologically the word *atonement* suggests *at-one-ment*, it feebly relates itself to the New Testament truth which presents Christ as the Lamb of God *taking away* the sin of the world.

II. EXPIATION

The New Standard Dictionary (1913 ed.) defines the meaning of this term thus: "The active means of expiating, or of making reparation or satisfaction, as for offense or sin; the removing of guilt by suffering punishment; atonement, or an atonement." In general, the term *expiation* is more inclusive and definite than *atonement*.

III. FORGIVENESS AND REMISSION

Much having been written previously in this work on the doctrinal significance of these terms, no more need be added here than to restate that divine forgiveness of sin is made possible only through the cross of Christ, and is never exercised apart from expiation—whether anticipated, as it was in the Old Testament, or realized, as it is in the New Testament economy.

IV. GUILT

Guilt (Gen. 42:21; Rom. 3:19; 1 Cor. 11:27; James 2:10), which means that the guilty one has offended God's character and will, is predicated of every person and in two respects:

1. As personal and thus related to the historical fact of actual sin. Such guilt is nontransferable. History and its records can never be changed.

2. As an obligation to justice, which is the theological use of the term *guilt*. This is transferable in the sense that an innocent person may discharge the obligation of one who is guilty.

V. JUSTICE

Generally speaking, whether as used in the Old Testament or the New Testament, the term *justice* is a synonym of righteousness. The conduct of one toward another is in view, and especially the truth that God acts toward men in justice. So perfect in itself is the plan of salvation through Christ, that God is said to be just (not, merciful) when He justifies the ungodly (Rom. 3:26; 4:5). God is ever just in all His ways.

VI. JUSTIFICATION

Theologically considered, the term *justification* means to be declared righteous. It is true that, being in Christ, the believer is righteous; but justification is the divine acknowledgment and declaration that the one who is in Christ is righteous. That which God thus publishes He defends. Justification is immutable.

VII. PENALTY

Though immeasurable by the finite mind, both reason and revelation assert that the penalty for sin is no more than that which God's holiness requires. It is God's judicial authority expressed. It is that which Christ satisfied. Whatever these demands were, it is now to be believed that Christ has met these demands for those who trust Him.

VIII. PROPITIATION

As already stated, propitiation is the Godward effect or value of the cross. Since Christ has died, God is propitious. This truth is the heart of the gospel and that which is to be believed.

IX. RECONCILIATION

Similarly, but a brief added word concerning reconciliation need be offered here. It represents the manward effect and value of the cross. Since the word signifies a complete change, the term cannot be applied properly to God who is immutable, but it does apply to man, who by the death of Christ is placed in a changed relation to God and to His judgments against man. By his own choice man may be turned about or converted respecting the rightful claims of God upon him.

X. REDEMPTION AND RANSOM

These two terms are practically the same in meaning. Redemption implies the payment of a ransom price, and, in the redemption which Christ has wrought, the divine judgments against sin having been measured out, these stand paid by Christ's voluntary sacrifice. This, again, is not something yet to be done; but, being already accomplished, is something to believe.

XI. SACRIFICE

While this term usually means to relinquish that which one may hold in possession, its doctrinal meaning is that of an offering to God. Thus every animal slain in the Mosaic economy was a sacrifice, and these looked on in anticipation to the one final and perfect sacrifice which Christ became for lost men (Heb. 9:26; 10:12).

XII. SATISFACTION

The forces of modern thought have been for nearly a century arrayed against the doctrine of satisfaction. The offense of this doctrine is the claim that God, having certain holy, inherent demands against sin, which claims arise from His outraged righteousness and character, has accepted as satisfying the payment which Christ has made. This doctrine must be considered at length in the following chapter of this thesis.

XIII. VICARIOUS AND SUBSTITUTIONARY

Again the two words being considered are identical in meaning and refer to the suffering of one in the place of another, in the sense that by that suffering on the part of one the other is wholly relieved. A vicar is an authorized or accepted substitute in office or service, and not merely anyone providing a benefit in general. Christ suffered and died that men might not be required to bear their burden of condemnation. To reject this truth is to reject the plainest doctrine of Scripture, to reject the gospel, and the only righteous ground on which God may exercise grace toward the lost.

Chapter VII

THEORIES FALSE AND TRUE OF THE
VALUE OF CHRIST'S DEATH

SYSTEMATIC THEOLOGY introduces no theme more difficult than an attempted analysis of the values secured by Christ in His death—with respect to its necessity; its effect upon God, upon man, upon angels; and the principles involved in its application. In approaching this subject, it may clarify the main discussion if certain truths are stated upon which any worthy attention to this aspect of doctrine must be based.

I. PRELIMINARY CONSIDERATIONS

1. GENERAL FACTS REVEALED. According to the Scriptures, the original harmony between God and man, from which Adam fell, must be treated as a fundamental reality. Though God was in the beginning in unbroken communion with man, He was, because of the sin of man, compelled to drive him from the garden and to proclaim that "without shedding of blood is no remission"; and though man was in the beginning in communion with God, he became estranged from God and is ever in unrest until through divine provisions he is restored to the righteousness of God. What may constitute the detail of those renewed relations has varied with different ages and in harmony with different divine purposes. The Israelite under his covenants, when restored to right relations with God, quite nearly duplicated the estate of unfallen man. He was in communion with God and blessed with a long life of tranquility on the earth. On the other hand, the Christian, when in that right relation to God which characterizes his saved estate, is conformed to Christ the Last Adam and all possessions, positions, life, and expectation are centered in that realm where his Living Head now is. Whether it be restricted to that estate which resembles the first Adam or whether it be the glorious transformation into the image of the Last Adam, the metamorphosis is a work of God for man, is wrought upon a righteous basis which God has constituted, and is available to man on such terms as God has determined. It may be reckoned as characteristic of both God and man that God seeks the man—as He did in Eden—and that

man hides from God and attempts—as symbolized by his apron of fig leaves—to clothe his nakedness from the eye of God. These three features of truth—God is man's Savior, God originates the plan by which man may be saved, and God determines the terms upon which man may be saved—are a reasonable starting-point for the study of the complex problem of those theories men have formed respecting the value of the thing which Christ accomplished by His death and the application of the value of that death to those who are estranged from God.

The fact that the Bible so exalts the importance of Christ's death—even making the world, if not the universe, *redempto-centric*—along with the corresponding human experience of sole relief and benefit in things spiritual by and through the cross, has compelled serious men to formulate theories respecting the whole divine undertaking. As the Bible offers no ready-made system of theology, in like manner it presents no ready-made theory of the value of Christ's work on the cross; however, there is little difficulty, comparatively, to be encountered when the plain teachings of the Word of God are taken in simple faith. The attempt to formulate a philosophy which purports to analyze God and all His works is fraught with insuperable problems. Inductions must be made and have been made with great care covering all that God has disclosed from Genesis 3:15 to the song of triumph with which the Bible closes. Out of such inductions certain truths emerge and these, when rightly arranged, might constitute a theory; but it is to be remembered that such a theory thus formed is, at best, characterized by the human element and is to that extent subject to error. A theory never creates a fact; it reaches its fruition when it explains a fact which already exists. Men have not originated any truth respecting the purpose and value of Christ's death; they have sought only to trace the meaning of that which God has accomplished. On this vital point, R. W. Dale has written:

The Idea of an objective Atonement invented by theologians to satisfy the exigencies of theological systems! It would be almost as reasonable to maintain that the apparent motion of the sun was invented by astronomers in order to satisfy the exigencies created by astronomical theories. The Idea has perplexed, and troubled, and broken up successive systems of theology. It was precisely because they failed to account for it that theological systems which were once famous and powerful, and from which their authors hoped for an immortal name, have perished. If it had been possible to expel the Idea from the faith of Christendom, the task of theology would have been made wonderfully easier. *The history of the doctrine is a proof that the idea of an objective Atonement was not invented by theologians.* . . . . It is true, and the truth has great significance, that the craving for a sacrifice for sin is one of the deepest instincts of the religious life of the race. It is also true that this craving is satisfied by the Christian Atonement. But that, apart from the clearest and most emphatic declarations of Christ Himself and His Apostles, the Church should ever have supposed that His Death could be the ground on which God forgives the sins of mankind, is incredible. . . . Had Moses perished at the hands of his inconstant and ungrateful and rebellious fellow-countrymen, I can imagine prophet after prophet insisting on his sufferings and death, in order to inspire the people with a fidelity to God like that which had been illustrated in the martyrdom of their great leader; and the Church might have made a similar use of His crucifixion. But what we have to account for is the universal prevalence of the idea that, while those who put Christ to death committed the greatest of human crimes, His Death was the Propitiation for the sins of the world. I can account for the prevalence of that idea in one way, and only in one way. It was a great and essential element in the original gospel which the Apostles were charged to preach to all nations. The Church received it from the Apostles. The Apostles received it from Christ.— *The Atonement*, 4th ed., pp. 299–300, 309–10

Primarily, the death of Christ answers a necessity and purpose in God. Human philosophy is strained beyond measure in its attempts to trace the majestic realities related to that death. Obviously, no theory can be formed by man respecting Christ's death that will be complete in all its parts. At best, what God has said should be received and believed. If such a procedure gives the intellectual pride of man no great latitude, perhaps by so much the truth may be preserved in its purity and simplicity.

2. THE DEATH OF CHRIST IS UNIQUE. Not only is Christ's death without a parallel in all human history both with regard to the way it was endured, and the measureless achievement said to have been wrought by it, but it was a *voluntary* crucifixion. He offered no resistance, for He had said, "No man taketh it [my life] from me, but I lay it down of myself" (John 10:18). It is far from natural for one who is innocent to an infinite degree, to project himself into a felon's death. Of no other could it be said that he is God's Lamb taking away the sin of the world, or that it pleased Jehovah to bruise him, and that Jehovah "laid on him the iniquity of us all" (Isa. 53:6, 10). The philosophies of men are no more qualified to penetrate into this the most crucial of all divine undertakings than they are prepared to penetrate into the realms of infinity or into the Person of God. Nevertheless, the burden laid on the theologian is in evidence here as elsewhere. His is the task of systematizing and interpreting the precise revelation God has given. Mere speculation is debarred; yet, in spite of this obvious truth, very

much of the literature bearing on the meaning of the death of Christ is permeated with human conjecture.

3. ITS EXTENT. The almost universal disposition to restrict the value of Christ's death to the one truth that it is a ransom or redemption from sin leads unavoidably to various errors. That His death is the ground of imputed righteousness and justification, that it is the basis on which a Christian may be forgiven and may walk in divine enablement, that it provides eternal blessedness for Israel, that it is the foundation on which an oncoming sinless eternity will rest, and that, objectively, it means more to God than it means to all men and angels combined, seems never to have occurred to many inventors of theories respecting the value of Christ's death. It is evident that a theory which comprehends no more than the forgiveness of sin—as glorious as that truth may be—will be more given to error than to truth.

4. ITS THREE DIRECTIONS. The problem of sin when restricted to unregenerate men is met by the death of Christ and that value points objectively in three directions—a redemption toward sin, a reconciliation toward man, and a propitiation toward God. Though all originates in God, it yet remains true that He who originates provides and receives a ransom; that He who originates provides and acknowledges His own Lamb as the One who bears away sin, thus providing a reconciliation; and He who originates provides, by Christ's death, that by which He Himself is propitiated. Though rationalism condemns these truths as being contradictory, they are the very heart of the divine revelation regarding the saving work and grace of God. It is but another instance added to many already encountered in which revelation surpasses reason and the devout soul may know by simple faith what he otherwise could never know.

It hardly need be indicated that a theory which purports to set forth the value of Christ's death and yet omits any part or parts of this threefold division of Christ's work upon the cross can only mislead and deceive.

5. DIVINE SATISFACTION THROUGH CHRIST'S DEATH IS NOT PERSONAL SALVATION. The satisfaction respecting the divine judgments against sin which Christ provided in His death does not itself constitute the salvation of those for whom He died. The unsaved are forgiven and justified not at the time of the cross nineteen hundred years ago, but when they believe; and the saved who sin are not forgiven and cleansed on the date of Calvary, but when they confess. Regardless of the truth that the disposition to believe, in the one case, and to confess,

in the other case, is wrought in the individual heart by the Holy Spirit, it yet remains true that these transforming blessings are conditioned on what is declared to be the elective choice of men. That treatment of the doctrine of satisfaction which invests it with those absolute provisions which necessitate the salvation of those for whom Christ died without regard for the element of human responsibility, is but another rationalistic deduction which is grounded on a partial revelation and, therefore, like all part-truth, is subject to great error.

6. TYPE AND ANTITYPE. None who accept the Scriptures as the Word of God can doubt the divine arrangement, purpose, and sanction of the truth as it lies paralleled between type and antitype. Since so much typology pertains to the death of Christ, this peculiar body of truth must be given its full import if the full value of Christ's death is to be recognized. That it is omitted from practically all theological discussions regarding Christ's death is a self-evident fact and the effect of its neglect is obvious.

7. THEORIES MAY BE QUESTIONED. Strictly speaking, there could be no theory relative to the value of Christ's death. That death is a *fact* and the Bible asserts its manifold effectiveness. Human speculation is ever active and reason has raised its objections to every divine revelation. That deep mystery is present in the greatest of all divine undertakings, should be no surprise or cause for distress to devout minds. The heart of man—however much it may be disciplined—can and should do no more than believe the record God has given concerning His Son. The careful study of all that is revealed to the end that its true message may be comprehended, is certainly enjoined (2 Tim. 2:15); but rationalistic arguments which contradict revelation are foreign to a true theological method.

II. HISTORICAL RECORD

The multiplied and complex views respecting the value of Christ's death which have obtained within the Christian era may be divided into three time-periods: (a) from the beginning to Anselm (c. 1100); (b) from Anselm to Grotius (c. 1600); and (c) from Grotius to the present time.

1. FROM THE BEGINNING TO ANSELM. It appears that no very definite attempt was made by men of the early church to formulate a doctrine relative to the value of Christ's death. The teachings of Christ and the Apostles were received in simplicity of faith. The

following from the *Epistle of Barnabas* (c. vii) will serve to indicate the belief of the men of earlier days: "If therefore the Son of God, who is Lord [of all things], and who will judge the living and the dead, suffered, that His stroke might give us life, let us believe that the Son of God *could not* have suffered except for our sakes." To this may be added a quotation from the *Epistle to Diognetus:*

> When our wickedness had reached its height, and it had been clearly shown that its reward, punishment and death, was impending over us; and when the time had come which God had before appointed for manifesting His own kindness and love—how the one love of God, through exceeding regard for men, did not regard us with hatred, nor thrust us away, nor remember our iniquity against us, but showed great long-suffering, and bore with us—He himself took on Him the burden of our iniquities, He gave His own Son as a ransom for us, the Holy One for transgressors, the Blameless One for the wicked, the Righteous One for the unrighteous, the Incorruptible One for the corruptible, the Immortal One for them that are mortal. For what other thing was capable of covering our sins than His righteousness? By what other One was it possible that we, the wicked and the ungodly, could be justified, than by the only Son of God? O sweet exchange! O unsearchable operation! O benefits surpassing all expectation! that the wickedness of many should be hid in a single Righteous One, and that the righteousness of One should justify many transgressors.— Chap. ix, both Fathers as cited by R. W. Dale, *Ibid.,* pp. 271–72

However, it was held from an early time and almost universally, in spite of voices raised against it, that the ransom which Christ provided was paid to Satan. Previously it has been pointed out (Chapter IV) that the death of Christ accomplished the judgment of Satan (John 12:31; 16:11; Col. 2:14–15), that Satan is that mighty foe who opened not the house of his prisoners (Isa. 14:17) and who was defeated by Christ in His death to the extent that Christ "opened the prison to them that are bound" (Isa. 61:1). It is evident that such Scriptures as these were given an exceedingly important place in the early days of the church. Here, as is so often recorded in all centuries of church history, confusion arises from the assumption that Christ wrought but one single thing in His death. Satan and his angels were judged, but the value of Christ's death is not restricted to that truth; nor is it given the important place. Most certainly there is no basis for the notion that Christ paid a ransom to Satan for the redemption of lost men. As an illustration of the protest which certain men raised against this unfounded conception, the following from Gregory Nazianzen is cited:

> To whom and on what account, was the blood which was shed on our behalf poured out, that precious and illustrious blood of Him who was God, and

both High Priest and Sacrifice? We were held fast by the devil since we were sold as slaves under sin, and had purchased pleasure by vice. If, now, the price of redemption is given only to him who has possession of the captives, then I ask, To whom was this ransom given, and on what ground? To the evil one? Oh, what a monstrous outrage! Then the robber received not merely a ransom from God, but received God Himself as the price of our redemption! Magnificent wages for his tyranny, on the payment of which justice required him to spare us! If, however, the ransom was paid to the Father, how, in the first place, can this be? for it was not God who had possession of us. And, in the second place, for what reason should the blood of His only begotten Son give any satisfaction to the Father, who did not even accept Isaac when his father [Abraham] offered him, but changed the sacrifice of a rational being into that of a ram? Is it not clear that the Father received the sacrifice, not because He Himself demanded or needed it, but for the sake of the Divine government of the universe . . . , and because man must be sanctified through the incarnation of the Son of God.—Opera. Cologne, 1680. I, 691–92, cited by Dale, *ibid.*, pp. 273–74

2. FROM ANSELM TO GROTIUS. The writing by Anselm in his *Cur Deus Homo* abruptly changed much of the former opinion. Anselm contended that the creature has wronged the Creator who has sovereign rights of ownership in that which He has made, and that a ransom was paid to God. The idea borders closely upon the truth of divine propitiation, and is, again, an almost exclusive emphasis upon one aspect of truth. The following quotations from *Cur Deus Homo* will indicate the positive character of the reasoning of Anselm, who is deemed the framer of the doctrine of satisfaction:

Sin is nothing else than not to render to God His due. . . . The entire will of a rational creature ought to be subject to the will of God. . . . He who does not render to God this honour which is due to Him, robs God of what is His own, and dishonours God; and this is what it is to sin. . . . Every one who sins [is] bound to pay back the honour of which he has robbed God; and this is the satisfaction which every sinner is bound to pay to God (c. xi.) . . . Nothing is less tolerable in the order of things than that a creature should rob his Creator of the honour due to Him and not repay Him that of which he robs Him. . . . If nothing be more great or good than God, nothing can be more just than that which preserves His honour in the disposing of events, even the Supreme Justice, which is nothing else than God Himself (c. xiii.). . . . That God should lose His own honour is impossible; for either the sinner of his own will pays what he owes, or God takes it from him against his will. For either man of his own free will exhibits that subjection to God which is due from him, whether by not sinning, or by making amends for his sin, or else God subjects him to Himself by tormenting him against his will, and by this means shows Himself to be his Lord, which the same refuses of his own will to acknowledge.—C. xiv., all cited by Dale, *ibid.*, pp. 280–81

Anselm made much of the representative character of Christ as the God-man, that it is impossible for fallen man to render satisfaction to God, and that Christ as the representative man, as well as very God, did render that satisfaction as a substitute, and thus the satisfaction was rendered both by God who alone could compass so great a requirement and by the representative Man.

During the period which began with Anselm's influence, certain other important and closely related subjects were under discussion, one of these being whether Christ actually became the sin which He bore—the sum total of all sinners—or whether, in a forensic sense, He bore the judgment of sin as is foreshadowed in the typical truth that a lamb was efficacious for an individual, as in the case of Abel, or for a family, as in the Passover, or for the nation, as in the case of the Day of Atonement. Martin Luther vigorously contended for the idea that Christ became the sin of all men and not merely the bearer of their judgments. In his commentary on Galatians 3:13 he declares:

The doctrine of the gospel (which of all others is most sweet and full of singular consolation) speaketh nothing of our works or of the works of the law, but of the inestimable mercy and love of God towards most wretched and miserable sinners: to wit, that our most merciful Father, seeing us to be oppressed and overwhelmed by the curse of the law, and so to be holden under the same, that we could never be delivered from it by our own power, sent His only Son into the world, and laid upon Him the sins of all men, saying, "Be Thou Peter, that denier; Paul, that persecutor, blasphemer, and cruel oppressor; David, that adulterer; that sinner which did eat the apple in Paradise; that thief which hanged upon the cross; and, briefly, be Thou the person which hath committed the sins of all men. See therefore that Thou pay and satisfy for them." Here now cometh the law, and saith, I find Him a sinner, and that such a one as hath taken upon Him the sins of all men, and I see no sins else but in Him, therefore let Him die upon the cross; and so he setteth upon Him, and killeth Him. By this means the whole world is purged and cleansed from all sins, and so delivered from death and all evils.—Cited by Dale, *ibid.*, p. 289

Another problem which received much consideration was one related to divine freedom as involved in the doctrine of satisfaction. If God must require just satisfaction—not being allowed to forgive sin as an act of sovereign leniency—is not His own freedom restricted and the exercise of His mercy limited? Francis Turretin (1682) contended that God's relation to fallen man is not private; it involves public interests which cannot be disregarded if the government of God is to stand.

The Socinians, in defense of their rationalistic interpretation of the value of Christ's death, contended that if Christ actually rendered satisfaction to God for fallen men then those for whom Christ died would be automatically saved by that death, which is universalism. An answer to that challenge was the theory of a limited redemption, which asserts that Christ died only for the elect, or for those who were, according to God's purpose, to be saved. Since this so important question must yet receive extended treatment (Chapters VIII–X), it will not be pursued at this point.

3. From Grotius to the Present Time. The Rectoral or Governmental Theory of the value of Christ's death was originated by Hugo Grotius (1583–1645) of Leyden, Holland. This theory, soon to be discussed more fully, has held a strong influence over men of liberal minds, and has been, since its introduction, about the only notable competitor against the time-honored doctrine of satisfaction, which doctrine, though formulated by Anselm, has been the accepted view of the believers who form the church in all her generations.

III. THEORIES IN GENERAL

Certain more or less well-defined theories or human philosophies have been set forth which attempt to explain that which Christ accomplished in His death. Each of these, in turn, has been subject to variations and modifications corresponding to the idea which any individual might wish to incorporate into a given scheme. Some writers have sought, even at great length, to list these theories. In the *New Schaff-Herzog Encyclopaedia of Religious Knowledge* (I, 349–56), Dr. B. B. Warfield presents the following fivefold classification of these theories:

(1) Theories which conceive the work of Christ as *terminating upon Satan,* so affecting him as to secure the release of souls held in bondage by him. (2) Theories which conceive the work of Christ as *terminating physically on man,* so affecting him as to bring him by an interior and hidden working upon him into participation with the one life of Christ; the so-called "mystical theories." (3) Theories which conceive the work of Christ as *terminating on man, in the way of bringing to bear on him inducements to action;* so affecting man as to lead him to a better knowledge of God, or to a more lively sense of his real relation to God, or to a revolutionary change of heart and life with reference to God; the so-called "moral influence theories." (4) Theories which conceive the work of Christ as *terminating on both man and God, but on man primarily and on God only secondarily* . . . the so-called "rectoral or governmental theories." (5) Theories which conceive the work of Christ as *terminating primarily on God and secondarily on man.* . . . This theory supposes that our Lord, by sympathetically entering into our condition . . . so keenly felt our sins as His own, that He could confess and adequately repent

of them before God; and this is all the expiation justice asks . . . the so-called "middle theory" of the Atonement.

As a further preparation for a right understanding of various theories regarding the value of Christ's death, certain schemes which assign little or no importance to the work of Christ should be identified by every student of Soteriology. Among these and quite unique in its claims is Universalism. With a positiveness that exceeds the Satisfactionists, this system declares that the whole race was ruined by sin. It also claims that Christ died for all men in the most absolute sense and that no other step is needed. All men are saved by the death of Christ. By some this salvation is made to extend to fallen angels, including Satan. Likewise schemes are proposed which claim that men may be forgiven by the sovereign act of God. This conception exists in the minds of multitudes and is the natural result of careless forms of preaching and writing which cast the unsaved directly on the mercy of God without reference to the imperative truth that divine mercy is possible only by and through the death of Christ as Redeemer, Reconciler, and Propitiator. The Scripture does not say, "Believe on the mercy of God and thou shalt be saved"; it rather asserts, "Believe on the Lord Jesus Christ, and thou shalt be saved." That the sinful, whether lost or saved, of the old order or of the new, are never forgiven apart from the blood of Christ, or that which typified it, is the constant teaching of the Bible. It is well stated in Hebrews 9:22, "And without shedding of blood is no remission." This notion of forgiveness by divine generosity is not only indifferent to the value of Christ's death, but disregards the issues respecting the divine Person and government which that death so perfectly protects. This notion also fails to recognize that, if one soul were ever forgiven one sin by the sovereign act of God apart from the righteous ground provided by Christ in His death, a principle is introduced thereby which would make it possible for God to forgive all sin by a sovereign act and thus render the death of Christ unnecessary. It is this same loose thinking which assumes that the sovereign love of God may be depended upon to keep souls from eternal perdition; yet no soul may be saved from perdition apart from the work of Christ. In this the Universalists are more consistent than those who magnify sovereign forgiveness. The Scripture most depended upon by the advocates of the idea of forgiveness by sovereignty is the parable of the "prodigal son." In that parable there is no efficacious blood, no regeneration, and no exercise of faith. There is confession and forgiveness such as is accorded a son restored to the Father's fellowship; and that forgiveness, it is assured, always rests upon the blood of Christ (cf. 1 John 1:7, 9).

Out of the welter of human opinion and the din of conflicting voices the Word of God brings a clear assurance regarding the value of Christ's death. However, several theories are to be considered specifically and the first three with brevity:

1. THE MARTURIAL THEORY. The appeal of the Marturial theory is that the moral disability of man is encouraged by Christ's death as a martyr, and by His resurrection. It is asserted that Christ died as a martyr because of the truth He taught and the life He lived, that by His death He gave the ultimate confirmation to His doctrine, and that by His death He demonstrated His own sincerity. The theory lacks a recognition of the necessity of sacrifice and may well be classed with those schemes which avoid any reference to objective expiation. It is clearly taught in the New Testament that Christ's death was wholly voluntary. The words of Christ are a final refutation of the Marturial theory: "From that time forth began Jesus to shew unto his disciples, how that he must go unto Jerusalem, and suffer many things of the elders and chief priests and scribes, and be killed, and be raised again the third day" (Matt. 16:21); "No man taketh it from me, but I lay it down of myself. I have power to lay it down, and I have power to take it again. This commandment have I received of my Father" (John 10:18). It is also recorded that when He died He, as the Sovereign of life, dismissed His own spirit: "And when Jesus had cried with a loud voice, he said, Father, into thy hands I commend my spirit: and having said thus, he gave up the ghost" (Luke 23:46). Only the ethical aspect of Christ's teachings as they bear on this life and the life to come are in view in this theory; these are made more effective, it is claimed, by a martyr's death.

2. THE MORAL INFLUENCE THEORY. This scheme of doctrine was originated by Faustus Socinus (1539–1604) and became a distinguishing belief of his followers. The theory asserts that the value of Christ's death is not objectively toward God, but fulfills its purpose in human salvation through the influence which that death exerts on the daily life of men. It aims at reformation, with no thought of regeneration in its Biblical sense. To the last degree this scheme should be classified among those that attempt no worthy recognition of the value of Christ's death. All of Christ's life, His teachings, His mighty works, His death, His resurrection, and His ascension serve but one objective purpose,

namely, to exert a moral influence over men. The theory lends itself to a great variety of ideas, but its essential principle is unchanged. Modern Unitarians, being the nearest representatives of the Socinian views, more nearly perpetuate the Moral Influence theory than any others of the present day. The advocates of this theory have never been concerned to interpret the teachings of the Bible. It is recognized by all students of the Scriptures that the death of Christ does have its effect on the lives of those who are saved. No text declares this more clearly than 2 Corinthians 5:15, which states: "And that he died for all, that they which live should not henceforth live unto themselves, but unto him which died for them, and rose again."

A theory closely related to the Moral Influence theory and to be classed with it contends that the death of Christ was an expression of the sympathy of God for the sinner. An illustration used by those who preach this idea is of a mother leaning over the cradle of her sick child, and there is more pain manifest on her face through sympathy than is manifest on the face of the suffering child; but Christ did not die merely to become a companion of men who die. He died that men might not have to die. He does not merely hold their hand while they suffer the judgments of their sins; rather, He bore that penalty that they might never have it to bear.

3. THE IDENTIFICATION THEORY. This estimation of the value of the death of Christ may be stated in few words: It is declared by those who defend this idea that Christ so identified Himself with men that He was able to represent them before God, and thus to confess their sins and to repent in their behalf. It is obvious that the essential element of expiation is not included and that God, again, is supposed to be justified in forgiving sovereignly those who repent, whether it be their own act or the act of another identified with them.

4. THE RECTORAL OR GOVERNMENTAL THEORY. In entering upon an analysis of the Rectoral or Governmental theory, it is acknowledged that it is different, indeed, from those theories already mentioned, it being the one and only theory which recognizes the need of an objective work of Christ with respect to God. Other theories seek no more than the remission of human sin, without regard for the deeper moral issues which arise when it is asserted that a holy God forgives sin apart from any penalty for the sin. There are but two theories—that of Satisfaction and the Rectoral or Governmental—which can claim the attention of sincere men who respect the holy character of God and the revelation He has given. Thus, and for this reason, these two interpretations are

placed over against each other in every worthy treatment of this great theme. It will likewise be necessary to hold these two systems in close comparison throughout this discussion.

The history of the Rectoral or Governmental theory has been traced above. There it was pointed out that, as a natural interpretation of the Scriptures, many believers from its beginning held the doctrine of divine satisfaction through the death of Christ, and, though the doctrine of satisfaction was systematized by Anselm in the eleventh century, the doctrine was held in general, as much as any truth obtained, throughout the Christian era. In the sixteenth century attacks were made upon the doctrine of satisfaction by the Socinians which were rationalistic and against the very Scriptures upon which the doctrine rests. These Scriptures were misinterpreted and rejected in the interest of human reason. It was then that Hugo Grotius, a jurist of Holland and a man of colossal intellect, undertook to devise a scheme of interpretation which would preserve some semblance of an objective value in Christ's death and yet avoid much of the rational criticism then being launched against the doctrine of satisfaction. Though men have departed to some extent from the Grotian philosophy, the essential features of his theory remain as he propounded them. This theory has been the refuge of Arminians, it is largely the belief of the theologians of continental Europe, and has been the accepted doctrine held by the independents of Great Britain and New England. In the latter region, this theory has been defended by such men as Joseph Bellamy, Samuel Hopkins, John Smalley, Stephen West, Jonathan Edwards, Jr., Horace Bushnell, and Edwards A. Park. The last-named stated that this theory was "the traditional orthodox doctrine of the American Congregationalists." Nevertheless, the doctrine of satisfaction has been, and is, held by all Calvinists and is that which appears in all the worthy creeds of the church.

These two systems of interpretation agree that the death of Christ and the shedding of His blood play a large part in the salvation of men. The doctrine of satisfaction embodies the conception of Christ's death, that it was a penal substitution which had the objective purpose of providing a just and righteous ground for God to remit the sins of those for whom Christ died. The equity, it is declared, is perfect, since the Substitute bore the penalty. This is expressed in the words, "that he might be just, and the justifier of him which believeth in Jesus" (Rom. 3:26). The Rectoral or Governmental theory contends that in His death Christ provided a vicarious suffering, but that it was in no way a bearing of punishment. The advocates of this theory object to the doctrine of imputation in all its forms, especially that human sin was ever imputed to Christ or that the righteousness of God is ever imputed to those who believe. They declare that a true substitution must be *absolute* and thus, of necessity, it must automatically remit the penalty of these for whom Christ died. Therefore, it is asserted that, since Christ died for all men and yet not all men are saved, the Satisfaction theory fails. That there was a substitution of the most absolute character both as respects merit and demerit, which does not become effective apart from a vital union with Christ—the result of saving faith—but does accrue to all who are in Christ, is rejected.

It is conceded that there are great difficulties which arise when finite minds attempt to reduce the divine mode of operation respecting the salvation of lost men—the greatest divine undertaking—to the limitations of a human theory. Believing that the death of Christ did provide an absolute satisfaction and was a complete substitution and to avoid the problem which is engendered by the fact that multitudes are not saved, a certain school of Calvinists have averred that Christ died only for the elect, or those who are saved. Some of the more extreme of this school contend that, in the case of the elect, saving faith is of minor importance since the death of Christ is automatically effective. The majority of Calvinists, however, recognize the obvious fact, that even the elect are no more saved than the nonelect until they believe on Christ.

Judging from their voluminous writings, it is not easy for the advocates of the Rectoral or Governmental theory to state precisely what they believe Christ accomplished by His death, and it is equally difficult to understand the exposition of the theory which they offer. To say, as they do, that Christ's sufferings were sacrificial but not punitive, is equal to saying that Christ answered by His death some divine necessity other than the penalty which sin incurs from divine holiness and divine government. It is asserted that the sin of man caused God to suffer and that that suffering fell on Christ, though the Father was in complete rapport with the Son in the hour of suffering. The sufferings are said to manifest thus divine compassion rather than penal judgment. When so estimated, it is declared, the sufferings are not lessened nor is their efficacy reduced. By these sufferings of Christ, God reveals His holy hatred for sin, and, by an actual demonstration in the cross, He displays the distress which sin causes Him. This is allowed to pass as an objective value of Christ's death Godward, and is as near to propitiation as the system is able to approach.

The plea of those who hold the Governmental theory is that, since God is love and ever has been, there is no occasion for Him to be propitiated. Yet the Scripture declares that the unsaved are "children of wrath" (Eph. 2:3), and that by His death Christ has rendered God propitious (1 John 2:2). In its objective value manward, or as it affects the sinner for whom He died, it can mean no more than a moral influence such as would arise in the mind of one who is impressed by the spectacle of divine sorrow for sin and compassion for the sinner. By so much, the death of Christ accomplishes no change in the estate of the sinner. This is as near to reconciliation as the theory may come; yet the Bible declares that God was in Christ reconciling the world unto Himself, and, by that death, so changed the estate of men that He is not now imputing their trespasses unto them (2 Cor. 5:19). Similarly, considering the value of Christ's death sinward, according to this theory God is safe, in a governmental sense, in forgiving the one who is rendered penitent by the recognition of the fact of Christ's death; and that is as near as the system may approach to a redemption. Yet this Christ, according to His own declaration, gave His life "a ransom for many" (Matt. 20:28; cf. Mark 10:45; 1 Tim. 2:6). The theory is exhausted by its one claim that, on the rectoral or governmental side of the divine requirements, having by Christ's death demonstrated the divine estimation of evil and by His sacrificial suffering displayed the divine compassion, God may with safety to His government pardon in a sovereign manner the sinner who, being influenced by the fact of Christ's death, is penitent. Divine government is thought to be protected sufficiently in the maintenance of its holy standards if forgiveness as a divine generosity is extended to the penitent. Labored arguments have been presented to demonstrate that a forgiveness based on an expression of divine displeasure concerning sin—which expression is accepted as a form of atonement for sin—is not a sovereign forgiveness, but is based on a worthy ground. Such arguments fail to carry any weight of conviction with those who oppose the theory.

From the above it may be concluded that Grotius, as those who follow him, distinguished between that which was *governmental* and that which is *personal* in God with respect to His judgment of sin. The theory proposes that God could not judge sin on a personal basis or as that which outrages His holiness, since He is love, but He must judge sin on the ground of His rectoral or governmental relation to men. No penalty falls on a substitute and the penitent sinner is forgiven as an act of divine compassion. Baur published an estimation of the work of

Grotius in *Bibliotheca Sacra* (IX, 259), and a brief quotation bearing on this phase of the theory is given here: "The fundamental error of the Socinian view was found by Grotius to be this: that Socinus regarded God, in the work of redemption, as holding the place merely of a creditor, or master, whose simple will was a sufficient discharge from the existing obligation. But, as we have in the subject before us to deal with punishment and the remission of punishment, God cannot be looked upon as a creditor, or an injured party, since the act of inflicting punishment does not belong to an injured party as such. The right to punish is not one of the rights of an absolute master or of a creditor, these being merely personal in their character; it is the right of a ruler only. Hence God must be considered as a ruler, and the right to punish belongs to the ruler as such, since it exists, not for the punisher's sake, but for the sake of the commonwealth, to maintain its order and to promote the public good" (cited by Miley, *Theology*, II, 161).

From this brief analysis it will be seen that two major ideas are paramount in this theory as presented by its advocates, namely, *penitence* and *forgiveness*, and no other aspects of the value of Christ's death are acknowledged and no other feature of the great work of God in the salvation of a soul is comprehended in this system. Should any question be raised about the need of an amercement or penalty that would uphold the sanctity of the law, the fact that Christ suffered sacrificially is deemed sufficient to meet the requirement. Grotius was Arminian in his theology and his theory is well suited to a system of interpretation of the Scriptures which is satisfied with modified and partial truths.

As for the methods employed by these two systems, it may be observed that the doctrine of satisfaction follows the obvious teachings of the Bible. It is the result of an unprejudiced induction of the Word of God as it bears on the death of Christ. On the other hand, the defenders of the Grotian theory build a philosophy which is not drawn from Scripture, and, having declared their speculations and reasonings, undertake to demonstrate that, by various methods of interpretation, the Scriptures may be made to harmonize with the theory. It is significant that Christians, being, in the main, subject to the Bible, have held the doctrine of satisfaction throughout all generations.

Of those who have expounded and defended the Rectoral or Governmental theory, none in the United States has given it more scholarly consideration than Dr. John Miley, the Arminian theologian. When stating his disagreement with the time-honored doctrine of satisfaction, Dr. Miley objects (1) to the doctrine of substitution as generally held.

It is his contention that neither the sin of man is imputable to Christ, nor the righteousness of God imputable to man; and (2) if man's sin is imputable to Christ, man does not need the personal faith which appropriates forgiveness, since nothing could remain to be forgiven. These are the major arguments which Socinus advanced and these, in turn, have been presented by many of the Arminian school. The fallacy involved will be given due consideration in the next division of this chapter. It is due Dr. Miley that a part, at least, of his own defense of the Rectoral or Governmental theory should be quoted here. Under the general division, "THEORY AND NECESSITY FOR ATONEMENT," he declares:

(1). *An Answer to the Real Necessity.*—The redemptive mediation of Christ implies a necessity for it. There should be, and in scientific consistency must be, an accordance between a doctrine of atonement and the ground of its necessity. The moral theory finds in the ignorance and evil tendencies of man a need for higher moral truth and motive than reason affords; a need for all the higher truths and motives of the Gospel. There is such a need—very real and very urgent. And Christ has graciously supplied the help so needed. But we yet have no part of the necessity for an objective ground of forgiveness. Hence this scheme does not answer to the real necessity for an atonement. Did the necessity arise out of an absolute justice which must punish sin, the theory of satisfaction would be in accord with it, but without power to answer to its requirement, because such a necessity precludes substitutional atonement. We do find the real necessity in the interests of moral government—interests which concern the divine glory and authority, and the welfare of moral beings. Whatever will conserve these ends while opening the way of forgiveness answers to the real necessity in the case. Precisely this is done by the atonement which we maintain. In the requirement of the sacrifice of Christ as the only ground of forgiveness the standard of the divine estimate of sin is exalted, and merited penalty is rendered more certain respecting all who fail of forgiveness through redemptive grace. And these are the special moral forces whereby the divine law may restrain sin, protect rights, guard innocence, and secure the common welfare. Further, the doctrine we maintain not only gives to these salutary forces the highest moral potency, but also combines with them the yet higher force of the divine love as revealed in the marvelous means of our redemption. Thus, while the highest good of moral beings is secured, the divine glory receives its highest revelation. The doctrine has, therefore, not only the support derived from an answer to the real necessity for an atonement, but also the commendation of a vast increase in the moral forces of the divine government.

(2). *Grounded in the Deepest Necessity.*—We are here in direct issue with the doctrine of satisfaction: for here its advocates make special claim in its favor, and urge special objections against ours. We already have the principles and facts which must decide the question. In their scheme, the necessity lies in an absolute obligation of justice to punish sin, simply as such, and ultimately in a divine punitive disposition. But we have previously shown that there is no such necessity. We have maintained a punitive disposition in God; but we also find in him a compassion for the very sinners whom his justice so condemns. And we may as reasonably conclude that his disposition of clemency will find its satisfaction in a gratuitous forgiveness of all as that he will not forgive any, except on the equivalent punishment of a substitute. Who can show that the punitive disposition is the stronger? We challenge the presentation of a fact in its expression that shall parallel the cross in expression of the disposition of mercy. And with no absolute necessity for the punishment of sin, it seems clear that but for the requirements of rectoral justice compassion would triumph over the disposition of a purely retributive justice. Hence this alleged absolute necessity for an atonement is really no necessity at all. What is the necessity in the governmental theory? It is such as arises in the rightful honor and authority of the divine Ruler, and in the rights and interests of moral beings under him. The free remission of sins without an atonement would be their surrender. Hence divine justice itself, still having all its punitive disposition, but infinitely more concerned for these rights and interests than in the mere retribution of sin, must interpose all its authority in bar of a mere administrative forgiveness. The divine holiness and goodness, infinitely concerned for these great ends, must equally bar a forgiveness in their surrender. The divine justice, holiness, and love must, therefore, combine in the imperative requirement of an atonement in Christ as the necessary ground of forgiveness. These facts ground it in the deepest necessity. The rectoral ends of moral government are a profounder imperative with justice itself than the retribution of sin, simply as such. One stands before the law in the demerit of crime. His demerit renders his punishment just, though not a necessity. But the protection of others, who would suffer wrong through his impunity, makes his punishment an obligation of judicial rectitude. The same principles are valid in the divine government. The demerit of sin imposes no obligation of punishment upon the divine Ruler; but the protection of rights and interests by means of merited penalty is a requirement of his judicial rectitude, except as that protection can be secured through some other means. It is true, therefore, that the rectoral atonement is grounded in the deepest necessity.

(3). *Rectoral Value of Penalty.*—We have sufficiently distinguished between the purely retributive and the rectoral offices of penalty. The former respects simply the demerit of sin; the latter, the great ends to be attained through the ministry of justice and law. As the demerit of sin is the only thing justly punishable, the retributive element always conditions the rectoral office of justice; but the former is conceivable without the latter. Penal retribution may, therefore, be viewed as a distinct fact, and entirely in itself. As such, it is simply the punishment of sin because of its demerit, and without respect to any other reason or end. But as we rise to the contemplation of divine justice in its infinitely larger sphere, and yet not as an isolated attribute, but in its inseparable association with infinite holiness, and wisdom, and love, as attributes of the one divine Ruler over innumerable moral beings, we must think that his retribution of sin always has ulterior ends in the interests of his moral government. We therefore hold all divine punishment to have a strictly rectoral function. Punishment is the ultimate resource of all righteous government.

Every good ruler will seek to secure obedience, and all other true ends of a wise and beneficent administration, through the highest and best means. Of no other is this so true as of the divine Ruler. On the failure of such means there is still the resource of punishment which shall put in subjection the harmful agency of the incorrigible. Thus rights and interests are protected. This protection is a proper rectoral value of penalty, but a value realized only in its execution. There is a rectoral value of penalty simply as an element of law. It has such value in a potency of influence upon human conduct. A little analysis will reveal its salutary forces. Penalty, in its own nature, and also through the moral ideas with which it is associated, makes its appeal to certain motivities in man. As it finds a response therein, so has it a governing influence, and a more salutary influence as the response is to the higher associated ideas. First of all, penalty, as an element of law, appeals to an instinctive fear. The intrinsic force of the appeal is determined by its severity and the certainty of its execution; but the actual influence is largely determined by the state of our subjective motivity. Some are seemingly quite insensible to the greatest severity and certainty of threatened penalty, while others are deeply moved thereby. Human conduct is, in fact, thus greatly influenced. This, however, is the lowest power of penalty as a motive; yet it is not without value. Far better is it that evil tendencies should be restrained, and outward conformity to law secured, through such fear than not at all. The chief rectoral value of penalty, simply as an element of law, is through the moral ideas which it conveys, and the response which it thus finds in the moral reason. As the soul answers to these ideas in the healthful activities of conscience and the profounder sense of obligation, so the governing force of penalty takes the higher form of moral excellence. As it becomes the clear utterance of justice itself in the declaration of rights in all their sacredness, and in the reprobation of crime in all its forms of injury or wrong, and depth of punitive desert, so it conveys the imperative lessons of duty, and rules through the profounder principles of moral obligation. Now rights are felt to be sacred, and duties are fulfilled because they are such, and not from fear of the penal consequences of their violation or neglect. The same facts have the fullest application to penalty as an element of the divine law. Here its higher rectoral value will be, and can only be, through the higher revelation of God in his moral attributes as ever active in all moral administration.

(4). *Rectoral Value of Atonement.*—The sufferings of Christ, as a proper substitute for the punishment, must fulfill the office of penalty in the obligatory ends of moral government. The manner of fulfillment is determined by the nature of the service. As the salutary rectoral force of penalty, as an element of law, is specially through the moral ideas which it reveals, so the vicarious sufferings of Christ must reveal like moral ideas, and rule through them. Not else can they so take the place of penalty as, on its remission, to fulfill its high rectoral office. Hence the vicarious sufferings of Christ are an atonement for sin as they reveal God in his justice, holiness, and love; in his regard for his own honor and law; in his concern for the rights and interests of moral beings; in his reprobation of sin as intrinsically evil, and utterly hostile to his own rights and to the welfare of his subjects. Does the atonement in Christ reveal such truths? We answer, Yes. Nor do we need the impossible penal element of the theory of satisfaction for any part of this revelation. God reveals his profound regard for the sacredness of his law, and for the interests which it conserves, by what he does for their support and protection. In direct legislative and administrative forms he ordains his law, with declarations of its sacredness and authority; embodies in it the weightiest sanctions of reward and penalty; reprobates in severest terms all disregard of its requirements, and all violation of the rights and interests which it would protect; visits upon transgression the fearful penalties of his retributive justice, though always at the sacrifice of his compassion. The absence of such facts would evince an indifference to the great interests concerned; while their presence evinces, in the strongest manner possible to such facts, the divine regard for these interests. The facts, with the moral ideas which they embody, give weight and salutary governing power to the divine law. The omission of the penal element would, without a proper rectoral substitution, leave the law in utter weakness. Now let the sacrifice of Christ be substituted for the primary necessity of punishment, and as the sole ground of forgiveness. But we should distinctly note what it replaces in the divine law and wherein it may modify the divine administration. The law remains, with all its precepts and sanctions. Penalty is not annulled. There is no surrender of the divine honor and authority. Rights and interests are no less sacred, nor guarded in feebler terms. Sin has the same reprobation; penalty the same imminence and severity respecting all persistent impenitence and unbelief. The whole change in the divine economy is this—that on the sole ground of the vicarious sacrifice of Christ all who repent and believe may be forgiven and saved. This is the divine substitution for the primary necessity of punishment. While, therefore, all the other facts in the divine legislation and administration remain the same, and in unabated expression of truths of the highest rectoral force and value, this divine sacrifice in atonement for sin replaces the lesson of a primary necessity for punishment with its own higher revelation of the same salutary truths; rather, it adds its own higher lesson to that of penalty. As penalty remains in its place, remissible, indeed, on proper conditions, yet certain of execution in all cases of unrepented sin, and, therefore, often executed in fact, the penal sanction of law still proclaims all the rectoral truth which it may utter. Hence the sacrifice of Christ in atonement for sin, and in the declaration of the divine righteousness in forgiveness, is an additional and infinitely higher utterance of the most salutary moral truths. The cross is the highest revelation of all the truths which embody the best moral forces of the divine government. The atonement in Christ is so original and singular in many of its facts that it is the more difficult to find in human facts the analogies for its proper illustration. Yet there are facts not without service here. An eminent lecturer, in a recent discussion of the atonement, has given notoriety to a measure of Bronson Alcott in the government of his school. He substituted his own chastisement for the infliction of penalty upon his offending pupil, receiving the infliction at the hand of the offender. No one can rationally think such a substitution penal, or that the sin of the pupil was expiated by the stripes which the master suffered instead. The substitution answered simply for the disciplinary ends of penalty. Without reference either to the theory of Bronson Alcott or to the interpretation of Joseph Cook, we so state the case as most obvious in the philosophy of its own facts. Such office it might well fulfill. And we accept the report of the very salutary result, not only as certified by the most reliable authority, but also as intrinsically most credible. No one in the school, and to be ruled by its discipline, could henceforth think less gravely of any offense against its laws. No one could think either that the master regarded with lighter reprobation the evil of such offense, or that he was less resolved upon a rigid enforcement of obedience. All these ideas must have been intensified, and in a manner to give them the most healthful influence. The vicarious sacrifice of the master became a potent and most salutary moral element in the government maintained. Even the actual punishment of the offender could not have so secured obedience for the sake of its own obligation and excellence. We may also instance the case of Zaleucus, very familiar in discussions of atonement, though usually accompanied with such denials of analogy as would render it useless for illustration. It is useless on the theory of satisfaction, but valuable on a true theory. Zaleucus was lawgiver and ruler of the Locrians, a Grecian colony early founded in southern Italy. His laws were severe, and his administration rigid; yet both were well suited to the manners of the people. His own son was convicted of violating a law, the penalty of which was blindness. The case came to Zaleucus both as ruler and father. Hence there was a conflict in his soul. He would have been an unnatural father, and of such a character as to be unfit for a ruler, had he suffered no conflict of feeling. His people entreated his clemency for his son. But, as a statesman, he knew that the sympathy which prompted such entreaty could be but transient; that in the reaction he would suffer their accusation of partiality and injustice; that his laws would be dishonored and his authority broken. Still there was the conflict of soul. What should he do for the reconciliation of the ruler and the father? In this exigency he devised an atonement by the substitution of one of his own eyes for one of his son's. This was a provision above law and retributive justice. Neither had any penalty for the ruler and father on account of the sin of the son. The substitution, therefore, was not penal. The vicarious suffering was not in any sense retributive. It could not be so. All the conditions of penal retribution were wanting. No one can rationally think that the sin of the son, or any part of it, was expiated by the suffering of the father in his stead. The transference of sin as a whole is unreasonable enough; but the idea of a division of it, a part being left with the actual sinner and punished in him, and the other part transferred to a substitute and punished in him, transcends all the capabilities of rational thought. The substitution, without being penal, did answer for the rectoral office of penalty. The ruler fully protected his own honor and authority. Law still voiced its behests and sanctions with unabated force. And the vicarious sacrifice of the ruler upon the altar of his parental compassion, and as well upon the altar of his administration, could but intensify all the ideas which might command for him honor and authority as a ruler, or give to his laws a salutary power over his people. This, therefore, is a true case of atonement through vicarious suffering, and in close analogy to the divine atonement. In neither case is the substitution for the retribution of sin, but in each for the sake of the rectoral ends of penalty, and thus constitutes the objective ground of its remissibility. We have, therefore, in this instance a clear and forceful illustration of the rectoral value of the atonement. But so far we have presented this value in its nature rather than in its measure. This will find its proper place in treating the sufficiency of the atonement.

(5). *Only Sufficient Atonement.*—Nothing could be more fallacious than the objection that the governmental theory is in any sense acceptilational, or implicitly indifferent to the character of the substitute in atonement. In the inevitable logic of its deepest and most determining principles it excludes all inferior substitution and requires a divine sacrifice as the only sufficient atonement. Only such a substitution can give adequate expression to the great truths which may fulfill the rectoral office of penalty. The case of Zaleucus may illustrate this. Many other devices were also at his command. He, no doubt, had money, and might have essayed the purchase of impunity for his son by the distribution of large sums. In his absolute power he might have substituted the blindness of some inferior person. But what would have been the signification or rectoral value of any such measure? It could give no answer to the real necessity in the case, and must have been utterly silent respecting the great truths imperatively requiring affirmation in any adequate substitution. The sacrifice of one of his own eyes for one of his son's did give the requisite affirmation, while nothing below it could. So in the substitution of Christ for us. No inferior being and no inferior sacrifice could answer, through the expression and affirmation of great rectoral truths, for the necessary ends of penalty. And, as we shall see in the proper place, no other theory can so fully interpret and appropriate all the facts in the sacrifice of Christ. It has a place and a need for every element of atoning value in his substitution.—*Ibid.*, II, 176–84

R. W. Dale is the outstanding English exponent of the Rectoral or Governmental theory, though he draws much nearer the doctrine of satisfaction than Dr. Miley. Only the most careful study of Dale's language will disclose the view which he evidently held. A brief portion of his writing is quoted here:

The Death of Christ may be described as an Expiation for sin, for it was a Divine act which renders the punishment of sin unnecessary. It was a Vicarious Death. He died "for us," "for our sins," "in our stead." For the principle that we deserved to suffer was asserted in His sufferings, that it might not have to be asserted in ours. He was forsaken of God, that we might not have to be forsaken. He did not suffer that He might merely share with us the penalties of our sin, but that the penalties of our sin might be remitted. It was a Representative Death, the Death of One whom the elder theologians were accustomed to describe as the new Federal Head of the human race, or of the Church. The technical language of theologians obscured and even concealed the truth which it was intended to express. The Lord Jesus Christ is in very truth, by the original law of the universe, the Representative of mankind. It may be described as a Ransom—an act of God by which we are delivered or redeemed from the calamities which threatened us so long as we were exposed to the punishment of sin, and by which we are also delivered or redeemed from those moral and spiritual evils from which there was no escape except through the restoration to us of the life of God. It was a Satisfaction to the righteousness of God, in whatever sense the punishment of the guilty can be spoken of as a Satisfaction to the righteousness of God. It was a Sacrifice for sin—an acknowledgment, such as we could never have made for ourselves, of the greatness of our guilt; an actual submission on our behalf to the penalty of guilt, and a confession that our very life had been justly forfeited by our sins. It was a Propitiation for sin—a Propitiation originated and effected by God himself, through which we are brought into such relations to God, that all moral reasons for withholding from us the remission of sins disappear. As an act of submission to the righteousness of the Law by which we were condemned, an act done in our name, and ultimately carrying our submission with it, it "has the property"—to quote the formal definition of a Propitiation given by one of our own theologians—"of disposing, inclining, or causing the judicial authority to *admit* the expiation; that is, to assent to it as a valid reason for pardoning the offender" (Dr. Pye Smith). Or, to state what seems to me to be the complete truth, the Death of Christ was a Propitiation for the sins of men because it was a revelation of the righteousness of God on the ground of which He can remit the penalties of sin; because it was an act of submission to the justice of those penalties on behalf of mankind, an act in which our own submission was really and vitally included; and because it secured the destruction of sin in all who through faith are restored to union with Christ. It is, therefore, the Supreme and irresistible argument by which we can now sustain our appeal to God's infinite mercy to grant us forgiveness of sin and deliverance from the wrath to come.—*Op. cit.,* pp. 432–34

As a summarization of this discussion of the Rectoral or Governmental theory, three indictments may be lodged against this system.

(a) It is a hypothesis which is based on human reason, which makes no avowed induction of the Scriptures on the theme which it essays to expound, but contends that the Scriptures, by special interpretation, can be made to harmonize with it.

(b) It attempts an impossible distinction between the sufferings of Christ as *sacrificial* in contrast to the sufferings of Christ as *penal.* The weakness of this distinction is well published in Dr. Miley's two illustrations, quoted above—the teacher punished in place of the pupil and Zaleucus who sacrificed his eye for the crime of his son. Of these, Dr. Miley asserts that they could not be penal. If he means that they rendered no satisfaction to God for sin as God saw it, none will contend with him; but within their own sphere as related to human laws and regulations, each became a definite penal substitute which not only upheld the law that was involved, but gave, so far as human standards may require, a righteous discharge of the offender. One fallacy which dominates this theory lies hidden in the unrecognized distinction which exists between divine and human governments.

(c) It restricts the scope of the value of Christ's death to the one issue of the forgiveness of the sins of the unsaved, the assumption being that fallen man—if, indeed, man be fallen at all—needs no more than the forgiveness of sin. The death of Christ unto the sin nature and the death of Christ as a ground for imputed righteousness are either neglected or rejected.

5. THE DOCTRINE OF SATISFACTION. As has been observed, the belief that Christ met the righteous demands of God against sin has been the view of true believers in all their history, and because of the fact that it is the plain testimony of the Word of God and the natural conclusion whenever an unprejudiced induction of the Bible teaching bearing on this theme is made. It remains, as it has been, the unquestioned belief of expositors, conservative preachers, and evangelists.

The doctrine of satisfaction falls into two general classifications or schools of interpretation—the absolute and the moderate. By the term *absolute* reference is made to a school of theologians who teach, with an emphasis upon the apparent reasonableness of the case, that if Christ rendered satisfaction to God for the sins of a person, that person is thereby constituted one of the elect and must, of necessity, be saved since the penalty no longer exists, having been perfectly borne by the substitute. The *moderate* interpretation of Christ's death contends that, on the authority of the Scriptures, Christ died for the whole *cosmos* world and that none are saved or immediately benefited by Christ's death until they believe. Since this phase of the discussion respecting the value of Christ's death occupies an entire division of this volume, next to be considered, it need not be pursued further in this connection. Under that division the various points of difference between the schools of thought of those who hold the doctrine of satisfaction will be examined.

As in contrast to all other theories regarding the value of the death of Christ—including the Rectoral or Governmental—which entire group restricts the work of Christ to the one undertaking of providing a way by which the sinner may be forgiven, the doctrine of satisfaction, because of its full accounting for *all* that the Bible affirms, recognizes and includes the typical foreshadowings of the Old Testament, and is as much concerned to be in accord with these as with the New Testament antitypical teachings; it sustains from the Word of God the actual substitution by Christ both in the field of disobedience which He bore ($\dot{a}\nu\tau\acute{\iota}$) in the room and stead of the sinner, and in the field of obedience which He offered to God in behalf of those who are void of obedience; it incorporates the truth that Christ by His death ended the entire merit-system for all who believe; it respects the peculiar and far-reaching doctrines of redemption, reconciliation, and propitiation; it gives unreserved consideration to the death of Christ in its relation to the sin nature and the personal sins which flow out of it; it accounts for those specific personal sins committed by Christians; it also advances into angelic realms and into heaven itself. Compared to all of this, a theory which cannot, by its limitations, expand beyond a gratuitous or sovereign forgiveness of the personal sins of those who are unsaved is less than a human gesture where naught but the mighty arm of the infinite One can avail. Nor should it be overlooked that so-called theories are not only hopelessly inadequate but they dishonor God by assuming that He can disregard, if not insult, His own holiness by an attitude of leniency toward sin; and, as has been stated, if divine leniency for sin is once admitted, a principle is introduced which denies the Word of God and besides, if extended to all sin, would account the death of Christ foolishness.

In view of the fact that this entire volume with its exposition of Soteriology is an elucidation of the doctrine of satisfaction and that this entire work on theology is grounded in that sublime reality, its more extended analysis is uncalled for here.

CONCLUSION

In an address—"Modern Theories of the Atonement"—delivered before the Religious Conference held in Princeton Seminary, October 13, 1902, and published in the Princeton Review of 1903, Dr. B. B. Warfield gave what, it is believed, is the most clarifying analysis of this subject ever published. This address is deemed of sufficient importance to every theological student to justify its reproduction here:

We may as well confess at the outset that there is no such thing as a modern theory of the Atonement, in the sense in which there is a modern theory, say, of the Incarnation—the *kenosis* theory to wit, which is a brand-new conception, never dreamed of until the nineteenth century was well on its course, and likely, we may hope, to pass out of notice with that century. All the theories of the Atonement now current readily arrange themselves under the old categories, and have their prototypes running back more or less remotely into the depths of Church history.

The fact is, the views men take of the atonement are largely determined by their fundamental feelings of need—by what men most long to be saved from. And from the beginning three well-marked types of thought on this subject have been traceable, corresponding to three fundamental needs of human nature as it unfolds itself in this world of limitation. Men are oppressed by the ignorance, or by the misery, or by the sin in which they feel themselves sunk; and, looking to Christ to deliver them from the evil under which they particularly labor, they are apt to conceive His work as consisting predominantly in revelation of divine knowledge, or in the inauguration of a reign of happiness, or in deliverance from the curse of sin.

In the early Church, the intellectualistic tendency allied itself with the class of phenomena which we call Gnosticism. The longing for peace and happiness that was the natural result of the crying social evils of the time, found its most remarkable expression in what we know as Chiliasm. That no such party-name suggests itself to describe the manifestation given to the longing to be delivered from the curse of sin, does not mean that this longing was less prominent or less poignant: but precisely the contrary. The other views were sloughed off as heresies, and each received its appropriate designation as such: this was the fundamental point of sight of the Church itself, and as such found expression in numberless ways, some of which, no doubt, were sufficiently bizarre—as, for example, the somewhat widespread representation of the atonement as centering in the surrender of Jesus as a ransom to Satan.

Our modern Church, you will not need me to tell you, is very much like the early Church in all this. All three of these tendencies find as full representation in present-day thought as in any age of the Church's life. Perhaps at no other period was Christ so frequently or so passionately set forth as merely a social Saviour. Certainly at no other period has His work been so prevalently summed up in mere revelation. While now, as ever, the hope of Christians at large continues to be set upon Him specifically as the Redeemer from sin.

The forms in which these fundamental types of thinking are clothed in our modern days, differ, as a matter of course, greatly from those they assumed in the first age. This difference is largely the result of the history of thought through the intervening centuries. The assimilation of the doctrines of revelation by the Church was a gradual process; and it was also an orderly process —the several doctrines emerging in the Christian consciousness for formal discussion and scientific statement in a natural sequence. In this process the doctrine of the atonement did not come up for formulation until the eleventh century, when Anselm gave it its first really fruitful treatment, and laid down for all time the general lines on which the atonement must be conceived, if it is thought of as a work of deliverance from the penalty of sin. The influence of Anselm's discussion is not only traceable, but has been determining in all subsequent thought down to to-day. The doctrine of satisfaction set forth by him has not been permitted, however, to make its way unopposed. Its extreme opposite—the general conception that the atoning work of Christ finds its essence in revelation and had its prime effect, therefore, in deliverance from error—was advocated in Anselm's own day by perhaps the acutest reasoner of all the schoolmen, Peter Abelard. The intermediate view which was apparently invented five centuries later by the great Dutch jurist, Hugo Grotius, loves to think of itself as running back, in germ at least, to nearly as early a date. In the thousand years of conflict which has raged among these generic conceptions each has taken on protean shapes, and a multitude of mixed or mediating hypotheses have been constructed. But, broadly speaking, the theories that have divided the suffrages of men easily take places under one or other of these three types.

There is a fourth general conception, to be sure, which would need to be brought into view were we studying exhaustive enumeration. This is the mystical idea which looks upon the work of Christ as summed up in the incarnation; and upon the saving process as consisting in an unobserved leavening of mankind by the inworking of a vital germ then planted in the mass. But though there never was an age in which this idea failed entirely of representation, it bears a certain aristocratic character which has commended it ordinarily only to the few, however fit: and it probably never was very widely held except during the brief period when the immense genius of Schleiermacher so overshadowed the Church that it could hardly think at all save in the formulas taught by him. Broadly speaking, the field has been held practically by the three theories which are commonly designated by the names of Anselm, Grotius, and Abelard; and age has differed from age only in the changing expression given these theories and the relative dominance of one or another of them.

The Reformers, it goes without saying, were enthusiastic preachers of the Anselmic conception—of course as corrected, developed, and enriched by their own deeper thought and truer insight. Their successors adjusted, expounded, and defended its details, until it stood forth in the seventeenth century dogmatics in practical completeness. During this whole period this conception held the field; the numerous controversies that arose about it were rather joined with the Socinian or the mystic than internal to the circle of recognized Church teachers. It was not until the rise of Rationalism that a widely spread defection became observable. Under this blight men could no longer believe in the substitutive expiation which is the heart of the Anselmic doctrine, and a blood-bought redemption went much out of fashion. The dainty Supranaturalists attained the height only of the Grotian view, and allowed only a "demonstrative" as distinguished from an "ontological" necessity for an atonement, and an "executive" as distinguished from a "judicial" effect to it. The great evangelical revivals of the eighteenth and early nineteenth centuries, however, swept away all that. It is probable that a half-century ago the doctrine of penal satisfaction had so strong a hold on the churches that not more than an academic interest attached to rival theories.

About that time a great change began to set in. I need only to mention such names as those of Horace Bushnell, McLeod Campbell, Frederick Dennison Maurice, Albrecht Ritschl, to suggest the strength of the assault that was suddenly delivered against the central ideas of an expiatory atonement. The immediate effect was to call out an equally powerful defense. Our best treatises on the atonement come from this period; and Presbyterians in particular may well be proud of the part played by them in the crisis. But this defense only stemmed the tide; it did not succeed in rolling it back. The ultimate result has been that the revolt from the conceptions of satisfaction, propitiation, expiation, sacrifice, reinforced continually by tendencies adverse to evangelical doctrine peculiar to our times, has grown steadily more and more widespread, and in some quarters more and more extreme, until it has issued in an immense confusion on this central doctrine of the gospel. Voices are raised all about us proclaiming a "theory" of the atonement impossible, while many of those that essay a "theory" seem to be feeling their tortuous way very much in the dark. That, if I mistake not, is the real state of affairs in the Modern Church.

I am not meaning to imply that the doctrine of substitutive atonement—which is, after all, the very heart of the gospel—has been lost from the consciousness of the Church. It has not been lost from the hearts of the Christian community. It is in its terms that the humble Christian everywhere still expresses the grounds of his hope of salvation. It is in its terms that the earnest evangelist everywhere still presses the claims of Christ upon the awakened hearer. It has not even been lost from the forum of theological discussion. It still commands powerful advocates wherever a vital Christianity enters academical circles: and, as a rule, the more profound the thinker, the more clear is the note he strikes in its proclamation and defense. But if we were to judge only by the popular literature of the day—a procedure happily not possible—the doctrine of a substitutive atonement has retired well into the background. Probably the majority of those who hold the public ear, whether as academical or as popular religious guides, have definitely broken with it, and are commending to their audiences something other and, as they no doubt believe, something very much better. A tone of speech has even grown up regarding it which is not only scornful but positively abusive. There are no epithets too harsh to be applied to it, no invectives too intense to be poured out on it. An honored bishop of the Methodist Episcopal Church tells us that "the whole theory of substitutional punishment as a ground either of conditional or unconditional pardon is unethical, contradictory, and self-subversive" (Bishop Foster, in his "Philosophy of Christian Experience": 1891, p. 113). He may rightly claim to be speaking in this sweeping sentence with marked discretion and unwonted charity. To do justice to the hateful theme requires, it seems, the tumid turmoil and rushing rant of Dr. Farrar's rhetoric. Surely if hard words broke bones, the doctrine of the substitutional sacrifice of the Son of God for the sin of man would long ago have been ground to powder.

What, then, are we offered instead of it? We have already intimated that it is confusion which reigns here: and in any event we cannot go into details. We may try, however, to set down in few words the general impression that the most recent literature of the subject makes.

To obtain a just view of the situation, I think we ought to note, first of all, the wide prevalence among the sounder thinkers of the Grotian or Rectoral theory of the atonement—the theory, that is, that conceives the work of Christ not as supplying the ground on which God forgives sin, but only as supplying the ground on which He may safely forgive sins on the sole ground of His compassion. The theory of hypothetical universalism, according to which Christ died as the proper substitute for all men on the condition, namely, that they should believe—whether in its Remonstrant or in its Amyraldian form—has in the conflict of theories long since been crushed out of existence—as, indeed, it well deserved to be. This having been shoved out of the way, the Grotian theory has come to be the orthodox Arminian view and is taught as such by the leading exponents of modern Arminian thought whether in Britain or America; and he who will read the powerful argumentation to that effect by the late Dr. John Miley, say, for example, will be compelled to agree that it is, indeed, the highest form of atonement-doctrine conformable to the Arminian system. But not only is it thus practically universal among the Wesleyan Arminians. It has become also, under the influence of such teachers as Drs. Wardlaw and Dale and Dr. Park, the mark also of orthodox Nonconformity in Great Britain and of orthodox Congregationalism in America. Nor has it failed to take a strong hold also of Scottish Presbyterianism: it is specifically advocated by such men of mark and leading as, for example, Dr. Marcus Dods. On the Continent of Europe it is equally widespread among the saner teachers: one notes without surprise, for example, that it was taught by the late Dr. Frederic Godet, though one notes with satisfaction that it was considerably modified upward by Dr. Godet, and that his colleague, Dr. Gretillat, was careful to correct it. In a word, wherever men have been unwilling to drop all semblance of an "objective" atonement, as the word now goes, they have taken refuge in this half-way house which Grotius has builded for them. I do not myself look upon this as a particularly healthful sign of the times. I do not myself think that, at bottom, there is in principle much to choose between the Grotian and the so-called "subjective" theories. It seems to me only an illusion to suppose that it preserves an "objective" atonement at all. But meanwhile it is adopted by many because they deem it "objective," and it so far bears witness to a remanent desire to preserve an "objective" atonement.

We are getting more closely down to the real characteristic of modern theories of the atonement when we note that there is a strong tendency observable all around us to rest the forgiveness of sins solely on repentance as its ground. In its last analysis, the Grotian theory itself reduces to this. The demonstration of God's righteousness, which is held by it to be the heart of Christ's work and particularly of His death, is supposed to have no other effect on God than to render it safe for Him to forgive sin. And this it does not as affecting Him, but as affecting men—namely, by awaking in them such a poignant sense of the evil of sin as to cause them to hate it soundly and to turn decisively away from it. This is just Repentance. We could desire no better illustration of this feature of the theory than is afforded by the statement of it by one of its most distinguished living advocates, Dr. Marcus Dods. The necessity of atonement, he tells us, lies in the "need of some such demonstration of God's righteousness as will make it possible and safe for Him to forgive the unrighteous." Whatever begets in the sinner true penitence and impels him toward the practice of righteousness will render it safe to forgive him. Hence Dr. Dods asserts that it is inconceivable that God should not forgive the penitent sinner, and that Christ's work is summed up in such an exhibition of God's righteousness and love as produces, on its apprehension, adequate repentance. "By being the source, then, of true and fruitful penitence, the death of Christ removes the radical subjective obstacle in the way of forgiveness."

"The death of Christ, then, has made forgiveness possible, because it enables man to repent with an adequate penitence, and because it manifests righteousness and binds men to God." There is no hint here that man needs anything more to enable him to repent than the presentation of motives calculated powerfully to induce him to repent. That is to say, there is no hint here of an adequate appreciation of the subjective effects of sin on the human heart, deadening it to the appeal of motives to right action however powerful, and requiring therefore an internal action of the Spirit of God upon it before it can repent: or of the purchase of such a gift of the Spirit by the sacrifice of Christ. As little is there any hint here of the existence of any sense of justice in God, forbidding Him to account the guilty righteous without satisfaction of guilt. All God requires for forgiveness is repentance: all the sinner needs for repentance is a moving inducement. It is all very simple; but we are afraid it does not go to the root of matters as presented either in Scripture or in the throes of our awakened heart.

The widespread tendency to represent repentance as the atoning fact might seem, then, to be accountable from the extensive acceptance which has been given to the Rectoral theory of the atonement. Nevertheless much of it has had a very different origin and may be traced back rather to some such teaching as that, say, of Dr. McLeod Campbell. Dr. Campbell did not himself find the atoning fact in man's own repentance, but rather in our Lord's sympathetic repentance for men. He replaced the evangelical doctrine of substitution by a theory of sympathetic identification, and the evangelical doctrine of expiatory penalty-paying by a theory of sympathetic repentance. Christ so fully enters sympathetically into our case, was his idea, that He is able to offer to God an adequate repentance for our sins, and the Father says, It is enough! Man here is still held to need a Saviour, and Christ is presented as that Saviour, and is looked upon as performing for man what man cannot do for himself. But the gravitation of this theory is distinctly downward, and it has ever tended to find its lower level. There are, therefore, numerous transition theories prevalent —some of them very complicated, some of them very subtle—which connect it by a series of insensible stages with the proclamation of human repentance as the sole atonement required. As typical of these we may take the elaborate theory (which, like man himself, may be said to be fearfully and wonderfully made) set forth by the modern Andover divines. This finds the atoning fact in a combination of Christ's sympathetic repentance for man and man's own repentance under the impression made upon him by Christ's work on his behalf—not in the one without the other, but in the two in unison. A similar combination of the revolutionary repentance of man induced by Christ and the sympathetic repentance of Christ for man meets us also in recent German theorizing, as, for example, in the teaching of Häring. It is sometimes clothed in "sacrificial" language and made to bear an appearance even of "substitution." It is just the repentance of Christ, however, which is misleadingly called His "sacrifice," and our sympathetic repentance with Him that is called our participation in His "sacrifice"; and it is carefully explained that though there was "a substitution on Calvary," it was not the substitution of a sinless Christ for a sinful race, but the substitution of humanity *plus* Christ for humanity *minus* Christ. All of which seems but a confusing way of saying that the atoning fact consists in the revolutionary repentance of man induced by the spectacle of Christ's sympathetic repentance for man.

The essential emphasis in all these transition theories falls obviously on man's own repentance rather than on Christ's. Accordingly the latter falls away easily and leaves us with human repentance only as the sole atoning fact —the entire reparation which God asks or can ask for sin. Nor do men hesitate to-day to proclaim this openly and boldly. Scores of voices are raised about us declaring it not only with clearness but with passion. Even those who still feel bound to attribute the reconciling of God somehow to the work of Christ are often careful to explain that they mean this ultimately only, and only because they attribute in one way or other to the work of Christ the arousing of the repentance in man which is the immediate ground of forgiveness. Thus Dean Fremantle tells us that it is "repentance and faith" that "change for us the face of God." And then he adds, doubtless as a concession to ingrained, though outgrown, habits of thought: "If, then, the death of Christ, viewed as the culminating point of His life of love, is the destined means of repentance for the whole world, we may say, also, that it is the means of securing the mercy and favour of God, of procuring the forgiveness of sins." And Dr. (now Principal) Forsyth, whose fervid address on the atonement at a great Congregationalist gathering a few years ago quite took captive the hearts of the whole land, seems really to teach little more than this. Christ sympathetically enters into our condition, he tells us, and gives expression to an adequate sense of sin. We, perceiving the effect of this, His entrance into our sinful atmosphere, are smitten with horror of the judgment our sin has thus brought on Him. This horror begets in us an adequate repentance of sin: God accepts this repentance as enough; and forgives our sin. Thus forgiveness rests proximately only on our repentance as its ground: but our repentance is produced only by Christ's sufferings: and hence, Dr. Forsyth tells us, Christ's sufferings may be called the ultimate ground of forgiveness.

It is sufficiently plain that the function served by the sufferings and death of Christ in this construction is somewhat remote. Accordingly they quite readily fall away altogether. It seems quite natural that they should do so with those whose doctrinal inheritance comes from Horace Bushnell, say, or from the Socinian theorizing of the school of Ritschl. We feel no surprise to learn, for example, that with Harnack the sufferings and death of Christ play no appreciable part. With him the whole atoning act seems to consist in the removal of a false conception of God from the minds of men. Men, because sinners, are prone to look upon God as a wrathful judge. He is, on the contrary, just Love. How can the sinner's misjudgment be corrected? By the impression made upon him by the life of Jesus, keyed to the conception of the Divine Fatherhood. With all this we are familiar enough. But we are hardly prepared for the extremities of language which some permit themselves in giving expression to it. "The whole difficulty," a recent writer of this class declares, "is not in inducing or enabling God to pardon, but in moving men to abhor sin and to want pardon." Even this difficulty, however, we are assured is removable: and what is needed for its removal is only proper instruction.

"Christianity," cries our writer, "was a revelation, not a creation." Even this false antithesis does not, however, satisfy him. He rises beyond it to the acme of his passion. "Would there have been no Gospel," he rhetorically demands—as if none could venture to say him nay—"would there have been no Gospel had not Christ died?" Thus "the blood of Christ" on which the Scriptures hang the whole atoning fact is thought no longer to be needed: the gospel of Paul, which consisted not in Christ *simpliciter* but specifically in "Christ as crucified," is scouted. We are able to get along now without these things.

To such a pass have we been brought by the prevailing gospel of the indiscriminate love of God. For it is here that we place our finger on the root of the whole modern assault upon the doctrine of an expiatory atonement. In the attempt to give effect to the conception of indiscriminate and undiscriminating love as the basal fact of religion, the entire Biblical teaching as to atonement has been ruthlessly torn up. If God is love and nothing but love, what possible need can there be of an atonement? Certainly such a God cannot need propitiating. Is not He the All-Father? Is He not yearning for His children with an unconditioned and unconditioning eagerness which excludes all thought of "obstacles to forgiveness"? What does He want but—just His children? Our modern theorizers are never weary of ringing the changes on this single fundamental idea. God does not require to be moved to forgiveness; or to be enabled to pardon; or even to be enabled to pardon safely. He raises no question of whether He can pardon, or whether it would be safe for Him to pardon. Such is not the way of love. Love is bold enough to sweep all such chilling questions impatiently out of its path. The whole difficulty is to induce men to permit themselves to be pardoned. God is continually reaching longing arms out of heaven toward men: oh, if men would only let themselves be gathered unto the Father's eager heart! It is absurd, we are told—nay, wicked —blasphemous with awful blasphemy—to speak of propitiating such a God as this, of reconciling Him, of making satisfaction to Him. Love needs no satisfying, reconciling, propitiating; nay, will have nothing to do with such things. Of its very nature it flows out unbought, unpropitiated, instinctively and unconditionally, to its object. And God is Love!

Well, certainly, God *is* Love. And we praise Him that we have better authority for telling our souls this glorious truth than the passionate assertion of these somewhat crass theorizers. God *is* Love! But it does not in the least follow that He is nothing but love. God *is* Love: but Love is not God and the formula "Love" must therefore ever be inadequate to express God. It may well be—to us sinners, lost in our sin and misery but for it, it must be—the crowning revelation of Christianity that God is love. But it is not from the Christian revelation that we have learned to think of God as nothing but love. That God is the Father of all men in a true and important sense, we should not doubt. But this term "All-Father"—it is not from the lips of Hebrew prophet or Christian apostle that we have caught it. And the indiscriminate benevolencism which has taken captive so much of the religious thinking of our time is a conception not native to Christianity, but of distinctly heathen quality. As one reads the pages of popular religious literature, teeming as it is with ill-considered assertions of the general Fatherhood of God, he has an odd feeling of transportation back into the atmosphere of, say, the decadent heathenism of the fourth and fifth centuries, when the gods were dying, and there was left to those who would fain cling to the old ways little beyond a somewhat saddened sense of the *benignitas numinis*. The *benignitas numinis!* How studded the pages of those genial old heathen are with the expression; how suffused their repressed life is with the conviction that the kind Deity that dwells above will surely not be hard on men toiling here below! How shocked they are at the stern righteousness of the Christian's God, who loomed before their startled eyes as He looms before those of the modern poet in no other light than as "the hard God that dwelt in Jerusalem"! Surely the Great Divinity is too broadly good to mark the peccadillos of poor puny man; surely they are the objects of His compassionate amusement rather than of His fierce reprobation. Like Omar Khayyam's pot, they were convinced, before all things, of their Maker that "He's a good fellow and 'twill all be well."

The query cannot help rising to the surface of our minds whether our modern indiscriminate benevolencism goes much deeper than this. Does all this one-sided proclamation of the universal Fatherhood of God import much more than the heathen *benignitas numinis?* When we take those blessed words, "God is Love," upon our lips, are we sure we mean to express much more than that we do not wish to believe that God will hold man to any real account for his sin? Are we, in a word, in these modern days, so much soaring upward toward a more adequate apprehension of the transcendent truth that God is love, as passionately protesting against being ourselves branded and dealt with as wrath-deserving sinners? Assuredly it is impossible to put anything like their real content into these great words, "God is Love," save as they are thrown out against the background of those other conceptions of equal loftiness, "God is Light," "God is Righteousness," "God is Holiness," "God is a consuming fire." The love of God cannot be apprehended in its length and breadth and height and depth—all of which pass knowledge—save as it is apprehended as the love of a God who turns from the sight of sin with inexpressible abhorrence, and burns against it with unquenchable indignation. The infinitude of His love would be illustrated not by His lavishing of His favor on sinners without requiring an expiation of sin, but by His—through such holiness and through such righteousness as cannot but cry out with infinite abhorrence and indignation—still loving sinners so greatly that He provides a satisfaction for their sin adequate to these tremendous demands. It is the distinguishing characteristic of Christianity, after all, not that it preaches a God of love, but that it preaches a God of conscience.

A somewhat flippant critic, contemplating the religion of Israel, has told us, as expressive of his admiration for what he found there, that "an honest God is the noblest work of man." There is a profound truth lurking in the remark. Only it appears that the work were too noble for man; and probably man has never compassed it. A benevolent God, yes: men have framed a benevolent God for themselves. But a thoroughly honest God, perhaps never. That has been left for the revelation of God Himself to give us. And this is the really distinguishing characteristic of the God of revelation: He is a thoroughly honest, a thoroughly conscientious God—a God who deals honestly with Himself and us, who deals conscientiously with Himself and us. And a thoroughly conscientious God, we may be sure, is not a God who can deal with sinners as if they were not sinners. In this fact lies, perhaps, the deepest ground of the necessity of an expiatory atonement.

And it is in this fact also that there lies the deepest ground of the increasing failure of the modern world to appreciate the necessity of an expiatory atonement. Conscientiousness commends itself only to awakened conscience; and in much of recent theologizing conscience does not seem especially active. Nothing, indeed, is more startling in the structure of recent theories of atonement, than the apparently vanishing sense of sin that underlies them. Surely, it is only where the sense of guilt of sin has grown grievously faint, that men can suppose repentance to be all that is needed to purge it. Surely it is only where the sense of the power of sin has profoundly decayed, that men can fancy that they can at will cast it off from them in a "revolutionary repentance." Surely it is only where the sense of the heinousness of sin has practically passed away, that man can imagine that the holy and just God can deal with it lightly. If we have not much to be saved from, why, certainly, a very little atonement will suffice for our needs. It is, after all, only the sinner that requires a Saviour. But if we are sinners, and appreciate what it means to be sinners, we will cry out for that Saviour who only after He was perfected by suffering could become the Author of eternal salvation.—*Studies in Theology,* pp. 283–97

DIVINE ELECTION

Chapter VIII

THE FACT OF DIVINE ELECTION

IN THIS PURSUANCE of the theme, divine election, a limited treatment is proposed in view of the extended consideration already given in Chapter XV of Volume I. Only the subdivision of the doctrine of decrees, namely, divine election, is directly germane to the more restricted field of Soteriology.

Though the doctrine of divine election presents difficulties which are insolvable by the finite mind, the fact of divine selection is not limited to God's choice of some out of the many for eternal glory; it is observable anywhere in the universe. There is a variety in all God's creation. There are classifications among the angels. One star is said to differ from another star in glory. Men are not born of the same race with the same advantages, nor with the same native abilities. These variations in the estates of men cannot be accounted for on the basis of the efficacy of the free will of man. Men do not choose their race, their life conditions, whether it be in civilization or in heathendom, nor do they choose their natural gifts. On the other hand, it is as clearly disclosed to those who will receive the revelation, that God's attitude toward the entire human family is one of infinite compassion and boundless sacrificial love. Though the two revealed facts—divine election and the universality of divine love—cannot be reconciled within the sphere of human understanding, here, as elsewhere, God may be honored by *believing* and by *resting* in Him. Therefore, to God be all the glory! And to Him be given the first consideration! Those systems of religious thought which require that the doctrine of God shall conform to the notion of the supremacy of man, which begin with man, defend man, and glorify man, are fundamentally wrong and therefore are productive of God-dishonoring error. The order of truth is established forever by the first phrase of the Bible—"In the beginning God." He it is who planned, He executes, and He it is who will realize to an infinite degree *all* that He has purposed. He will never be defeated nor disappointed.

The true system of religious thought begins with God, defends God, and glorifies God; and the creature is conformed to the plan and purpose of the Creator. The fall of man alone can account for the wickedness of heart which resists the divine supremacy.

Having declared the believer to be blessed "with all spiritual blessings in heavenly places in Christ" (Eph. 1:3), the Apostle proceeds to enumerate some of those measureless possessions and positions in Christ; and what could be more orderly than that the contemplation of the divine dealing with man should begin with a declaration of God's sovereignty in election? Whatever God bestows upon His creatures must, of necessity, be absolute in its nature. He discovers nothing in fallen man other than an object of His superabounding grace. The first man, Adam, stood before God on the ground of a natural perfection, being the true representation of God's creative purpose; but Adam fell from the estate of natural perfection and from that time, both for Adam and his posterity, only regenerative grace could commend any human being to God. No obligation rests upon God in the exercise of His grace. He may, and does, choose whom He will. He neither sees, nor foresees, any good in man which might form a basis of His blessings. Whatever good is found in redeemed man is wrought in him by divine grace. God does design for those whom He chooses that they shall be "holy and without blame before him"; but this is the result which is wrought by God in grace, and is never wrought by man. Certainly man has not chosen God. Christ emphasized this when He said, "Ye have not chosen me, but I have chosen you." Even the first man when unfallen and wholly free to choose, did not choose God; how much more is it certain that fallen man will not of himself choose God! Therefore the provision of the ground of redemption is not enough in itself; the perverted will of man must be divinely moved. The unregenerate heart must be rendered willing as well as transformed in its essential character. All of this God undertakes and accomplishes in sovereign grace. He elects, He calls, He inclines the heart, He redeems, He regenerates, He preserves, and He presents faultless before His glory those who are the objects of His sovereign grace. On the other hand, He employs means to the accomplishment of His purpose. On the divine side, the awful demands of sin must be met by the sacrifice of His only begotten Son. It is not enough that sin shall be *declared* to be sinful; it is required that its curse shall be *borne* by the Lamb of God, the will of man must be moved, regeneration must be wrought by the Spirit, and every spiritual and heavenly blessing must be secured by the setting up of an actual union with Christ. On the human side, when man's opposition to God is divinely broken down, he then believes to the saving of his soul. So demanding and real are all the divine means employed for the saving of the lost, that it is as much required of man that he believe and thus elect to be saved by the divine grace, as that actual redemption shall be wrought for him on Calvary's cross. In the realm of human experience man is conscious only of his power to choose, or reject, the salvation that is in Christ; and, because of the reality of this human choice, he is saved or lost according to his belief, or disbelief, in Christ as his Savior.

While there is very much in the doctrine of divine election which transcends the limitations of the finite understanding, it is true that man originates nothing—not even sin, since sin began with the angels of God. It is God who hath chosen His elect; and while this selection is both sovereign and final, nevertheless not one human being who desires to be saved and who complies with the necessary terms of the gospel, will ever be lost.

The wickedness of fallen man is disclosed in his natural disposition to withhold from his Creator the honor and obedience which is due from the creature. Man's inability to recognize the measurements of the estate into which he has been placed by creation, or to be satisfied therewith, is a primary evidence of the fall. Nothing, indeed, will arise in the natural man that might be a basis of divine favor. Such a basis must originate in the sovereign grace of God, and that which does thus arise is perfect and worthy of God.

The treatment of the doctrine of election falls into two major parts, namely, (a) the fact of divine election and (b) the order of elective decrees.

This study of the fact of divine election may be subdivided into four features, which are, (a) the terms used, (b) a clear revelation, (c) essential truths embraced, and (d) objections to the doctrine of election.

I. THE TERMS USED

1. BIBLICAL USAGE. In Biblical usage, the word *election* designates a sovereign divine purpose so formulated as to be independent of human merit, descent, or cooperation. The entire doctrine is in harmony with the truth, previously observed, that, in God's creation, both variety and selection are everywhere present. The term is used of Israel (Isa. 65:9, 22), of the Church (Rom. 8:33; Col. 3:12; 2 Tim. 2:10; 1 Thess. 1:4; 1 Pet. 5:13), and of Christ (Isa. 42:1; 1 Pet. 2:6).

2. Chosen. This word is but a synonym of the word *election*. Those elected of God are chosen by Him from all eternity. Like *election,* the term is applied to Israel (Isa. 44:1), and to the Church (Eph. 1:4; 2 Thess. 2:13; 1 Pet. 2:9), and is also used of the apostles (John 6:70; 13:18; Acts 1:2).

3. Drawing. There is a general drawing as mentioned in John 12:32, "And I, if I be lifted up from the earth, will draw all men unto me"; and an irresistible drawing which Christ mentioned, "No man can come to me, except the Father which hath sent me draw him: and I will raise him up at the last day" (John 6:44).

4. Calling. This feature of divine activity is similar to drawing. No Scripture defines the divine call, with all that it means in its effectiveness, better than Romans 8:30: "Moreover whom he did predestinate, them he also called: and whom he called, them he also justified: and whom he justified, them he also glorified."

5. Divine Purpose. Again, that which is closely akin to election is suggested by the word *purpose.* It is written, "Having made known unto us the mystery of his will, according to his good pleasure which he hath purposed in himself" (Eph. 1:9); "According to the eternal purpose which he purposed in Christ Jesus our Lord" (Eph. 3:11).

6. Foreknowledge. This specific term means merely that God knows beforehand. It is used of Israel (Rom. 11:2) and of the Church (Rom. 8:29).

7. Foreordination and Predestination. These words, almost complete synonyms, are used in the New Testament to declare the truth that God determines what shall be before it comes to pass. These words are more concerned with that to which men are divinely appointed than with the men themselves. God's foreordination and predestination precede all history. As foreknowledge recognizes the certainty of future events, foreordination and predestination make those events sure. The two divine activities of foreseeing and foreordaining could not function separately. They do not occur in succession, but are dependent on each other and either one is impossible without the other.

II. A CLEAR REVELATION

Whatever reaction to the fact of divine election may be recorded by the mind of man, the doctrine stands as an unequivocal revelation. This is not to say that it is free from complexity, or that problems are involved in the doctrine which are insuperable; and, as before noted under like circumstances, where human apprehension reaches its utmost boundary, faith is still a guiding factor. A few moments of unprejudiced reflection will serve much, to the end that a very simple proposition may be accepted, which is, that this is God's universe; all created intelligences are the work of His hands and therefore are to be disposed of as He shall choose. It only remains to discover, what is equally true, that what He determines is directed by infinite understanding, executed by infinite power, and is the manifestation of infinite love. How terrible might be the estate of the creature were he in the hands of an insane, fiendish despot! How universal, too, is the confidence in the mind of man that God is good! Why should it not be so? But why, when His goodness is even dimly recognized, is it not a ground of rest and trust? Is it not clear to all that to question the divine elective plan is to question the very wisdom and worthiness of God? Angels, who know vastly more of God's Being, cease not to adore Him throughout all ages. To do less than that would be, for them, to descend to the level of satanic infamy. In view of the truth that God has designed, created, and executed all that is, and that it goes on to the consummation He has foreordained, it should not be thought strange or unreasonable that He determines the course and destiny of human history. Men choose their course by what seems to them a free will and they glory in the fact that they are wise enough to adjust themselves to circumstances, but God is the Author of circumstances. Man blindly responds to the emotions of his heart, but God searches the heart of man and is able to create and control every sentiment which sways the mind of men. No equal game of competition for supremacy is on between God and man. When all the vain conceit of man is at its superlative manifestation, he is still the creature functioning as God created him to do. It is common sanity to give God His rightful place and to acknowledge His sovereign elective purpose in all that He has made to exist. The Bible is adjusted to the truth that God is supreme, with the authority and sovereign right in creation that belongs normally to the Creator. He may give latitude to men, but their sphere of freedom is never outside the larger sphere of His eternal purpose. Certain Scriptures may well be cited which mark off the uncompromised authority of God.

No more striking example of election could be found than that asserted by Jehovah when He utters His seven "I will's" which form the unconditional covenant with Abraham. "I will bless thee, I will make of thee a great nation, in thee shall all the families of the earth be blessed." These purposes, centered in one man apart from any human conditions to be fulfilled, reach out to the whole earth and imply the divine ascendancy and jurisdiction over not one human destiny alone, but over governments and nations to the end of time. In this light it will not be difficult to observe that the election of one person is a small issue compared to the outreach of such a covenant, and that Abraham is the elect of God for this distinction. Attention should be given to the prediction, which has never failed to be executed, in which Jehovah declared to Abraham, "I will bless them that bless thee, and curse him that curseth thee." When the nations who are thus to be judged stand before the throne of Christ's glory (Matt. 25:31–46), the King will say to those on the right hand "Come, ye blessed," and to those on the left hand, "Depart . . . ye cursed." However, it is to be observed that in predestination a kingdom is prepared from the foundation of the world for those on the right hand; but no specific preparation is indicated for those on the left hand. They go to the lake of fire prepared for the devil and his angels. Men have no rightful part in that destiny, but only as they have cast in their lot with the enemies of God and have, like Satan, repudiated the Creator's authority. Multitudes of men lived in Abraham's generation, but God prepared and spoke to Abraham alone. It would be rationalistic to contend with Jehovah because of the fact that He did not do for every person precisely what He did for Abraham and because of the fact that what He did was wrought in sovereign grace apart from any consideration of merit or demerit on Abraham's part.

In His early ministry, Christ asserted the unwelcome truth of divine election when He said, "But I tell you of a truth, many widows were in Israel in the days of Elias, when the heaven was shut up three years and six months, when great famine was throughout all the land; but unto none of them was Elias sent, save unto Sarepta, a city of Sidon, unto a woman that was a widow. And many lepers were in Israel in the time of Eliseus the prophet; and none of them was cleansed, saving Naaman the Syrian" (Luke 4:25–27).

Why, indeed, should an obscure maiden be chosen to be the mother of the Redeemer? Were there not a multitude to resent this on the ground of seeming partiality? Yet the angel said unto Mary, "Hail, thou that art highly favoured, the Lord is with thee: blessed art thou among women" (Luke 1:28).

Were certain men chosen to be apostles at random? Did Christ pick the first men that He met after He determined to associate men with Himself, or were these men chosen in the divine counsels of eternity? Was it a mere coincidence that Saul of Tarsus was prepared by education and called to the greatest of all human tasks—the formation of Christian doctrine? God could say, as well, to Pharaoh, "Even for this same purpose have I raised thee up, that I might shew my power in thee, and that my name might be declared throughout all the earth" (Rom. 9:17). Thus it is disclosed that a mighty purpose is served through Pharaoh; yet Pharaoh did not understand it. Doubtless he considered himself to be worthy of all the credit for what he was, being as self-centered as any other "self-made" man.

The case of Cyrus is equally instructive. God called him by name when Cyrus had not known Him. This mighty king was called that he might know that Jehovah is the God of Israel, and that Cyrus might know Jehovah. The prophet declares: "Thus saith the LORD to his anointed, to Cyrus, whose right hand I have holden, to subdue nations before him; and I will loose the loins of kings, to open before him the two leaved gates; and the gates shall not be shut; I will go before thee, and make the crooked places straight: I will break in pieces the gates of brass, and cut in sunder the bars of iron: and I will give thee the treasures of darkness, and hidden riches of secret places, that thou mayest know that I, the LORD, which call thee by thy name, am the God of Israel. For Jacob my servant's sake, and Israel mine elect, I have even called thee by thy name: I have surnamed thee, though thou hast not known me" (Isa. 45:1–4). Why, indeed, of two of earth's greatest kings —Pharaoh and Cyrus—to be elected thus, should one be to a hardened heart and the other to know Jehovah? The Scriptures do not leave room for an implication that these destinies were due to human designs or traits; the testimony in each instance is that Jehovah did precisely what occurred in each case. God is not asking to be relieved of such responsibility. Why should God elect Jacob and reject Esau? Why should the seed be called in Isaac and not in Ishmael? Only because God willed it so; and shall it be said that there was no worthy reason for these divine selections? Should it be said that there is no reason for any of God's actions in election and only because of the fact that men, perchance, do not understand them? Is any life ever lived—whether it be on the plane of Pharaoh or on the plane of an apostle—that does not serve the purpose of its Creator? Is it not true that no two human beings are alike as seen by God and that no one could serve as a substitute for another; or could the divine purpose for one be extended, as men would require, to others?

It is rational, to say the least, for each person to enter gladly into the will of God for himself and especially since, within His eternal purpose,

He extends the gracious invitation "Whosoever will may come." It is not to be expected that the unsaved will accept truth respecting divine sovereignty in election. The mind energized by Satan (Eph. 2:2) will not yield any point to the authority of God. The entire theme concerns those only who are regenerated and should never be presented to, or even discussed in the presence of, the unsaved.

III. ESSENTIAL TRUTHS EMBRACED

1. GOD HAS BY ELECTION CHOSEN SOME TO SALVATION, BUT NOT ALL. This truth, too often resisted for want of an understanding of the nature of God, or of the position He occupies in relation to His creatures, is reasonable; but it is distinctly a revelation. This, as before stated, cannot be doubted by those who are amenable to the Word of God. It is disclosed concerning individuals that they were chosen in the Lord (Rom. 16:13), chosen to salvation (2 Thess. 2:13), chosen in Him before the foundation of the world (Eph. 1:4), predestined to the adoption of sons (Eph. 1:5), elect according to the foreknowledge of God (1 Pet. 1:2), vessels of mercy which He hath before prepared unto glory (Rom. 9:23). There can be no question raised but that these passages contemplate an act of God by which some are chosen, but not all. The idea of election, or selection, cannot be applied to an entire class as unrelated to any others. Hidden in the word *election* is the implied truth, which is unavoidably a part of it, that others are not chosen, or are passed by. This suggests again the distinction, already particularized when discussing the divine decrees, that predestination points either to election or retribution, and that election cannot be understood in any other light than that others—the nonelect—are passed by. The thought expressed by the word *election* cannot be modified. It asserts an express intention on the part of God to confer salvation on certain persons, but not all. It is not a mere purpose to give salvation to those who may believe; it rather determines who will believe.

2. DIVINE ELECTION WAS ACCOMPLISHED IN ETERNITY PAST. All things which related to human history were determined in the eternal counsels of God before man was created. Three passages serve to state this truth: "According as he hath chosen us in him before the foundation of the world, that we should be holy and without blame before him in love" (Eph. 1:4); "Who hath saved us, and called us with an holy calling, not according to our works, but according to his own purpose

and grace, which was given us in Christ Jesus before the world began" (2 Tim. 1:9); "Known unto God are all his works from the beginning of the world" (Acts 15:18). Some have held that election takes place in time and that it was the sending of the gospel to men which God purposed in past ages. Men are elect, it is claimed, only as they exercise their own wills in accepting the offers of divine grace. To such, one passage of Scripture provides a correction: "But we are bound to give thanks alway to God for you, brethren beloved of the Lord, because God hath from the beginning chosen you to salvation through sanctification of the Spirit and belief of the truth: whereunto he called you by our gospel, to the obtaining of the glory of our Lord Jesus Christ" (2 Thess. 2:13–14). Thus it is said that election to salvation is "from the beginning," which corresponds to that beginning cited in John 1:1. The gospel, it is said, served as the call which fulfilled the eternal election to salvation.

3. ELECTION DOES NOT REST MERELY ON FOREKNOWLEDGE. The obvious distinction between foreknowledge and foreordination, or predestination, has been the occasion for much discussion, there being those who assert that God, by His foreknowledge, discriminated between those who by their own choice would accept salvation and those who would not, and, being thus informed, God was able to predestinate those He knew would believe. The superficial character of this notion is seen (1) in the fact that foreknowledge and foreordination, or predestination, could not be placed in a sequence. Nothing could be foreknown as certain that had not been made certain by foreordination, nor could anything be foreordained that was not foreknown. Of three passages bearing on the relationship between these two divine activities, two mention foreknowledge first in order, while the other reverses this arrangement. In Romans 8:29 it is written, "For whom he did foreknow, he also did predestinate"; and in 1 Peter 1:2 believers are addressed as "elect according to the foreknowledge of God." But in Acts 2:23, where the divine purpose in Christ's death is in view, it is said: "him being delivered by the determinate counsel and foreknowledge of God." (2) The Scriptures declare that that which cometh to pass is foreordained of God and not merely foreknown. Salvation is by grace apart from works. Men are not saved because of good works whether anticipated or realized. Election is according to grace and not according to works. If salvation be by grace, it is no more of works, and if it be by works, it is no more of grace (Rom. 11:5–6). In the light of this revelation, it is

impossible to build a foreseen structure of works as the ground of any person's salvation. Similarly, there is divine authority for denying that faith and personal holiness, even foreseen, determine divine election. The Bible reverses this order by declaring that election is unto faith and holiness. It is no slight error to confuse these issues and make faith and holiness the cause and election the effect. Faith can serve no greater purpose than to be the means by which that which God has determined may be realized. Referring again to passages already cited, it will be seen that God chose from the beginning those to be saved, and predestinated them to "belief of the truth" (2 Thess. 2:13); and He chose some before the foundation of the world that they should be holy and without blame before Him in love (Eph. 1:4). Thus it is revealed that men are not first holy and then elect; but they are first elect and that election is unto holiness. As an illustration of this order in the truth, the Apostle refers to the divine choice of Jacob over Esau before they were born and before they had done either good or evil. All this, it is said, is to the end that the divine election might stand, not of works, but of Him that calleth (Rom. 9:10–13). It may be added that acceptable works and qualities are not resident in any fallen human being, except these characteristics are wrought in the human heart by divine energy. It would therefore be folly to expect that God would foresee in men what could never exist. Doubtless, multitudes of people cling to a conditional election lest they be forced to recognize the depravity of man.

4. DIVINE ELECTION IS IMMUTABLE. Not only will that which was determined in past ages be brought to fruition, but it is immutable. It is claimed by those who give an undue emphasis to the ability of the human will, that God's purposes in salvation may be frustrated, that the elect of today may, because of human determination, become the nonelect of tomorrow. It is implied that God can do no more than to adjust Himself to the will of man, and His determination concerning His creatures may change. In reply to this idea, it may be remarked that God has never created a human will as an instrument to defeat His own purpose. He creates them that they may serve His immutable will. Since God is the Creator of all things, it is absurd to suppose that He who creates cannot determine the choice and destiny of that which He has wrought. Referring to those who had erred and by their unbelief had "overthrown the faith of some," the Apostle declares in assuring terms, "Nevertheless the foundation of God [His eternal purpose] standeth sure, having this seal, The Lord knoweth them that are his" (2 Tim.

2:18–19). Human language cannot express a more positive assertion than that which appears in Romans 8:30: "Moreover whom he did predestinate, them he also called: and whom he called, them he also justified: and whom he justified, them he also glorified." The text, in harmony with all the Bible, states that *all* who are predestinated are called, that *all* who are called are justified, and that *all* who are justified are glorified. There could not be one more or one less, else God has failed in the realization of His good pleasure.

5. ELECTION IN RELATION TO CHRIST'S MEDIATION. In theological investigation, a problem arises which sustains no close relation to the believer's daily life and service but which relates to the order of elective decrees—to be considered in Chapter IX—whether Christ died for men because of their election to salvation, or whether they are elect because Christ died for them. The question introduces nothing chronological. It has to do with that which is logical, or the matter of cause and effect in the mind of God. In other words, since it is so evident that God was not influenced in His elective choice by foreseen faith and obedience of the elect, was He influenced by the foreseen relation of the elect to the Savior? This much may be known: There was that in God which impelled Him to give His Son for the world (John 3:16). From this and other Scriptures it may be concluded that, though the Lamb was slain from the foundation of the world (Rev. 13:8), the election of some to salvation through the Lamb's death established the necessity for that death. By this interpretation, election stands first in the order uninfluenced by other issues, and is thus distinctly an election according to grace. The whole theme is exceedingly abstruse and it may be well to be reminded here of Romans 11:34: "Who hath known the mind of the Lord? or who hath been his counsellor?" If the best of men were to devise a program for the Almighty, it is probable they would not include election at all, and it is more than certain that their scheme would not start with election in sovereign grace apart from all values of human merit.

The doctrine of election is not without its difficulties—precisely such, indeed, as are normal when the finite mind assays to trace the paths of infinity. Within his own consciousness, man recognizes little outside his own power of determination; however, in the end and regardless of the means by which man has reached his destiny, it will be that destiny which was not only foreseen, but was divinely purposed. Such must be the conviction of every devout soul that contemplates the obvious truth, that the Creator is as resourceful in executing His purposes as He is in originating them.

IV. OBJECTIONS TO THE DOCTRINE OF ELECTION

In his *Systematic Theology,* Dr. Augustus H. Strong has presented the usual objections to election and refuted them in a manner so brief and yet so conclusive that it seems well to restate his material here. A part only of his argument in each instance is here quoted:

(*a*) It is unjust to those who are not included in this purpose of salvation. —Answer: Election deals, not simply with creatures, but with sinful, guilty, and condemned creatures. That any should be saved, is matter of pure grace, and those who are not included in this purpose of salvation suffer only the due reward of their deeds. There is, therefore, no injustice in God's election. We may better praise God that he saves any, than charge him with injustice because he saves so few. . . .

(*b*) It represents God as partial in his dealings and a respecter of persons. —Answer: Since there is nothing in men that determines God's choice of one rather than another, the objection is invalid. It would equally apply to God's selection of certain nations, as Israel, and certain individuals, as Cyrus, to be recipients of special temporal gifts. If God is not to be regarded as partial in not providing a salvation for fallen angels, he cannot be regarded as partial in not providing regenerating influences of his Spirit for the whole race of fallen men. . . .

(*c*) It represents God as arbitrary.—Answer: It represents God, not as arbitrary, but as exercising the free choice of a wise and sovereign will, in ways and for reasons which are inscrutable to us. To deny the possibility of such choice is to deny God's personality. To deny that God has reasons for his choice is to deny his wisdom. The doctrine of election finds these reasons, not in men, but in God. . . .

(*d*) It tends to immorality, by representing men's salvation as independent of their own obedience.—Answer: The objection ignores the fact that the salvation of believers is ordained only in connection with their regeneration and sanctification, as means; and that the certainty of final triumph is the strongest incentive to strenuous conflict with sin. . . .

(*e*) It inspires pride in those who think themselves elect.—Answer: This is possible only in the case of those who pervert the doctrine. On the contrary, its proper influence is to humble men. Those who exalt themselves above others, upon the ground that they are special favorites of God, have reason to question their election. . . .

(*f*) It discourages effort for the salvation of the impenitent, whether on their own part or on the part of others.—Answer: Since it is a secret decree, it cannot hinder or discourage such effort. On the other hand, it is a ground of encouragement, and so a stimulus to effort; for, without election, it is certain that all would be lost (*cf.* Acts 18:10). While it humbles the sinner, so that he is willing to cry for mercy, it encourages him also by showing him that some will be saved, and (since election and faith are inseparably connected) that he will be saved, if he will only believe. . . .

(*g*) The decree of election implies a decree of reprobation.—Answer: The decree of reprobation is not a positive decree, like that of election, but a permissive decree to leave the sinner to his self-chosen rebellion and its natural consequences of punishment.—Pp. 431–34

CHAPTER IX

THE ORDER OF ELECTIVE DECREES

OF ALL THE DECREES of God, reaching out as they do to infinity, five are related directly to the purpose of God in election as it pertains to those who comprise the Church, the Body of Christ. The problem which presents itself to the mind of thoughtful and devout men is with respect to the order which these five decrees maintain in the mind of God. The arrangement, being logical rather than chronological, is somewhat speculative and yet great issues are involved. By the term *logical* is meant that, though the entire program is as one thought in the mind of God, the principle of cause and effect is evidently involved. That is, one issue may prepare the way for and thus become the cause of another. These specific decrees are here named, but without regard at this time for the right order which they sustain.

(1) The decree to elect some to salvation and leave others to their just condemnation.
(2) The decree to create all men.
(3) The decree to permit the fall.
(4) The decree to provide salvation for men.
(5) The decree to apply salvation to men.

Four schools of interpretation are recognized, each contending for a specific order in the arrangement of these elective decrees. These schools are: the *supralapsarian,* the *infralapsarian,* the *sublapsarian,* and the *Arminian,* the first three being classed as Calvinistic. Though the defense of these varying orders concerns primarily the one subject—the election of some to be saved and the leaving of others to a just condemnation—the titles by which three of these schools are identified relates them to the fall of man. The word *lapsarian* refers to one who believes in the doctrine that man is a fallen being. Of this particular line of investigation, Dr. Charles Hodge writes this qualifying word: "It is to be borne in mind that the object of these speculations is not to pry into the operation of the divine mind, but simply to ascertain and exhibit the relation which the several truths revealed in Scripture concerning the plan of redemption bear to each other" (*Systematic Theology,* II,

321). A more detailed consideration of each of the claims advanced by each of these schools is here presented:

I. THE ORDER SET FORTH BY THE SUPRALAPSARIANS

This group is sometimes styled the *High Calvinists* or the *Ultra Calvinists*. The primary issue in the order proposed by this school of interpreters is that the decree to elect some and to reprobate all others stands first in the order of decrees, and by this disposal God is declared to have elected men to their destiny before they were created and before the fall. In reality, by this system men are consigned to perdition before they sin and without a cause, except it be by the sovereign will of God. It is true that God, as First Cause, effected man's existence knowing who would be reprobate, but this responsibility, like that of the presence of sin in the world, is never reckoned from the creature back upon God. Earlier in this immediate discussion, it was concluded that divine election precedes the determination to provide a Savior. The present issue is with respect to the order which obtains between the decree to elect and the decree to permit the fall.

The order as defended by the supralapsarians is:

(1) Decree to elect some to be saved and to reprobate all others.

(2) Decree to create men both elect and nonelect.

(3) Decree to permit the fall.

(4) Decree to provide salvation for the elect.

(5) Decree to apply salvation to the elect.

On this view as held by the supralapsarians, Dr. Wm. G. T. Shedd remarks:

The supralapsarian theory places, in the order of decrees, the decree of election and preterition before the fall, instead of after it. It supposes that God begins by decreeing that a certain number of men shall be elected, and reprobated. This decree is prior even to that of creation, in the logical order. . . . The objections to this view are the following: (*a*) The decree of election and preterition has reference to a non-entity. Man is contemplated as creatable, not as created. Consequently, the decree of election and preterition has no real object. . . . Man is only ideally existent, an abstract conception; and therefore any divine determination concerning him, is a determination concerning non-entity. But God's decrees of election and reprobation suppose some actually created beings, from which to select and reject. "On *whom* he will, he hath mercy; and *whom* he will, he hardeneth," Rom. 9:18. The first decree, in the order of nature, must therefore be a decree to create. God must bring man into being, before he can decide what man shall do or experience. It is no reply to say, that man is created in the Divine idea, though not in reality, when the decree of predestination is made. It is equally true that he is fallen in the Divine idea, when this decree is made. And the question is, What is the logical order, *in the divine idea,* of the creation and the fall? (*b*) The Scriptures represent the elect and non-elect, respectively, as taken out of an existing aggregate of beings. John 15:19, "I have chosen you out of the world." (*c*) The elect are chosen to justification and sanctification. Eph. 1:4–6; 1 Pet. 1:2. They must therefore have been already fallen, and consequently created. God justifies "the ungodly," Rom. 4:5; and sanctifies the unholy. (*d*) The supralapsarian reprobation is a Divine act that cannot presuppose sin, because it does not presuppose existence. But the Scriptures represent the non-elect as sinful creatures. In Jude 4, the men who were "of old ordained to this condemnation" are "ungodly men, turning the grace of God into lasciviousness." Accordingly, the Westminster Confession (III.7) affirms that God passes by the non-elect, and "ordains them to dishonor and wrath for their *sin,* to the praise of his glorious justice." The supralapsarian quotes Rom. 9:11, in proof of his assertion that election and preterition are prior to the creation of man. "The children being not yet born, neither having done any good or evil," Jacob was chosen and Esau was left. This is an erroneous interpretation. Birth is not synonymous with creation. Parents are not the creators of their children. Man exists before he is born into the world. He exists in the womb; and he existed in Adam.—*Dogmatic Theology,* I, 442–43

II. THE ORDER SET FORTH BY THE INFRALAPSARIANS

According to this school—properly called *moderate* Calvinists—the distinctive issue is that the decree to elect some and to leave others in retribution follows the fall, the order they defend being:

(1) Decree to create all men.

(2) Decree to permit the fall.

(3) Decree to provide salvation for men.

(4) Decree to elect those who do believe and to leave in just condemnation all who do not believe.

(5) Decree to apply salvation to those who believe.

Dr. Charles Hodge is one, among several, who makes no distinction between the infralapsarian and sublapsarian views by not mentioning the latter. What he writes, therefore, combines these to some extent. Of the infralapsarians he says:

That this view is self-consistent and harmonious. As all the decrees of God are one comprehensive purpose, no view of the relation of the details embraced in that purpose which does not admit of their being reduced to unity can be admitted. In every great mechanism, whatever the number or complexity of its parts, there must be unity of design. Every part bears a given relation to every other part, and the perception of that relation is necessary to a proper understanding of the whole. Again, as the decrees of God are eternal and immutable, no view of his plan of operation which supposes Him to purpose first one thing and then another can be consistent with their nature. And as God is absolutely sovereign and independent, all his purposes must be determined from within or according to the counsel of his own will. They cannot be supposed to be contingent or suspended on the action of his creatures, or upon anything out of Himself. The infralapsarian scheme, as held by most Augustinians, fulfils all these conditions. All the particulars form one comprehensive whole. All follow in an order which supposes no change of purpose; and all depend on the infinitely wise, holy, and righteous will of God. The final end is the glory of God. For that end He creates the world, allows the fall; from among fallen men He elects some to everlasting life, and leaves the rest to the just recompense of their sins. Whom He elects He calls, justifies, and glorifies. This is the golden chain the links of which cannot be separated or transposed. This is the form in which the scheme of redemption lay in the Apostle's mind as he teaches us in Rom. viii. 29, 30.—*Op. cit.*, p. 320

III. THE ORDER SET FORTH BY THE SUBLAPSARIANS

This arrangement sustained by a group who are also styled *moderate* Calvinists, differs but slightly from the order proposed by the infralapsarians. Technically, the infralapsarians place election after the decree to provide salvation, though Dr. Hodge, quoted above, does not recognize this feature when listing the order of decrees as proposed by the infralapsarians. The sublapsarians are identified by the placing of the decree to elect to follow the decree to permit the fall. In general, the sublapsarian order is a refutation of the supralapsarian order. Dr. Hodge's theological position classes him more reasonably with this school. The distinction between the infralapsarian and the sublapsarian is that the infralapsarian school places the decree to provide salvation before the decree to elect, while the sublapsarian places the decree to elect before the decree to provide salvation. The infralapsarian order, which places the decree to provide salvation before the decree to elect, allows possibly for the contention that Christ wrought an unlimited redemption, whereas the sublapsarian order, which places the decree to elect before the decree to provide salvation, favors the theory of a limited redemption. The order prescribed by the sublapsarians is:

(1) Decree to create all men.
(2) Decree to permit the fall.
(3) Decree to elect those who do believe and to leave in just condemnation those who do not believe.
(4) Decree to provide salvation for men.
(5) Decree to apply salvation to those who believe.

IV. THE ORDER SET FORTH BY THE ARMINIANS

Here the order is identical with that of the infralapsarian view, with one exception: The Arminian view of election, which they make to follow the decree to provide salvation, is by the Arminians made to depend on foreseen human virtue, faith, and obedience, whereas the infralapsarian view of election invests it with sovereign choice apart from any foreseen human merit whatsoever.

Refuting the Arminian idea of election, Dr. Shedd exposes the position of Richard Watson—the chief of Arminian theologians—as follows:

Respecting election, Watson (Institutes, II. 338) remarks as follows: "To be elected is, to be separated from the world ('I have chosen you out of the world'), and to be sanctified by the Spirit ('elect unto obedience'). It follows, then, that election is not only an act of God in *time*, but also that it is *subsequent* to the administration of the means of salvation. Actual election cannot be eternal, for from eternity the elect were not actually chosen out of the world, and could not be actually sanctified unto obedience." This explanation makes election to be sanctification itself, instead of its cause. "To be elected, is to be separated from the world, and to be sanctified." The term "separate" is used here by Watson not as St. Paul uses it to denote election, when he says that God "separated him from his mother's womb" (Gal. 1:15); but in the sense of sanctification, as St. Paul employs it in 2 Cor. 6:17, "Be ye separate, and touch not the unclean thing." By this interpretation, election is made to be the same thing as sanctification, instead of being an act of God that produces it; as is taught in Eph. 1:4, "He hath chosen us that we should be holy," and in 1 Pet. 1:2, "Elect unto obedience."—*Op. cit.*, p. 449

CONCLUSION

It will be observed from the foregoing that the differences represented in these various orders of decrees, though they seem highly speculative to some, do represent vital doctrine at its very foundation. The three schools of Calvinists contend alike that divine election is the sovereign choice of God which expresses His grace apart from every form of human works foreseen or actual; and that the Arminian school, by making election to be no more than foreknowledge of human merit, asserts that, in the end, man elects himself by his faith and obedience. The Calvinistic schools are the result of a faithful induction of the Word of God bearing on the elective decrees, whereas the Arminian school is an intrusion of human reason.

Chapter X

FOR WHOM DID CHRIST DIE?

THIS CHAPTER UNDERTAKES the discussion of a question which for many centuries has divided and yet divides some of the most orthodox and scholarly theologians. On the one hand, those who according to theological usage are known as *limited redemptionists* contend that Christ died only for that elect company who in all dispensations were predetermined of God to be saved; and, on the other hand, those who according to the same theological usage are known as *unlimited redemptionists* contend that Christ died for all men who live in the present age, which age is bounded by the two advents of Christ, and that His death has other and specific values in its relation to the ages past as well as the ages to come. The issue is well defined, and men of sincere loyalty to the Word of God and who possess true scholarship are found on both sides of the controversy. It is true that the doctrine of a limited redemption is one of the five points of Calvinism, but not all who are rightfully classified as Calvinists accept this one feature of that system. It is equally true that all Arminians are unlimited redemptionists, but to hold the doctrine of unlimited redemption does not necessarily constitute one an Arminian. There is nothing incongruous in the fact that many unlimited redemptionists believe, in harmony with all Calvinists, in the unalterable and eternal decree of God whereby all things were determined after His own will; and in the sovereign election of some to be saved, but not all; and in the divine predestination of those who are saved to the heavenly glory prepared for them. Without the slightest inconsistency the unlimited redemptionists may believe in an election according to sovereign grace, that *none* but the elect will be saved, that *all* of the elect will be saved, and that the elect are by divine enablement alone called out of the estate of spiritual death from which they are too impotent to take even one step in the direction of their own salvation. The text, "No man can come to me, except the Father which hath sent me draw him" (John 6:44), is as much a part of the one system of doctrine as it is of the other.

It is not easy to disagree with good and great men. However, as they appear on each side of this question, it is impossible to entertain a conviction and not oppose those who are of a contrary mind. The disagreement now under discussion is not between orthodox and heterodox men; it is within the fellowship of those who have most in common and who need the support and encouragement of each other's confidence. Few themes have drawn out more sincere and scholarly investigation.

I. CLASSIFICATION OF VIEWS

When recognizing more specifically the divisions of theological thought concerning the extent of the value of the death of Christ, it will be found that the limited redemptionists are divided into two general groups, and that the unlimited redemptionists are likewise divided into two general groups, making in all four divisions or parties in relation to this question. The position held by these may be defined briefly as follows:

1. THE EXTREME LIMITED REDEMPTIONISTS. This group is sometimes styled the High, or Ultra, Calvinist. It includes the supralapsarians who, as has been seen, assert that the decree of divine election stands first in the order of elective decrees—before the decree to create men, before the decree to permit the fall, and before the decree to provide salvation. Such a view could make no place for an unlimited redemption, nor could it encourage the preaching of the gospel to those who, they contend, were reprobated from the beginning.

2. THE MODERATE CALVINISTS WHO ARE LIMITED REDEMPTIONISTS. The appellation *Moderate Calvinist*, in this instance, is based on their belief that the decree to elect is preceded by the decree to create and the decree to permit the fall. Though they contend for a limited redemption, they make a place for world-wide preaching of the gospel and grant certain concessions not possible to the extreme Calvinists.

3. THE MODERATE CALVINISTS WHO ARE UNLIMITED REDEMPTIONISTS. The men who belong to this school of interpretation defend all of the five points of Calvinism excepting one, namely, "Limited Atonement," or what has been termed "the weakest point in the Calvinistic system of doctrine." This form of moderate Calvinism is more the belief of Bible expositors than of the theologians, which fact is doubtless due to the truth that the Bible, taken in its natural terminology and apart from those strained interpretations which are required to defend a theory, seems to teach an unlimited redemption. Men of this group believe that Christ died actually and fully for all men of this age alike, that God has ordained that the gospel shall be preached to all for whom

Christ died, and that through the proclamation of the gospel He will exercise His sovereign power in saving His elect. This group believe in the absolute depravity of man and his total inability to believe apart from the enabling power of the Spirit, and that the death of Christ, being forensic, is a sufficient ground for any and every man to be saved, should the Spirit of God choose to draw him. They contend that the death of Christ of itself saves no man, either actually or potentially, but that it does render all men *savable;* that salvation is wrought of God alone, and at the time the individual believes.

4. The Arminians. An exhaustive study of the Arminian view is not called for here, this being a consideration of those variations which obtain among Calvinists. Enough will be presented if it be remarked that the Arminians hold that Christ's death was for all men alike, and that it secures for everyone a measure of common grace whereby all are able to believe if they will. Men are, according to this view, subject to divine judgment only on the ground of their wilful rejection of Christ's salvation.

Besides, mention may be made of a theory advanced by F. W. Grant which maintains that Christ's death is a *propitiation* for the whole world and a *substitution* for the elect; but Grant has failed to disclose how God could be propitious toward the world apart from the substitutionary aspect of Christ's death. Grant is doubtless seeking to distinguish between that which is *potential* for all mankind and that which has been *consummated* in, and *applied* to, the elect who are saved.

II. POINTS OF AGREEMENT AND DISAGREEMENT BETWEEN THE TWO SCHOOLS OF MODERATE CALVINISTS

First, it is a common belief that all men are not to be saved. Both schools will unite in a rejection of any form of universalism or restitutionism. An innumerable company are to be saved and an innumerable company are to be lost. *Second,* it is a common belief that the death of Christ is suitable in the sense that it would answer the need of every fallen man. *Third,* it is a common belief that men could be saved by no other means than the death and resurrection of Christ. *Fourth,* the gospel is to be preached to all, but the underlying freedom to preach is different within one group than it is within the other. *Fifth,* faith must be wrought in the unsaved by the Holy Spirit. *Sixth,* only the elect will be saved. *Seventh,* whatever Christ did, whether for the elect or non-elect, is suspended awaiting compliance on the part of the unsaved with the divinely imposed conditions. No person is born forgiven or justified. *Eighth,* the belief of one group is that God provides salvation for the elect to the end that the elect might be saved. The belief of the other group is that God provided salvation for all men to the end that the elect might be saved. Both schools appeal to the Scriptures, though the one is forced, because of its restricted nature, to make strained interpretations of the so-called universal passages. Reference will be made to these strained interpretations as this chapter advances.

No concessions are required on the part of the unlimited redemptionists. Their system is not complicated or involved. The limited redemptionist concedes that what Christ did would be sufficient to save the nonelect were any such to believe; but the ultra Calvinist could not concede that the elect would be lost if such a one were not to believe, since under that system the death of Christ for a soul becomes the surety for that soul to such a degree that it could not be lost.

In this connection it is well to observe that salvation is vastly more than the forgiveness of sins. It is not difficult to demonstrate that sins are accounted for by the fact that Christ bore them on the cross, but to assert that the bearing of sin is equivalent to the salvation of the one for whom Christ suffered is quite another thing. Certain features of man's salvation through Christ are directly secured through the cross of Christ—forgiveness, eternal life, justification, all his positions in Christ, and some aspects of sanctification. However, other features of salvation —a place in the family and household of God, adoption, heavenly citizenship, access to God, freedom under grace from the merit system—are wrought by God as the expression of divine benevolence and are related to the death of Christ only as God is rendered free through Christ's death to act in behalf of those who believe. It is therefore both unscriptural and misleading to imply that there is no distinction to be drawn between that particular aspect of the saving work of God in providing a Savior, and the saving work of God in which the mighty transformations which constitute a Christian what he is, are accomplished. No responsibility of faith is laid on the sinner to provide the values of Christ's death, but salvation itself is only realized in answer to saving faith. There is nothing inconsistent, if God so wills, in a circumstance which leaves even the elect in a lost estate until they believe; nor is there any inconsistency if one, for whom Christ died, shall be left in a lost estate forever. The limited redemptionist considers the death of Christ as actual for the elect and of no saving benefit for the nonelect, while the unlimited redemptionist considers the death of Christ as actual for the elect and potential and provisional for the nonelect. The notion is without foundation which assumes that a thing is less real because its acceptance may be uncertain or conditional.

The human estimation of the immeasurable value of Christ's death in behalf of lost men is in no way lessened or discredited by the belief that its value is received at the time that saving faith is exercised, rather than at the time the Savior died. The unlimited redemptionist is in no way forced, because of his belief, to take a second place in magnifying the glorious saving work of the Lord Jesus Christ.

The highway of divine election is quite apart from the highway of redemption. With respect to election it is declared that "whom he did predestinate, them he also called: and whom he called, them he also justified: and whom he justified, them he also glorified" (Rom. 8:30), and in this great certainty every believer may rejoice. In respect to redemption it is written that Christ died for fallen men and that salvation, based on that death, is proffered to all who believe; and that condemnation rests on those who do not believe, and on the ground that they refuse that which has been provided for them. It would seem unnecessary to point out that men cannot reject what does not even exist, and if Christ did not die for the nonelect, they cannot be condemned for unbelief (cf. John 3:18). Both salvation and condemnation are conditioned on the individual's reaction to one and the same thing, namely, the saving grace of God made possible through the death of Christ.

In the former connection, the extent of the outreach of Christ's death has been considered. In all, fourteen measureless divine achievements have been enumerated. Only a restricted portion of these achievements is involved in this discussion. In the light of the great and complex work of Christ reaching out to past ages and to ages to come, to an entire elect nation, to the disannulling of the entire merit system, to angelic spheres, to heaven itself, to the judgment of the sin nature, to the propitiation for the Christian's sins, and to the delay of righteous judgments against all sin, the question of whether He died for the elect or the whole world is reduced, comparatively, to a small issue. The limited redemptionist concedes, with his opponent, that divine judgments are delayed on the ground of a universal thing which Christ accomplished in His death; but, by so much, the principle of a universal value in His death is acknowledged and the step is indeed insignificant from that position to the position occupied by the universal redemptionist.

Within the range of human reason, a problem arises which has been the point of attack against Calvinists by Socinians and by Arminians

—that if Christ bears the sin of any person, that person should benefit by this divine sacrifice and be free from the judgment which the Savior bore. To avoid this problem, the limited redemptionist contends that Christ died for the elect only. The unlimited redemptionist believes that, while Christ died provisionally for all men, the benefit is applied only when the condition of personal saving faith is met. The limited redemptionist of the moderate school believes with his opponent that none are forgiven until they believe, and by so much he fails to solve the problem which his system was originated to disentangle. To the unlimited redemptionist, the seeming inequity of a judgment falling upon a person after Christ has borne that judgment is but one more mystery which the finite mind cannot understand. The unlimited redemptionist recognizes two revelations which are equally clear—that Christ died for the *cosmos* world, and that His death is the ground of salvation for those who believe and the ground of condemnation for those who do not believe. That men are saved on the one condition of personal faith and that men are condemned for want of that faith are plain teachings of the New Testament. It is equally as great a mystery and one which is closely related to the present problem that, though faith is divinely wrought in the human heart, men are treated as though faith originated in them. They are blessed eternally who have that faith, and are condemned eternally who have it not. The devout soul must recognize his own limitations and here, as elsewhere, be satisfied to receive as true what God has spoken.

Much of the truth incorporated into these introductory remarks will be treated more fully in the following pages. This proposed discussion of this issue which divides the two schools of moderate Calvinists will pursue the following order: (a) dispensational aspects of the problem; (b) three doctrinal words; (c) the cross is not the only saving instrumentality; (d) universal gospel preaching; (e) is God defeated if men are lost for whom Christ died? (f) the nature of substitution; (g) the testimony of the Scriptures.

III. DISPENSATIONAL ASPECTS OF THE PROBLEM

Judging from their writings, the limited redemptionists frequently ignore dispensational distinctions, recognizing, as they usually do, but one elective purpose of God, in which they include all within the human family from Adam to the present generation who have experienced any divine favor. By this method of interpretation the pre-Israelite patriarchs, the Israelites, and the New Testament Church are assumed to be but one unbroken succession. Without hesitation they draw material for argument from the Old Testament relationships, and assume that whatever may have been true in previous dispensations is comparable and applicable in the present age, whereas the informed, unlimited redemptionist recognizes the dispensational features of God's dealings with men, and contends that the universal aspect of the value of Christ's death could apply only to the present age of the outcalling of that elect company which comprises the Church, which is the Body of Christ—an age differing, as it does, from all other ages in many respects, notably, that in it a universal gospel is to be preached, all distinctions between Jews and Gentiles are broken down (Rom. 3:9; 10:12; Eph. 3:6), and tremendous changes are wrought by the death and resurrection of Christ which place the people of this age in a position of responsibility toward God heretofore unknown.

It should be recognized that Israel is an elect *nation* into which each of her succeeding generations entered by physical birth, and that there is no basis in the fact of Israel's *national* election for comparison with the Church which is composed of elect *individuals*, both Jews and Gentiles, each one predestined, called, justified, and glorified (Rom. 8:30), and commissioned to proclaim a world-wide gospel, which responsibility was wholly unknown in previous ages. It is true that a door was open for proselytes to enter Jewry; but whatever may have been the facts, nothing is said of their being foreordained to do so, or that they exercised saving faith, or that they were regenerated as men are now regenerated, or that a gospel was ever preached unto them. The striking inability to see divine distinctions and purposes concerning humanity is disclosed in the pamphlet, *The Redeemed, Who Are They?*, by Rev. James Mortimer Sanger, B.A. Contending for the opinion that in all ages there are but two classes of people in the world—the good and the bad—this author further claims that Genesis 3:15 anticipates two lines of seed, and that Christ died for the seed of the woman, but not for the seed of Satan. Unfortunately for this theory the seed of the woman is Christ Himself, and none can doubt from Ephesians 2:1–2 that salvation has since come to some, at least, who were originally vitally related to Satan as fully as any unregenerate ever could be.

National election, too often confused with individual election (note the Apostle's warning to the nation Israel on this point as recorded in Rom. 9:4–13), anticipates no more than the ultimate blessing of Israel as a nation and their national preservation unto that end. Ahab and Jezebel, along with Abraham and Sarah, were partakers alike in Israel's national election. However, a judgment day for Israel is predicted when multitudes will be rejected (Ezek. 20:33–44; Dan. 12:1–3). There is, nonetheless, a recognition in the Bible of a spiritual remnant in all Israel's generations; but that spiritual group shared no additional covenants, their distinction being due to their willingness to be more faithful to those relations to Jehovah which were the privileges extended to all in Israel. The remnant out of Israel in this age is "a remnant according to the election of grace" (Rom. 11:5), and is composed of those who are saved by faith in Christ, and therefore partake of the heavenly calling which pertains to the Church. It is not until a Deliverer comes out of Zion that all Israel will be saved (Rom. 11:27), and that salvation will not only be unto the realization of all their national, earthly covenants, but also unto the taking away of their sins (cf. Jer. 31:34). In the present time, as above stated, only a remnant out of Israel are being saved as *individuals,* which is according to the divine election in grace and unto the heavenly glory of the Church. Nor is there assurance that all Gentiles will be saved in this dispensation. God is rather visiting the Gentiles to take out of them a people for His name (Acts 15:14). Eventually world-wide blessings for Gentiles will be experienced (Acts 15:18), but not until the promised One returns and rebuilds the tabernacle of David which is fallen down (Acts 15:16–17). Therefore, the issues relative to limited or unlimited redemption must be confined to the present age with its divine purpose in the outcalling of the Church, or hopeless confusion must result—such, indeed, as does prevail to a large extent at the present time. Problems relative to God's ways with people of other ages are important in their place, but are not germane to this discussion.

IV. THREE DOCTRINAL WORDS

Though common to theological usage, the terms *limited redemption* and *unlimited redemption* are inadequate to express the whole of the problem which is under consideration. There are three major aspects of truth set forth in New Testament doctrine relative to the unmeasured benefits which are provided for the unsaved through the death of Christ, and redemption is but one of the three. Each of these aspects of truth is in turn expressed by one word, surrounded as each word is by a group of derivatives or synonyms of that word. These three words are: ἀπολύτρωσις, translated *redemption,* καταλλαγή, translated *reconcil-*

iation, and ἱλασμός, translated *propitiation.* The riches of divine grace which these three words represent transcend all human thought or language; but these truths must be declared in human terms if declared at all. As it is necessary to have four Gospels, since it is impossible for one, two, or even three, to present the full truth concerning our Lord Jesus Christ, so the Scriptures approach the great benefit of Christ's death for the unsaved from three angles, to the end that what may be lacking in the one may be supplied in the others. There are at least four other great words—*forgiveness, regeneration, justification,* and *sanctification*—which represent spiritual blessings secured by the death of Christ; but these are to be distinguished from the three already mentioned in one important particular, namely, that these four words refer to aspects of truth which belong only to those who are saved. Over against these, the three words—*redemption, reconciliation,* and *propitiation*—though incorporating in the scope of their meaning vital truths belonging to the state of the saved, refer in particular to that which Christ wrought for the unsaved in His death on the cross. What is termed *the finished work of Christ* may be defined as the sum total of all that these three words connote when restricted to those aspects of their meaning which apply alone to the unsaved. *Redemption* is within the sphere of relationship which exists between the sinner and his sins, and this word, with those grouped with it, contemplates sin as a slavery, with the sinner as the slave, and freedom to be secured only through the redemption, or ransom, which is in Christ Jesus (John 8:32–36; Rom. 6:17–20; 8:21; 2 Pet. 2:19; Gal. 5:1). *Reconciliation* is within the sphere of relationship which exists between the sinner and God, and contemplates the sinner as at enmity with God, and Christ as the maker of peace between God and man (Rom. 5:10; 8:7; 2 Cor. 5:19; James 4:4). *Propitiation* is also within the sphere of relationship which exists between God and the sinner, but *propitiation* contemplates the larger necessity of God being just when He justifies the sinner, and Christ as an Offering, a Sacrifice, a Lamb slain, who, by meeting every demand of God's holiness against the offender, renders God righteously *propitious* toward that offender (Rom. 3:25; 1 John 2:2; 4:10). Thus it may be seen that redemption is the *sinward* aspect of the cross, reconciliation is the *manward* aspect of the cross, and propitiation is the *Godward* aspect of the cross, and that these three great doctrines combine to declare, as best any human terms are able, one divine undertaking.

From the foregoing it will be seen that the question at issue between the limited redemptionists and the unlimited redemptionists is as much a question of limited or unlimited reconciliation, and limited or un-limited propitiation, as it is one of limited or unlimited redemption. Having made a careful study of these three words and the group of words which must be included with each, one would hardly deny but that there is a twofold application of the truth represented by each.

There is the aspect of redemption which is represented by the word ἀγοράζω, translated *redeem*, which word means *to purchase in the market;* and, while it is used to express the general theme of redemption, its technical meaning implies only the *purchase* of the slave, but does not necessarily convey the thought of his *release* from slavery. The word ἐξαγοράζω, also translated *redeem*, implies much more, in that ἐξ, meaning *out of*, or *out from*, is combined with ἀγοράζω and thus indicates that the slave is *purchased out of the market* (note here, also, the even stronger terms λυτρόω and ἀπολύτρωσις with their meanings *to loose* and *deliverance*). There is, then, a redemption which *pays the price,* but does not of necessity *release* the slave, as well as redemption which is unto *abiding freedom.* It is probable that the reference to redemption in VIII, 6, and VIII, 8 of the Westminster Confession has the efficacious redemption in view which is completed in those who are saved.

According to 2 Corinthians 5:19 there is a reconciliation declared to be world-wide and wrought wholly of God; yet, in the verse which follows in the context, it is indicated that the individual sinner has the responsibility, in addition to the universal reconciliation wrought of God, to be reconciled himself to God. What God has accomplished has so changed the world in its relation to Himself that He, agreeable to the demands of infinite righteousness, is satisfied with Christ's death as a solution of the sin question for each one. The *desideratum* is not reached, however, until the individual, already included in the world's recon-ciliation, is himself satisfied with that same work of Christ which has satisfied God as the solution of his own sin question. Thus there is a reconciliation which of itself saves no one, but which is a basis for the reconciliation of any and all who will believe. When they believe, they are reconciled experimentally and eternally, and become the children of God through the riches of His grace.

In one brief verse, 1 John 2:2, God declares that there is a propitia-tion for our (Christians') sins, and not only for our sins, but also for the sins of the whole world. While due recognition will be given later on to the interpretation of this and similar passages offered by the limited redemptionists, it is obvious that the same twofold aspect of truth—that applicable to the unsaved and that applicable to the saved —is indicated regarding propitiation as is indicated in the case of both redemption and reconciliation.

From this brief consideration of these three great doctrinal words it may be seen that the unlimited redemptionist believes as much in unlimited reconciliation and unlimited propitiation as he does in unlimited redemption. On the other hand, the limited redemptionist seldom includes the doctrines of reconciliation and propitiation specifically in his discussion of this issue.

V. THE CROSS IS NOT THE ONLY SAVING INSTRUMENTALITY

It is one of the points most depended upon by the limited redemptionists to claim that redemption, if wrought at all, *necessitates* the salvation of those thus favored. According to this view, if the redemption price is paid by Christ it must be ἐξαγοράζω or ἀπολύτρωσις, rather than ἀγοράζω, in every instance. It is confidently held by all Calvinists that the elect will, in God's time and way, every one, be saved, and that the unregenerate believe only as they are enabled by the Spirit of God; but the question here is whether the sacrifice of Christ is the only divine instrumentality whereby God *actually* saves the elect, or whether that sacrifice is a divine work, finished, indeed, with regard to its scope and purpose, which renders all men *savable,* but one applied in sovereign grace by the Word of God and the Holy Spirit only when the individual believes. Certainly Christ's death of itself forgives no sinner, nor does it render unnecessary the regenerating work of the Holy Spirit. Any one of the elect whose salvation is predetermined, and for whom Christ died, may live the major portion of his life in open rebellion against God and, during that time, manifest every feature of depravity and spiritual death. This alone should prove that men are not severally saved by the act of Christ in dying, but rather that they are saved by the divine *application* of that value when they believe. The blood of the passover lamb became efficacious only when applied to the door post. The fact that an elect person does live some portion of his life in enmity toward God and in a state in which he is as much lost as any unregenerate person, indicates conclusively that Christ must not only die to provide a righteous basis for the salvation of that soul, but that that value must be *applied* to him at such a time in his life as God has decreed, which time, in the present generation, is almost two thousand years subsequent to the death of Christ. By so much it is proved that the priceless value in

Christ's death does not save the elect, nor hinder them from rejecting the mercies of God in that period of their life which precedes their salvation.

The unlimited redemptionist claims that the value of Christ's death is extended to all men, but the elect alone come, by divine grace wrought by an effectual call, into its fruition, while the nonelect are not called, but are those passed by. They hold that God indicates who are the elect, not at the cross, but by the effectual call and at the time of regeneration. It is also believed by the unlimited redemptionists that it pleased God to place the whole world in a position of infinite obligation to Himself through the sacrifice of Christ, and though the mystery of personal condemnation for the sin of unbelief when one has not been moved to faith by the Spirit cannot be solved in this world, the unregenerate, both elect and nonelect, are definitely condemned for their unbelief so long as they abide in that estate (John 3:18). There is nothing more clarifying in connection with this agelong discussion than the recognition of the fact that while they are in their unregenerate state, no vital distinction between the elect and the nonelect is recognized in the Scriptures (1 Cor. 1:24 and Heb. 1:14 might suggest this distinction along lines comparatively unimportant to this discussion). Certainly, that form of doctrine which would make redemption equivalent to salvation is not traceable when men are contemplated in their unregenerate state, and that salvation which is delayed for many years in the case of an elect person might be delayed forever in the case of a nonelect person whose heart God never moves. Was the objective in Christ's death one of making the salvation of all men *possible,* or was it the making of the salvation of the elect *certain?* Some light is gained on this question when it is thus remembered that the consummating divine acts in the salvation of an individual are wrought when he believes on Christ, and not before he believes.

VI. UNIVERSAL GOSPEL PREACHING

A very difficult situation arises for the limited redemptionist when he confronts the great commissions which enjoin the preaching of the gospel to *every* creature. How, it may be urged, can a universal gospel be preached if there is no universal provision? To say, at one time, that Christ did not die for the nonelect and, at another time, that His death is the ground on which salvation is offered to all men, is perilously near contradiction. It would be mentally and spiritually impossible for a limited redemptionist, if true to his convictions, to urge with sincerity those who are known to be nonelect to accept Christ. Fortunately, God has disclosed nothing whereby the elect can be distinguished from the nonelect while both classes are in the unregenerate state. However, the gospel preacher, if he entertains a doubt respecting the basis for his message in the case of even one to whom he is appealing, if sincere, does face a real problem in the discharge of his commission to preach the gospel to every creature. To believe that some are elect and some non-elect creates no problem for the soul-winner provided he is free in his convictions to declare that Christ died for everyone to whom he speaks. He knows that the nonelect will not accept the message. He knows, also, that even an elect person may resist it to near the day of his death. But if the preacher believes that any portion of his auditors are destitute of any basis of salvation, having no share in the values of Christ's death, it is no longer a question in his mind of whether they will accept or reject; it becomes rather a question of *truthfulness* in the declaration of the message. As Dr. W. Lindsay Alexander points out: "On this supposition [that of a limited atonement] the general invitations and promises of the gospel are without an adequate basis, and seem like a mere mockery, an offer, in short, of what has not been provided. It will not do to say, in reply to this, that as these invitations are actually given we are entitled on the authority of God's word to urge them and justified in accepting them; for this is mere evasion" (*A System of Biblical Theology*, II, 111). Representing the other side of the question, another Britisher, writing as late as 1919, declares: "Alas for the consummate folly of would-be theologians possessing Bibles, yet forever harping upon such mere pickings as 'whosoever believeth' and 'whosoever will!'" Almost every theologian has discussed in his writings the question of a limited or unlimited redemption, and clarifying quotations might be multiplied indefinitely could space be given to them. On the question of the beliefs of sincere gospel preachers, it would repay the reader to investigate how, universally, all great evangelists and missionaries have embraced the doctrine of unlimited redemption, and made it the very underlying structure of their convincing appeal.

VII. IS GOD DEFEATED IF MEN ARE LOST FOR WHOM CHRIST DIED?

Back of this phase of this subject is the conviction oft expressed by limited redemptionists, that for Christ to die for those who are never saved is to experience defeat on His part. Of course, it must be conceded that if the finished work is a *guarantee* of salvation to those for whom Christ died, there is a very noticeable defeat if one fails to be saved. But it is merely *assumed* that redemption is a guarantee of salvation. Christ becomes the surety of salvation when one believes. Christ's death is a finished transaction, the value of which God has not ever applied to any soul until that soul passes from death unto life. It is *actual* in its availability, but *potential* in its application. To state that the value of Christ's death is suspended until the hour of regeneration, is not to intimate that its value is any less than it would be were it applied at any other time. There are reasons which are based on the Scriptures why God might provide a redemption for *all* when He merely proposed to save *some*. He is justified in placing the whole world in a particular relation to Himself that the gospel might be preached with all sincerity to all men, and that, on the human side, men might be without excuse, being judged, as they are, for their rejection of that which is offered unto them. Men of this dispensation are condemned for their unbelief. This is expressly declared in John 3:18 and implied in John 16:7-11, in which latter context the Spirit is seen in His work of convincing the world of but one sin, namely, that "they believe not on me." But to reject Christ and His redemption, as every unbeliever does, is equivalent to the demand on his part that the great transaction of Calvary shall be reversed and that his sin, which was laid upon Christ, shall be retained by himself with all its condemning power. It is not asserted here that sin is thus ever retained by the sinner. It is stated, however, that since God does not apply the value of Christ's death to the sinner until that sinner is saved, God would be morally free to hold the sinner who rejects Christ, as being accountable for his sins, and to this unmeasured burden would be added all the condemnation which justly follows the sin of unbelief. In this connection, reference is made by the limited redemptionists to three passages which it is argued indicate that impenitent men die with their sins upon them and, therefore, it is asserted, Christ could not have borne their sins. These passages are:

John 8:24. "If ye believe not that I am he, ye shall die in your sins." This is a clear statement that calls for little exposition. It is a case of believing on Christ or dying in the condemnation of sin. It is not alone the one sin of unbelief, but "your sins" to which Christ refers. There is occasion for some recognition of the fact that Christ spoke these words *before* His death and, also, that He here requires them to believe that He is the "I AM"—Jehovah. These facts are of importance in any specific consideration of this text; but enough may be said, if it be pointed out that the issue is as much a problem for one side of this discussion as for the other. If it be claimed by the limited redemptionists that these people to whom Christ spoke would die in their sins because they were nonelect and, therefore, their sins were not borne by Christ, it may be replied (1) that the condition indicated by Christ on which they may avoid dying in their sins is not based on His not dying for them, but rather their *believing* on Him, and (2) were it true that they die in their sins because of their position as nonelect for whom Christ did not die, it would be equally true that those among them who were of the elect (cf. verse 30) and whose sins were laid on Christ, would have no need to be saved from a lost estate. In other words, this important passage teaches that the value of Christ's death, as marvelous and complete as it is, is not applied to the unregenerate until they *believe*. It is the effectual calling of the Spirit which indicates God's elect and not some partial, unidentified, and supposed discrimination wrought out in the death of Christ.

Ephesians 5:6. "Because of these things cometh the wrath of God upon the children of disobedience." The designation *children of disobedience* does not refer to the personal disobedience of any individual in this class, but rather to the fact that all unregenerate people are disobedient in the natural headship of Adam. This includes the elect and nonelect in their unsaved state; but it should be noted that those elect saved people to whom the Apostle is writing were, until saved, not only children of disobedience, but under the energizing power of Satan, being in a state of spiritual death (Eph. 2:1–2). Thus, again, it is proved that the value of Christ's death is applied to the elect, not at the cross, but when they believe.

Revelation 20:12. "And the dead were judged out of those things which were written in the books, according to their works." This scene is related to the great white throne judgment of all the unregenerate of all the ages, and it should be noted that, in other ages, men were placed more upon a covenant of works than they are now. The sum total of sin in the present age is *unbelief* (John 16:9), as the sum total of human responsibility toward God in securing a right relation to God is *belief* (John 6:29). It is very possible that those of this vast company who were of this dispensation may be judged for the one inclusive sin of unbelief, while those of other ages may be judged for many and specific sins; but from the foregoing proofs it is evident that it is in no way unscriptural to recognize that the impenitent of this age are judged according to their own specific sins, since the value of Christ's death is not applied to or accepted for them until they believe, and all these it is evident have never believed.

At this point, and in this connection, it is appropriate to consider the challenge which the limited redemptionists universally advance—that if Christ bore the sins of the nonelect, they could not be lost; for it is claimed even the condemning sin of unbelief would thus be borne and, therefore, have lost its condemning power. By this challenge the important question is raised of whether Christ bore all the individual's sins except *unbelief*. On this aspect of this theme, John Owen wrote nearly three centuries ago: "God imposed His wrath due unto, and Christ underwent the pains of hell for, either all the sins of all men, or all the sins of some men, or some sins of all men. If the last, some sins of all men, then have all men some sins to answer for, and so no man shall be saved. . . . If the second, that is what we affirm, viz. that Christ in their stead and room suffered for all the sins of all the elect in the world. If the first [viz. that Christ died for all the sins of all men], then why are not all freed from the punishment of all their sins? You will say, Because of their unbelief; they will not believe. But this unbelief, is it a sin or is it not? If not, why should they be punished for it? If it be, then Christ underwent the punishment due to it or not. If He did, why must that hinder, more than their other sins for which He died, from partaking of the fruit of His death? If He did not, then He did not die for all their sins" (cited by W. L. Alexander, *ibid.*, II, 109–10).

To this it may be replied that the sin of unbelief assumes a specific quality, in that it is man's answer to that which Christ wrought and finished for him when bearing his sins on the cross. There is, doubtless, divine freedom secured by Christ's death whereby God may pardon the sin of unbelief since he freely forgives *all* trespasses (Col. 2:13), and there is, therefore, now no condemnation to them that are in Christ Jesus (Rom. 8:1). The sin of unbelief, being particular in character, is evidently treated as such in the Scriptures. Again, if Christ bore the sin of unbelief along with the other sins of the elect, then no elect sinner in his unregenerate estate is subject to any condemnation, nor does he require to be forgiven or justified in the sight of God.

If it be inquired at this point, as it frequently is, whether the general call of God (John 12:32) could be sincere in every instance since He does not design the salvation of the nonelect, it may be asserted that, since the inability of the nonelect to receive the gospel is due to human sin, from His own standpoint, God is justified in extending the invitation to them. In this connection there is an important distinction to be observed between the sovereign *purpose* of God and His *desires*. For specific and worthy reasons, God, as any other being, may purpose to do more or less than He desires. His desire is evidently toward the whole world (John 3:16), but His purpose is as clearly revealed to be toward the elect. In the important passage, "who would have all men to be saved" (1 Tim. 2:4, R.V.), this distinction is seen in that the passive rather than the active form of the verb *save* is used.

VIII. THE NATURE OF SUBSTITUTION

The limited redemptionists sincerely believe that Christ's substitution for a lost soul *necessitates* the salvation of that soul. The following is another argument from John Owen: "For whom Christ died, He died as their sponsor, in their room and stead, that He might free them from guilt and desert of death (Isa. 53:5, 6; Rom. 5:6–8; Gal. 3:13; 2 Cor. 5:21). Evidently He changeth turns with us, that we might be made the righteousness of God in Him. . . . Christ dying for men made satisfaction for their sins, that they should not die. Now, for what sins He made satisfaction, for them the justice of God is satisfied; which surely is not done for the sins of the reprobates, because He justly punisheth them to eternity upon themselves (Matt. 5:26)" (as summarized by Alexander, *ibid.*, p. 108). This is a fair issue and there is some light available through the careful consideration of the precise nature of substitution itself.

Man did not first discover the necessity of a substitute to die in his room and stead; this necessity was in the heart of God from all eternity. Who can declare what sin actually is in the sight of infinite rectitude? Who will assume to measure the ransom price God must require for the sinner? Who can state what the just judgments of outraged holiness were, which were required by the Father and rendered by the Son? Or who can declare the cost to God of the disposition of sin itself from His presence forever?

Two Greek prepositions are involved in the doctrine of substitution: (1) Ὑπέρ (translated *for*), which word is broad in its scope and may mean no more than that a thing accomplished becomes a benefit to others. In this respect it would be declared by this word that Christ's death became a benefit to a greater or less degree to those for whom He died. This word is, however, at times invested with the most absolute substitutionary meaning (cf. Heb. 2:9; Titus 2:14; 1 Pet. 2:21;

3:18; 4:1). (2) Ἀντί (also translated *for*), which word conveys the thought of complete substitution of one thing or person in the place of another. Orthodox men, whether of one school or the other, will contend alike that Christ's death was *for* men in the most definite sense. However, substitution may be either *absolute* or *conditional*, and in the case of Christ's death for the sinner it was both absolute and conditional. Marshall Randles in his book on *Substitution*, page 10, states this twofold aspect of truth thus: "Substitution may be absolute in some respects, and conditional in others, *e.g.*, a philanthropist may pay the ransom price of an enslaved family, so that the children shall be unconditionally freed, and the parents only on condition of their suitably acknowledging the kindness. Similarly the substitution of Christ was partly absolute, and partly conditional, in proportion to man's capacity of choice and responsibility. His death availed for the rescue of infants from the race-guilt; their justification, like their condemnation, being independent of their knowledge and will, and irrespective of any condition which might render the benefit contingent. But for the further benefit of saving men who have personally and voluntarily sinned, the death of Christ avails potentially, taking effect in their complete salvation if they accept Him with true faith."

It is not a question of the perfect character of Christ's substitution; His substitution is as complete whether applied at one time or another, or if it never be applied. It is not a question of the ability or the inability of the sinner to believe apart from divine enablement. It is rather a question of whether the full value of Christ's death might be *potentially* provided for the nonelect, even though they never benefit by it, but are only judged because of it. The limited redemptionists, it may be restated, believe that the elect are saved because it is *necessary* for them to be saved in view of the fact that Christ died for them. The unlimited redemptionists believe that the substitutionary death of Christ accomplished to infinite perfection all that divine holiness could ever require for every lost soul of this age; that the elect are saved on the ground of Christ's death for them through the effective call and divine enablement of the Spirit; that the value of Christ's death is rejected even by the elect until the hour that they believe; and that that value is rejected by the nonelect forever, and for this rejection they are judged.

It has been objected at this point that the belief of the unlimited redemptionist results in the end in man being his own savior; that is, he is saved or lost according to his works. The question of whether believing on Christ is a saving work has been considered earlier in this thesis. One passage of Scripture will suffice to clear this matter. In Romans 4:5 it is written: "But to him that worketh not, but believeth on him that justifieth the ungodly, his faith is counted for righteousness." Here the thought is not that the candidate for salvation performs no works *except* belief, but rather that by believing he turns from all works of his own, on which he might depend, and confides in Another to do that which no human works could ever do. By so much the determination rests with man, though it is recognized that no man possesses saving faith apart from a divine enablement to that end. Recognition must be given by all to the fact—to be expanded later on—that the peculiar manner in which God enlightens the mind and moves the heart of the unsaved to the end that they gladly accept Christ as Savior, is in no way a coercion of the will; rather the human volition is strengthened and its determination is the more emphatic. It is futile to attempt to dismiss the element of human responsibility from the great gospel texts of the New Testament.

It is both reasonable and Scriptural to conclude that a perfect substitution avails for those who are saved: that, in the case of the elect, it is delayed in its application until they believe and in the case of the nonelect, it is never applied at all.

IX. THE TESTIMONY OF THE SCRIPTURES

In the progress of the discussion between the limited redemptionists and the unlimited redemptionists, much Scripture is noted on each side and, naturally, some effort is made by each group to harmonize that which might seem to be conflicting between these lines of proof. Some of the passages cited by the limited redemptionists are:

John 10:15. "I lay down my life for the sheep." This statement is clear. Christ gave His life for His elect people; however, it is to be observed that both Israel's election and that of the Church are referred to in this text (vs. 16).

John 15:13. Christ laid down His life for His friends.

John 17:2, 6, 9, 20, 24. In this most important Scripture Christ declares that He gives eternal life to as many as are given to Him, that an elect company has been given to Him, that He prays now only for this elect company, and that He desires that this elect company may be with Him in glory.

Romans 4:25. Christ is here said to have been delivered for *our* (the elect) sins and raised again for *our* (the elect) justification. This, too, is specific.

Ephesians 1:3–7. In this extended text the fact that Christ is the Redeemer of His elect people is declared with absolute certainty.

Ephesians 5:25–27. In which passage Christ is revealed as both loving the Church and giving Himself for it, that He might bring it with infinite purity and glory into His own possession and habitation.

In contemplating the Scriptures cited above, and many others of the same specific character, the unlimited redemptionists assert that it is the primary purpose of Christ to bring many sons into glory and that He never lost sight of this purpose; that it actuated Him in all His sufferings and death is beyond question, and that His heart is centered on those who are thus given to Him of the Father. However, not once do these passages exclude the truth, equally emphasized in the Scripture, that He died for the whole world. There is a difference to be noted between the *fact* of His death and the *motive* of His death. He may easily have died for all men with a view to securing His elect. In such a case, Christ would have been actuated by two great purposes: one, to pay the forensic ransom price for the world; the other, to secure His elect Body and Bride. The former of these purposes seems to be implied in such texts as Luke 19:10, "For the Son of man is come to seek and to save that which was lost," and John 3:17, "For God sent not his Son into the world to condemn the world; but that the world through him might be saved," while the latter seems to be implied in such passages as John 10:15, "As the Father knoweth me, even so know I the Father: and I lay down my life for the sheep." The Scriptures do not always include all the truth involved in the theme presented, at a given place. Similarly, if the fact that any reference to the nonelect world is omitted from these passages (which refer only to the elect) is a sufficient ground for the contention that Christ died only for the elect, then it could be argued with inexorable logic that Christ died only for Israel (cf. John 11:51; Isa. 53:8); and that He died only for the Apostle Paul, for Paul declares "who loved me, and gave himself for me" (Gal. 2:20). As well might one contend that Christ restricted His prayers to Peter because of the fact that He said to Peter: "But I have prayed for thee" (Luke 22:32). To the unlimited redemptionist these Scriptures present not the slightest difficulty. He interprets these great passages precisely as does his opponent. He believes in the sovereign election of God and the one and only heavenly purpose to gather out a redeemed people for heaven's glory. However, the limited redemptionist is not able to deal with the unlimited redemption passages as easily. Important passages may be grouped together thus:

1. PASSAGES WHICH DECLARE CHRIST'S DEATH TO BE FOR THE WHOLE WORLD (John 3:16; 2 Cor. 5:19; Heb. 2:9; 1 John 2:2). The limited redemptionist states that the use of the word *world* in these and similar passages is restricted to mean the world of the elect, basing the argument on the fact that the word *world* may at times be restricted in the extent of its scope and meaning. They claim that these universal passages, to be in harmony with the revelation that Christ died for an elect company, must be restricted to the elect. According to this interpretation, John 3:16 would read: "God so loved the elect, that He gave His only begotten Son, that whosoever [of the elect] believeth in Him should not perish, but have everlasting life." 2 Corinthians 5:19 would read: "God was in Christ, reconciling the elect unto Himself." Hebrews 2:9 would read: "He tasted death for every man of those who comprise the company of the elect." 1 John 2:2 would read: "He is the propitiation for our [the elect] sins: and not for our's only, but also for the sins of those who comprise the world of elect people." John 1:29 would read: "Behold the Lamb of God, which taketh away the sin of the elect."

A study of the word *cosmos* has been presented in Volume II. There it was seen that usually this word refers to a satanic system which is antigod in character, though in a few instances it refers to the unregenerate people who are in the *cosmos*. Three passages serve to emphasize the antipathy which obtains between the saved, who are "chosen out of the world," and the world itself: "If the world hate you, ye know that it hated me before it hated you. If ye were of the world, the world would love his own: but because ye are not of the world, but I have chosen you out of the world, therefore the world hateth you" (John 15:18–19); "They are not of the world, even as I am not of the world" (John 17:16); "And we know that we are of God, and the whole world lieth in wickedness" (1 John 5:19). Yet, in support of a theory, it is claimed that the elect, which the world hates and from which it has been saved, is the "world." Dr. Shedd points to certain specific passages. To quote: "Sometimes it is the world of believers, the church. Examples of this use are: John 6:33, 51, 'The bread of God is he which giveth life to the world' [of believers]. Rom. 4:13, Abraham is 'the heir of the world' [the redeemed]. Rom. 11:12, 'If the fall of them be the riches of the world.' Rom. 11:15, 'If the casting away of them be the reconciling of

the world.' In these texts, 'church' could be substituted for 'world' "
(*Dogmatic Theology*, II, 479). It is an assumption, quite foreign to Dr.
Shedd, to declare that the word *ecclesia*—called-out ones—should be
substituted for the word *cosmos* in these passages. Not one of them requires consideration in any other light than that usually accorded to
the satanic system.

2. PASSAGES WHICH ARE ALL-INCLUSIVE IN THEIR SCOPE (2 Cor.
5:14; 1 Tim. 2:6; 4:10; Titus 2:11; Rom. 5:6). Again, the limited redemptionist points out that in various passages the word *all* is restricted
to the elect. Indeed, such passages must be restricted if the cause of
the limited redemptionist is to stand—but are these properly so restricted? By the limited redemptionist's interpretation, 2 Corinthians
5:14 would read: "If one died for the elect, then were the elect dead."
1 Timothy 2:6 would read: "who gave Himself a ransom for the elect,
to be testified in due time." 1 Timothy 4:10 would read: "who is the
Saviour of the elect, especially of those who believe." Titus 2:11 would
read: "The grace of God that bringeth salvation hath appeared unto
the elect." Romans 5:6 would read: "In due time Christ died for the
elect, in their ungodly estate."

3. PASSAGES WHICH OFFER A UNIVERSAL GOSPEL TO MEN (John
3:16; Acts 10:43; Rev. 22:17, etc.). The word *whosoever* is used at least
110 times in the New Testament, and always with the unrestricted
meaning.

4. A SPECIAL PASSAGE, 2 Peter 2:1, wherein the ungodly false teachers of the last days who bring swift destruction upon themselves are said
to "deny the Lord that bought them." Men are thus said themselves
to be ransomed who deny the very ground of salvation and who are
destined to destruction.

Two statements may be in order in concluding this division of this
discussion:

(a) The interpretation of John 3:16 which the limited redemptionist offers tends to restrict the love of God to those among the unregenerate who are the elect. In support of this, passages are quoted
which declare God's peculiar love for His saved people. There is no
question that there is a "much more" expression of the love of God
for men after they are saved than before (Rom. 5:8–10), though His
love for unsaved men is beyond measure; but to assert that God loves
the elect in their unregenerate estate more than the nonelect, is an
assumption without Scriptural proof. Some limited redemptionists have
been bold enough to say that God does not love the nonelect at all.

(b) What if God did give His Son to die for all men of this dispensation in an equal sense, to the end that all might be legitimately invited to gospel privileges, could He, if actuated by such a purpose, use any more explicit language than He has used to express such an intent?

CONCLUSION

Again let it be said that to disagree with good and worthy teachers is undesirable, to say the least; but when these teachers appear on both sides of a question, as in the present discussion, there seems to be no alternative. By an inner bent of mind some men tend naturally to accentuate the measureless values of Christ's death, while others tend to accentuate the glorious results of the application of those values in the immediate salvation of the lost. The gospel must be understood by those to whom it is preached; and it is wholly impossible for the limited redemptionist, when presenting the gospel, to hide with any completeness his conviction that the death of Christ is only for the elect. And nothing could be more confusing to an unsaved person than to be drawn away from the consideration of the saving grace of God in Christ, to the contemplation of the question whether he is elect or not. Who can prove that he is of the election? If the preacher believes that some to whom he addresses his message could not be saved under any circumstances, those addressed have a right to know what the preacher believes and in time will know. Likewise, it is not wholly sincere to avoid the issue by saying the preacher does not know whether any nonelect are present. Are they absent from every service? Is it not reasonable to suppose that they are usually present when such a vast majority of humanity will probably never be saved at all? In this discussion of this and other problems respecting the value of Christ's death, no greater wrong could be imposed than that, by a philosophical contemplation of truths that are throbbing with glory, light, and blessing, the evangelistic fervor of even one who is called to preach salvation through Christ to lost men should be dampened. May the God who loved a lost world to the extent that He gave His own Son to die for that world, ever impart that passion of soul to those who undertake to convey the message of that measureless love to men!

THE SAVING WORK OF THE
TRIUNE GOD

CHAPTER XI

THE FINISHED WORK OF CHRIST

RESPECTING THE THEME now under consideration, no words of Scripture more accurately or completely describe the destiny-determining truth that God is the Author, Executor, and Consummator of man's salvation than Jonah 2:9 and Psalm 3:8. These texts assert: "Salvation is of Jehovah" and "Salvation belongeth unto Jehovah." Though the references, like all in the Old Testament, contemplate those aspects of salvation which are peculiar to the old order—often extending no further than to imply that God's covenant people were delivered from their enemies—these uncomplicated and conclusive declarations serve as well to set forth the truth regarding the broader field of divine undertaking in man's salvation as recorded in the New Testament. The gospel preacher should ever be on his guard lest by so much as an inference or intimation he violate or contradict the transcendent revelation that salvation is of Jehovah. Not the slightest insinuation should ever be advanced which implies that man might share in, or contribute to, that final consummation in eternal glory. Again, reason as well as revelation may serve to guide the mind; for, it will be seen, every step of the way from the divine election from before the foundation of the world (Eph. 1:4) to the presentation in faultless perfection in glory is superhuman and therefore must be wrought, if wrought at all, by Another who is mighty to save. At no point has Arminianism—and with it all other forms of rationalism—missed the way more completely than it has respecting the truth that salvation is of Jehovah, being misled—often in real sincerity—by the wholly irrelevant fact that God does instruct the one who is saved about his manner of life. Confusion and contradiction arise when these later life-responsibilities are allowed to enter as a part of the human requirements in salvation. By such teachers it is claimed that man is saved by the power of God through faith, provided he continues by good works to adorn the doctrine which he professes. No less subversive of the truth of divine grace is that disposition to require of the unsaved some form of meritorious works as a part of the human step in the initial stage of salvation. That salvation from its beginning to its end is all a work of God in response to saving faith uncomplicated by any form of human merit, virtue, or works, is the cornerstone in the whole structure of Soteriology. It is true, a saved person may do things for God; but the reality of his salvation is due alone to the truth that God has done things for him. Too often this essential feature of salvation is acknowledged as a theory and then, for want of due consideration or consistency, such human requirements are imposed on the unsaved as the condition of their salvation as deny the fundamental truth that salvation is by faith alone. In this introductory word only a passing reference to these issues may be made, which issues, later on (Chapter XX), must be considered with utmost attention.

To the same end that clarity may prevail, it is essential to recognize that the "salvation [which] is of Jehovah" includes the three Persons of the Godhead as actively engaged in the realization of this stupendous undertaking. It has been demonstrated in previous pages that the central truth of Soteriology is the fact that the Second Person became incarnate and died a sacrificial death; however, when salvation is viewed in its broader aspects, it is seen to be wrought as fully by the First Person and the Third Person. In every aspect of saving grace the three Persons are concurring. Even when hanging on the cross, the Son was not alone in His vast achievement. It was God who was in Christ reconciling the world unto Himself; the Father was offering His Lamb; and that sacrifice was offered through the eternal Spirit (Heb. 9:14).

The entire scope of the divine undertaking by which a person may be saved and presented faultless before the presence of His glory is here to be contemplated—and without reference to that divine election which was before all time—under seven general divisions, namely, (1) the finished work of Christ, (2) the convicting work of the Spirit (Chap. XII), (3) the riches of divine grace (Chap. XIII), (4) the doctrine of security (Chaps. XIV–XVII), (5) deliverance from the reigning power of sin, (6) deliverance from human limitations (Chap. XVIII), and (7) the believer presented faultless (Chap. XIX).

No apology is to be made for the renewal of the discussion of the finished work of Christ. It inheres as an essential factor of the present theme. The consideration of it again is safe for the student since it is fundamental to a right understanding of the gospel of divine grace, and must undergird every worthy presentation of it.

Attention has been called before to the truth that what is termed *the finished work of Christ* includes a threefold contemplation of the value of Christ's death as related to the unsaved. That death is a redemption toward sin, a reconciliation toward man, and a propitiation toward God. No one, or even two, of these aspects of Christ's death for the unsaved will represent a full exhibition of that specific phase of His death. All three are required; but the three together form a perfect whole which is properly termed *the finished work of Christ*. No aspect of the sin problem can be conceived which does not find its solution in this three-fold achievement. With sufficient consideration of these aspects of doctrine, the student will early arrive at the point where the theological usage by which all that Christ wrought in His death is referred to as *redemption* will be judged as misleading, and the mind will require as clear a recognition of the facts of *reconciliation* and *propitiation* as of *redemption*. He will as certainly depart from the theological tradition that these are synonymous terms which relate to one and the same thing. Since these three aspects of Christ's accomplishment in His death are so foundational to all features of Soteriology, reference must be made to them in subsequent discussion, as they have been considered in that which has gone before.

Argument could not arise against the truth that the finished work of Christ is altogether and only a work of God for man to which man could make no contribution whatever. Men, indeed, had their part in the crucifixion of Christ (Acts 4:27–28), but only as the perpetrators of the greatest crime in the universe. These effective factors in Christ's death for the unsaved are not even remotely within the range of human cooperation. In relation to this threefold work of Christ, man can sustain no part in it other than to *believe* that it avails for him. To those who believe, the whole value of Christ's finished work is reckoned and, because of that reckoning, they stand at once redeemed from condemnation because of sin, reconciled with respect to their own relation to God, and sheltered perfectly under that satisfaction which Christ offered to outraged holiness. By so much, the one who believes is forevermore upon a peace footing with God (Rom. 5:1). These immeasurable benefits to fallen man are incomprehensible; but though the sum total of all the divine blessings which are gained through the death of Christ be added into one vast whole, that mighty sum is small indeed as compared with the value to God Himself of that which Christ wrought by His death upon the cross.

As a designed purpose, the salvation of men had its origin in God and accomplishes an objective which answers the divine intent with that infinity of perfection which characterizes every work of God. As for relative importance, the realization of His aim is not only the major goal in view, but is the whole of that aim. That men are rescued from eternal misery is but an integral aspect of the entire objective; for it will not be overlooked that neither the creation of the universe, including all moral beings, nor the fall of man was imposed upon God as a necessity. It is not difficult to deduce from that supreme divine pronouncement—Colossians 1:15–19: "Who is the image of the invisible God, the firstborn of every creature: for by him were all things created, that are in heaven, and that are in earth, visible and invisible, whether they be thrones, or dominions, or principalities, or powers: all things were created by him, and for him: and he is before all things, and by him all things consist. And he is the head of the body, the church: who is the beginning, the firstborn from the dead; that in all things he might have the preeminence. For it pleased the Father that in him should all fulness dwell"—that creation, including angels and men, is wrought by the Second Person, the Savior of the world, and for Him, and that every adhesion by which the universe holds together and every progression in the march of time is due to His immediate presence, support, and power. Supreme above all is His headship in relation to the Church, and by the Church all fulness of satisfaction is secured to God; for there is that in the Church which corresponds to "the riches of the glory of his inheritance in the saints." Upon the divine side, the salvation of men is not merely a rescuer's expedition or heroism. It is of surpassing import to fallen men that they may be saved; but back of that is a divine project the realization of which is in itself important enough to justify the creation of a universe, the incarnation of the Second Person, and His sacrificial death. It follows that the bringing of many sons unto glory (Heb. 2:10) achieves more for the One by whom it is designed and wrought than for the sons who are glorified. Every step God is taking in this great achievement makes its permanent contribution to that which will glorify Him henceforth and forever.

It may be concluded that, by the death of Christ as a redemption toward sin, a reconciliation toward man, and a propitiation toward God, a higher morality is developed by which the Holy One, who cannot look upon sin with the least degree of allowance, is able to remain just while He justifies the ungodly who do no more than to believe in Jesus (Rom. 3:26; 4:5).

CHAPTER XII

THE CONVICTING WORK OF THE SPIRIT

WHAT IS PRESENTED in this general division is based on the truth that there are two necessities underlying the salvation of a soul, namely, (1) a righteous dealing with the problem of human sin—and this God has consummated in the gift of His Son as the Lamb who took away the sin of the world—and (2) a free choice of salvation on the part of man and in view of the fact that God recognizes the free will of man for what He created it to be. It is reasonable to conclude that as man by an act of his will renounced God at the beginning, in like manner he, by the act of his own will, must return to God. It matters nothing at this point that man cannot of himself turn to God and that he must be enabled to do so. In the end, though enabled, he acts by his own will and this truth is emphasized in every passage wherein the salvation of man is addressed to his will. "Whosoever will may come."

The present chapter aims to point out that aspect of the saving work of God by which He, by the Spirit, exerts an influence upon the unsaved by which they may make an intelligent acceptance of Christ as Savior and by which they are caused to desire the salvation which Christ provides. It is as definitely contended that, apart from this divine influence, no unregenerate person will ever turn to God. From this it will be seen that, next to the accurate and faithful presentation of the gospel of saving grace, no truth is more determining respecting all forms of evangelism than this. It is in connection with this specific enabling work of the Spirit that the sovereign election of God is manifested. Only those are included whom God *calls, draws,* and *enlightens.* The gospel is to be preached to all, but not all will respond to it. Because of the fact that not all do respond to the gospel, earnest evangelists and preachers have often been distressed, supposing that stronger appeals, mightier arguments, and greater personal influence would bring those who are indifferent to Christ as Savior, thus ignoring this all-determining preliminary work of the Spirit by which alone unregenerate people may believe. Outward actions have been stressed in soul-winning—actions which may be performed apart from any heart-acceptance of Christ as Savior.

These outward professions have too often been counted as salvation. Because of the fact that such superficial avowals prove spurious, doctrines have been encouraged which allow for the possibility of surrendering saving faith. Since it is clearly indicated that one hundred percent of those predestinated are called, and one hundred percent of those called are justified, and one hundred percent of those justified are glorified (Rom. 8:30), the evangelist does well to consider the importance of the divine call by which the heart is inclined and sufficiently enlightened to act intelligently on its own account and by its own volition in the glad acceptance of Christ as Savior. Only confusion and spiritual darkness can result when, apart from this illuminating divine call, the unsaved are forced by human pressure into professions which have no origin in the heart itself. No ground is found in the Bible for the Arminian notion of a general bestowment of grace whereby all men are able to respond to the gospel appeal; yet such a belief, along with the added error that those once saved can be lost again, has encouraged soul-winners to press the unsaved into outward assumptions and expressions which have no depth of conviction behind them. Such profession must end in failure; but little consideration has been given to the damage which is done to the soul that attempts such man-impelled professions and finds them to fail. Any method or appeal which encourages men to do aught other than to *believe* on Christ is fraught with dangers which are infinite and eternal. It is true that only the elect will believe; but what misrepresentation of, and insult to, God's faithfulness is engendered when, because of wrong doctrine and misleading appeals, a theory must be propounded and defended which contradicts God's unconditional covenant that those predestinated will be called, justified, and glorified.

The extended truth related to that work of the Spirit in the human heart which precedes salvation and which makes salvation possible will be considered under three divisions, namely, (1) the need of the Spirit's work, (2) the fact of the Spirit's work, and (3) the result of the Spirit's work.

I. THE NEED OF THE SPIRIT'S WORK

Dr. A. A. Hodge distinguishes three meanings in the word *inability* as it applies to men—it is *absolute*, *natural*, and *moral*. He writes:

It is *absolute* in the proper sense of that term. No unregenerate man has power either directly or indirectly to do what is required of him in this respect; nor to change his own nature so as to increase his power; nor to *prepare* himself for grace, nor in *the first instance* to co-operate with grace, until in the act of regeneration God changes his nature and gives him through grace gracious ability to act graciously in constant dependence upon grace. It is *natural* in the sense that it is not accidental or adventitious but innate, and that it belongs to our fallen nature as propagated by natural law from parent to child since the fall. It is *not* natural in *one* sense, because it does not belong to the nature of man as created. Man was created with plenary ability to do all that was in any way required of him, and the possession of such ability is always requisite to the moral perfection of his nature. He may be a real man without it, but can be a perfect man only with it. The ability graciously bestowed upon man in re-generation is not an endowment extra-natural, but consists in the restoration of his nature, in part, to its condition of primitive integrity. *It* is *not* natural in another sense, because it does not result in the least from any constitutional deficiency in human nature as it now exists as to its rational and moral faculties of soul. This inability is purely *moral,* because while every responsible man possesses all moral as well as intellectual faculties requisite for right action, the moral *state* of his faculties is such that right action is impossible. Its *essence* is in the inability of the soul to know, love, or choose spiritual good, and its *ground* exists in that moral corruption of soul whereby it is blind, insensible, and totally averse to all that is spiritually good.—*Outlines of Theology,* pp. 340–41

And Dr. W. Lindsay Alexander also states:

The inability of man to deliver himself from guilt and condemnation arises from want of power to do what is requisite for the attaining of the object; the inability of man to be good and holy arises from a want of will or inclination to do what he has the power physically to do. Strictly speaking, the inability in this latter case is simply confirmed indisposition to do what is right, arising from spiritual blindness and depravity. Man has not lost the capacity to be holy; he has not ceased to be a free agent, choosing what he prefers, and determining his own acts; he is under no external force preventing him from being holy. The spiritual inability under which he lies is that of a mind set against God, destitute of the principle of spiritual vitality and activity, through carnality and worldliness and sinful indulgence incapable of discerning the beauty of holiness, and so environed and permeated by selfishness that all true love to God is excluded from it. This is a real inability, inasmuch as it hinders and prevents man from being holy, though it does not destroy his capacity for being holy.—*System of Biblical Theology,* I, 324

However, the objective in the immediate discussion is not to demonstrate the general inability of fallen man—to which fact the Scriptures bear abundant proof—but to make evident the more specific truth that unregenerate men are not able to take one step, apart from the enabling power of the Spirit, in the direction of their salvation. The Arminian error which avers that a general and universal grace is given to all men by which they, if they will, may turn to God is exposed and reproved by a large body of Scripture, and no Scripture is found which sustains this error. Several of these vital passages may well be considered at this point:

Romans 3:10–18. "As it is written, There is none righteous, no, not one: there is none that understandeth, there is none that seeketh after God. They are all gone out of the way, they are together become unprofitable; there is none that doeth good, no, not one. Their throat is an open sepulchre; with their tongues they have used deceit; the poison of asps is under their lips: whose mouth is full of cursing and bitterness: their feet are swift to shed blood: destruction and misery are in their ways: and the way of peace have they not known: there is no fear of God before their eyes."

Following the disclosure set forth in Romans 3:9 of the age-characterizing truth that Jews and Gentiles are now alike divinely reckoned to be "under sin," which means that they are without merit in respect to their salvation, an unqualified condemnation, asserted in verses 10–18, is said to rest upon all men. Of the various affirmations in this context, one directly precludes the idea that unregenerate people of this age have ability in themselves to turn to God. This Scripture declares: "There is none that seeketh after God." In spite of this far-reaching statement, men have too often been urged to "seek the LORD while he may be found" (Isa. 55:6), not discovering the wide difference between the restoration of a covenant people and the present estate of the human race—Jew and Gentile alike—"under sin." In the present age there is but One that is seeking. Luke 19:10 records Christ's own words, "For the Son of man is come to seek and to save that which was lost." Thus it is seen to be by divine initiative alone that any from among the lost are, in this age, brought to the place where they embrace the salvation which is in Christ Jesus. A portion of this Romans passage, it will be seen, is quoted from Psalm 14:1–3; yet it is clear that, while the Psalm exhibits the natural wickedness of man as common to all ages and a distinct Old Testament revelation, it omits the *specific* declaration that none are seeking after God, thus perhaps implying that the inability to seek is not only true, but has a particular manifestation in the present age of grace.

1 Corinthians 2:14. "But the natural man receiveth not the things of the Spirit of God: for they are foolishness unto him: neither can he know them, because they are spiritually discerned."

The "things of the Spirit of God" which the unregenerate man is here said to be unable to receive include a vast field of revelation, but none more in evidence than the Scriptures which invite men to God and which extend to them the many wonderful promises. To the unsaved, these Scriptures are "foolishness," and, owing to their inability, they are disqualified from knowing or receiving these things of God. Romans 8:7 bears on this same incapacity: "Because the carnal mind is enmity against God: for it is not subject to the law of God, neither indeed can be." Likewise, Romans 1:21 asserts that, having rejected God in the beginning of the human race, men "became vain in their imaginations, and their foolish heart was darkened." Here, as before, much more than depravity is published. It is the inability of man to turn to God apart from divine enablement, which is disclosed.

2 Corinthians 4:3–4. "But if our gospel be hid, it is hid to them that are lost: in whom the god of this world hath blinded the minds of them which believe not, lest the light of the glorious gospel of Christ, who is the image of God, should shine unto them."

This will be concluded at once to be the most direct and decisive passage bearing on the question whether the unsaved have any power, apart from immediate divine enlightenment, to turn to God in saving faith. It is the gospel—by which alone men are saved—which has been veiled by Satan to the end that its truth should not reach them. Men are not blinded with regard to morals, education, and those things which make for refinement. Upon those and similar themes all may attend without difficulty and within the range of their native ability. On the other hand, as all experienced soul-winners must recognize, the unsaved remain unimpressed with the way of salvation until they are awakened by the Spirit, and when awakened, their response and enthusiasm is a marvel to behold. This blinding is said to be wrought by Satan, and it is implied that it is one of his strategies in the execution of his purpose to defeat God in His grace toward lost men. This satanic effort to defeat God is to be expected from all that has transpired between God and Satan in past ages, and in the light of the fact that a soul when saved is translated "from the power of darkness" (Col. 1:13) and becomes a witness against Satan in this sphere of his activity. The same truth that the mind of the unsaved is blinded is declared in Ephesians 4:18: "having the understanding darkened, being alienated from the life of God through the ignorance that is in them, because of the blindness of their heart." In the light of this Scripture, little ground remains on which the notion may rest which avers that man is able, apart from immediate divine enablement, to turn to God in saving faith.

Ephesians 2:1–3. "And you hath he quickened, who were dead in trespasses and sins: wherein in time past ye walked according to the course of this world, according to the prince of the power of the air, the spirit that now worketh in the children of disobedience: among whom also we all had our conversation in times past in the lusts of our flesh, fulfilling the desires of the flesh and of the mind; and were by nature the children of wrath, even as others."

An estate in spiritual death is by the Apostle thus said to characterize all the "children of disobedience"; and since this disobedience refers to the first sin of the federal head of the race, the term *children of disobedience* includes all who are unsaved—those who have not, by being united to the resurrected Christ, come under the blessing made possible through the obedience of Christ (Phil. 2:8). The estate of spiritual death is universal, and no more should be expected of a spiritually dead person than he is able to produce. Being, as this passage declares, under Satan's control, no revolutionary, independent turning to God will be permitted. Those in Satan's power will turn to God only as One who is greater in power than Satan moves them so to turn.

Akin to this specific revelation is that written in 1 John 5:19: "And we know that we are of God, and the whole world lieth in wickedness." It requires more understanding concerning angelic realities than human beings possess to comprehend the meaning of the word κεῖμαι, here translated *lieth*, which implies a vital, if not organic, union between the unsaved and Satan. Out of such a relationship no individual may hope to be released apart from divine deliverance.

John 3:3. "Jesus answered and said unto him, Verily, verily, I say unto thee, Except a man be born again, he cannot see the kingdom of God."

According to this passage, the incapacity of the unsaved is to a marked degree emphasized by Christ. The kingdom of God is that spiritual realm into which one may enter only by a birth from above, and which, though infinitely real and rich in its essentials, cannot be seen or comprehended by unregenerate men. There is special force in this unqualified assertion by Christ in view of the fact that it was addressed to one of the most faithful and religious men of his day. The truth that the most conscientious of Judaism needed a new birth, which evidently he little understood, should not be overlooked. No discredit is implied respecting the great factors and blessings which Judaism secured; but it is clearly demonstrated here, as everywhere that this truth appears, that a new and marvelous reality is introduced by the death and resurrection of Christ and by the advent of the Holy Spirit. It is in the range of these new and measureless blessings that the inability of the unsaved to "see the kingdom of God" is demonstrated.

John 6:44. "No man can come to me, except the Father which hath sent me draw him: and I will raise him up at the last day."

The counterpart passage—"No man cometh unto the Father, but by me" (John 14:6)—declares the truth that there is but one way for the lost to be saved (cf. Acts 4:12; Heb. 7:25); but the passage under consideration discloses the truth that none will ever come to the Savior apart from the immediate drawing power of God. The statement is unqualified and final. The message presented is so important that the Savior goes on to say: "It is written in the prophets, And they shall be all taught of God. Every man therefore that hath heard, and hath learned of the Father, cometh unto me" (John 6:45).

The present discussion involves the whole doctrine of the divine call. There is a general drawing which is exercised wherever and whenever Christ is preached as Savior (John 12:32), but such should not be confused with the specific and irresistible drawing to which reference is made in John 6:44. Of all who are thus drawn, the Savior could say with an unqualified assurance, "And I will raise him up at the last day." Likewise, there is a general call which may be felt whenever the gospel is preached, and it, too, may be resisted, as it often is; but over against this is the efficacious call of Romans 8:30. In this passage, as before observed, it is assured that everyone whom God predestinates is called, and the precise numerical company, again, of those called are justified, and that same company—no more and no less—are to be glorified. The lost are not said here, or elsewhere, to originate their own steps toward God; rather it is as His sovereignty determines.

Ephesians 2:8–9. "For by grace are ye saved through faith; and that not of yourselves: it is the gift of God: not of works, lest any man should boast."

So conclusive is this passage relative to man's inability in the field of saving faith that much has been attempted in the way of exegesis which proposes to make the salvation the gift of God, rather than the faith which receives it. When thus interpreted, the phrase "through faith" is practically eliminated and serves no purpose. The contrast which the passage sets up between faith and works becomes a contrast between salvation and works, for which there is no ground either in Scripture or reason. If the passage stood alone in the Word of God, declaring a truth not elsewhere propounded, some reason might be assigned to such exegetical attempts which divest the context of its assured meaning;

but, when rightly interpreted, it stands out as but one of many of the same general character.

Though much Scripture of an indirect nature might be cited, enough has been presented to establish the doctrine of man's natural inability to exercise saving faith. Were men able to move themselves toward God, there would be no provision from God for this need. The fact that such enablement is provided argues in favor of man's inability. It is too often supposed that the only restraint upon unregenerate persons in the sphere of their ability to turn to God, is their natural disinclination or prejudice. The Arminian error regarding a universal grace is largely responsible for such suppositions. If Christian workers cannot move the unsaved out of the power of Satan by argument and persuasion, a far more effective way is open and that is prayer. It is probable that God has included prayer as one of the divinely ordained means for the calling out and saving of His elect people. Prayer is not a provision by which men may secure something outside the elective will of God; it is rather one of the ordained steps in the realization of that will.

II. THE FACT OF THE SPIRIT'S WORK

One passage, which records the words of Christ in the upper room and which anticipates the peculiar features of the present age, declares specifically the fact that the Holy Spirit undertakes a work in the hearts of unregenerate men which is quite evidently not their regeneration, but may be defined as a preparation of the mind to the end that an intelligent choice of Christ as Savior may be made. In the light of the Scriptures just considered, there would be no hope of the salvation of any individual in this age apart from this particular ministry of the Spirit. The passage which stands quite alone respecting this work of the Spirit, reads as follows: "Nevertheless I tell you the truth; It is expedient for you that I go away: for if I go not away, the Comforter will not come unto you; but if I depart, I will send him unto you. And when he is come, he will reprove the world of sin, and of righteousness, and of judgment: of sin, because they believe not on me; of righteousness, because I go to my Father, and ye see me no more; of judgment, because the prince of this world is judged" (John 16:7–11).

Evidently, this specific work is wrought in behalf of the *cosmos* world, but, of necessity, it is directed, not to the *cosmos* as a whole, but to the individual. All that the Spirit undertakes in this ministry is indicated by the word ἐλέγχω, which has been variously translated *reprove, con-*

vince, convict, etc. The word determines so much at this point that it must not be passed over lightly.

The thought expressed by ἐλέγχω is not at all of the creation of sorrow in the heart, but rather of an illumination or enlightenment respecting certain truths which the Lord was careful to enumerate; that is, the enlightenment will be along three lines—"sin, because they believe not on me"; "righteousness, because I go to my Father, and ye see me no more"; and "judgment, because the prince of this world is judged." This ministry is one which is accomplished in the heart itself, by which the whole being responds to realities which had not been recognized before. In contrast with this ministry to the unsaved, an enlightening, or teaching, ministry is undertaken on a much wider scale in the heart of the one who is saved. This wider ministry is described and defined in the verses which follow in the same context (John 16:12–15).

These three features of revelation now under consideration—sin, righteousness, judgment—as defined in their scope by the Lord, constitute the essentials of the gospel of divine grace.

1. "OF SIN." In view of a finished work by Christ wherein sin is borne and all blessings are secured, the immeasurable failure for the individual for whom Christ has died is that he does not *believe* on Him. It is noticeable, though contrary to general opinion, that the Spirit does not enlighten the mind with respect to all the sins the individual has committed. It is not a matter of creating shame or remorse concerning sin, nor is it so much as a reminder of sin that has been committed—though there is nothing, on the other hand, to preclude sorrow or consciousness of sin; it is rather that, since sin has been borne by Christ, there remains the one great and only responsibility of one's attitude toward the Savior who bore the sin. This unbelief the Lord declared is the basis of final condemnation, when He said: "He that believeth on him is not condemned: but he that believeth not is condemned already, because he hath not believed in the name of the only begotten Son of God" (John 3:18). To make the unsaved realize this is a task too great for the preacher; it must be accomplished by the Holy Spirit, and He will so reveal this specific truth to the unsaved, within the elective divine purpose, as the gospel is preached to them. The fact indicated in this text, that the one ground of condemnation is the failure to *believe* on Christ as Savior, confirms the truth, restated more than one hundred times in the New Testament, that the one and only condition of salvation is faith in Christ as Savior. Only the elect will believe and even these will do so through the enlightening ministry of the Spirit alone. However,

though no complete explanation is given of all that is involved, those who do not believe, as indicated in John 3:18, are held accountable for not believing. Unfallen man would experience no such difficulty in the realms of faith; and since his present incapacity is so largely due to that original separation from God which the first sin wrought, there is, possibly, a partial solution to this problem which these Scriptures set up.

The testimony of this portion of the truth is, then, that it is the work of the Spirit to enlighten the unsaved with respect to the one determining sin, that they believe not on Christ.

2. "OF RIGHTEOUSNESS." Since imputed righteousness is the only form of righteousness included in salvation by grace and since this context presents only those most vital truths related to man's salvation which the Holy Spirit reveals, it is clear that the reference here is to imputed righteousness—that perfect righteousness of God which Christ is and which the believer becomes when in Christ. The whole issue is of a perfect standing before God—far more, indeed, than the removal of sin by forgiveness. It is that which God bestows on "him that worketh not" (Rom. 4:5); and of the greatest importance is the truth that the one who would be saved shall come to know that he is not entering into a merit arrangement, which would demand of him that he produce his own righteousness as a basis of acceptance before God. Gospel preaching has made much of the remission of sin through the redemption that is in Christ Jesus, and not more than should be; but a deplorable neglect has been accorded the equally requisite truth that a perfect standing is imputed also to the one who believes. The truth of the gospel, as outlined in John 16:7-11, is presented in a full-orbed perfection. Wherein it exceeds man's restricted discernment of the gospel will but serve to demonstrate the inattention of men to the paramount theme. As over against this careless notion that any kind of a statement will serve as a gospel message, attention should again be drawn to the unrevoked anathema of Galatians 1:8-9. So little, indeed, is the fact and value of imputed righteousness comprehended—due to a large extent to the neglect of it—that it is not easy to develop this truth to the same level of realization to which the more accentuated verity of forgiveness of sin has attained. There can be no question that the two ideas—imputed righteousness and remission of sin—are, as a challenge to the human understanding, incomparable, largely due, it would seem, to the obvious fact that remission of sin is a more or less common experience in human relationships, while the imputation of righteousness has no parallel in human experience outside that set forth in the gospel. However, were these to be compared,

that which is constructive and positive, as imputed righteousness is, will be held in higher regard by those who understand it than remission of sin, which is only negative in character. What could contribute more to peace of mind and heart than the consciousness that one has become the assured recipient of a perfect and eternal standing before God?

To the extent that the great truth of imputed righteousness is foreign to human experience and to the extent that it is grounded on an invisible Person in heaven rather than on self or any human ability or character, to that degree its presentation to darkened, unregenerate minds must be supernaturally wrought by the Holy Spirit. This is precisely what He does when He convicts of righteousness. It is not affirmed that the unsaved individual must understand the complex doctrine of imputed righteousness before he can be saved; it is rather maintained that the truth that a complete standing and acceptance before God, which renders unnecessary all works of human merit, shall be comprehended and that this perfect standing proceeds from Christ and is based on a new and vital union set up between Christ and the one who believes. Here is introduced a supernatural feature of the gospel. Divine forgiveness of sin is also a supernatural accomplishment when based on the death of Christ; but far too often forgiveness of sin is computed to be no more than a divine benevolence or generosity.

A marked distinction is to be noted between that form of righteousness which man produces and proposes to offer to God as the basis of his acceptance, and that form of righteousness which God has made available and presents to man. In God's plan of salvation, man ceases from his own works and enters into rest; for there remaineth an unending sabbath rest from all works of merit for those who believe (Heb. 4:9–10). So far as the unsaved are concerned, the requirements are met when by the specific enlightenment of the Spirit they recognize that Christ as Savior answers every need of the human heart for time and eternity. This is a far different overture than the proposition that sin may be forgiven. It extends to the larger constructive fact that a perfect righteousness is imputed to all who believe. The essential fact that the Holy Spirit is appointed so to enlighten the mind of unsaved man respecting imputed righteousness, indicates conclusively that this great truth should be included as a major factor in all gospel preaching to the unsaved. The ambitious student, bent on excelling as an effective and accurate preacher of the gospel, would do well to learn—even by tireless effort—the great doctrine of imputed righteousness.

3. "OF JUDGMENT." No reference is made by this phrase to a judg-

ment to come; the reference is rather to the greatest of all judgments, which is now past and was accomplished by Christ as Substitute when He died the Just for the unjust, when the immeasurable billows of God's hatred of sin swept over the One who had become a sin offering for those for whom He died. This judgment, it is revealed, did concern Satan the prince of this world, but in a sense far deeper than a mere judgment of the person of that great being. The judgment accomplished infinite results for the unsaved and of these results the Holy Spirit would cause them to be enlightened.

The human mind can conceive of nothing more hopeless or helpless than a fallen human being for whom Christ did not die. Such, to an unrevealed degree, was the estate of humanity before the cross—excepting those of one nation with whom covenants were made and who had the advantage of animal sacrifices that anticipated the values of Christ's death. It is true that the privilege of animal sacrifices was extended to humanity before the nation Israel began its history; but what the precise value of these sacrifices was is not revealed and the people did not long claim their benefits (Rom. 1:21). Apparently the very fact that no sacrifices were offered by these multitudes became the ground on which the people were claimed by Satan as his own subjects. In Isaiah 14:17, among the stupendous undertakings of Satan there enumerated, it is affirmed that Satan "opened not the door of his prisoners." Whether it was in his power to release them is, at this juncture, an unimportant question. It is enough to know that they were helpless in Satan's power. These people, with respect to helplessness, were not unlike the fallen angels for whom no sacrifice, so far as Scripture discloses, has ever been made. In the description of the mighty realities which Christ would accomplish in His first advent and which He Himself asserted were fulfilled when He came the first time, it is said that He came "to proclaim liberty to the captives, and the opening of the prison to them that are bound" (Isa. 61:1; cf. Luke 4:16–21).

The same truth—that Satan held a vast authority over men and that that authority was broken by Christ in His death—is recorded in Colossians 2:14–15, which reads: "Blotting out the handwriting of ordinances that was against us, which was contrary to us, and took it out of the way, nailing it to his cross; and having spoiled principalities and powers, he made a shew of them openly, triumphing over them in it." Here, as in John 16:11, it is taught that it was by and through the cross that Christ triumphed over Satan and his fallen angels. The passage (John 16:11) hardly declares that men are redeemed by Christ's triumph over Satan and his angels; it is rather that men are redeemed by the same death which served as a judgment of Satan and his angels, and by that death are released from that power which Satan exercised over them—as indicated in Colossians 1:13: "Who hath delivered us from the power of darkness, and hath translated us into the kingdom of his dear Son," and 1 John 5:19: "And we know that we are of God, and the whole world lieth in wickedness."

It is indicated that the Spirit will enlighten the unsaved with respect to judgment—both that their sins are judged and that the one is judged who, because of his assumed authority over the unsaved, holds them in his power. A central truth of the gospel is that Christ in His death as Substitute bore the sins of those who are lost, and there is no truth which needs more the illumination of the Spirit if it is to be disclosed to Satan-blinded minds. This enlightenment is of a work that is finished, to which nothing need be added and to which nothing could be added. It is a work finished as a redemption toward sin, a reconciliation toward the sinner, and propitiation toward God. The work is not something the sinner must persuade God to do, but is something perfectly accomplished, to which the unsaved can sustain no other relation than to believe what God has wrought in his behalf.

Thus it may be deduced that John 16:7–11 presents a truth of measureless import—a threefold work of the Spirit in behalf of the unsaved which is not to be confused with His larger ministries when, as a part of the salvation of men, He regenerates, indwells, baptizes, and seals; nor is this specific ministry of the Spirit in enlightening the unsaved to be confused with His service to those who are saved when He bears fruit in them, exercises gifts, teaches the Word of God, and intercedes in them. When the Spirit enlightens the Satan-blinded mind regarding sin, righteousness, and judgment, that otherwise blinded mind is at once more than normally enabled to understand the three great foundational truths that sin has been judged, righteousness is available in and through Christ, and the condemning sin is failure to believe that which God now offers the sinner, namely, a perfect salvation in and through Christ the Savior. No soul can be saved apart from this enlightenment, for no other power is sufficient to break through the blindness which Satan has imposed on the minds of those who are lost. It therefore follows that evangelism which is adjusted to God's Word will make a large place for this preliminary work of the Spirit and recognize that in answer to prayer alone the souls of lost men may be moved to believe on Christ.

III. THE RESULTS OF THE SPIRIT'S WORK

To a degree which allows of no exception, the Scriptures assert the supernatural inability of fallen men to turn to God in saving faith, apart from the supernatural unveiling of the mind which Satan has darkened. It is equally true that this divine enlightenment results in an ability to understand the gospel, which ability is augmented beyond that which is the natural competency of the individual thus blessed. Those thus favored enter into the riches of divine grace by a faith which God engenders. That faith, it is declared, is "not of yourselves: it is the gift of God" (Eph. 2:8). Such imparted or inwrought faith leads on to a personal transaction with Christ—that specific commitment without which no adult or accountable person will be saved. In this enlightenment the natural faculties of seeing and hearing are also enlarged. The blind receive their sight and can say, "Whereas I was blind, now I see"; and the deaf hear. Such likewise was the spiritual meaning of those miracles in which Christ gave sight to blind eyes and opened deaf ears. To these realities He referred when He said: "And this is the Father's will which hath sent me, that of all which he hath given me I should lose nothing, but should raise it up again at the last day. And this is the will of him that sent me, that every one which seeth the Son, and believeth on him, may have everlasting life: and I will raise him up at the last day. . . . It is written in the prophets, And they shall be all taught of God. Every man therefore that hath heard, and hath learned of the Father, cometh unto me" (John 6:39–40, 45). These passages exhibit the sovereignty of God, and no Scripture is more absolute about divine determination than verse 44 of this same context: "No man can come to me, except the Father which hath sent me draw him: and I will raise him up at the last day." It is here in the sphere of an effectual call that the divine election is realized. It is not determined on the basis of a theory that there is a selected company for whom alone Christ has died, nor are men saved because of anything good—actual or foreseen—in them. In sovereign grace God predestined and those whom He predestined, He called—no more and no less—and whom He called, He justified—no more and no less—and whom He justified, He glorified—no more and no less. The Arminian practice of intruding into this passage the human element by such phrases as, "if they will to hear the call" and, "if they remain faithful," etc., deserves the rebuke which belongs to those who distort the Word of God by adding thereto. By these four divine actions—predestinating, calling, justifying, glorifying—the sovereign elective choice of God is disclosed. Not one of these is so related to the death of Christ that it can be claimed that it is by His death God marks off those whom He has chosen for His eternal glory. The elect and no more will be called, justified, and glorified, and evangelism would do well to conform to this revelation and not pursue Arminian misunderstandings which propose that by methods incorporating human works of merit any person can, if he will, respond to the gospel of divine grace.

It is yet to be observed that the individual, unregenerate person must believe for himself. The reception of Christ as Savior must be by a choice which arises in the center of his own being and be a reflection of his own intelligent preference. Too often methods have been employed requiring mere outward actions which, though sincere, may indicate no heart experience; and those outward actions may be motivated by the earnest appeal of loved ones and friends who, being themselves saved, do appreciate the importance of a decision for Christ. The pressure of these outside influences has been, in many instances, the chief dependence of the evangelist for his apparent success in his work. It is often recognized that the evangelist to be a success must possess a dominating and even overpowering personality. This with other psychological influences which are skilfully employed amount to what is almost an irresistible effect. All this mass of influence may be focused upon the unsaved individual to compel him to do something which perchance is no choice of his own, nor has it a vestige of virtue in the realm of that which constitutes a decision for Christ. A few "converts" have held out and these have justified the methods used without due regard to the disastrous effect upon a soul of the one who, under such irrelevant influences, has made professions and taken positions which were unrelated to a true acceptance of Christ as Savior. The lost are saved when they hear the gospel under divine illumination, that is, when they hear and believe. "So then faith cometh by hearing, and hearing by the word of God" (Rom. 10:17). As certainly as this is true, it is the preacher's part to expect that souls will be saved *while* he is preaching, rather than after he has concluded his message and has given the unsaved something to do that they may be saved. There is a public testimony on the part of those who are saved; but this should not be confused with the simple requirement that the lost may be saved by personal faith in Christ as Savior. The appeal of the soul-winner is of value, for it has pleased God to commit the proclamation of the gospel to those who are appointed to preach the glad tidings.

Chapter XIII

THE RICHES OF DIVINE GRACE

THIS ASPECT of the saving work of the triune God, though restricted to those transformations which are divinely wrought for the individual at the moment he believes, is not only supremely important since it defines the character of salvation, but is almost limitless in extent. The restrictions imposed demand that a clear distinction be made between that which has been divinely undertaken by way of preparation for the salvation of a soul, and the salvation itself. Included in the sphere of preparation are such achievements as the finished work of Christ, the enlightening work of the Spirit, and all other influences which provide the righteous ground upon which a lost soul may be saved. It is no small undertaking so to deal with the sin question that there is infinite freedom accorded God in saving the lost; nor is it a small endeavor so to move the Satan-blinded individual that he will act by his own choice in the receiving of Christ as his Savior. These two problems, it will be remembered from previous statements, form the total of that which hinders the salvation of fallen men. To satisfy the divine demands, a perfect redemption, reconciliation, and propitiation are required, while the problem on the human side is that of man's free, moral agency and the need of such influences as shall insure the right choice of the human will. A clear distinction is also required between the divine work in the immediate salvation of the soul and those responsibilities and activities which belong to the Christian life and service. Many new realities are created by regeneration and all aspects of human experience are affected by the mighty transformation which salvation secures. With respect to the distinction between salvation itself and the life responsibilities which follow, Arminianism has again wrought confusion by its misunderstandings, assuming, as that system does, that the immediate salvation—whatever it is conceived to be—is probationary and therefore made to depend, with reference to its permanence, upon holy living and faithfulness. None would deny that a holy life becomes the Christian in view of the fact that he is a child of God and also of the truth that he is a member of Christ's Body; but to make sonship, which by its nature is interminable and is a position before God which rests wholly on the merit of Christ, to be conditioned by and dependent upon human worthiness is to contradict the whole order of divine grace and to make impotent man to be, in the end, his own savior.

The significant phrase, the "things that accompany salvation" (Heb. 6:9), may be interpreted as referring to those mighty positions and possessions which are wrought instantaneously and simultaneously by God at the instant an individual exercises saving faith in Christ. When recorded in detail—as they will yet be—it will be seen that there are at least thirty-three of these stupendous, supernatural divine undertakings and that the sum total of these achievements is the measure of the difference between one who is saved and one who is lost. The essential and all-determining fact that these divine accomplishments are wrought instantaneously and simultaneously and are never a progressive order or sequence, establishes the truth that all human beings may be, at a given time, classified as either perfectly lost—God having wrought none of these features of salvation for them—or perfectly saved—God having wrought completely and finally all that enters into the immediate salvation of a soul. There are no intermediate estates. Of no human being could it be said that he is partly saved and partly lost. In conformity with the New Testament, it must be maintained that all cultured, refined, educated, moral, and religious people—regardless of outward professions—who have not been saved by a personal faith in Christ are lost, and as perfectly lost as they would be had they none of these characteristics which, in their place, are of great value. It may be a problem whether an individual has entered into saving grace through Christ—and here there is need of a clear apprehension of the Biblical evidence of so great a change (cf. 2 Cor. 13:5; 1 John 5:13)—but there could be no problem involved with respect to the essential truth that, until perfectly saved by the infinite work of God, the soul is perfectly lost.

Similarly, the messages to be preached to these two classes—those perfectly lost and those perfectly saved—are, of necessity, different in every particular. It is to be doubted whether any text of Scripture will be found to be applicable to both classes alike. To the unsaved, God makes no appeal with regard to their manner of life; no improvement or reformation is required of them. Society and civil governments may press their claims upon unregenerate people as also upon regenerate people to the end that prescribed ideals may be realized, but this fact—in so far as it obtains—must not be confused with the uncompromised attitude of God in His relation to these classes. He requires of the unsaved that they hear and heed the gospel only. Over against this, every divine injunction concerning a God-honoring faithfulness is addressed to the Christian and from the moment he is saved. There are no elementary, curtailed, or diminished requirements which are tempered to those who are beginners in the great responsibility of Christian living. The Scriptures recognize "babes in Christ," but they are not such because of immaturity; they are babes because of carnality (1 Cor. 3:1–2), and that form of carnality may be exhibited by those who have been Christians for fifty years.

Next to the delinquency of misstating the gospel with its immeasurable penalty (Gal. 1:8–9), is the so prevalent practice on the part of preachers of presenting Christian-life truth to the unsaved without warning them that such truth is not addressed to them. By this performance, every suggestion which might arise in the mind of the unsaved that a vital difference might exist between themselves and Christians is obliterated, and the unsaved are encouraged to believe that a Christian is one who merely acts in a certain way and such actions are all that God requires of any person. No matter how unimportant it may seem to the preacher, he cannot afford ever to address Christians about their specific duties and not remind the unsaved, if such be present, that the word being spoken can have no application to them. Such faithful discrimination will have the effect, at least, of creating a consciousness in the minds of unregenerate people that they are lost.

The thirty-three divine undertakings in the salvation of a soul, which are here designated as *the riches of grace,* represent all that God can do to satisfy His own infinite love for the sinner. If at first consideration this statement seems to be extreme, it, in due time, will be demonstrated to be true. As asserted of an earlier point in this treatment of Soteriology, the primary motive which actuates God in the salvation of the lost is the satisfying of His own love. To the end that infinite love may be gratified, He accomplishes infinite transformations. Compared to this, the thought that men are rescued from their plight, though an achievement which transcends all human understanding and naturally appeals to the mind of man, is secondary to the extent that man is secondary to God. The truth that the salvation of men affords an opportunity for God to gratify His infinite love for His creatures, is a theme which is too often neglected. It will always be remembered that because of His divine character of holiness, God can do nothing for sinners until satisfaction for their sin has been secured—this is accomplished in the finished work of Christ— and that because of God's recognition of the free, moral agency of man,

God can do nothing apart from man's own elective choice of Christ as Savior—even though that choice is engendered in the heart of man by the enlightenment of the Spirit. But when these fundamental conditions are met, every barrier is removed and infinite love instantly responds by lavishing on the man who exercises saving faith the whole measure of divine benefit, even the riches of grace in Christ Jesus. This, it will be seen, is no less than the greatest thing that Almighty God can do. One consideration alone will serve to demonstrate this truth, namely, that the saved one is destined to be conformed to the image of Christ. Infinity can conceive of nothing beyond that exalted reality, nor can omnipotence accomplish more. To be conformed to the image of Christ, to have been purified to infinite perfection by the blood of cleansing, to have received the gift of eternal life, to be clothed upon with the righteousness of God, and to have been constituted a citizen of heaven disposes practically of all that enters into the estate of fallen humanity. This great transformation is well described by the words: "the Father, which hath made us meet to be partakers of the inheritance of the saints in light" (Col. 1:12); yet, of all these marvels, none could be greater than that of being conformed to the image of Christ (Rom. 8:29; 1 John 3:2).

Another revelation, which as perfectly demonstrates the truth that salvation in its immediate aspect is the supreme divine achievement, is recorded in Ephesians 2:7. In preparation for this declaration, the Apostle has mentioned one out of all the believer's possessions, namely, the gift of eternal life—announced by the words, "hath quickened us together with Christ"—and from all the believer's positions, one, namely, "in Christ Jesus," and these two represent the great reality of eternal salvation. The answer to the question of why God should undertake the measureless benefit for which these representative possessions and positions stand, is that by so great salvation God may manifest the attribute of grace, which could be manifested in no other way. Ephesians 2:7 declares: "That in the ages to come he might shew the exceeding riches of his grace in his kindness toward us through Christ Jesus." There was that in God which no created being had ever seen. They had seen His glory, His majesty, His wisdom, and His power; but no angel or man had ever seen His grace. Other attributes might be subject to a variety of demonstrations; but the manifestation of grace is restricted to what God may do for those among men who, in spite of the fact that they deserve His judgments, are objects of His grace. As every other attribute or capacity of God must have its perfect exercise and exhibition—even for His own satisfaction—in like manner His grace must also have its infinitely perfect revealing within the restricted undertaking by which He saves the lost. To say that a sinner is saved by grace is to declare that, on the ground of a Substitute's death and in response to faith in that Savior, God has wrought a work so perfect in its entirety and so free from the cooperation of other beings that it is a complete all-satisfying-to-God demonstration of His grace. A statement of this kind may be made as easily as words may form a sentence; but who on earth or in heaven is able to comprehend the infinity of such a salvation? This demonstration, it should be added, will, by the very nature of the case, have its outshining in the life of each individual thus saved. It may be assumed that, had but one of all the human family been selected for the supreme honor of exhibiting eternally before all created beings the infinity of sovereign grace, the salvation of that one would be no different than the salvation of any one of the unnumbered throng from every kindred, tribe, and people who are saved by grace.

Too often it is assumed that divine grace in salvation is a willingness on the part of God to complete in each person's life what, perchance, may be lacking when the individual's own merit has been duly valued, the thought being that, as some, because of human virtue and faithfulness in character, are possessed of more worthiness than others, less grace would be required for those of supposed merit than would be required for those of little or no merit. The truth, already treated at length in Volume II, is that all men are now divinely reckoned and declared to be "under sin"—a state in which no merit of man is accepted by God—to the end that a standardized grace, wholly complete in itself, may be bestowed upon all alike. Were men permitted to contribute the smallest fraction toward their salvation, it would cease to be a grace manifestation and become an imperfect display of one of God's most glorious attributes. No thoughtful person will conclude that a fallen being could, under any circumstances or to any degree, cause a divine attribute to become an experienced reality. Man may become the recipient of grace, but he cannot contribute to it in the sense that he enables it to become what it is. No more conclusive setting forth of this sublime truth will be found than that recorded in Romans 4:16, "Therefore it is of faith [nothing on man's part], that it might be by grace [everything on God's part]; to the end the promise might be sure to all the [Abrahamic] seed" (that which is of the flesh, Israel, and that which is of the Spirit, the elect from among the Gentiles). On what other basis than faith on man's part and grace on God's part could any divine promise or purpose be *sure?*

In concluding these introductory words, it may be restated that saving grace is that which God accomplishes on the ground of Christ's death —accomplished and provided as a divine responsibility—and in response to the individual's faith in Christ—a human responsibility. This general division of this theme will be presented in three parts: (1) the estate of the lost, (2) the essential character of God's undertakings, and (3) the riches of divine grace.

I. THE ESTATE OF THE LOST

The word *lost* is used in the New Testament in two widely different ways. An object may be lost in the sense that it needs to be found. This use of the word does not imply that a change in the structure or character of the lost object is thereby indicated. It is lost only to the extent that it is out of its rightful place. Israel wandering from their covenants were styled by Christ as "the lost sheep of the house of Israel" (Matt. 10:6). In like manner, a Christian who is out of fellowship with God because of sin is misplaced; yet he remains unchanged with respect to the essential realities which make him a child of God—eternal life, imputed righteousness, and union with God. The God-given illustration of this wonderful truth is declared in the threefold parable of Luke 15. A sheep is lost and is "found." It was a sheep all the time, but was out of its place. A coin is lost from its place in the woman's headdress and is "found." It was the same coin all the time. A son was lost and is "found." And he was a son in every step of his wanderings. On the other hand, a person may be lost in such a manner as to need to be *saved*. "The Son of man is come to seek and to save that which was lost" (Luke 19:10). It is because of the fact that in salvation the structural changes are such as to demand divine provisions and divine creative powers, that the transition from the lost estate to that of the saved can be wrought only by God.

The body of truth now being considered contemplates at least four reasons why those who are of this fallen race are lost:

1. The lost soul has attained to none of the eternal realities that make a Christian what he is. All that may be said of the unsaved is *negative*. No Scripture makes this clearer than Ephesians 2:12, in which the Ephesian Christians are reminded of the lost estate from which they were saved: "That at that time ye were without Christ, being aliens from the commonwealth of Israel, and strangers from the covenants of promise, having no hope, and without God in the world."

2. Individuals are lost, also, because of the fact that they are born with a fallen, sinful nature. This is no doubt the most condemning feature of man's lost estate. When Adam sinned, he experienced a conversion downward. He became an entirely different kind of being. After the fall, he could propagate only "in his own likeness," and his first son was a murderer. Adam—in whom Eve is reckoned as one—is the only human being who ever became a sinner by sinning. All other members of the race commit sin because they are born sinners. Though this evil nature remains in the Christian as long as he is in the world, it was judged for the Christian by Christ on the cross (Rom. 6:10), and its condemnation removed. The death of Christ unto the sin nature is also the ground of the believer's deliverance by the Holy Spirit from the power of inbred sin. It is true that men are lost because of personal sins; but, since personal sins are the normal fruit of the evil nature, they should never be made the only, or even important, basis upon which a soul is lost. In reply to a claim that he is lost because of personal sin, an unregenerate person might easily assert that he had never been one percent as evil as he might have been, therefore he is only one percent lost. The lost estate consists primarily in a fallen nature, which is one hundred percent evil. An effort to be good or to form a worthy character is a poor remedy for a fallen nature. Only the grace of God acting on the ground of the death of His Son will avail.

3. Again, men are lost because of a decree which God has made concerning all who live on earth—Jew and Gentile alike—in the present age, which age is bounded by the two advents of Christ. It is written: "What then? are we better than they? No, in no wise: for we have before proved both Jews and Gentiles, that they are all under sin" (Rom. 3:9); "But the scripture hath concluded all under sin, that the promise by faith of Jesus Christ might be given to them that believe" (Gal. 3:22). The phrase "under sin" means, as stated above, that God will accept the merit of no person as a contributing factor in his salvation. This decree, which eliminates all human merit, is essential if salvation is to be by grace. This does not imply that a good life is not of value in its place; but the issue under consideration is the problem of how a holy God can *perfectly* save those who, in His sight, are *perfectly* lost. He disregards that which men deem to be good—and some possess more of this goodness than others—that He may replace it with the perfection of Christ. What, for the moment, seems to be a complete loss, thus in the end becomes an infinite gain. Since, by the very way in which He saves the lost, God is preparing the material for a heavenly demonstra-

tion of the unsearchable riches of His grace (Eph. 2:7), the inclusion in this salvation of any human element is impossible.

4. Similarly and finally, men are lost because of the fact that they are under the power of Satan. Only the Word of God can speak with authority on this theme. But four passages need be cited:

2 Corinthians 4:3–4. This text declares that the unsaved are blinded in their minds by Satan, lest the saving gospel of Christ should shine unto them.

Ephesians 2:1–3. The testimony at this point is that the unsaved are "children of disobedience"—being in the headship of disobedient Adam —and that everyone is energized by Satan. In contrast to this it would be well to note Philippians 2:13, where, by use of the same word, the Christian is said to be energized by God.

Colossians 1:13. This text points to the striking fact that a soul when saved is translated out of the power of darkness, in which darkness it naturally dwells.

1 John 5:19 (R.V.). The *cosmos,* it is asserted, including the unregenerate (as being a part of it), "lieth in" the wicked one. The word *wickedness,* found in the Authorized Version, is better translated *evil* or *wicked one* (note the preceding verse where the same word occurs). Likewise, the phrase *lieth in* is deeply suggestive, indicating as it does that in some measure the unsaved are *in Satan,* while the Christians are *in Christ.*

There is strong enough intimation with regard to the condemnation that rests upon the unsaved in the Scriptures, to assert that when they are saved it is from the curse of the law (Gal. 3:13), from wrath (1 Thess. 5:9; John 3:36), from death (2 Cor. 7:10), and from destruction (2 Thess. 1:9).

II. THE ESSENTIAL CHARACTER OF GOD'S UNDERTAKINGS

Before entering upon an enumeration of the thirty-three supernatural divine achievements which constitute the riches of grace, it is important to observe something of the essential character of these riches. Of these, seven vital singularities appear: (a) they are not experienced; (b) they are not progressive; (c) they are not related to human merit; (d) they are eternal in their character; (e) they are known only by revelation; (f) they are wrought by God alone; (g) they are not wrought by man.

1. THEY ARE NOT EXPERIENCED. This is not to imply that these riches are not real; it is rather to point out that they do not manifest their

reality to the emotional nature or through the medium of the nervous system. No better illustration of this fact will be found than is afforded by the supreme divine undertaking of justification; for, obviously, justification is not felt. There is no sensation which gives corroborative evidence that the believer is justified; it rests wholly on the testimony of God. So, likewise, it is with all these riches. They are not such as human experience can identify.

2. THEY ARE NOT PROGRESSIVE. This feature of these riches is of major importance. Since it is the way of almost every human experience, it is natural to conclude that whatever God may undertake will begin with immaturity and progress by degrees to eventual completion. However, in the case of these riches, it will be discovered that the process is different. Every divine undertaking is instantly wrought to that degree of infinite perfection which it will exhibit in the eternal ages to come. Sonship well illustrates this truth. There are many features of the relation between father and son which are subject to progression and change; but sonship itself knows no advancement or development. A child is as much a son at birth as he is at any subsequent point in his existence. Thus it is with every divine accomplishment that enters into the immediate salvation of men.

3. THEY ARE NOT RELATED TO HUMAN MERIT. Beneath this truth, which truth is foreign to all human processes of life and experience, is the sovereign purpose of God to do all that He does according to His own good pleasure, and this He is free to do because the believer is seen to be —as he really is—a member in the Body of Christ, and therefore meet to be blessed with all spiritual blessings in Christ Jesus. Whatever would be accorded the Son of God will be accorded a member in His Body. It is thus that these riches of grace are built solely on the merit of the Son of God, and, for that reason, are as abiding as the merit on which they rest.

4. THEY ARE ETERNAL IN THEIR CHARACTER. As stated above, the work of God for the believer is based on the enduring perfection of Christ and is not, therefore, subject to the variations which characterize a vacillating human experience. As in the case of imputed righteousness, wherein no trace of human worthiness can be included, every work of God in the immediate salvation of the lost is divinely sustained and consequently eternal in its nature. The gift of eternal life is of that divine nature which has existed from all eternity and will exist forever. God's election of believers is never a fortuity.

5. THEY ARE KNOWN ONLY BY REVELATION. Human imagination and

speculation can serve to no degree in attaining to the knowledge of all that God achieves when His love is released by the death of His Son and by the faith of the sinner. No title deed or earthly record ever tabulated such treasures. Their knowledge-surpassing blessedness can be approached only as they are considered one by one in the light of all that God has declared respecting them.

6. THEY ARE WROUGHT BY GOD ALONE. By their very nature, the riches of grace are of necessity the work of God for man. Who could so save himself that he will be on a peace footing with God forever, and eternally justified? Who can translate himself out of the power of darkness into the kingdom of the Son of God's love? Who can constitute himself a citizen of heaven, or write down his name there? God alone is able to save, according to those marvels which He declares are the portion of all who put their trust in Him.

7. THEY ARE NOT WROUGHT BY MAN. In certain respects this declaration is but the negative of the preceding assertion; however, it may be observed that one who is a sinner can take no step in the direction of his own redemption. He who is on earth can devise nothing for himself in heaven. He who is only a creature cannot conform himself to the likeness of his Creator. He who is of time cannot design and execute for eternity. Salvation is more than the continued existence of a good man; it provides the most radical transformations, the acquiring of infinite possessions, and the entering into positions which are in the sphere of heaven and of God. "And ye are complete in him" (Col. 2:10).

III. THE RICHES OF DIVINE GRACE

As the thirty-three stupendous works of God which together comprise the salvation of a soul are now presented, the essential facts, already tabulated, respecting these vast realities should be borne in mind. They are wrought of God; they are wrought instantaneously; they are wrought simultaneously; they are grounded on the merit of Christ; and, being grounded on the merit of Christ, are eternal. It follows that each person of the human family at a given moment is either perfectly saved, being the recipient of every spiritual blessing in Christ Jesus, or perfectly lost, being without one of these spiritual blessings—in the estate of those who are condemned because of a sin nature, because of personal sins, because of an estate under sin, and because they are to such a degree under the power of Satan. These thirty-three riches of grace are:

1. IN THE ETERNAL PLAN OF GOD. To be in the eternal plan of God

is a position of surpassing importance both with regard to the reality itself and its timeless character. The human mind cannot grasp what it means to be in the divine purpose from all eternity, nor what is indicated when it is declared that the same divine purpose extends into eternity to come—"whom he predestinated, he glorified." Whatever may be required as intermediate steps between the predestination and the glory will be under the absolute control of God and wrought of God regardless of the human element that may of necessity enter into it. No human will was ever created to defeat the will of God, but rather the human will is one of the instruments by which God realizes His purposes for humanity. It has always been thus and must be so of necessity, since God is what He is. The student who meditates on the Person of God, the eternity of God, the omnipotence of God, the sovereignty of God as Creator of, and Ruler over, all things, and the elective purpose of God, will be fortified against that form of rationalism—subtle in character and natural to the human heart—which imagines that, in His creation, God has unwittingly so tied His own hands that He cannot with that absoluteness which belongs to infinity realize His eternal purpose.

Five terms are employed in the New Testament to represent aspects of the truth respecting the sovereign purpose of God.

Foreknown. As difficult as it may be for a finite being to grasp the thought, it yet remains true that God foreknew from all eternity every step in the entire program of this universe to its minutest detail. The doctrine of the divine foreknowledge is properly restricted, since it is outside the range of that in God which causes things to come to pass. It is just what the term implies and no more—merely that God knows beforehand. Closely akin to foreknowledge is *foreordination* (Acts 2:23; 1 Pet. 1:2, 20).

Predestinated. As used in the New Testament, this great doctrinal word declares that God determines beforehand that which comes to pass. Destination is determined. In its New Testament use it refers only to that which God has predetermined for His elect. It should therefore not be used in reference to the nonelect and their destiny, though there can be no reasonable doubt but that, in ways beyond human understanding, the destiny of the nonelect is in the mind of God from all eternity. The question of whether, in point of time, foreknowledge precedes predestination, or predestination precedes foreknowledge, is not only useless but wholly uncalled for. God could not predestinate what He did not foreknow. Nor could He foreknow as certain to come to pass that which He had not made certain by predestination. Three passages are in evidence and in two of them foreknowledge stands first: "For whom he did foreknow, he also did predestinate to be conformed to the image of his Son, that he might be the firstborn among many brethren" (Rom. 8:29); "elect according to the foreknowledge of God the Father, through sanctification of the Spirit, unto obedience and sprinkling of the blood of Jesus Christ" (1 Pet. 1:2), while, in the third, foreknowledge is second: "Him, being delivered by the determinate counsel and foreknowledge of God, ye have taken, and by wicked hands have crucified and slain" (Acts 2:23). The two ideas which these words represent must of necessity be stated in sequence; but there could be no sequence in their relation the one to the other. It is, therefore, God's message to every believer that he has been both foreknown in predestination and predestinated through foreknowledge to the unending realization of all of God's riches of grace.

Elect of God. The term *elect,* as related to Christians, is distinctive in that it designates those who are predestinated, but with only an implication relative to destiny. They are the elect in the present age and will manifest the grace of God in future ages (cf. 1 Thess. 1:4; 1 Pet. 1:2; Rom. 8:33; Col. 3:12; Titus 1:1).

Chosen. Again an important aspect of truth is indicated by a specific word. The term *chosen,* when referring to that which God has wrought in behalf of the saved, emphasizes the peculiar act of God which separates unto Himself His elect who are both foreknown and predestinated. The Christian bears the high distinction that he has been chosen in Christ before the foundation of the world (Eph. 1:4).

Called. As far as New Testament terms have been traced, the words *predestination, elect,* and *chosen* are not used of those whom God has selected for salvation when still in their unregenerate state. The word *called,* however, may include in the breadth of its meaning those who, at a given time, are unregenerate but who in the divine purpose are to become regenerate. The angels are not only ministering spirits in behalf of those who are now saved, but of them also who shall be heirs of salvation (Heb. 1:14). "Faithful is he that calleth you, who also will do it" (1 Thess. 5:24). Reference in all this discussion is to an *effectual* call, such as is indicated in Romans 8:30, implying that God not only gives an invitation, but inclines the heart to glad acceptance of it.

How great, then, is this characterizing work of distinctive position! and how immeasurable the opulence of the one who is included in the eternal purpose of God!

2. REDEEMED. Redemption, as a doctrine and as it obtains in the present age, is properly subject to a threefold classification: (1) It

is universal in character in the sense that it includes the whole world
and provides a sufficient ground of righteousness upon which God may
save those who are lost. (2) It is specific when contemplated as the position into which the saved one has been brought. He is purchased out of
the bond slave market and set free with that liberty which is the rightful
portion of the sons of God (Gal. 5:1). It is not a position to be sought
or secured by faithfulness; it is that which God has wrought in behalf
of every regenerate person. The exercise of divine grace—even to the
finality of justification—is said to be "through the redemption that is in
Christ Jesus" (Rom. 3:24). It is in connection with redemption that
the believer has "forgiveness of sins," and this is "according to," and a
part of, "the riches of his grace" (Eph. 1:7). (3) There is yet a redemption of the body of the believer and for that redemption the Christian is waiting (Rom. 8:23). The thought here, as in all the riches of
grace, is that redemption is a position of transforming reality and is the
possession of all who are saved.

3. RECONCILED. Again, a special reconciliation is in view, one which
reaches far beyond that aspect of it which contemplates the whole world.
It is the reconciliation of the believer to God as presented in 2 Corinthians 5:20. A difference will be recognized between the reconciliation
of the world—as declared in 5:19—and the reconciliation of the individual—as declared in 5:20–21. The reconciliation of the world does not
obviate the reconciliation of the individual. The latter is that form of
reconciliation which is applied to the believer's heart and results in a
perfect and unending peace between God and the reconciled believer. To
be perfectly reconciled to God on the ground of the merit of Christ, as is
true of every child of God, is a position of blessedness indeed and is one
of the riches of divine grace.

4. RELATED TO GOD THROUGH PROPITIATION. The central truth contained in this doctrine—and more engaging than any other aspect of it
—is the abiding fact that God *is* propitious. He has been rendered free
toward sinners by the death of His Son for them. That which constitutes
the divine problem in the salvation of sinners, namely, the solution of
the problem of sin, has been solved perfectly. In the case of the unsaved, that which remains is the human responsibility of saving faith.
The truth that all that enters into the divine responsibility has been
perfectly wrought indicates that God is propitious toward sinners; but
He is also propitious toward His blood-bought child who has sinned,
which sin Christ bore on the cross. The truth is of greatest import that
"He is the propitiation for our sins" (1 John 2:2). The ever recurring

need of adjustment between the Christian and his Father is possible on the ground of the truth that the Father is propitious. To be in that relation to God in which He is propitious toward the specific sins of the child of God is a benefit of infinite grace. It is a position more advantageous than heart or mind can comprehend.

5. FORGIVEN ALL TRESPASSES. In the sense that there is now no condemnation to them which are in Christ Jesus, believers are forgiven all trespasses. The declaration of Colossians 2:13—"having forgiven you all trespasses"—covers all trespasses, past, present, and future (cf. Eph. 1:7; 4:32; Col. 1:14; 3:13). In no other way than to be wholly absolved before God, could a Christian be on an abiding peace footing with God or could he be, as he is, justified forever.

The divine dealing with sin is doubtless difficult for the human mind to grasp, especially such sins as have not yet been committed. However, it will be remembered that all sin of this age was yet future when Christ died. Its power to condemn is disannulled forever. In this connection the Holy Spirit inquires, "Who shall lay anything to the charge of God's elect?" and, "Who is he that condemneth?" The inspired answers are conclusive: God justifies rather than charges with sin; and condemnation has been laid upon Another, who died, who is risen, who is at the right hand of God for us, and who also maketh intercession for us" (Rom. 8:33–34). This chapter of Romans which begins with "no condemnation" ends with "no separation"; but such complete forgiveness is possible only on the ground of Christ's work in bearing sin and in releasing His merit to those who are saved through His mediation and are in Him. Men either stand in their own merit or in the merit of Christ. If they stand in their own merit—the only conception that is within the range of reason and that which is advocated by the Arminian system —there is only condemnation for each individual before God; but if they stand in the merit of Christ, being in Him—whether all its righteous ground is comprehended or not—there remains naught but continued union with God and therefore no condemnation and no separation.

At this point a distinction is called for between this abiding judicial forgiveness and the oft-repeated forgiveness within the family of God. The seeming paradox that one is forgiven and yet must be forgiven, is explained on the ground of the truth that there are two wholly and unrelated spheres of relationship between the believer and God. Regarding his *standing*, which like his Sonship is immutable since it is secured by his place in Christ, he is not subject to condemnation and will never be unjustified or separated from God. Regarding his *state*, which like the daily conduct of a son is mutable and is wholly within the family relationship, he must be both forgiven and cleansed (1 John 1:9). The writer to the Hebrews declares that, had the old order of sacrifices been as efficacious as the sacrifice of Christ, those presenting an animal sacrifice for their sin would "have had no more conscience of sins" (10:2). On the other hand, it is the believer's portion to be free from the sense of the condemnation of sin—he never thinks of himself as a lost soul, if at all instructed in God's Word; however, this is not to say that the Christian will not be conscious of the sins he commits. Sin, to the believer, is more abhorrent than ever it could have been before he was saved; but, when sinning, he will not have broken the abiding fact of his union with God though he has injured his communion with Him. Within the family relation—which relation cannot be broken—he may sin as a child (without ceasing to be a child) and be forgiven, and restored back into the Father's fellowship on the basis of his own confession of his sin and the deeper truth that Christ has borne the sin which otherwise would condemn.

None of the believer's positions before God, when rightly apprehended, is more a blessing to the heart than the fact that all condemnation is removed forever, God for Christ's sake having forgiven all trespasses.

6. VITALLY CONJOINED TO CHRIST FOR THE JUDGMENT OF THE OLD MAN "UNTO A NEW WALK." The essential doctrine of union with Christ appears as the basis of many of these riches of divine grace. In the present aspect of truth, only that which has to do with the death of Christ unto the sin nature is in view, and the central passage which declares this truth is Romans 6:1–10. This important Scripture will be brought forward in various places in this work on theology, but always it will be pointed out that it refers neither to self-judgment by self-crucifixion nor to a mode of ritual baptism. If the passage does not contemplate more than these interpretations imply, one of the most vital truths of the New Testament is deprived of its most important affirmation. The death of Christ, quite apart from its achievement as a final dealing with sins, is a judgment of the sin nature, which judgment does not mean that that nature is rendered incapable of action or that it is changed in its character; it does mean that a perfect judgment is gained against it and that God is now righteously free to deal with that nature as a judged thing. The evil character of that nature does not, after it is judged, restrain the Holy Spirit from curbing its power for us. Thus, by faith in the indwelling Spirit, the believer may

be delivered from the reigning power of sin and on the ground of Christ's death as a judgment of the sin nature. This feature of Christ's death is substitutionary to the last degree. The central passage asserts that the death of Christ is so definitely an act in behalf of the believer, that it is a cocrucifixion, a codeath, a coburial, and a coresurrection (cf. Col. 2:12). The application of this truth is not an injunction to enact all or any part of it; it is rather something about himself which the Christian is to believe or reckon to be true, being, as it is, the ground upon which he may by an intelligent faith claim deliverance from the power of the inbred sin nature.

To be placed thus permanently before God as one for whom Christ has died a judgment death against the sin nature is a position of privilege of infinite blessedness.

7. FREE FROM THE LAW. As now considered, the law is more than a code or set of rules governing conduct. Too often it is thought that to be free from the law is to be excused from doing the things which the law prescribes, and, because the law is "holy, and just, and good," it is difficult for many to accept the New Testament teaching that the law is not the prescribed rule of life for the believer. Why, indeed, it is inquired, should the believer do other than to pursue that which is holy, just, and good? Over against this idea is the uncompromising warning to the Christian that he by the death of Christ is free from the law (cf. John 1:17; Acts 15:24–29; Rom. 6:14; 7:2–6; 2 Cor. 3:6–13; Gal. 5:18). In one passage alone—Romans 6:14—the child of God is told that he is not under the law, and in another—Romans 7:2–6—he is said to be both dead to the law and delivered from the law. Since every ideal or principle of the law, except the fourth commandment, is carried forward and restated and incorporated in the grace manner of life, it hardly seems reasonable to contend that the believer should be warned so positively against doing the things contained in the law. The solution of the problem is to be found in the fact that the law is a system demanding human merit, while the injunctions addressed to the Christian under grace are unrelated to human merit. Since the child of God is already accepted in the Beloved and stands forever in the merit of Christ, application of the merit system to him is both unreasonable and unscriptural. When the principles contained in the merit system reappear in the grace injunctions, it is always with this vital change in the character. It is one thing to do a thing that is contained in the law in order that one may be accepted or blessed; it is a wholly different thing to do

those same things because one is accepted and blessed. Freedom from the merit obligation is that "liberty" to which reference is made in Galatians 5:1. It is not liberty to do evil; but it is a perfect relief from the crushing burden—the yoke of bondage (Acts 15:10)—of works of merit.

To be "free from the law" (Rom. 8:2), to be "dead to the law" (Rom. 7:4), and to be "delivered from the law" (Rom. 7:6; cf. Rom. 6:14; 2 Cor. 3:11; Gal. 3:25), describe a position in grace before God which is rich and full unto everlasting blessing.

8. CHILDREN OF GOD. To be born anew by the regenerating power of the Holy Spirit into a relationship in which God the First Person becomes a legitimate Father and the saved one becomes a legitimate child, is a position which is but dimly apprehended by any human being in this world. This far-flung reality is more a matter of heavenly values than of the earth. Nevertheless, this very regeneration is one of the foundational realities of everyone who has believed upon Christ as Savior. This birth from above accomplishes a measureless transformation. To be born into an earthly home of outstanding character is of great advantage, but to be born of God with every right and title belonging to that position—an heir of God and a joint heir with Jesus Christ—passes the range of human understanding. This new existence is not only intensely real, but it, like all begotten life, is everlasting in its very nature. The theme is so vast that it includes other positions and possessions which, in turn, will be mentioned as this analysis progresses.

Varied terms are used in the New Testament to identify this new birth. Each of these is distinct in itself and revealing.

Born again. It is of more than passing import that the Lord Jesus Christ selected Nicodemus, the most religious and ideal man of his day in Judaism, to whom and as applied to himself Christ declared the necessity of the new birth. The word ἄνωθεν is rendered *anew,* and its implication is that it is not only an actual birth, but it is new in the sense that it is no part of that first birth which is after the flesh. It is not a reordering or revising of the birth by the flesh. It is new in the sense that it is complete in itself and no product of the flesh. Of this distinction Christ said, "That which is born of the flesh is flesh; and that which is born of the Spirit is spirit" (John 3:6). Other confirming passages are John 1:12–13; 1 Peter 1:23.

Regenerated. This expressive term, which appears in Titus 3:5— "by the washing of regeneration"—conveys the same idea of a rebirth.

The passage relates a cleansing to this birth, but the birth does not consist in a mere cleansing of the old being; it is rather that a cleansing, like forgiveness, accompanies the regeneration.

Quickened. The word *quickened* expresses the thought that an object is made alive that did not possess that life before. Through regeneration by the Spirit, as in the case with the flesh, there is an impartation of life. Regeneration imparts the divine nature. Attention should be given also to Ephesians 2:1 and Colossians 2:13.

Sons of God. This title, used many times (cf. 2 Cor. 6:18; Gal. 3:26, R.V.; 1 John 3:2), publishes the true relationship between God and those who are saved. They are sons of God, not by a mere title or pretense, but by actual generation the offspring of God. The reality which the title designates cannot be taken too literally.

A new creation. Thus again, and by language both appropriate and emphatic, the mighty creative power of God is seen to be engaged in the salvation of men. As respects their salvation it is said that they are His workmanship, created in Christ Jesus. That exalted new creation is not only the direct work of God, but owes all that it is to its vital relation to Christ Jesus.

9. ADOPTED. The peculiar position of one who is adopted is an important feature of the riches of divine grace. Its unique place in the following passage indicates its major import: "According as he hath chosen us in him before the foundation of the world, that we should be holy and without blame before him in love: having predestinated us unto the adoption of children by Jesus Christ to himself, according to the good pleasure of his will" (Eph. 1:4–5). In attempting to discover what this position really is, it is needful to recognize that divine adoption has almost nothing in common with that form of it as accepted and practiced among men. According to human custom, adoption is a means whereby an outsider may become a member of a family. It is a legal way to create father and son relationship as a substitute for father and son reality. On the other hand, divine adoption, while referring both to Israel's kinship to God (Rom. 9:4) and to redemption of the believer's body (Rom. 8:23), is primarily a divine act by which one already a child by actual birth through the Spirit of God is placed forward as an adult son in his relation to God. At the moment of regeneration, the believer, being born of God and therefore the legitimate offspring of God, is advanced in relationship and responsibility to the position of an adult son. All childhood and adolescent years, which are normal in human experience, are excluded in spiritual sonship and the newly born

believer is at once in possession of freedom from tutors and governors —who symbolize the law principle—and is responsible to live the full-orbed spiritual life of an adult son in the Father's household. No period of irresponsible childhood is recognized. There is no body of Scripture which undertakes to direct the conduct of beginners in the Christian life as in distinction to those who are mature. Whatever God says to the old and established saint, He says to every believer—including those most recently regenerated. There should be no misunderstanding respecting the "babe in Christ," mentioned in 1 Corinthians 3:1, who is a babe because of carnality and not because of immaturity of years in the Christian life. In human experience legitimate birth and adoption never combine in the same person. There is no occasion for a father to adopt his own child. In the realm of divine adoption, every child born of God is adopted at the moment he is born. He is placed before God as a mature, responsible son. Thus adoption becomes one of the important divine undertakings in the salvation of men and is a position of great importance.

10. ACCEPTABLE TO GOD BY JESUS CHRIST. As a position before God, none could be more elevated or consummating than that a believer should be "made accepted in the beloved" (Eph. 1:6) and "acceptable to God by Jesus Christ" (1 Pet. 2:5). Such an estate is closely akin to that already mentioned wherein there is no condemnation, and to that, yet to be considered, of justification; but this aspect of truth not only announces the marvelous fact that the Christian is accepted, but grounds that acceptance in the position which he holds in Christ. As definitely as any member that might be joined to a human body would partake of all that the person is to whom it is joined—honor and position—so perfectly and rightfully a member joined to Christ by the baptism of the Spirit partakes of all that Christ is. In respect to this union with Christ and that which it provides, wonderful declarations are made:

a. MADE RIGHTEOUS. Reference here is neither to any merit nor good works on the part of the individual believer, nor has it the slightest reference to the unquestioned truth that God is Himself a righteous Being. It rather represents that standing or quality which Christ released by His death according to the sweet-savor aspect of it, and which rightfully becomes the believer's portion through his living union with Christ. It is righteousness imputed to the believer on the sole condition that he has believed on Christ as his Savior. Two major realities which constitute a Christian are: imparted eternal life (John 20:31) and imputed righteousness (2 Cor. 5:21). Of the two great salvation books in the New Testament, it may be said of John's Gospel that it stresses the gift of eternal life, and it may be said of the Epistle to the Romans that it stresses imputed righteousness. Eternal life is defined as "Christ in you, the hope of glory" (Col. 1:27), and imputed righteousness is based on the truth that the believer is in Christ. These two supreme truths are compressed by Christ into seven brief and simple words, when He said: "ye in me, and I in you" (John 14:20). Whether it be the reception of eternal life or of imputed righteousness, but one condition is imposed on the human side, namely, to believe on Christ as Savior (John 3:16; Rom. 3:22).

In an earlier treatment of this theme the essential features of imputed righteousness have been recorded and the extended body of Scripture bearing on this doctrine has been cited. The believer is "acceptable to God," even the infinitely holy God, since he has been *made* accepted in the Beloved; and this constitutes a transforming feature of the riches of divine grace.

b. SANCTIFIED POSITIONALLY. That there is a *positional* sanctification which is secured by union with Christ has too often been overlooked, and, because of this neglect, theories of a supposed sinless perfection in daily life have been inferred from those Scriptures which assert the truth that the believer has been "perfected for ever" through his sanctification. The point of misunderstanding is with regard to the *design* of sanctification, which may be defined as the setting apart of a person or thing, a classifying. It is thus that Christ sanctified Himself by becoming the Savior of the lost with all that that involved (John 17:19), which sanctification certainly could not imply any improvement in moral character on His part. Likewise, the sanctification of an inanimate object, such as the gold of the temple or the gift on the altar (Matt. 23:17, 19), indicates that a moral change in the thing sanctified is not demanded. Thus, in the case of the sanctification of a person, the moral change in that person's life may not be the result of sanctification; but no person or thing is sanctified without being set apart or classified thereby. Christ has been "made unto us . . . sanctification" (I Cor. 1:30), and the Corinthians—even when being corrected for evil practices—are assured that they were not only "washed" and "justified," but that they were "sanctified" (1 Cor. 6:11). Such sanctification was neither the estate of those believers nor did it refer to their ultimate transformation when they would appear in glory (Eph. 5:27; 1 John 3:2). It evidently indicated that greatest of all classifications, which resulted in the standing and position of every believer when he enters the New Creation through being joined to Christ and partakes of all that Christ is. This truth is declared in the phrase,

c. PERFECTED FOREVER. This consummating phrase appears in Hebrews 10:14 and applies equally to every believer. It, too, relates to the Christian's standing and position in Christ. Such a union with Christ secures the perfection of the Son of God for the child of God.

d. MADE ACCEPTED IN THE BELOVED. The student would do well to observe the force of the word *made* as it appears in a considerable number of passages, where it indicates that the thing accomplished is not wrought by the believer for himself, but is the work of God for him. If he is made something which he was not before, it is evidently the work of another in his behalf. In this instance, the believer is said to be *made accepted*. He is accepted on the part of God who, because of His infinite holiness, could accept no one less perfect than Himself. All of this is provided for on the basis of the truth that the believer is made accepted "in the beloved" (Eph. 1:6). Without the slightest strain upon His holiness, God accepts those who are in union with His Son; and this glorious fact, that the one who is saved is accepted, constitutes a measureless feature of divine grace.

e. MADE MEET. Here, again, the word *made* with all its significance appears, but with respect to that requirement which must be demanded of all who would appear in the presence of God in heaven. The text in which this assuring phrase occurs is Colossians 1:12, and it asserts that the believer is, even now, fitted for that celestial glory: "giving thanks unto the Father, which hath made us meet to be partakers of the inheritance of the saints in light." No mere pretense or bold assumption is indicated in this passage. The least believer, being in Christ, is even now *made meet* to be a partaker of the inheritance of the saints in light. It therefore becomes no arrogance or vainglory to accept this statement of God's Word as true, and as true from the moment one believes on Christ as Savior.

To be acceptable to God by Jesus Christ (1 Pet. 2:5), is a reality in every aspect of it and this truth, incomprehensible as it is, constitutes an important item in the whole field of the riches of grace in Christ Jesus.

11. JUSTIFIED. No present position in which the believer is placed is more exalted and consummating than that of being justified by God. By justification the saved one is lifted far above the position of one who depends on divine generosity and magnanimity, to the estate of one

whom God has declared justified forever, which estate the holy justice of God is as much committed to defend as ever that holy justice was before committed to condemn. Theological definitions respecting justification are more traditional than Biblical. Only inattention to Scripture can account for the confusion of justification with divine forgiveness of sin. It is true that each of these is an act of God in response to saving faith, that none are forgiven who are not justified, and that none are justified who are not forgiven; but in no particular do these great divine undertakings coalesce. Likewise, though they are translated from the same Greek root, the terms *righteousness* (imputed) and *justification* represent wholly different conceptions. The believer is constituted righteous by virtue of his position in Christ, but he is justified by a declaratory decree of God. Righteousness imputed is the abiding fact, and justification is the divine recognition of that fact. In other considerations of the doctrine of justification incorporated in this general work, a more exhaustive treatment is undertaken, including the scope of this divine enterprise in which God justifies the ungodly (Rom. 4:5) without a cause (Rom. 3:24), and on a ground so worthy, so laudable, and so unblemished that He Himself remains just when He justifies. He reserves every aspect of this measureless benefit to Himself, for the only human obligation is that of *believing* in Jesus (Rom. 3:26). It is the Christian's right to count this work done and to say, as in Romans 5:1, "Therefore being justified by faith . . ." Though language may describe it, only the Spirit of God can cause the mind to realize this essential position so elevated and so glorified.

12. MADE NIGH. The saved one, according to Ephesians 2:13, is said to be "made nigh." This text states: "But now in Christ Jesus ye who sometimes were far off are made nigh by the blood of Christ." As seen before, the word *made* is significant in that it assigns the whole undertaking to another than the one who receives the blessing. Various terms are employed in the New Testament to describe the close relation which is set up and exists between God and the believer. To be "made nigh" is not only a work of God, but is to be brought into a relationship to God which is of infinite perfection and completeness. To it nothing could be added in time or eternity. What such a nearness may mean to the Christian when he is present with the Lord cannot be anticipated in this life; nevertheless, the reality which the phrase *made nigh* connotes is as cogent an acquirement at the inception of the Christian's salvation as it will be at any point in eternity.

Divinely wrought positions are often accompanied by a corresponding

Christian experience. This is true of the subject in hand. While, as has been stated, the position which is described as nigh to God is itself complete and final, the one who is thus *nigh* is exhorted to "draw nigh" to God. It is written: "Draw nigh to God, and he will draw nigh to you. Cleanse your hands, ye sinners; and purify your hearts, ye double minded" (James 4:8); "Let us draw near with a true heart in full assurance of faith, having our hearts sprinkled from an evil conscience, and our bodies washed with pure water" (Heb. 10:22). These exhortations belong wholly in the realm of Christian experience, in which realm there may be a consciousness, more or less real, of personal fellowship with the Father and the Son (1 John 1:3). The process by which a believer may draw nigh—as required by James and in response to which God will Himself draw nigh to the believer—is that of a confession of sin and an adjustment of one's life to the will of God. Over against this it will be observed that, whether in fellowship or out of fellowship as respects conscious experience, the Christian is, because of his position in Christ, ever and always made nigh.

13. DELIVERED FROM THE POWER OF DARKNESS. As declared in Colossians 1:13, this special position, as described here in this passage, may be taken as representative of all the Scripture bearing on the Christian's deliverance from the power of Satan and his evil spirits. Previously, certain passages have been cited relative to the power of Satan over the unsaved. One passage, 2 Corinthians 4:3-4, reveals the blinding power of Satan over the unregenerate person's mind respecting the gospel; Ephesians 2:1-2 declares the whole company of the lost—designated "children of disobedience" (disobedient in the headship of disobedient Adam)—to be energized by Satan; 1 John 5:19 states that the *cosmos* world, in contrast to believers who are of God, "lieth in" the wicked one. The passage under consideration—Colossians 1:13—reads: "who hath delivered us from the power of darkness, and hath translated us into the kingdom of his dear Son." It will be observed that all these passages, to which reference is made, assert that the unsaved are under the power of Satan and that the believer is delivered from that power, though he must continue to wage a warfare against these powers of darkness; and the Apostle assures the Christian of the victory made possible by an attitude of faith in the Lord (Eph. 6:10–12). The same Apostle, when relating his own divine commission, mentions one certain result of his ministry, namely, that the unsaved were to be turned "from darkness to light, and from the power of Satan unto God" (Acts 26:18).

To be liberated thus is a great reality and constitutes one of the major positions into which the believer is brought through divine grace.

14. TRANSLATED INTO THE KINGDOM OF THE SON OF HIS LOVE. As Dean Alford points out in exposition of Colossians 1:13 (*N.T. for English Readers,* new ed., *in loc.*), the translation *into the kingdom* is "strictly local"; that is, it is *now* that it is accomplished, when saving faith is exercised, and the entrance is into the present form of the kingdom of God and of Christ. Two other passages shed light upon this great change which is experienced by all who pass from the lost estate to the saved estate: "that ye would walk worthy of God, who hath called you unto his kingdom and glory" (1 Thess. 2:12); "For so an entrance shall be ministered unto you abundantly into the everlasting kingdom of our Lord and Saviour Jesus Christ" (2 Pet. 1:11). In Colossians 1:13, the term "translated" evidently refers to the removal from the sphere of Satan's dominion to that of Christ. The kingdom is that of God, which may be considered also the kingdom of the Son of His love. Entrance into the kingdom of God is by the new birth (John 3:5). Such a position is far more than merely to be delivered from darkness, however much the advantage of that may be; it is to be inducted into and established in the kingdom of God's dear Son.

15. ON THE ROCK, CHRIST JESUS. In the consideration of divine grace as exercised in behalf of the lost, it is essential, as in other matters of similar import, to distinguish between the foundation and the superstructure. In the parable of the two houses—one built upon the rock and one built upon the sand (Matt. 7:24–27)—Christ made no reference to the superstructure, but rather emphasized the importance of the foundation. The smallest edifice built on the rock will endure the tests which try foundations, and only because the rock endures. Over against this, the Apostle writes (1 Cor. 3:9–15) of the superstructure which is built upon the rock, which superstructure is to be tested by fire. Reference is thus made, not to salvation, but to the works in which the Christian engages. It is not character building, but Christian service. There are, again, two general classes of superstructure being built upon Christ the Rock, and these are likened to gold, silver, and precious stones, on the one hand, and to wood, hay, and stubble, on the other hand. As gold and silver are refined by fire, and wood, hay, and stubble are consumed by fire, so the judgment of Christian service is likened to fire in which the gold and silver will stand the test and receive a reward, while that which corresponds to wood, hay, and stubble will suffer loss. It is declared, however, that the believer who suffers loss in respect to his

reward for service will himself be saved, though passing through that fire which destroys his unworthy service.

The important truth to be recognized at this point is that, while the unsaved build upon the sand, all Christians are standing and building on the Rock, Christ Jesus. They are thus secure with respect to salvation through the merit of Christ, apart from their own worthiness or faithfulness. While this figure used by Christ does not lend itself to a literal development in every particular, it is clearly stated by this object lesson that Christ is the Foundation on which the Christian stands and on which he builds. To be taken off the sand foundation and to be placed on the enduring Rock which is Christ, constitutes one of the richest treasures of divine grace.

16. A GIFT FROM GOD THE FATHER TO CHRIST. No moment in the history of the saints could be more laden with reality than that time when, as a consummation of His redemptive mission—foreseen from all eternity and itself the determining factor in the character of all ages to come— the Lord Jesus Christ reviewed in prayer to the Father that which He had achieved by His advent into this *cosmos* world. He fully intended for His own who are in this world to hear what He said in that incomparable prayer (John 17:13). Devout minds will ponder eagerly every word spoken concerning themselves under such august and solemn circumstances. What, indeed, would be the designation by which believers will be identified by the Son? What appellation is proper in such converse? What cognomen answers the highest ideal and conception in the mind of Deity with respect to Christians? Assuredly, the superlative title, whatever it is, would be employed by the Son when He presents formally His own, and petitions the Father in their behalf. Seven times in this prayer by one form or another and quite exclusively His saved ones are referred to as *those whom Thou hast given Me*. Nothing but ignorance of the great transaction which is intimated in this title will explain the inattention of Christians to this descriptive name. When it is considered, it is seen that in the background are two important doctrines, namely, that all creatures belong inherently to their Creator and, hence, that in sovereign election He has determined in past ages a company designed to be a peculiar treasure for His Son; but the title itself tells its own story of surpassing interest and importance, which is, that the Father has given each believer to the Son. This is not the only instance in which the Father gives a company of people to the Son. In Psalm 2:6–9 it is predicted that, at His second advent and when He is seated upon the Davidic throne, the then rebellious and raging nations

will be given by Jehovah to the Messiah. The imagination will not have gone far astray if it pictures a situation in eternity past when the Father presents individual believers separately to the Son—each representing a particular import and value not approached by another. Like a chest of jewels, collected one by one and wholly diverse, these love gifts appear before the eyes of the Son of God. Should one be missing, He, the Savior, would be rendered inexpressibly poor. Immeasurable and unknowable riches of grace are latent in that superlative cognomen, *those whom Thou hast given Me*.

Dr. C. I. Scofield's comment on this truth is clear and forceful: "Seven times Jesus speaks of believers as given to Him by the Father (vs. 2, 6 [twice], 9, 11, 12, 24). Jesus Christ is God's love-gift to the world (John 3:16), and believers are the Father's love-gift to Jesus Christ. It is Christ who commits the believer to the Father for safe-keeping, so that the believer's security rests upon the Father's faithfulness to His Son Jesus Christ" (*Scofield Reference Bible*, p. 1139).

17. CIRCUMCISED IN CHRIST. One of the Apostle's threefold divisions of humanity is the "Uncircumcision" with reference to unregenerate Gentiles, "the Circumcision in the flesh made by hands" with reference to Israel, and "the circumcision made without hands" with reference to Christians (Eph. 2:11; Col. 2:11). However, the important truth that the believer has been circumcised with a circumcision made without hands and wholly apart from the flesh, is the grace position which is now in view. In the Colossians passage (2:11), the believer's spiritual circumcision is said to be the "putting off the body of the sins of the flesh by the circumcision of Christ." Two closely related words occur in this passage, namely, *body* ($\sigma\hat{\omega}\mu\alpha$) and *flesh* ($\sigma\acute{\alpha}\rho\xi$). The physical body does not commit sin except as it is dominated by the flesh—which flesh includes the soul and spirit, and manifests that fallen nature which all possess, saved and unsaved alike. The physical body is not put off in a literal sense, but, being the instrument or sphere of sin's manifestation, the flesh with its "body of sin" may be annulled (Rom. 6:6), or rendered inoperative for the time being. As the sin nature was judged by Christ in His death, so the believer, because of his vital place in Christ, partakes of that "putting off" which Christ accomplished, and which fell as a circumcision upon Him and becomes a spiritual circumcision to the one for whom Christ substituted. It is a circumcision made "without hands." To stand thus before God as one whose sin nature, or flesh, has been judged and for whom a way of deliverance from the dominion

of the flesh has been secured, is a position which grace has provided, and is blessed indeed.

18. PARTAKERS OF THE HOLY AND ROYAL PRIESTHOOD. In his First Epistle, Peter declares that the believers form a holy priesthood (2:5) and a royal priesthood (2:9), and their royalty is again asserted by John when in Revelation 1:6 (R.V.) they are titled "a kingdom . . . priests," or according to another reading (A.V.), "kings and priests." The truth that Christ is a king-priest is reflected here. The believer derives all his positions and possessions from Christ. The child of God is therefore a priest now because of his relation to Christ the High Priest, and he will yet reign with Christ a thousand years—when Christ takes His earthly throne (Rev. 5:10; cf. 2 Tim. 2:12).

Priesthood has passed through certain well-defined stages or aspects. The patriarchs were priests over their households. Later, to Israel was offered the privilege of becoming a kingdom of priests (Ex. 19:6); but it was conditional and Israel failed in the realization of this blessing, and the priesthood was restricted to one tribe or family. On a grace basis, in which God undertakes through the merit of His Son, in the New Testament is introduced the true and final realization of a kingdom of priests. Every saved person in the present age is a priest unto God. The Old Testament priest is the type of the New Testament priest. Israel had a priesthood; the Church is a priesthood. To be a priest unto God with the certainty of a kingly reign is a position to which the one who believes on Christ is brought through the saving grace of God.

19. A CHOSEN GENERATION, A HOLY NATION, A PECULIAR PEOPLE. All three of these designations (1 Pet. 2:9) refer to one and the same general idea, namely, that the company of believers of this age—individuals called out from the Jews and Gentiles alike—are different from the unsaved Jew and Gentile to the extent to which thirty-three stupendous miracles transform them. They are a *generation,* not in the sense that they are restricted to one span of human life, but in the sense that they are the offspring of God. They are a *nation* in the sense that they are separate, a distinct grouping among all the peoples of the earth. They are a *peculiar people* in the sense that they are born of God and are therefore not of this *cosmos* world. They are not enjoined to try to be peculiar; any people in this world who are citizens of heaven, perfected in Christ, and appointed to live in the power of and to the glory of God, cannot but be peculiar.

These three designations represent permanent positions to which the

believer has been brought and they, likewise, make a large contribution
to the sum total of all the riches of divine grace.

20. HEAVENLY CITIZENS. Under this consideration, commonwealth
privilege, or what is better known as *citizenship*, is in view. Writing of
the estate of the Ephesians, who were Gentiles before they were saved,
the Apostle states that they were "aliens from the commonwealth of Israel." Israel's citizenship, though earthly, was specifically recognized by
God as separate from all other peoples. Into this position no Gentile
could come except as a proselyte. Thus it is said that the Gentile, being a
stranger to Israel's commonwealth, had not so much as any divine
recognition; yet immeasurably removed and heaven-high above even
Israel's commonwealth is the Christian's citizenship in heaven. Of
Christians it is written, "For our citizenship is in heaven" (Phil. 3:20,
R.V.); their names are written in heaven (Luke 10:20), and they are
said to have "come unto Mount Sion, and unto the city of the living
God, the heavenly Jerusalem" (Heb. 12:22). To enforce the same truth,
the Apostle also writes, "Now therefore ye are no more strangers and
foreigners, but fellow citizens with the saints, and of the household of
God" (Eph. 2:19). Actual presence in heaven is an assured experience
for all who are saved (2 Cor. 5:8); but citizenship itself—whether
realized at the present moment or not—is an abiding position accorded
to all who believe. In truth, the occupation of that citizenship by instant
removal from this sphere would be the normal experience for each
Christian when he is saved. To remain here after citizenship has been
acquired in heaven creates a peculiar situation. In recognition of this
abnormal condition, the child of God is styled a "stranger and pilgrim"
(1 Pet. 2:11; cf. Heb. 11:13) 'as related to this *cosmos* world-system.
In like manner, he is said to be an "ambassador" for Christ (2 Cor.
5:20). To remain here as a witness, a stranger, a pilgrim, and an ambassador is but a momentary experience; the heavenly citizenship will
be enjoyed forever. It is a glorious feature of the riches of divine grace.

21. OF THE FAMILY AND HOUSEHOLD OF GOD. Closely akin to citizenship and yet more restricted in their extent, are the positions the Christian is said to occupy in the family and household of God. As has been
observed, there are various fatherhood relations which God sustains;
but none in relation to His creatures is so perfect, so enriching, or so
enduring as that which He bears to the household and family of the
saints. So great a change has been wrought in the estate of those who are
saved respecting their kinship to God, that it is written of them: "Now
therefore ye are no more strangers and foreigners, but fellowcitizens

with the saints, and of the household of God" (Eph. 2:19). With this position an obligation arises which makes its claim upon every member of the household. Of this claim the Apostle writes: "As we have therefore opportunity, let us do good unto all men, especially unto them who are of the household of faith" (Gal. 6:10). In the present human relationship sustained in the *cosmos* world, there is, of necessity, but a limited difference observable between the saved and unsaved; yet those who comprise the household of faith are completely separated unto God, and into that family none could ever enter who sustains no true relation to God as his Father. Human organizations, including the visible church, may include a mixed multitude, but "the foundation of God standeth sure, having this seal, The Lord knoweth them that are his" (2 Tim. 2:19). In a great house there are some vessels to honor and some to dishonor, some of gold and silver, and some of wood and of earth. If a man purge himself from vessels of dishonor, he shall be a vessel unto honor, sanctified, and meet for the Master's use, and prepared unto every good work (2 Tim. 2:20-21). This picture of household relationships does not imply that there are those in the family of God who are not saved; the truth set forth is that not all believers are, in their daily life, as yielded to God as they might be, and that by self-dedication they may be advanced from the position of vessels of dishonor—of wood or of earth—to the position and substance of vessels of honor—of gold and of silver.

Like citizenship in heaven, a participation in the household and family of God is a position exalted as high as heaven itself, and honorable to the degree of infinity. Thus there is correspondence with all other features of the riches of divine grace.

22. IN THE FELLOWSHIP OF THE SAINTS. As Christian citizenship pertains to a relation to heaven, and as the household pertains to God, so the fellowship of the saints pertains to their relation the one to the other. The fact of this kinship and the obligation it engenders is stressed in the New Testament. The fact of kinship reaches out to incomparable realities. Through the baptism of the Spirit—by which believers are, at the time they are saved, joined to the Lord as members in His Body—an affinity is created which answers the prayer of Christ when He petitioned the Father that the believers might all be one. Being begotten of the same Father, the family tie is of no small import, but to be fellow members in the Body of Christ surpasses all other such conceptions. To be begotten of God results in sonship; but to be in Christ results in a standing as exalted as the standing of God's Son. To be partners in this

standing added to regeneration's brotherhood, constitutes that vital relationship for which Christ prayed when He asked "that they all may be one; as thou, Father, art in me, and I in thee" (John 17:21). A repetition of any statement as it occurs in the Bible is for emphasis. It would seem, however, that, when speaking to His Father, there would be little occasion for reiteration; yet in that one priestly prayer Christ prays four times directly and separately that believers may be *one*, and once that they may be *one* in their relation to the Father and to Himself (John 17:11, 21–23). With all this in view, it must be conceded that few, if any, truths are so emphasized in the Word of God as the unity of believers. This prayer of Christ's began to be answered on the Day of Pentecost when those then saved were fused into one corporate Body, and it has been answered continuously as, at the moment of believing, those saved are also joined to Christ's Body by the same operation of the Holy Spirit.

An unknowable unity exists between the Father and the Son. It is the mystery of the Trinity itself; yet it is on this very level that Christ has requested that believers may stand in relation to each other—"that they all may be one; as thou, Father, art in me, and I in thee . . . that they may be made perfect in one" (John 17:21–23). This prayer, as all that Christ ever prays, is answered, and the fact of oneness between the saints of God is a present truth whether anyone ever comprehends it in this world or not.

This marvelous unity between believers becomes the logical ground for all Christian action, one toward another. Such action should be consistent with the unity which exists. Never are Christians exhorted to *make* a unity by organization or combines; they are rather besought to *keep* the unity which God by His Spirit has created (Eph. 4:1–3). This can be done in but one way, namely, by recognizing and receiving, as well as loving and honoring, every other child of God. The spirit of separation from, and of exclusion of, other believers is a sin that can be measured only in the light of that ineffable union which separation and exclusion disregard.

To be in the fellowship of the saints is a position in grace too exalted and too dignified for mere human understanding.

23. A HEAVENLY ASSOCIATION. What is termed "the heavenly places" is a phrase which is peculiar to the Ephesian Letter and has no reference to heaven as a place or to specific places of spiritual privilege here on earth; but it does refer to the present realm of association with Christ, which association is the inherent right of all those who are in Christ

Jesus. The association is a partnership with Christ which incorporates at least seven spheres of common interest and undertaking.

a. PARTNERS WITH CHRIST IN LIFE. The New Testament declares not only that the believer has partaken of a new life, but asserts that life to be the indwelling Christ. In Colossians 1:27 a mystery is revealed which is "Christ in you, the hope of glory"; and in Colossians 3:4 it is also said that "Christ . . . is our life." Likewise in 1 John 5:11–12 it is written: "And this is the record, that God hath given to us eternal life, and this life is in his Son. He that hath the Son hath life; and he that hath not the Son of God hath not life." Upwards of eighty times in the New Testament the truth appears, that among the major features which characterize a Christian is the impartation of a new life from God. Thus a unique partnership in life is established between Christ and all who believe which is both a position and a possession.

b. PARTNERSHIP IN POSITION. As an incomparable position, the Christian is raised with Christ (Col. 3:1), and seated with Christ in the heavenly association. This truth is clearly revealed in Ephesians 2:6, which declares, "And hath raised us up together, and made us sit together in heavenly places in Christ Jesus." To be raised with Christ and to be seated with Christ is a partnership in position which is real and abiding. Its contribution to the entire fact of the believer's association with Christ is enough to characterize the whole. The honor and glory of it are knowledge-surpassing.

c. PARTNERS WITH CHRIST IN SERVICE. A number of passages unite in a testimony that the service of the Christian is one of copartnership with Christ. Of these, none is more direct and convincing than 1 Corinthians 1:9, which reads: "God is faithful, by whom ye were called unto the fellowship of his Son Jesus Christ our Lord." In the A.V. the word κοινωνία is rendered *fellowship*. As the word is at times rendered *communion* (cf. 2 Cor. 6:14) with the thought of agreement or partnership, and to be in harmony with the message of Christian service, which theme characterizes this Epistle, the idea of joint undertaking may be read into this passage. Some, as Meyer and Alford, see a sharing here in Christ's coming glory; but as this Epistle is almost wholly one parenthesis which begins with the verse following this notable text and ends with 15:57, it is important to observe the next verse in the direct course of the message, namely, 15:58. With the rendering of κοινωνία by *partnership*, the two dominant and connecting verses would read: "God is faithful, by whom ye were called unto the partnership of his Son Jesus Christ our Lord. . . . Therefore, my beloved brethren, be ye stedfast, unmoveable, always abounding in the work of the Lord, forasmuch as ye know that your labour is not in vain in the Lord." The same Epistle states, "For we are labourers together with God" (3:9); and 2 Corinthians 6:1 designates the believers as "workers together with him"—in the same context they are said to be "ministers of God" (6:4) and "ministers of the new testament" (3:6). To be thus in partnership with Christ is a position of limitless responsibility as well as exalted honor.

d. PARTNERS WITH CHRIST IN SUFFERING. Of the entire field of the doctrine of human suffering, a well-defined feature of that experience is *suffering with Christ.* "If we suffer, we shall also reign with him" (2 Tim. 2:12). Likewise, "For unto you it is given in the behalf of Christ, not only to believe on him, but also to suffer for his sake" (Phil. 1:29); and, again, "Beloved, think it not strange concerning the fiery trial which is to try you, as though some strange thing happened unto you: but rejoice, inasmuch as ye are partakers of Christ's sufferings; that, when his glory shall be revealed, ye may be glad also with exceeding joy" (1 Pet. 4:12–13). The Apostle testified of himself, "who now rejoice in my sufferings for you, and fill up that which is behind of the afflictions of Christ in my flesh for his body's sake, which is the church" (Col. 1:24), and, "For I reckon that the sufferings of this present time are not worthy to be compared with the glory which shall be revealed in us" (Rom. 8:18); similarly, "That no man should be moved by these afflictions: for yourselves know that we are appointed thereunto" (1 Thess. 3:3).

While the child of God may suffer the reproaches of Christ, which is a definite form of copartnership suffering with Christ, the form of fellowship suffering which is closest to the heart of the Savior is to share with Him His burden for lost souls—those for whom He died. Such longings are not natural to any human nature, but are generated in the heart by the Holy Spirit who causes the yielded believer to experience the compassion of God. It is written, "The fruit of the Spirit is love" (Gal. 5:22), and, "The love of God is shed abroad in our hearts by the Holy Ghost which is given unto us" (Rom. 5:5). As an illustration of this ability of the believer to experience the compassion of Christ, the Apostle testifies of himself thus, "I say the truth in Christ, I lie not, my conscience also bearing me witness in the Holy Ghost, that I have great heaviness and continual sorrow in my heart. For I could wish that myself were accursed from Christ for my brethren, my kinsmen according to the flesh" (Rom. 9:1–3). Partnership with Christ in suffering is real and reflects the fact that the Christian occupies a position of untold distinction.

e. PARTNERS WITH CHRIST IN PRAYER. The very act of praying in the name of Christ is in itself an assumption that He also makes petition to the Father for those things that are in the will of God and for which the Christian prays. The central passage bearing on this aspect of partnership is John 14:12–14: "Verily, verily, I say unto you, He that believeth on me, the works that I do shall he do also; and greater works than these shall he do; because I go unto my Father. And whatsoever ye shall ask in my name, that will I do, that the Father may be glorified in the Son. If ye shall ask any thing in my name, I will do it." "Greater works" are to be done by the Son of God in answer to the believer's prayer in His name. The partnership in responsibility is defined thus, "If ye shall ask . . . I will do."

f. PARTNERS WITH CHRIST IN BETROTHAL. To be betrothed to a person is a position which is both definite and demanding. It is also a partnership. The Church is espoused as a bride to Christ. The marriage day is that of His return to receive her unto Himself. It was the Apostle's desire that he might present believers a chaste virgin (not *as* a chaste virgin) to Christ (2 Cor. 11:2); and from Ephesians 5:25–27 it is to be understood that Christ loves the Church as a bridegroom might love a bride and that He gave Himself for His Bride.

g. PARTNERS IN EXPECTATION. The "blessed hope" (Titus 2:13) is ever the expectation of the instructed Christian; for the coming of Christ will be the moment of release from these limitations into the fulness of glory, and the moment of seeing Him who is the center of all reality for the believer. But Christ, too, is now "expecting" (Heb. 10:13), and His longings to claim His bride are as great as ever His willingness to die for her.

All partnerships in human relations create their corresponding positions and possessions; in like manner the sevenfold partnership which the child of God sustains with Christ creates positions and possessions, and these are riches of divine grace.

24. HAVING ACCESS TO GOD. Could any human being catch but one brief vision of the glory, majesty, and holiness of God, from that time forth that one would marvel that any human being—even if he were unfallen—could have access to God; yet, through Christ as Mediator, sinners are provided with an open door into the presence of God. In attempting to understand what is granted in that access to God, it would be well to pursue certain revealed truths in a purposeful order.

a. ACCESS INTO HIS GRACE. Divine grace in action is that achievement which God is free to undertake because of the satisfaction respecting sin which Christ provided by His death and resurrection; therefore, access into the grace of God is access into the value of His finished work. This door is open to all; but only those who have believed have entered in. Of this position which Christ procured, it is written: "By whom also we have access by faith into this grace wherein we stand" (Rom. 5:2). The believer is not only *saved* by grace (Eph. 2:8), but he *stands* in grace. He is ensphered in divine grace. The same grace that saved him sustains him. The same principle upon which he is saved when he believes, is continually applied to him for safekeeping throughout his earthly pilgrimage. Of the ensphering grace, Peter wrote these words, "But grow in grace, and in the knowledge of our Lord and Saviour Jesus Christ" (2 Pet. 3:18). The thought seems to be that the Christian, being in grace, is appointed therein to grow in the knowledge of Christ. Certainly no one who has not found entrance into divine grace through faith, will grow. It is not a matter of growing more gracious, but of coming to know Christ, which knowledge is possible since the believer has entered the sphere of grace (cf. 2 Cor. 3:18).

b. ACCESS UNTO THE FATHER. Of this specific access it is written: "For through him we both have access by one Spirit unto the Father" (Eph. 2:18). All three Persons of the Godhead appear in this brief text. It declares that both Jew and Gentile, being saved, have access through Christ and by the Spirit unto the Father. The essential part which Christ has accomplished has been considered at length, but there is also a part which the Holy Spirit undertakes. The Christian's apprehension (1 Cor. 2:10), communion (2 Cor. 13:14), and much of his qualification for the divine presence (1 Cor. 12:13), are directly the work of the Holy Spirit. The all-important truth—marvelous beyond comprehension— is that each believer has perfect and immutable access unto the Father.

c. ACCESS IS REASSURING. So perfect, indeed, is this admission into the divine presence and favor that the Christian is urged to come *boldly*. In this instance, boldness becomes the believer, since every obstacle has been removed. Two passages, both in the Epistle to the Hebrews, enjoin this boldness: "Let us therefore come boldly unto the throne of grace, that we may obtain mercy, and find grace to help in time of need" (4:16); "having therefore, brethren, boldness to enter into the holiest by the blood of Jesus, by a new and living way, which he hath consecrated for us, through the veil, that is to say, his flesh" (10:19–20).

To be one to whom unrestrained access into the presence of God is accorded is to occupy a position of superior privilege and standing, whether it be measured by the standards of heaven or of earth.

25. WITHIN THE MUCH MORE CARE OF GOD. It will be conceded by all who are awake to the divine revelation, that the love of God for the unsaved is as immeasurable as infinity; yet there is clear revelation that the expression of divine love for those who are saved is even "much more." The argument is that, if God loved sinners and enemies enough to give His Son to die for them, His attitude will be "much more" toward them when they are reconciled and justified. The Apostle states: "But God commendeth his love toward us, in that, while we were yet sinners, Christ died for us. Much more then, being now justified by his blood, we shall be saved from wrath through him. For if, when we were enemies, we were reconciled to God by the death of his Son, much more, being reconciled, we shall be saved by his life" (Rom. 5:8–10). This inconceivable devotion on the part of God for those He has saved leads on to various blessings for them.

a. OBJECTS OF HIS LOVE. The unchangeable love of God underlies all that He undertakes. It was His love that originated the way of salvation through Christ and thus by infinite grace. It is true that God is propitious; that is, He is able through the death of Christ to receive the sinner with unrestrained favor. The death of Christ did not cause God to love sinners; it was His love which provided that propitiation in and through Christ (John 3:16; Rom. 5:8; 1 John 3:16). The satisfaction which Christ rendered released the love of God from that demand which outraged holiness imposed against the sinner. The love of God knows no variations. It experiences no ups and downs, moods and tenses. It is the love of One who is immutable in all His character and ways.

b. OBJECTS OF HIS GRACE. Men are not saved into a state of probation, but into the sphere of infinite grace—a sphere in which God deals with them as those for whom Christ has died, and whose sins are already borne by a Substitute. That grace contemplates:

(1) *Salvation.* Thus it is written: "that in the ages to come he might shew the exceeding riches of his grace in his kindness toward us through Christ Jesus. For by grace are ye saved through faith; and that not of yourselves: it is the gift of God: not of works, lest any man should boast" (Eph. 2:7–9).

(2) *Safekeeping.* As the Scripture declares: "By whom also we have access by faith into this grace wherein we stand" (Rom. 5:2).

(3) *Service.* Of this it is said: "As thou hast sent me into the world,

even so have I also sent them into the world" (John 17:18); "But unto every one of us is given grace according to the measure of the gift of Christ" (Eph. 4:7).

(4) *Instruction.* So, also, it is asserted: "teaching us that, denying ungodliness and worldly lusts, we should live soberly, righteously, and godly, in this present world; looking for that blessed hope, and the glorious appearing of the great God and our Saviour Jesus Christ" (Titus 2:12–13).

c. OBJECTS OF HIS POWER. A full induction of all passages in which God is said to be *able* to work in behalf of those who trust Him will prove a real help to the student. It will be seen that infinite power is ever actively engaged in the support and defense of the believer. It is written: "And what is the exceeding greatness of his power to us-ward who believe, according to the working of his mighty power" (Eph. 1:19); "For it is God which worketh in you both to will and to do of his good pleasure" (Phil. 2:13).

d. OBJECTS OF HIS FAITHFULNESS. Limitless comfort is provided for those who recognize the faithfulness of God. It is said: "I will never leave thee, nor forsake thee" (Heb. 13:5); "being confident of this very thing, that he which hath begun a good work in you will perform it until the day of Jesus Christ" (Phil. 1:6); "Faithful is he that calleth you, who also will do it" (1 Thess. 5:24).

e. OBJECTS OF HIS PEACE. Not only is that peace *with* God in view (Rom. 5:1) which is due to the fact that all condemnation is removed, but the imparted, experimental peace is promised also: "Peace I leave with you, my peace I give unto you: not as the world giveth, give I unto you. Let not your heart be troubled, neither let it be afraid" (John 14:27); "And let the peace of God rule in your hearts, to the which also ye are called in one body; and be ye thankful" (Col. 3:15), and "The fruit of the Spirit is . . . peace" (Gal. 5:22).

f. OBJECTS OF HIS CONSOLATION. Respecting divine consolation it is written: "Now our Lord Jesus Christ himself, and God, even our Father, which hath loved us, and hath given us everlasting consolation and good hope through grace, comfort your hearts, and stablish you in every good word and work" (2 Thess. 2:16–17).

g. OBJECTS OF HIS INTERCESSION. While it is revealed that the Holy Spirit "maketh intercession" for the saints according to the will of God (Rom. 8:26) and they are enjoined to pray "in the Spirit" (Eph. 6:18; Jude 1:20), it is also indicated that one of the present ministries of Christ in heaven is His unceasing intercession for the saints. In His

Priestly prayer He said that He prayed not for the *cosmos* world, but for those the Father had given Him; and it is probable that His present intercession, like this Priestly prayer, is restricted to His own who are in the world. Three passages assert this heavenly intercession: "Who is he that condemneth? It is Christ that died, yea rather, that is risen again, who is even at the right hand of God, who also maketh intercession for us" (Rom. 8:34); "Wherefore he is able also to save them to the uttermost that come unto God by him, seeing he ever liveth to make intercession for them" (Heb. 7:25); "For Christ is not entered into the holy places made with hands, which are the figures of the true; but into heaven itself, now to appear in the presence of God for us" (Heb. 9:24).

To be included thus in the "much more" love and care of God becomes a position in divine grace which is of surpassing value.

26. HIS INHERITANCE. A partial anticipation of this position in grace has been expressed under the previous heading, which announced that each Christian is a gift of the Father to the Son; however, beyond the treasure which he is to Christ as a gift from the Father, Ephesians 1:18 asserts that the believer is also the inheritance of the Father. This exalted truth is the subject of the Apostle's prayer. As though, apart from the supernatural revelation of the Holy Spirit, they could not understand, he prays "the eyes of your understanding being enlightened; that ye may know what is the hope of his calling, and what the riches of the glory of his inheritance in the saints" (Eph. 1:18). Much is promised the believer respecting his future place in glory. It is written: "And the glory which thou gavest me I have given them; that they may be one, even as we are one" (John 17:22); "Moreover whom he did predestinate, them he also called: and whom he called, them he also justified: and whom he justified, them he also glorified" (Rom. 8:30); "When Christ, who is our life, shall appear, then shall ye also appear with him in glory" (Col. 3:4). It is only by such changes as He shall have wrought in fallen sinners that God will be glorified. They will reflect the "glory of his grace" (Eph. 1:6). Each child of God will serve as a medium or material by which the Shekinah glory of God will be seen.

27. THE INHERITANCE OF THE SAINTS. Far easier to comprehend than that just considered is the truth that the believer has an inheritance in God. The believer's inheritance is God Himself and all that God bestows. This is asserted by Peter thus: "An inheritance incorruptible, and undefiled, and that fadeth not away, reserved in heaven for you" (1 Pet. 1:4). The present blessings which the Spirit brings into the

Christian's heart and life are likened to an earnest or comparatively small payment of all that is yet to be bestowed. The Apostle writes: "which is the earnest of our inheritance until the redemption of the purchased possession, unto the praise of his glory" (Eph. 1:14); "knowing that of the Lord ye shall receive the reward of the inheritance: for ye serve the Lord Christ" (Col. 3:24). An eternal inheritance (Heb. 9:15) is a possession under grace; its specifications are unknowable until they are claimed in heaven.

28. LIGHT IN THE LORD. As presented in the Scriptures with its symbolic meaning, an extensive body of truth is related to the general theme of light. Above all and supreme is the revelation that "God is light" (1 John 1:5). The meaning of this term as thus applied to God is that He is transparently holy and in Him is no moral darkness at all. That holy light which God is, has its manifestation on the face of Christ (2 Cor. 4:6). The believer has, by divine grace, become light (Eph. 5:8)—not merely that divine light shines upon him, but *is* light in the Lord. This great reality does not dismiss the truth that the believer is commanded to "walk in the light" (1 John 1:7), the light which God is. Both truths obtain and each engenders its own obligation. To walk in the light is not to become the light; it is rather to be wholly subject to the mind and will of God and adjusted to the holy character of God. In this respect, the Bible is a lamp to the feet and a light upon the path (Ps. 119:105). However, with regard to the light which the believer is, it may be observed that to have received the light into one's being is a possession and to be light in the Lord is a position. No person becomes the light by attempting to shine; rather, having become light in the Lord and that as a divine achievement, he is appointed to shine as a light in a dark world. It is reasonable to conclude that the light which the believer is may be identified as the indwelling divine nature, and that that light is veiled in this world, but will have its manifestation in glory.

29. VITALLY UNITED TO THE FATHER, THE SON, AND THE HOLY SPIRIT. As perplexing as it may be to the human mind, the Scriptures advance six distinct revelations regarding relationships between the Godhead and the believer, and these relationships represent realities which find no comparisons in the sphere of human intercourse. It is said (1) that the believer is in God the Father (1 Thess. 1:1), (2) that God the Father is in the believer (Eph. 4:6), (3) that the believer is in the Son (Rom. 8:1), (4) that the Son is in the believer (John 14:20), (5) that the believer is in the Spirit (Rom. 8:9), and (6) that the Spirit is in the believer (1 Cor. 2:12). The force of these stupendous declara-

tions is centered in the intensity of meaning which must be assigned to the word *in* as used in each of these six declarations. It is evident that to be in the Father, or the Son, or the Holy Spirit is a position; and for the Father, or the Son, or the Holy Spirit to be in the believer constitutes a possession. A corresponding truth grows out of all this which is a result of it, namely, that the believers are one in each other as the Father is in the Son and the Son is in the Father (John 17:21). Since the believer's physical body is a corporate entity, it is not as difficult to think of that body as an abode; and the body is termed a temple of the Holy Spirit (1 Cor. 6:19). On the other hand, it is exceedingly difficult to understand the truth asserted that the believer is in the Father, the Son, and the Holy Spirit. This peculiar relationship to the Son is amplified by a sevenfold declaration or under seven figures: (1) the believer is a member in Christ's Body (1 Cor. 12:13), (2) the believer is to Christ as a branch to the vine (John 15:5), (3) the believer is to Christ as a stone in the building of which Christ is the Chief Cornerstone (Eph. 2:19–22), (4) the believer is to Christ as a sheep in His flock (John 10:27–29), (5) the believer is a part of that company who forms the Bride of Christ (Eph. 5:25–27), (6) the believer is a priest in a kingdom of priests over which Christ is High Priest forever (1 Pet. 2:5, 9), and (7) the believer is a part of the New Creation over which Christ as the Last Adam is the Head (2 Cor. 5:17). In John 14:20: "At that day ye shall know that I am in my Father, and ye in me, and I in you," three great truths are declared as those which the believer is to know specifically in this age, namely, (1) Christ is in the Father, (2) the believer is in Christ, and (3) Christ is in the believer.

Similarly, there is much in the New Testament respecting the relationship which obtains between the Holy Spirit and the believer, which will yet be considered more fully in Volume VI.

The truths declared and distinguished under this heading represent not only the most vital positions and possessions which infinite grace can create, but are the very heart of Christianity, being never intimated in the Old Testament.

30. BLESSED WITH THE EARNEST OR FIRST-FRUITS OF THE SPIRIT. As before intimated, the immeasurable blessings which come to the child of God because of his relation to the Holy Spirit are as a comparatively small down-payment which binds with certainty the larger gifts of heaven's glory. These present ministries of the Spirit are said to be an "earnest" (2 Cor. 1:22; Eph. 1:14) and "firstfruits" (Rom. 8:23) of the Spirit. There are five of these present riches: (1) The

believer is *born* of the Spirit (John 3:6), by which operation Christ is begotten in the one who exercises saving faith. (2) The believer is *baptized* by the Spirit (1 Cor. 12:13), which is a work of the Holy Spirit by which the believer is joined to Christ's Body and comes to be in Christ, and therefore a partaker of all that Christ is. (3) The believer is *indwelt* or *anointed* by the Spirit (John 7:39; Rom. 5:5; 8:9; 2 Cor. 1:21; Gal. 4:6; 1 John 2:27; 3:24), by which Presence the believer is equipped for every conflict and service. (4) The believer is *sealed* by the Spirit (2 Cor. 1:22; Eph. 4:30), which is the work of God the Holy Spirit by which the children of God are made secure unto the day of redemption. (5) The believer may be *filled* with the Spirit (Eph. 5:18), which ministry of the Spirit releases His power and effectiveness in the heart in which He dwells.

The Spirit's work in and through the Christian results in both positions and possessions that are themselves marvelous realities of the riches of divine grace, and all of these together form but a foretaste of the glory which is assured in heaven.

31. GLORIFIED. What God has determined, though it be yet future, is properly looked upon as sufficiently certain to be considered a present achievement. He is the One "who . . . calleth those things which be not as though they were" (Rom. 4:17). Awaiting the child of God is a surpassing heavenly glory—even partaking of the infinite glory which belongs to the Godhead. Of this fact it is written: "For I reckon that the sufferings of this present time are not worthy to be compared with the glory which shall be revealed in us" (Rom. 8:18); "When Christ, who is our life, shall appear, then shall ye also appear with him in glory" (Col. 3:4). It is not to be concluded that there is a present and a future glory which are unrelated. The present glory is the divine reckoning of the future glory to be even a present reality. No passage more clearly asserts this fact than Romans 8:30, which states: "Moreover whom he did predestinate, them he also called: and whom he called, them he also justified: and whom he justified, them he also glorified."

To be a glorified saint is a position in divine grace of immeasurable riches and, in the certainty of the divine purpose, it becomes a possession.

32. COMPLETE IN HIM. This, with the theme which follows, serves as a conclusion of that which has gone before in this attempt to record the riches of divine grace; yet these are specific disclosures of all that enters into the exceeding grace of God. What may be included in the word *complete* when the Apostle says, "For in him dwelleth all the fulness of

the Godhead bodily. And ye are complete in him, which is the head of all principality and power" (Col. 2:9–10), is beyond the range of human understanding. No careless use of terms will be discovered in any Scripture, and this passage presents the voice of the Holy Spirit declaring that, to the degree by which God values things and according to those standards which God employs, the child of God is complete; but so great a transformation is due to the all-determining fact that he is in Christ. The truth is thus once more presented that, because of his vital union with Christ, the believer partakes of all that Christ is. The Father finds infinite delight in the Son, nor can He find delight in that which is less than the perfection of the Son. While men may ever be before the Father as the creatures of His hand, those who are saved are, even now, perfected in His sight by and through their vital relation to the Son. Thus a principle is introduced which is far removed from human custom or practice and, naturally, beyond human understanding, but not beyond the range of human acceptance or belief, since it is declared in the Word of God. To be complete in Christ is a glorious reality and is a portion of that grace which is extended to all who believe.

33. POSSESSING EVERY SPIRITUAL BLESSING. No text of Scripture more perfectly accounts for *all* the riches of grace than Ephesians 1:3, which reads: "Blessed be the God and Father of our Lord Jesus Christ, who hath blessed us with all spiritual blessings in heavenly places in Christ." All the riches of grace tabulated in the thirty-two points made before are to be included in this sweeping term—"all spiritual blessings." These are again and finally declared to be realized on the basis of the believer's relation to Christ. Thus all positions and possessions which together measure the riches of divine grace are traced to the believer's place in Christ. These are accorded the one who believes on Christ to the saving of his soul.

CONCLUSION

It would hardly be amiss to restate the truth that salvation is a work of God for man and not a work of man for God. It is what God's love prompts Him to do and not a mere act of pity which rescues creatures from their misery. To realize the satisfaction of His love God has been willing to remove by an infinite sacrifice the otherwise insuperable hindrance which sin has imposed; He is, likewise, overcoming the wicked opposition to His grace which the fallen human will presents by inclining His elect ones to exercise saving faith in Christ. When the way is thus clear, God is free to do all that infinite love dictates. Nothing short of transformations which are infinite will satisfy infinite love. An inadequate record of these riches of grace which together represent the infinity of saving grace has been submitted; but it still remains true that "the half has never been told." The student who is ambitious to be accurate in gospel preaching will not only observe but ever contend for the truth that all these riches are purely a work of God, and that to secure them the individual could do no more than to receive at the hand of God what He is free to give in and through Christ Jesus. Those who believe on Christ in the sense that they receive Him (John 1:12) as their Savior enter instantly into all that divine love provides. These thirty-three positions and possessions are not bestowed in succession, but simultaneously. They do not require a period of time for their execution; but are wrought instantaneously. They measure the present difference which obtains between one who is saved and one who is not saved.

> "Oh to grace how great a debtor
> Daily I'm constrained to be!
> Let thy goodness, like a fetter,
> Bind my wandering heart to Thee."

THE ETERNAL SECURITY OF
THE BELIEVER

Chapter XIV

INTRODUCTION TO THE DOCTRINE
OF SECURITY

THIS ASPECT of Soteriology, commonly styled by earlier theologians *the perseverance of the saints,* contends that no individual once the recipient of the saving grace of God will ever fall totally and finally from that estate, but that he shall be "kept by the power of God through faith unto salvation" (1 Pet. 1:5). The doctrine of security is one of the five points of the Calvinistic system, but it is more distinguished by the fact that it is set forth in the New Testament in the most absolute terms and is there seen to be an indivisible feature of that which God undertakes when a soul is saved. This major doctrine is well stated in the *Westminster Confession of Faith,* which declares: "They whom God hath accepted in his Beloved, effectually called and sanctified by his Spirit, can neither totally nor finally fall away from the state of grace; but shall certainly persevere therein to the end, and be eternally saved" (17.1).

That the Scripture on this theme requires careful exposition to the end that it may not even seem to contradict itself is readily conceded, and this feature of this truth will not be overlooked. In such a consideration, a "verily, verily" should not be countermanded by an "if." The words of certainty must stand as they appear on the Sacred Page.

The Calvinistic system, which is here both held and defended as being more nearly Pauline than any other, is built upon a recognition of four basic truths, each of which should be comprehended in its basic character. These truths are: (1) *Depravity,* by which term is meant that there is nothing in fallen man that could commend him to God. He is an object of divine grace. (2) *Efficacious grace,* by which term is meant that fallen man, in being saved, is wrought upon wholly by God— even the faith which he exercises in his salvation is a "gift of God" (Eph.

267

2:8). (3) *Sovereign and eternal election,* by which term is meant that those who are saved by efficacious grace from the estate of depravity have been chosen of God for that blessedness from before the foundation of the world (Eph. 1:4; Rom. 8:30). (4) *Eternal security,* by which term it is meant that those chosen of God and saved by grace are, of necessity, preserved unto the realization of the design of God. Since sovereign election purposes this and sovereign grace accomplishes it, the Scriptures could not—being infinitely true—do other than to declare the Christian's security without reservation or complication. This the Scriptures assuredly declare.

Rationalism in its varied forms and Arminianism in particular challenge these sovereign verities. To the Arminian the limiting effect of depravity is annulled to a large degree by the supposed bestowment upon all men of a so-called "common grace" which provides ability on the sinner's part to turn to Christ. According to this belief, men are saved by divine grace into a momentary right relation with God from which they can fall. The continuation in that right relation with God—regardless of the fact that it is the realization of the divine purpose—is made by the Arminian to depend on human merit and conduct. Similarly, sovereign election is to the Arminian no more than divine foreknowledge by which God is able to make choice of those who will act righteously in respect to His offers of grace—a foreseeing and consequent recognition of human merit, which recognition contradicts the doctrine of sovereign grace (Rom. 11:6).

Of all New Testament doctrines two—sovereign election and sovereign grace—are most closely related to the doctrine of eternal security. This is obvious. Personal election, which is that form of it that is alone involved, is distinctly unto eternal realities which, of necessity, can be realized only by the safekeeping to final fruition of all who are included in election. Similarly, it is to be seen that the ground upon which sovereign grace advances provides a holy God with the requisite freedom, not merely to save those who are unworthy, but to preserve them after they are saved—even when, as all are, they are unworthy. It is in this larger field of operation for the grace of God, when not comprehended, that Arminian notions of insecurity arise.

Therefore, if God in sovereign election has determined in eternal past ages that some shall be "before him" in glory (Eph. 1:4) and these are predestined to that glory (Rom. 8:30), and if God in sovereign grace has removed every barrier to that purpose which sin and the human will impose, security is assured, and to deny it is to contend that either sovereign election or sovereign grace (or both together) is impotent. By such a line of indisputable reasoning, it is concluded that the doctrine of security is an indispensable feature of Pauline and Calvinistic theology.

On the vital importance of this aspect of truth in its relation to a right understanding of Biblical doctrine, Principal Cunningham in his *Historical Theology* (3rd ed., II, 493) writes:

If it be true that God has, from eternity, absolutely and unconditionally chosen some men, certain persons, to eternal life, these men assuredly will all infallibly be saved. If it be also true that He has arranged that no man shall be saved, unless upon earth he be brought into a state of grace, unless he repent and believe, and persevere in faith and holiness, He will assuredly give to all whom He has chosen to life faith and holiness, and will infallibly secure that they shall persevere therein unto the end. And as it is further taught by Calvinists, that God produces in some men faith and conversion in the execution of His decree of election, just because He has decreed to save *these* men, —and does so for the purpose of saving them,—the *whole* of what they teach under the head of perseverance is thus effectually provided for, and thoroughly established,—faith and regeneration being never produced in any except those whose ultimate salvation has been secured, and whose perseverance, therefore, in faith and holiness must be certain and infallible. All this is too plain to require any illustration; and Calvinists must of course, in consistency, take the responsibility of maintaining the certain perseverance of all believers or saints,—of all in whom faith and holiness have been once produced.

To this may be added the testimony of Dr. Ralph Wardlaw, who writes:

Respecting this doctrine we may observe in general, that it follows as a necessary sequence from the doctrine of personal election which we have just been endeavouring to illustrate in its scriptural meaning, and to establish on the basis of scriptural authority. Election is election to salvation; not to privilege merely, or the enjoyment of the means of salvation, but, through these means, to salvation itself. If this be the Bible doctrine, then it follows inevitably, that all who are elected to salvation shall obtain salvation. To hold the former, and question the latter, would be self-contradictory. Perseverance is a consequence of election, and involved in it. There can properly be no personal election to salvation without it. The one doctrine is necessary to the integrity of the other. Instead of being distinct doctrines, they are integrant parts of the same doctrine. To suppose any who are of the elect to fail of final salvation, is to render election altogether nugatory. The arguments, therefore, on these two of the five points are clearly reciprocal; that is, every proof of election is a proof of perseverance, and every proof of perseverance is a proof of election. —*System of Theology*, II, 550

While Christians and their creeds are divided into the two groups—Calvinists with their certainty of security and Arminians with their doubts and imaginary dangers—it will be found that belief or disbelief in security is personal and individual, depending on the degree of understanding of the Word of God and conformity to that Word which the individual possesses. Many members in Calvinistic churches are, for want of training in doctrine, unable to rise above the rationalism of the Arminian view, while a few who are enrolled in Arminian memberships have discovered the gracious reality of eternal security. The significant fact will speak for itself, that great multitudes upon right instruction turn from Arminianism to Calvinism, while, on the other hand, none have been known to turn from an instructed, intelligent Calvinism to Arminianism.

At least three exceptional beliefs which are outside the range of either Calvinism or Arminianism should be noted: (1) Augustine held that some might be saved who were not of the elect and that these might fall away. His view never gained a worthy following. Of this Augustinian view Principal Cunningham has written:

Augustine seems to have thought that men who were true believers, and who were regenerated, so as to have been really brought under the influence of divine truth and religious principle, might fall away and finally perish; but then he did not think that those persons who might, or did, thus fall away and perish belonged to the number of those who had been predestinated, or elected, to life. He held that all those who were elected to life must, and did, persevere, and thus attain to salvation. It was of course abundantly evident, that if God chose some men, absolutely and unconditionally, to eternal life,—and this Augustine firmly believed,—these persons must, and would, certainly be saved. Whether persons might believe and be regenerated who had not been predestinated to life, and who, in consequence, might fall away, and thereby fail to attain salvation, is a distinct question; and on this question Augustine's views seem to have been obscured and perverted by the notions that then generally prevailed about the objects and effects of outward ordinances, and especially by something like the doctrine of baptismal regeneration, which has been, perhaps, as powerful and extensive a cause of deadly error as any doctrine that Satan ever invented. Augustine's error, then, lay in supposing that men might believe and be regenerated who had not been elected to life, and might consequently fail of ultimate salvation; but he never did, and never could, embrace any notion so irrational and inconsequential, as that God could have absolutely chosen some even to life, and then permitted them to fall away and to perish; and the negation of this notion, which Augustine never held, constitutes the sum and substance of what Calvinists have taught upon the subject of perseverance.—*Op. cit.,* p. 490

(2) Arminius, whatever his followers have embraced of part-truth or error, did not himself renounce the belief in security. To quote Principal Cunningham again:

Arminius never wholly renounced the doctrine of the certain perseverance of all believers, even after he had abandoned all the other principles of Calvinism, but spoke of this as a point on which he had not fully made up his mind, and which, he thought, required further investigation,—thus virtually bearing testimony to the difficulty of disposing of the scriptural evidence on which the doctrine rests. His immediate followers, likewise, professed for a time some hesitation upon this point; but their contemporary opponents do not seem to have given them much credit for sincerity in the doubts which they professed to entertain regarding it, because, while they did not for a time directly and explicitly support a negative conclusion, the whole current of their statements and arguments seemed plainly enough to indicate that they had already renounced the generally received doctrine of the Reformed churches upon this subject. They very soon, even before the Synod of Dort, openly renounced the doctrine of the perseverance of the saints, along with the other doctrines of Calvinism; and I am not aware that any instance has since occurred, in which any Calvinist has hesitated to maintain this doctrine, or any Arminian has hesitated to deny it.—*Ibid.*, pp. 490–91

(3) Certain Lutherans have contended that one once saved might fall away, but that such a one would, with absolute certainty, be restored and saved in the end. This conception, too, has secured no following.

It hardly seems necessary to point out that this discussion concerns those only who are saved in the New Testament meaning of that word. Obviously, there are those who are mere professors who possess every outward appearance—baptism, church affiliation, sympathy, and service—who are lacking features that really identify a saved person. It is assured that mere professors "go out" eventually from the company of the believers. The Apostle John states respecting mere professors that "they went out from us, but they were not of us; for if they had been of us, they would no doubt have continued with us: but they went out, that they might be made manifest that they were not all of us" (1 John 2:19). In the words "They went out from us," there is a superficial relationship acknowledged. Similarly, in the words "They were not of us," another relationship is recognized. The former could mean no more than a profession, while the latter implies the existence of the eternal bonds which those who went out did not share. God does not fail to discern the true classification of men. It is written of Him: "Nevertheless the foundation of God standeth sure, having this seal, The Lord knoweth them that are his. And, Let every one that nameth the name of Christ depart from iniquity" (2 Tim. 2:19). None could go out from the company of believers who had not first been with them; and those thus with them, of whom it could be said that they were not of them, could be *with* them only in the sense that they were mere professors (cf. Matt. 13:3–7).

The keeping power of God is vouchsafed only to those who are saved. When Arminians assert that supposed Christians have ceased to function as such, it is well to recall the sifting process which is described by the words, "They went out from us . . . that they might be made manifest that they were not all of us."

In concluding this word of introduction, it may serve a worthy purpose to point out (1) that the truth of eternal security is inherent in the nature of salvation itself. This fact, it is anticipated, will be made clear in the discussion which follows, as it has been made clear from the analysis of divine grace which has gone before. If salvation is no more than a detached coin which one holds in the hand and is secure only by virtue of a feeble human grasp, it might easily, nay, almost certainly, be lost. On the other hand, if salvation is the creation of a new being composed of unchangeable and imperishable elements, and in every aspect of it is made to depend on the perfect and immutable merit of the Son of God, there can be no failure. Indeed there can be, and too often is, personal sin on the part of the one who is saved; but, as has been seen, that is accounted for to the infinite satisfaction of God's holiness upon another and all-sufficient basis. (2) Actually, there are no proper grounds for drawing a distinction between salvation and safekeeping, though for practical purposes such a distinction may be set up. The conclusion of the preceding discussion on that which God undertakes when He saves a soul, demonstrates the truthfulness of the assertion that God is not offering a salvation to men which is not eternal in its very nature; and in spite of all human experience, which is too often cited as a determining factor, it is true that no soul once saved has ever been, or ever will be, lost again. Doubts about the security of those who are saved may be traced almost universally to a failure to comprehend the reality of that which God accomplishes in sovereign grace.

These declarations, confessedly dogmatic, will be defended in the following pages. This thesis will follow a twofold analysis in the next two chapters, namely, (1) the Arminian view and (2) the Calvinistic view.

CHAPTER XV

THE ARMINIAN VIEW OF SECURITY

THOUGH BUT LITTLE reference has been made in this work to one of them, three systems of theology have flourished which offer their varying contentions in the field of Soteriology. These systems are Socinianism, Arminianism, and Calvinism. Socinianism and Calvinism are as far removed the one from the other as midnight and noontime. Socinianism in its day denied almost every feature of Christian doctrine, while Calvinism adheres rigidly to the revelation God has given. It is Calvinism which seeks to honor God—Father, Son, and Spirit—by its views respecting depravity, human guilt, and human helplessness, and these in the light of divine sovereignty, divine supremacy, and the sufficiency of divine grace. On the other hand, Arminianism sustains an intermediate ground between the rationalism of Socinianism and the determined Biblical character of Calvinism. A certain group of Arminians have leaned toward Socinianism and were these advocates consistent, they, like the Socinians, would deny the work of Christ and much of the work of the Holy Spirit. The more conservative Arminians—such as Arminius himself—though inconsistent with themselves and steeped with Socinian rationalism in their approach to every soteriological truth, do evince a degree of amenability to the Word of God and the doctrines which that Word exhibits.

There are truths, such as the lost estate of man through sin and the need of salvation, that are common to Arminians and Calvinists alike. On the ground of these common beliefs a degree of united effort in evangelism has been possible between the representatives of these two systems. The real controversy between the two, however, has not been abandoned, nor could it be. It will be found that in the case of each major theme related to Soteriology the Arminian position is weak and inaccurate and to that extent misleading. The instructed preacher and teacher will contend for the precise meaning of the Scriptures. What may be passed over in the interests of harmony in united Christian service cannot as easily be passed over when a worthy declaration of truth is called for. Along with this, it should be pointed out—and history will verify the assertion—that sustained, extended, unprejudiced study of the Sacred Text must and, therefore, does lead to the Calvinistic position. It is conceivable hypothetically that both Arminianism and Calvinism are wrong, but it is wholly impossible for both to be right. The Bible offers no contradictions. If one system is right, the other is wrong. There is no compromise possible. Through extended study uncounted multitudes have turned from Arminianism to Calvinism; but history offers few, if any, examples of an opposite movement.

It will be remembered that, after all, the appellations *Arminianism* and *Calvinism* are no more than convenient names for general systems and that in each of these systems there is represented a wide latitude of variation in the doctrine being held. As already indicated, Arminius himself did not hold the extreme views which some of his followers have advanced, yet they retain the Arminian name. In like manner, the very fact that there are at least two schools of Calvinists precludes the possibility of Calvin being the promoter of every form of doctrine which appears under his name. Under other disciplines the student would do well to read attentively the extended history covering the development of each of these systems.

In respect to the truth of eternal security, it will be noted, as of other major doctrines, that it is impossible to be in agreement with all sincere men. In the light of the disagreement which obtains, the student can do no more than to be amenable to the Word of God. The two claims—that the Christian is secure and that he is insecure—present a complete contradiction and no middle ground of compromise could possibly be found.

While the doctrine of security may not represent the most important difference which exists between these two theological systems, neither the claim respecting security nor the claim respecting insecurity can be maintained apart from the effort to harmonize each with the whole body of soteriological truth. Bitterness between the advocates of these divergent systems could hardly be avoided when there is no way of reconciliation between them; and this controversy is greatly stimulated by the immeasurable importance of the question. The issue that is paramount is whether the saving work of Christ on the cross includes the safekeeping of the one who trusts Him, or not. This is the central and precise issue in the controversy. Either Christ did enough by His death concerning the believer's sins that it can be said that "there is therefore now no condemnation to them which are in Christ Jesus" (though it is not said that there is no chastisement), or He did not. Again, either Christ did enough by His death and resurrection in fulfilling the sweet savor type, that it can be said that the believer possesses eternal life and the perfect standing of the Son of God, being in Him, or He did not. If there is no sufficient ground for the removal of condemnation and no sufficient ground for the impartation of eternal life and the imputing of Christ's merit, then the most vital teachings of the New Testament are rendered void. It is these so-compelling features of truth which are conspicuous by their absence from Arminian writings. Arminian theologians are a product of the limited teachings which are presented in their schools from generation to generation, and therefore the deeper realities are not known by them. To know these realities is to embrace them, for they constitute the warp and woof of the Pauline gospel.

The Arminian view may be divided for convenience into three general features: (1) the Arminian view of major soteriological doctrines, (2) the Arminian emphasis upon human experience and reason, and (3) the Arminian appeal to the Scriptures.

I. THE ARMINIAN VIEW OF MAJOR SOTERIOLOGICAL DOCTRINES

The field is properly restricted in this discussion to problems of soteriological doctrine. The consideration of the Arminian view of the value of Christ's death is not entered upon here and this is due to the fact that it has had an extended treatment in an earlier portion of this work. The doctrines to be noted are: (a) the Arminian view of original sin, (b) the Arminian view of universal and efficacious calling, (c) the Arminian view of divine decrees, (d) the Arminian view of the fall, (e) the Arminian view of omniscience, (f) the Arminian view of divine sovereignty, and (g) the Arminian view of sovereign grace.

1. THE ARMINIAN VIEW OF ORIGINAL SIN. It is exceedingly difficult for a system of doctrine, which builds so much on the freedom of the human will and contends that all men are by virtue of a common grace enabled to act without natural or supernatural restraint in the matter of their own salvation, to defend unconditionally the doctrine of total depravity. It is observable that Arminianism has put but little emphasis upon the teaching respecting that inability which is the nature and essence of original sin. The Arminian notion of depravity, whatever it is supposed to be in its original form, is largely overcome, it is contended, by a fancied common grace. However, in the working of this scheme, one of the Arminian inconsistencies—a withdrawing with one hand what is bestowed with the other—is displayed. It is rather too much

to suppose that a common grace—itself without Biblical justification—is a complete corrective of total depravity; and it will not be without explanation, in part at least, if, starting with such a premise as their idea of common grace provides, the Arminians drift into equally unscriptural notions respecting sanctification and sinless perfection. Naturally, the will of man, which is supposed to be emancipated by common grace, may, as effectually, defeat the realization of that which is best. It is certain that, when given an unrestrained freedom of volition, that volition will not always turn in the right direction or toward God. It may as readily turn from God, and that, it is contended, even after years of life and experience in a regenerate state. Over against this fallacious rationalism—this unsupported theory and feeble deification of man—the Scriptures assert, and in accordance therewith the Calvinists teach, that man is totally depraved, that God must and does move in behalf of fallen man for his salvation—even engendering saving faith—and that salvation, being distinctly a work of God, is, like all His works, incapable of failure. It is thus demonstrated that the erroneous exaltation of the human ability in the beginning becomes man's effectual undoing in the end. Over against this, the man who is totally incompetent, falling into the hands of God, who acts in sovereign grace, is saved and safe forever. For such an achievement the glory is not to be shared by fallen man but is altogether due God alone.

2. THE ARMINIAN VIEW OF UNIVERSAL AND EFFICACIOUS CALLING. Without reference to a limited or an unlimited redemption—which theme some theologians are determined to bring into the discussion of an efficacious call and which it is believed has but a remote relation to the subject in hand—the real question is whether, as the Arminian contends, the divine influence upon men whereby they are enabled to receive the gospel and to be saved is that common grace which the Arminian claims is bestowed upon all men, or whether that divine enablement, as the Calvinist declares, is a specific, personal call of the individual by which the Holy Spirit moves that one to understand and intelligently to accept the saving grace of God as it is in Christ Jesus. If the contention of the Arminian be true—that God gives no more enablement to one than to another—the fact that, when the gospel is preached alike to each, one is saved and another is not, becomes a matter of the human will which, it is claimed, either accepts or rejects the gracious invitation. Such an arrangement might seem plausible were it not for that array of Scripture, already considered in another connection, which declares that man has no power to move himself toward

God. The New Testament not only lends no support to the Arminian notion of common grace, but definitely teaches that men are helpless in their fallen estate (cf. Rom. 3:11; 1 Cor. 2:14; 2 Cor. 4:3–4; Eph. 2:8–9). On the other hand, the Calvinist contends that, when God by His Spirit inclines one to receive Christ, that one, in so doing, acts only in the consciousness of his own choice. It is obvious that to present a convincing argument to a person which leads that person to make a decision, does not partake of the nature of a coercion of the will. In such a case, every function of the will is preserved and, in relation to the gospel, it remains true that "whoever will may come"; yet back of this truth is the deeper revelation that no fallen man wills to accept Christ until enlightened by the Holy Spirit (John 16:7–11). Principal Cunningham writes on this general problem as follows:

It is important to fix in our minds a clear conception of the *alternatives* in the explanation of this matter, according as the Calvinistic or the Arminian doctrine upon the subject is adopted. The thing to be accounted for is,— the positive production of faith and regeneration in some men; while others continue, under the same outward call and privileges, in their natural state of impenitence and unbelief. Now this is just virtually the question, Who maketh those who have passed from death to life, and are now advancing towards heaven, to differ from those who are still walking in the broad way? Is it God? or is it themselves? The Calvinists hold that it is God who makes this difference; the Arminians—however they may try to conceal this, by general statements about the grace of God and the assistance of the Spirit—virtually and practically ascribe the difference to believers themselves. God has given sufficient grace— everything necessary for effecting the result—to others as well as to them. There is no difference in the call addressed to them, or in the grace vouchsafed to them. This is equal and alike. There is a difference in the result; and from the sufficiency and consequent substantial equality of the universal grace vouchsafed, this difference in the result must necessarily be ascribed, as to its real adequate cause, to something in themselves,—not to God's grace, not to what He graciously bestowed upon them, but to what they themselves were able to do, and have done, in improving aright what God communicated to them. If sufficient grace is communicated to all who are outwardly called, then no more than what is sufficient is communicated to those who actually repent and believe; for, to assert this, is virtually to deny or retract the position, that what was communicated to those who continue impenitent and unbeliev- ing, *was sufficient or adequate,* and thus to contradict their fundamental doc- trine upon this whole subject. And when the true state of the question, and the real alternatives involved, are thus brought out, there is no difficulty in seeing and proving that the Arminian doctrine is inconsistent with the plain teaching of Scripture,—as to the great principles which regulate or determine men's spiritual character and eternal destiny,—the true source and origin of all that is spiritually good in them,—the real nature of faith and regeneration, as implying changes which men are utterly unable to produce, or even to co-operate, in the first instance, in originating; and as being not only the work of God in men,—the gift of God to men,—but also, and more particularly, as being in every instance the result of a special operation of the Holy Ghost,—an operation represented as altogether peculiar and distinguishing,—bestowed upon some and not upon others, according to the counsel of God's own will, and *certainly* or infallibly effecting, wherever it is bestowed, all those things that accompany salvation.—*Historical Theology*, 3rd ed., II, 404–5

Again it will be seen that the Arminian exaltation of the human will in the matter of personal salvation encourages those same Arminians to contend, as they do, that the same free will by which the individual accepts Christ is itself able to depart from God after he is saved. To such rationalistic conclusions, the Word of God, which asserts the inability of man to turn to God, lends no support. It is rather revealed that, after one is saved, "it is God which worketh in you both to will and to do of his good pleasure" (Phil. 2:13); nor does this continuous inclination by the Spirit of the Christian's volition partake in any respect of a coercion of the human will.

3. THE ARMINIAN VIEW OF DIVINE DECREES. Under this aspect of the general theme, this solemn truth respecting God is approached again. None but the most careless will fail to recognize that the subject of divine decrees, with its corresponding doctrines of predestination, election, and reprobation, involves the contemplation of the most fathomless, inaccessible, and mysterious themes to which the human mind may be addressed. To comprehend this vast subject would be equivalent to comprehending the mind of God. That difficulties arise in the mind of man when reflecting on so great a subject is to be expected, since it could not be otherwise. Similarly, it is generally conceded that this topic in all its bearings—philosophical, theological, and practical—has been more considered than any other; yet the mysteries involved must remain inscrutable until the greater light of another world breaks upon the human mind.

In its simple form, the question now in view may be stated thus: Did God have a plan in eternity past which He is executing in time? The two extreme positions—Socinianism and Calvinism—may well be compared at this point. The former held that all future events which depend upon secondary causes, such as the human will, are by necessity unknowable even to God, while the Calvinists maintain that God has not only ordained whatsoever cometh to pass, but is executing the same through His providence. Midway between these so divergent conceptions is the position of the Arminians—a position in which conflicting ideas appear. Arminians have not been willing to deny the foreknowledge of God in agreement with the Socinians; nor have they been willing to accept that estimation of God which accords to Him the unconditional authority to act, power to achieve, and purpose to govern, in all that cometh to pass. Therefore, the doctrines of divine decrees, of predestination, of sovereign election, and of retribution are by the Arminians either directly denied or explained away by recourse to reason. At times the plain assertions of the Sacred Text have been distorted in this effort. They claim that God had no other decree respecting the salvation of men than that He would save those who believe, and condemn and reprobate those who do not believe. Beyond this, man is responsible apart from any divine relationship. Having sent His Son into the world to remove the insuperable obstacle of sin and having removed man's inability by a bestowal upon him of a supposed common grace, man is left to make his own choice, though, of course, the gospel must be preached unto him. According to this plan, God determines nothing, bestows nothing apart from the removal of inability, and secures nothing. Certain individuals are chosen of God only in the sense that He foresaw their faith and good works—which faith and good works arise in themselves and are not divinely wrought. In the end, according to this system, man is his own savior. A salvation which originates in such uncertainties, builds upon mere foreknowledge of human merit, and exalts the human will to the place of sovereignty, cannot make place for the doctrine of security, since eternal security of those who are saved depends on the sovereign undertakings of God.

4. THE ARMINIAN VIEW OF THE FALL. A return to a full discussion of the fall of man, already pursued at length in Volume II, is uncalled for here. What has been written before must serve as a background for this brief reference to a theme so extended and mysterious.

Far more than is sometimes realized, the doctrine of the fall of man is closely related to the whole Biblical scheme of predestination. Apart from the fall with its complete ruin of the race, there could be no sufficient basis for the doctrine of sovereign grace with its utter disregard for human merit, nor for a defense against the notion that sovereign election represents a respect of personal qualities in man on the part of God. Arminians of the older school have not denied the fall of man, or the extent of that fall. They suppose, however, no matter how complete the fall, that it is overcome by the bestowal of common grace. From the moment that grace is bestowed, the case of a man is different. Ability on man's part to act for or against the will of God becomes the cornerstone of the Arminian structure of Soteriology. The supposed ability to reject God not only conditions and makes contingent the salvation of men to the extent that God may assume no more than to foreknow what man will do, but that supposed ability survives after regeneration and renders it possible for the redeemed to degenerate back to their original lost estate. Calvinists maintain that men are wholly unable to deliver themselves or to take one step in the direction of their own salvation, that men have no claim upon God for salvation because of merit, and that the salvation of men is a divine undertaking built upon a righteous ground which not only provides a holy God with freedom to save meritless men, but provides as well the same righteous freedom on God's part by which He can keep them saved forever.

When this divinely wrought arrangement for the salvation of men through grace is abandoned and a merit system for man is substituted, as the Arminians choose to do, they find themselves beset with fears, backslidings, and failures which have no recognition in the New Testament. A grave question arises under the Arminian system, namely, whether men who have been impressed with the notion that they are to a large degree their own saviors and keepers, will ever find the rest and peace which is the portion of those who have ceased from their own works and are wholly cast upon God.

5. THE ARMINIAN VIEW OF OMNISCIENCE. No slight difficulty for the Arminian system arises from the obvious fact that God could foreknow nothing as certain in the future unless He had Himself made it certain by foreordination. Neither could foreknowledge function apart from foreordination, nor foreordination apart from foreknowledge. Merely to foreknow what will be determined by secondary causes, leaves the entire program of events adrift without chart or compass. According to His Word, God assuredly foreknows, foreordains, and executes. Every prediction of the Bible incorporates these elements, and nowhere more conclusively than in the events connected with the death of Christ. God foreknew that His Son would die upon a cross, but He did more about it than merely to foreknow. Peter declares that Christ as the Lamb was "foreordained before the foundation of the world" (1 Pet. 1:20); and so great an event could not be left to the uncertainties of human wills. "Wicked hands" crucified the Son of God, but this was according to the "determinate counsel and foreknowledge of God" (Acts 2:23). The salvation of each individual who believes on Christ is no more an accident of human determination than is the death of

Christ. The Arminian idea of election to eternal glory on the part of some, is that it includes those who believe on Christ, persevere, and die in the faith, whereas the Scriptures teach that certain men believe, persevere, and die in the faith because of the fact that they are elect and destined to eternal glory. When man is given the responsibility of working out his own eternal destiny, as Arminianism expects him to do, it will be remembered that all this could be done as effectively whether God foreknew it or not. Security, according to the Arminian conception of it, is that which God foreknew men would do in their own behalf and, since the human element bulks largely in it, the actual arrival of a soul in heaven's glory is more or less accidental—certainly not predetermined and executed by God.

6. THE ARMINIAN VIEW OF DIVINE SOVEREIGNTY. It is conceded by all who are of a pious mind that God is the Supreme Ruler of the universe and that He exercises His authority and power to that end. That He is putting into effect precisely what He had before designed, would not create prejudice as a proposition by itself, were it not for the fact that such an admission leads on logically to the Calvinistic position respecting the predestination, justification, and glorification of all whom He has chosen for eternal salvation. Calvinists contend that God acts in perfect reason, but upon a level much higher than may be comprehended by the human understanding; and therefore they do not assume to assign a reason for all of God's ways in the universe and with men. Arminians, however, seek to assign a reason for God's dealings with men and do, by so much, deny His sovereignty. It is a worthy attitude to believe that God rules over all things, executing precisely His own will and purpose, and that in doing this He acts always within the limitations which His adorable attributes impose. It follows, also, that, because of His omnipotence, God could have prevented any and every form of evil, and that, as evil is present, it is serving a purpose which is worthy of God and which will, in the end, be recognized as worthy by all intelligences. Arminians tend to discredit the sovereignty of God by assuming that events are not necessarily to be considered as having a place or part in the divine will. This has led to much discussion regarding the divine volition. Arminians are wont to distinguish an antecedent will from a consequent will in God. The former moves Him to save all men, while the latter is conditioned by the conduct of men. The antecedent will is not a sovereign will; it, too, is restricted by human action. Such a conception is far removed from the Calvinistic teaching concerning the efficacious will of God—that which not only elects to save

some, but actually does save them and preserve them, having anticipated all things requisite to that end and having provided those requisite things. As before stated, the two impediments or barriers which
stood in the way were sin and the freedom of the human will. In the
sacrificial death of His Son, God dealt finally with the obstacle which
sin engenders. By moving the hearts of men to desire His saving grace
(which acts have no semblance to coercion), He removes the obstruc-
tion which the free will of man might impose. The two systems—Arminianism and Calvinism—are each consistent at this point within
themselves. The Arminian contends that man is supreme and that God
is compelled to adjust Himself to that scheme of things. The Calvinist
contends that God is supreme and that man is called upon to be conformed to that revelation. The Arminian is deprived of the exalted blessing which is the portion of those who believe the sublime facts of predestination, election, and the sovereignty of God, because he hesitates
to embrace them in their full-orbed reality. Having incorporated into
his scheme the finite human element, all certainty about the future is
for the Arminian overclouded with doubts. Having made the purpose of
God contingent, the execution of that purpose must be contingent. By
so much the glorious, divine arrangement by which the ungodly may go
to heaven, is replaced by the mere moral program in which only good
people may have a hope.

7. THE ARMINIAN VIEW OF SOVEREIGN GRACE. As certainly as there
are two widely separated and divergent forms of religion in the world—
in the one, God saves man and in the other, man saves himself—so
definitely Calvinism and Arminianism are withdrawn the one from the
other. All the forms of religion that men cherish are, with one exception,
in the class which is identified by the obligation resting upon man to
save himself; and in this group, because of its insistence that the element
of human merit must be recognized, the Arminian system is classed.
Standing alone and isolated by its commitment to the doctrine of pure
uncompromising grace, the true Christian faith, as set forth by the great
Apostle and later defended by Calvin and by uncounted theologians before and since his day, is a system of Soteriology characterized by its
fundamental feature that God, unaided and to His own unshared and
unchangeable glory, originates, executes, and consummates the salvation of man. The sole requirement on the human side is that man receive
what God has to give. This he does, he is told, by believing upon Christ
as his Savior. Arminianism distorts this sublime, divine undertaking by
the intrusion of human features at every step of the way. It can rise no

higher in the interpretation of the Word of God respecting sovereign election, than to claim that it consists in the action of divine foreknowledge by which God foresees the men of faith, holiness, and constancy. This interpretation not only reverses the order of truth—the Scriptures declare that men are elected unto holiness and not on account of holiness—but intrudes at the very beginning of the divine program in salvation the grace-destroying element of human merit. In the matter of the one condition of believing on Christ for salvation, the Arminians have constantly added various requirements to the one which is divinely appointed, and all of these infringe upon this one essential of pure grace by adding to it the element of human works. Similarly, in the sphere of the believer's safekeeping, which is declared to be altogether a work of God, Arminianism makes security to be contingent upon human conduct. Arminians seem strangely blinded in the matter of comprehending the divine plan by which, apart from all features of human merit, sinners are elected in past ages without respect to future worthiness, saved at the present time on the sole condition of faith in Christ, and kept to the eternal ages to come through the power of God on a basis which sustains no relation to human conduct. In reality, to assert so much is to declare that Arminians are blind to the true gospel of divine grace which is the central truth of Christianity—that is, if the Pauline revelation is to be considered at all. Over against this and in conformity to the New Testament, Calvinists assert that election is on a basis of grace which foresees no human merit in those chosen, that present salvation is by faith or belief alone, and that those saved are kept wholly by divine grace without reference to human worthiness.

It would seem wholly unnecessary to remind the student again that there is an important body of truth which conditions the believer's daily life after he is saved, and that his life is motivated, not by a requirement that works of merit must be added to the perfect divine undertaking and achievement in saving grace, but is motivated by the most reasonable obligation to "walk worthy of the vocation [calling] wherewith he is called" (Eph. 4:1). Behaving well as a son is far removed in principle from the idea of behaving well to become a son. It is the blight of Arminian soteriology that it seems incapable of recognizing this distinction, and therefore does not allow a place for the action of pure grace in the realization of the sovereign purpose of God through a perfect salvation and an eternal safekeeping apart from any and every form of human merit or cooperation.

Though much must be made of this theme in other connections, a word is in order at this point respecting the meaning of the term *sovereign grace*—a term employed by Calvinists with genuine satisfaction, but both rejected and avoided by Arminians. Sovereign grace originates and is at once a complete reality in the mind of God when He, before the foundation of the world, elects a company who are by His limitless power to be presented in glory conformed to the image of His Son. By so much they are to be to all intelligences the means by which He will manifest the exceeding riches of His grace (Eph. 2:7). This manifestation will correspond to His infinity and will satisfy Him perfectly as the final, all-comprehensive measurement of His attribute of grace. Two obstacles, allowed by Him to exist, must be overcome—sin and the will of man. That His grace may be manifest and its demonstration enhanced, He undertakes by Himself—for no other could share in its achievement—to overcome the obstacle of sin. That this obstacle is overcome is declared in many texts of the Scriptures. Two may be quoted here: "The next day John seeth Jesus coming unto him, and saith, Behold the Lamb of God, which taketh away the sin of the world" (John 1:29); "to wit, that God was in Christ, reconciling the world unto himself, not imputing their trespasses unto them; and hath committed unto us the word of reconciliation" (2 Cor. 5:19). There remains, therefore, but the obstacle of the human will. Having designed that man as creature shall be possessed of an independent will, no step can be taken in the accomplishment of His sovereign purpose which will even tend to coerce the human volition. He does awaken the mind of man to spiritual sanity and brings before him the desirability of salvation through Christ. If by His power, God creates new visions of the reality of sin and of the blessedness of Christ as Savior and under this enlightenment men choose to be saved, their wills are not coerced nor are they deprived of the action of any part of their own beings. It is the unreasoned objection of Arminians that the human will is annulled by sovereign election. On this important point Principal Cunningham writes:

The Arminians usually object to these views about the certain efficacy or insuperability of the grace of God in conversion, that they are inconsistent with the nature of the human will, and with the qualities that attach to it. They usually represent our doctrine as implying that men are forced to believe and to turn to God against their will, or whether they will or not. This is a misrepresentation. Calvinists hold no such opinion; and it cannot be shown that their doctrine requires them to hold it. Indeed, the full statement of their doctrine upon the subject excludes or contradicts it. Our Confession of Faith, after giving an account of effectual calling, which plainly implies that the grace of God in conversion is an exercise of omnipotence, and cannot be successfully resisted, adds, "Yet so as they come most freely, being made willing by His grace." That special operation of the Spirit, which cannot be overcome or frustrated, is just the renovation of the will itself, by which a power of willing what is spiritually good—a power which it has not of itself in its natural condition, and which it could not receive from any source but a divine and almighty agency—is communicated to it. In the exercise of this new power, men are able to co-operate with the Spirit of God, guiding and directing them; and they do this, and do it, not by constraint, but willingly,—being led, under the influence of the news concerning Christ, and the way of salvation which He has opened up to and impressed upon them, and the motives which these views suggest, to embrace Christ, and to choose that better part which shall never be taken away from them. In the commencement of the process, they are not actors at all; they are wholly passive,—the subjects of a divine operation. And from the time when they begin to act in the matter, or really to *do* anything, they act freely and voluntarily, guided by rational motives, derived from the truths which their eyes have been opened to see, and which, humanly speaking, might have sooner led them to turn to God, had not the moral impotency of their wills to anything spiritually good prevented this result. There is certainly nothing in all this to warrant the representation, that, upon Calvinistic principles, men are forced to repent and believe against their wills, or whether they will or not.—*Ibid.,* pp. 413–14

After all, though the human will is preserved in its normal freedom throughout the process by which men are brought into eternal glory, the all-important factor in the undertaking is the will of God. The Arminian contention that the will of the creature may defeat the will of the Creator is both dishonoring to God and a deification of man. It is nearly puerile to assert that He who creates all angels, all material things, all human beings by the word of His command, He who preserves all things and by whom they hold together, He who can promise to Abraham that through him all nations shall be blessed, and to David that a kingdom will be his portion forever, He who has made innumerable predictions concerning His purpose in future times which necessitate the immediate direction of the lives of countless beings, that He cannot guide the destiny of one soul in the way of His choosing.

No Arminian has questioned that God desires to keep those whom He has saved through Christ; their sphere of doubt is simply that God *cannot* do what He desires, even though He has removed every obstacle that could hinder Him.

It is thus demonstrated that the Arminian view of seven major soteriological doctrines tends to dishonor God, to pervert and distort the doctrine of divine grace, and that it displays unbelief toward the revelation God has given.

II. THE ARMINIAN EMPHASIS UPON HUMAN
EXPERIENCE AND REASON

Though Scripture is cited by Arminians to defend their contention that the Christian is not secure—and these Scriptures are yet to be considered—their appeal is usually more to experience and reason than to the testimony of the Bible. When turning thus to experience, it is often recounted that some individual has first been a Christian and then, later, became unsaved; but in every such instance two unsupportable assumptions appear. It could not be demonstrated finally that the person named was saved in the first place, nor could it be established that he was unsaved in the second place. If Demas be cited because he forsook the Apostle Paul (2 Tim. 4:10), it will be remembered that that is far removed from the idea that God forsook Demas. Similarly, if it be observed that Judas—one of the twelve—went to his own place, it is also as clearly stated by Christ that he was "the son of perdition" (John 17:12) with no implication that he was ever saved. On the question which Judas engenders, Dr. Wardlaw remarks:

(1). There is no evidence of anything like true grace in Judas, but evidence to the contrary (John vi.64). The only thing that can be advanced against this is the passage in which he seems to be spoken of as one of those given unto Christ (John xvii.12). This leads me to observe—(2). That in the context of these words, Jesus says things regarding "those given to Him," which could not possibly be true of Judas (John xvii.2, 6, 9, 11, 12). Surely, if Judas had been "kept" as the rest were, he could not have been the "son of perdition." It follows that he was not among the "given" and the "kept." (3). In this passage, it is true, the phrase is used which usually denotes exception:—"None of them is lost, but," etc. (εἰ μή.) It may be remarked, however, that there are instances in which εἰ μή is used, not exceptively, but adversatively, in the same sense as ἀλλά (Gal. i.7; Rev. ix.4; xxi.27). This explanation may be confirmed by the consideration that to interpret otherwise is to make the Saviour contradict Himself (John vi.39). If Judas was of those given to Him and perished, what Jesus says would not be true. (4). It is true that Judas is spoken of as chosen (John vi.70, 71). It is obvious, however, that this choice relates exclusively to office. The very terms of the verses quoted may suffice to show this. As to the reason for which Jesus did choose such a character to be one of the Twelve, that is a totally distinct question, having nothing to do with our present inquiry. We have further proof that the choice was not personal but official (John xiii.10, 11, 16). From these verses it appears that Judas was not one of His chosen; and had not, like them, the cleansing of His Spirit. When we distinguish between the two meanings of "chosen," all is plain. (5). On the principle so repeatedly adverted to, of persons being spoken of according to profession, appearance, and association, Judas appeared amongst the

Twelve as one of them; and might be included under the same general designations with them, though not spiritually, or in strict propriety of speech, belonging to those given Him of the Father (John xv.2; Mat. xv.13).—*System of Theology*, II, 570

At this point the extended New Testament doctrine relative to the fact of the Christian's sin and the divine provision for that sin through the death of Christ and on the condition that the sin is confessed, is logically introduced—a doctrine greatly neglected and by none more than the Arminian theologian. Recognition of the sublime truth that, by His bearing all sin on the cross, Christ has secured a propitious attitude on the part of God the Father toward "our sins" (the sins of the Christian) and toward "the sins of the whole world" (the sins of the unsaved), is lacking in the Arminian way of thinking. This lack is seen in the almost universal reply which is made to the question of what power or agency might serve to render a true child of God unregenerate again. The answer is that it is *sin* that unsaves the Christian—not little sins such as all Christians commit, else none could hold out an hour, but great and terrible sins—but, if this were true, then there are sins which the Christian may commit which Christ did not bear on the cross, and these still have condemning power over the believer who has been sheltered under the provisions of the cross. As for this the Scriptures declare: "He that believeth on him is not condemned: but he that believeth not is condemned already, because he hath not believed in the name of the only begotten Son of God" (John 3:18); "Verily, verily, I say unto you, He that heareth my word, and believeth on him that sent me, hath everlasting life, and shall not come into condemnation; but is passed from death unto life" (5:24); "There is therefore now no condemnation to them that are in Christ Jesus" (Rom. 8:1, R.V.); "Who is he that condemneth? It is Christ that died, yea rather, that is risen again, who is even at the right hand of God, who also maketh intercession for us" (Rom. 8:34); "For if we would judge ourselves, we should not be judged. But when we are judged, we are chastened of the Lord, that we should not be condemned with the world" (1 Cor. 11:31–32). These are positive, unconditional covenants giving the assurance that the believer will never be condemned. It is certain from the last of these passages that the Christian who sins will be chastened, and, indeed, God is a faithful disciplinarian and His child in His household will not escape correction if he sins; but chastisement and condemnation are wholly unrelated. So, also, the corresponding contrast is again in evidence at this point. Union, which depends altogether on the merit which is secured by being in Christ, is far removed in its essential character from communion, which depends on the believer observing to do all the will of God. Union with Christ, being based on the unchanging merit of Christ—He is the same yesterday, today, and forever—must and does continue forever, and all problems respecting the believer's daily life are, of necessity, dealt with upon a wholly different ground. To base the Christian's continuance in the saved state upon his daily life is to demand of him that which no Christian ever experienced in this world— sinless perfection. Holding over Christians the requirement of sinlessness as the only hope of security—as Arminians do—is to call forth that peculiar form of carelessness or discouragement which is the reaction of every serious person when confronted with an impossibility. All of this becomes another approach to the same misunderstanding that is the curse of that form of rationalism which cannot comprehend the gospel of divine grace. Such a rationalism plans it so that good people may be saved, be kept saved because of their personal qualities, and be received into heaven on their merit. The gospel of divine grace plans it so that bad people—which wording describes every person on earth— may be saved, be kept saved as they were saved through the saving work and merit of Christ, and be received into heaven, not as specimens of human perfection, but as objects of infinite grace. Arminianism, with its emphasis upon human experience, human merit, and human reason, apparently has little or no comprehension of the revelation that salvation is by grace alone, through faith.

Few Arminians have been consistent in the matter of the effect of sin on the child of God. They seem not to know of a vast body of Scriptures which disclose the entire truth of sin and its cure as related to the believer, but, if logical, must require as many regenerations as there are separate sins. Arminians are not consistent at this point; being confronted by the obvious, indisputable fact that Christians do remain saved who are confessedly imperfect, they advance the notion, before cited, that it is only extreme forms of wickedness that are able to unsave the believer. God declares of Himself that He cannot with allowance look on sin and in His own holiness there is not so much as a shadow of turning, and to infer that He is not disturbed by lesser sins is not only contrary to truth but a flagrant insult to Him. Calvinism, because it follows the truth contained in the divine revelation, imposes no such outrage upon divine holiness, but rather follows the divine arrangement by which all sin, both before and after conversion, is righteously dealt with, but to the glory of God and the eternal salvation of the believer. After all, in view of the demands of divine holiness, there are but two alternatives, namely, either to stand in the perfection of Christ or to be sinless in one's self. The latter is impossible and could exist, if it existed at all, wholly apart from the saving intervention of the Son of God; the former is possible to all and is offered to all on the sole ground of faith in the Savior that God has provided. Salvation through Christ is the essence of Christianity, while salvation through personal worthiness is no better than any pagan philosophy, and it is of this notion, so foreign to the New Testament revelation, that Arminianism partakes.

Another experimental consideration of the Arminian is the claim that if, as the Calvinist teaches and as is certainly set forth in the New Testament, the believer will not be lost because of sin, the effect of that doctrine is to license the saved one to sin, thus tending to antinomianism. In other words, God has no other motive to hold before the believer that will insure a faithful manner of life, than the one impossible proposition that he will be lost unless he is faithful. As one man declared, "If I believed that I am safe as a Christian, I would at once engage in the fullest possible enjoyment of sin." This sentiment will be recognized as the mind of an unregenerate person. The saved person's answer to the question, "Shall we continue in sin, that grace may abound?" is "God forbid." That is, though the mind of the flesh is present in the Christian and he does have that tendency to evil, he also has the mind of the Spirit and that voice is never wholly silent. Security does not mean, as the Arminian supposes, that God merely keeps unholy people saved regardless of what they do. He has made immeasurable divine provisions respecting the daily life of the believer, namely, the Word of God which may be hid in the heart that one thus fortified may not sin against God, the presence of the victorious Spirit as a delivering power in every believer's life, and the incomparable sustaining power of the unceasing prayer of Christ for those who are saved. If one who professed to be saved, later departed from the way of truth and evinced no desire for a holy life, he would give no assurance that he had ever been saved and would, by so much, be an exception and not an exhibition of that which is true of a Christian. No system of theology may boast that its scheme of doctrine guarantees that those who are saved will never sin. It would be difficult to prove, though constantly asserted by Arminians, that those, like the Puritans, who believe they are secure in Christ, were and are greater sinners than Arminian adherents who make no such claim. It may be repeated that the greatest incentive in any person's life is that which rightfully impels a true believer and which no Arminian has given a worthy trial in his own life, namely, to honor God in his life because he believes he is saved and safe in the redeeming grace of God, rather than to attempt to honor God because by so much he hopes to be saved and safe. Doing right never saved a sinner nor did it ever preserve a saint; but it is true that being divinely saved and preserved is the most imperative obligation to do right.

In conclusion, it may be restated that, as for human experience which the Arminian believes is at times a proof that one once saved can be lost again, it cannot be proved that such a case ever existed. On the contrary, revelation so defines the saving and keeping power of God that it can be said with all assurance, that not one of those who have been truly regenerated has ever been lost nor could such a one be lost. As for human reason, which the Arminian employs against the doctrine of security, it need only be pointed out that no human reason is able to trace the divine undertaking which provides both salvation and safekeeping on the ground of the sacrifice and imputed merit of the Son of God, and with no other requirement resting on the sinner than that he believe on Christ as his Savior. What God accomplishes is according to reason, but it is that higher reason which characterizes every divine undertaking.

III. THE ARMINIAN APPEAL TO THE SCRIPTURES

Of all the contentions offered by the Arminians, their appeal to the Scriptures is that feature most worthy of candid consideration; for it will be admitted by all who attempt to expound the Word of God that there are several passages which, when taken in what appears on the surface to be their meaning, do seem to imply that one once saved might be lost again. The challenge is one respecting the exact meaning of the portions of Scripture involved and how in the divine mind, since the Word of God cannot contradict itself, they are to be harmonized with a much greater array of Scripture testimony—a body of truth which Arminians seldom essay to discuss—which permit of no varied interpretations and which dogmatically assert the eternal security of the true child of God. The challenge is also how these supposed insecurity passages may be made to harmonize with the truth of the believer's position both in the elective purpose of God, as an object of sovereign grace, and in the Body of Christ with all that that membership secures. It will be seen, also, that there is no strain placed upon those Scriptures, when so interpreted that they harmonize with the passages which declare the safekeeping of Christians. Over against this, the passages asserting security, along with the demands of the doctrines of sovereign election and sovereign grace, can be interpreted in but one way, unless great violence is done to them by the taking from or adding to them of mere human opinions. That Arminians do not discuss them is a significant fact in itself.

With respect to the place the doctrine of security fills in its relation to other great doctrines, an observing student of Bible teachings will recognize the fact that the Arminian contention does not broaden out to contemplate with any fullness the doctrines of sovereign election and sovereign grace. It is satisfied to present a partial consideration of the doctrine of security; and yet both sovereign election, with its unalterable purpose to bring those whom God has predestinated into eternal glory, and sovereign grace, which answers every requirement that is involved and meets to the point of infinite perfection every issue that can arise in the process of bringing a lost sinner into that glory, are censurably neglected. These two doctrines are supreme and, comparatively, the doctrine of security is no more than a straw floating on the surface of those unplumbed depths of divine reality—*sovereign election* and *sovereign grace*. Upon any worthy consideration of these great doctrines, an unprejudiced person will concede that were God to fail in His eternal purpose for even one soul, after having wrought every provision in grace to meet every existing obstacle, He would become thereby a colossal failure. The reason for this disproportionate emphasis, on the part of Arminians, upon the one doctrine of security is not hard to recognize. The surface question of whether a Christian will continue saved is easily apprehended, while the themes of sovereign election and sovereign grace are too involved for certain types of minds.

Good men may be cited as authority on either side of this controversy and any man may be mistaken; but the Word of God is not in error, nor does it contradict itself. It does not present alternative systems of theology from which men may choose. Divine election is either sovereign and therefore as unalterable as the character of God, or it is not. Saving and sustaining grace is either infinitely capable of presenting the chief of sinners faultless before the holy divine presence, or it is not. The one for whom, by regeneration, God has begun a good work will have this continued and consummated unto the day of Jesus Christ (Phil. 1:6), or he will not. Intermediate or compromising positions on these great propositions are impossible. God is either supreme, with all that such a statement implies, or He is not; and those who doubt His supremacy may well examine themselves to see whether they be in the faith at all (2 Cor. 13:5). A collection of mere negatives sustained by human guesses has no claim to the title *a system of Christian theology*.

For clarity and for convenience the passages—even those obviously misunderstood—which the Arminians present in defense of their claim of insecurity are here grouped in various classifications with the implication that what is true of one passage in a group is more or less true of all in that classification. In entering upon a consideration of these passages, certain underlying facts should be restated, namely, (1) that the issues do not concern any merely nominal professor of the faith who is not actually regenerate after the manner set forth in the New Testament; (2) that a doubtful passage—one concerning which worthy expositors disagree—shall not be made to annul a positive statement of Scripture over which, in its intended meaning, no question can arise; and (3) all recourse to human experience or even to human reason, valuable as these may be in their place, cannot be allowed to serve as a contradiction, or even a qualification, of the direct declarations of revelation.

The passages involved in this aspect of this discussion are:

1. SCRIPTURES DISPENSATIONALLY MISAPPLIED. Like "the love of money," failure rightly to divide the word of truth is a root of (doctrinal) evil. Under the present division, it is largely a failure to distinguish the primary from the secondary application of a text.

Matthew 24:13. "But he that shall endure unto the end, the same shall be saved."

The context is altogether of a coming tribulation (cf. vss. 21–22) and the address is to Israel. Their identification as those to whom Christ is speaking appears in numerous parts of the Olivet Discourse, but in none more clearly than in verse 9 where it is predicted, "And ye shall be hated of all nations for my name's sake." The passage in question accords with all Scripture bearing on the experience of Israel in the coming tribulation. She shall be saved out of it (Jer. 30:7). Of this time the Savior said to the Jews to whom He was speaking, "He that endureth to the end, the same shall be saved." Over against this, it will be remembered that the Christian is *now* saved when he believes (John 3:36; 5:24). Had the passage been addressed to Christians, it, to be in keeping with Christian doctrine, would read, *He that is saved will endure to the end* (cf. John 3:16; 10:28).

Matthew 18:23–35. This extended passage sets forth a law of forgiveness, namely, that the one who is forgiven should himself forgive.

To make what is distinctly said of the King in relation to the kingdom of heaven (vs. 23) to apply to the Church is a confusion of truth for which there is no excuse. Also, to make the mere act of forgiveness to be equivalent to eternal salvation is likewise all but unpardonable. If the King's salvation is equal to the salvation of those forgiven, their obligation is to save their debtors by forgiving them. A Christian in Christ and under the protection of infinite grace, is not to be delivered to the tormentors until he pays a debt which Christ has already paid.

Ezekiel 33:7–8. "So thou, O son of man, I have set thee a watchman unto the house of Israel; therefore thou shalt hear the word at my mouth, and warn them from me. When I say unto the wicked, O wicked man, thou shalt surely die; if thou dost not speak to warn the wicked from his way, that wicked man shall die in his iniquity; but his blood will I require at thine hand."

It would seem wholly irrelevant to bring forward a passage which is so clearly a warning and instruction addressed to Israel through the prophet in the time of their dispersion; yet this passage, like Ezekiel 18:20–26, is constantly used by Arminians as evidence that the Christian may suffer the awful consequences of bearing the blood of some lost soul. Additional passages in this class are Psalm 51:11; 2 Thessalonians 2:3.

2. PASSAGES RELATED TO THE FALSE TEACHERS OF THE LAST DAYS. The period identified as the "last days" for the Church, though exceedingly brief, as compared to other ages and dispensations, occupies a disproportionate place in the New Testament. The time is the very end of the Christian era, and immediately preceding the removal of the Church from the earth and the introduction of the tribulation into the world. These "last days" are characterized by false teachers. These teachers are never said to be saved, but, because of the peculiar character of their wickedness, they bring swift destruction upon themselves. They appear only in the "last days" and are therefore not a part of the age as a whole. Three passages are especially in evidence:

1 Timothy 4:1–2. "Now the Spirit speaketh expressly, that in the latter times some shall depart from the faith, giving heed to seducing spirits, and doctrines of devils; speaking lies in hypocrisy; having their conscience seared with a hot iron."

Not all of this context is quoted, but enough is presented to indicate that by a peculiar and unequivocal inspiration it is said that men of authority in the church will, in the latter times, turn from that system of doctrine which is termed *the faith*, and substitute in its place doctrines of demons. Some suppose, without warrant, that these teachers are believers who become unregenerate apostates. The passage, in harmony with other Scriptures bearing on the same general truth, asserts no more than that these important persons, having had some understanding of "the faith" (cf. Jude 1:3), reject it to the extent that they turn from it and embrace in its place the doctrines of demons. The notion that some once saved are lost again, receives no support from this Scripture.

2 Peter 2:1–22. This passage, too extended for quotation, is largely an identification of the teachers of the last days. They are said to bring in heresies, they discount former divine judgments, they despise angels and divine governments, and they have forsaken the right way. These, having escaped the pollution of the *cosmos* world through the knowledge of the Lord and Savior Jesus Christ—not through the acceptance of Christ as Savior but being indebted to Christ for much truth, which truth they forsake and pervert—they turn from what they know. Instead of being blessed and saved by the truth, they turn to heresies. To them—perhaps as ordained ministers—was committed "the way of righteousness" and the "holy commandment"; yet they turn to that which marks them as false teachers. They are likened to a dog and to a sow. In the present day there should be no hesitation in the recognition of unregenerate clergy. On this passage Burt L. Matthews in a tract which is in reply to one by Millard respecting security (p. 23), writes:

If the writer had considered the 22nd verse he would have understood the one quoted. Read it—"the dog is turned to his own vomit again, and the sow that was washed to her wallowing in the mire." This is true of the best bred dog, and of the prize blue-ribboned sow, because their natures remain unchanged. It is likewise true of those who know the way of righteousness, but turn according to their unchanged nature to unholy things. They have never been born again, and received a new nature, and become a new creation in Christ. Consulting the 20th verse, how many unnumbered thousands have escaped the pollutions of the world through the knowledge of the Lord and Saviour Jesus Christ, by being born in a Christian home and in a nation where the ethics of Christ have raised the morals of living, and have never acknowledged their debt by the personal acceptance of Jesus Christ as Saviour? How many have turned to the pollutions of the nations that know not God, and how much worse is their state, than if they had never known the way of righteousness? Light and knowledge increase responsibility.

Jude 1:3–19. Again, the passage in question exceeds the reasonable bounds of a quotation. As Jude is like a second witness to the truth that the Apostle Peter presents in the above passage, there is similarity to be noted. Jude's specific identification of the false teachers is disclosed in verses 4 and 16–19, which read: "For there are certain men crept in unawares, who were before of old ordained to this condemnation, ungodly men, turning the grace of our God into lasciviousness, and denying the only Lord God, and our Lord Jesus Christ. . . . These are murmurers, complainers, walking after their own lusts; and their mouth speaketh great swelling words, having men's persons in admiration because of advantage. But, beloved, remember ye the words which were spoken before of the apostles of our Lord Jesus Christ; how that they told you there should be mockers in the last time, who should walk after their own ungodly lusts. These be they who separate themselves, sensual, having not the Spirit."

Little thought is given to this and other passages related to the false teachers of the last days when it is claimed that, because of the course pursued by these false teachers with respect to the truth of God, Christians might be expected to apostatize. Granting for the moment that which is not true, namely, that these are degenerated believers, it will be seen that there is no claim to be set up here respecting believers who do not live in the last days, and that there is no reference to people of that period in general, but only to the false teachers themselves.

3. A MERE REFORMATION OR OUTWARD PROFESSION. A wide range of human experience is accounted for under this division of this theme. If there is to be any clear understanding of the facts involved, it is essential that precisely what enters into salvation shall be kept in mind. Four passages call for special consideration:

Luke 11:24–26. "When the unclean spirit is gone out of a man, he walketh through dry places, seeking rest; and finding none, he saith, I will return unto my house whence I came out. And when he cometh, he findeth it swept and garnished. Then goeth he, and taketh to him seven other spirits more wicked than himself; and they enter in, and dwell there: and the last state of that man is worse than the first."

The Savior is here presenting a phase of truth related to demonology which is not even remotely related to salvation by grace. A demon going out of a person, leaving that former abode free from such an unholy tenant, may return, taking with him other demons worse in character than the first tenant. The fallacy of the use of this Scripture to teach insecurity is seen in the fact that the removal of a demon is not the equivalent of salvation, in which salvation the divine nature is imparted. Likewise, the presence of the divine nature in any individual is a certain guarantee that no demon can enter (1 John 4:4). This incident may represent a reformation or improvement in the case of a suffering one, but it contributes nothing to the question of whether one once saved might be lost again.

Matthew 13:1–8. This parable doubtless anticipates conditions which obtain in the present age, and warning is given that there will be profession without possession on the part of many. Whatever seeming reality may be attached to the experience of those who are represented by that which fell by the wayside, or by seed that fell in stony places, or by seed that fell among thorns, the determining test is that these did not mature into *wheat,* as did the seed which fell into good ground. The three failures do not represent three classes of people, but rather the effect of the Word of God on various people. That Word does move many superficially, but those who are saved by it are likened to wheat. The three failures do not represent those who first became wheat and after that were reduced to nothing.

1 Corinthians 15:1–2. "Moreover, brethren, I declare unto you the gospel which I preached unto you, which also ye have received, and wherein ye stand; by which also ye are saved, if ye keep in memory what I preached unto you, unless ye have believed in vain."

The Apostle is not implying that some of the Corinthian believers were lost for want of faith; rather it is that their faith has never been sufficient for salvation (cf. 2 Cor. 13:5).

Hebrews 3:6, 14. "But Christ as a son over his own house; whose house are we, if we hold fast the confidence and the rejoicing of the hope firm unto the end. . . . For we are made partakers of Christ, if we hold the beginning of our confidence stedfast unto the end."

In both of these verses but one thought about security obtains, namely, that the genuine endures and that which fails—except it be accounted for otherwise—is proved to be false.

The entire field of profession is recognized in the New Testament and with this body of truth in hand there is little excuse for misunderstanding. The general theme of profession appears directly or indirectly in more than one of these divisions of this general subject. It is important to note again the divine discrimination and the final disposition of that which God classes as mere profession. The fact of the divine penetration is published in 2 Timothy 2:19: "Nevertheless the foundation of God standeth sure, having this seal, The Lord knoweth them that are his." And the final disposition of profession is announced in 1 John 2:19: "They went out from us, but they were not of us; for if they had been of us, they would no doubt have continued with us: but they went out, that they might be made manifest that they were not all of us." The "going out" indicates that those who go out "are not of us," and they go out that this, so important fact may be made "manifest."

4. A TRUE SALVATION IS PROVED BY ITS FRUITS. In the parable just considered respecting wheat, the thought of fruitage represents the reality which the Christian is. In the present field of discussion, fruit depicts the normal expression of a genuine regeneration—a reasonable test of that regeneration. It will be remembered, however, that there is such a condition possible as a Christian who, for a time, may be out of fellowship with Christ. In such a state there will be no fruit borne. Such a situation is exceptional rather than normal when the test of salvation by its fruits is made. Both lines of truth—that salvation is to be tested by its fruits, and that a believer may be for a time out of fellowship with his Lord—are abundantly sustained in the text of the New Testament.

John 8:31. "Then said Jesus to those Jews which believed on him, If ye continue in my word, then are ye my disciples indeed."

There is no implication to be admitted here that these Jews have the obligation of keeping themselves in the disciple's place; it is rather that, if they are true disciples, they will continue in the words of Christ. It should be noted, also, that Christ has indicated no more than that these Jews were *disciples,* which could mean simply that they were *learners.* However, the same principle obtains whether it be in the case of a true Christian or a mere learner—that which is genuine continues.

James 2:17–18, 24, 26. "Even so faith, if it hath not works, is dead, being alone. Yea, a man may say, Thou hast faith, and I have works: shew me thy faith without thy works, and I will shew thee my faith by my works. . . . Ye see then how that by works a man is justified, and not by faith only. . . . For as the body without the spirit is dead, so faith without works is dead also."

The entire context, James 2:14–26, will be recognized as the central passage bearing on the general Biblical contention that a true regeneration is demonstrated by its fruits. The Apostle Paul discloses the truth in Romans 5:1 that the requirement on the human side for justification before God is *faith;* but the Apostle James declares that the requirement on the human side for justification before men is *good works.* It is a supreme divine undertaking for a sinner to be justified eternally before God which can neither be recognized nor understood by the *cosmos* world; and it is of such a nature that the one who is the object of that justification can sustain no other relation to it than to receive it, with all other divine riches, from the hand of God on the principle of faith. The outmost bounds of the discernment of those who are of this world consists in the quiet reasonable demand, that the one who professes to be saved shall live on a plane which corresponds to that profession. It is to be expected that the world will judge and reject the profession which does not meet their own ideals respecting what a Christian should be, namely, what he pretends to be. The ideals of the world are far below those which God marks out for His child; but of this, as in the fact of justification by faith, the world knows nothing. Nevertheless, in the sphere of the Christian's testimony, the Scriptures stress the reaction of the world to the Christian's profession as of vital importance. The believer is appointed to "walk in wisdom toward them that are without" (outside the family of God—Col. 4:5). The believer's security is not in the hands of the *cosmos* world, but, like justification, is wholly in the grace-empowered hand of God. This passage by James lends no support to an Arminian claim that believers are insecure.

John 15:6. "If a man abide not in me, he is cast forth as a branch, and is withered; and men gather them, and cast them into the fire, and they are burned."

Arminian writers generally look upon John 15:6 as the most formidable Biblical testimony in behalf of their claims in the field of insecurity. The passage merits consideration and, like many others, requires that attention be given to its context. The real question at issue concerning the passage is whether Christ, by His use of the figure of the vine and the branches and His call for an abiding life, is referring to the Christian's *union* or the Christian's *communion* with Himself. Unless this doctrinal distinction is apprehended, there can be no basis for a right understanding of the text in question. The idea of abiding in Christ as a branch in a vine could serve as an illustration of either union or communion with Him. It is easily discernible that He is employing this figure to represent communion with Himself. Union with Him is a result of the baptism of the Spirit, by which divine operation believers are joined to the Lord (cf. 1 Cor. 6:17; 12:13; Gal. 3:27). That such an eternal union with Christ does not, and could not, depend upon human effort or merit is a fundamental truth. On the other hand, communion with Christ does depend on the Christian's faithfulness and adjustment to God. John declares that "if we walk in the light, as he is in the light, we have fellowship [communion] one with another"—that is, the believer has communion with Christ (1 John 1:7). The term *walk* refers to the daily life of the believer. As might be expected in respect to a matter so vital and yet so easily misunderstood, Christ defines precisely the use He is making of the term *abide*—whether it be *union* depending on divine sufficiency, or *communion* depending on human faithfulness. Christ removed all uncertainty when He said, "If ye keep my commandments, ye shall abide in my love; even as I have kept my Father's commandments, and abide in his love" (John 15:10). To keep Christ's commandments is a human responsibility—akin to walking in the light. As a parallel He cites the fact that He abode in His Father's love, or communion, by doing His Father's will. It is certain that Christ was not attempting to preserve *union* with His Father—the fact of the eternal Trinity—by obedience; to give it the human resemblance, He was not "attempting to keep saved."

Still another declaration by Christ in this same context—equally as conclusive—is found in the words, "Every branch in me that beareth not fruit he taketh away" (vs. 2). It is distinctly a branch *in Him,* which is union with Him, that is not bearing fruit. Certainly, if union with Christ depended on fruit bearing, few would pass the test. That the unfruitful branch is "taken away"—literally, lifted up out of its place— is a reference to that removal from this life which God reserves the right to accomplish for the one who is persistently unfaithful (cf. 1 Cor. 11:30; 1 John 5:16). The word $αἴρω$, here to be translated "lifteth it up," occurs many times in the New Testament and almost universally means a removal from one place or position to another. Significant, indeed, is its use with the prefix $ἐπί$ in Acts 1:9, where the Lord is said to have been "taken up" out of their sight (cf. John 17:15; Acts 8:33). It does not follow that the death of any Christian may be identified as a divine removal on account of fruitlessness. If, as is doubtless true, no person knows of such an instance, that fact only confirms the truth that the matter is a divine responsibility which does not concern other Christians to the slightest degree. If it is claimed that an unfruitful Christian should not go to heaven, it will be remembered that the assurance of heaven does not depend on communion, or fruit bearing, but on union with Christ. It is also to be considered that all Christian success or failure is to be judged at the *bema*—the judgment seat of Christ in heaven—and that the fruitless Christian must thus go to heaven before he can appear before that tribunal. If entering heaven is not due to a divine undertaking in behalf of all who are in union with Christ and apart from every aspect of human merit, there is little hope for anyone on this earth.

It may be concluded, then, that in this context Christ is dealing with the Christian's communion with Himself, which communion depends upon human faithfulness. It is also important to observe that it is the lack of this very faithfulness which is condemned by the world.

With the background of what has gone before, approach may be made to John 15:6, in which the truth is declared that if a man abide not in Christ, he will come under the condemning judgment of men. The believer's testimony to the world becomes as a branch "cast forth" and "withered." The judgment of the world upon the believer is described in the severest of terms—"Men gather them, and cast them into the fire, and they are burned." To read into this passage the idea that God casts them forth and that God burns them is to disregard important language, and to contradict the great truths which belong to salvation by grace alone. If it be asked how in practical experience men burn each other, it will be seen that this language is highly figurative, for men do not in any literal sense burn each other; but they do abhor and repel an inconsistent profession. This passage and its context witness to the truth that communion, which depends on the believer, may fail, but it does not declare that union, which depends on Christ, has ever failed or ever will fail.

2 Peter 1:10–11. "Wherefore the rather, brethren, give diligence to make your calling and election sure: for if ye do these things, ye shall never fall: for so an entrance shall be ministered unto you abundantly into the everlasting kingdom of our Lord and Saviour Jesus Christ."

At the outset, it is important to observe that the word πταίω, here translated *fall,* is properly translated *stumble* (cf. Rom. 11:11; Jude 1:24), and that an abundant entrance into the everlasting kingdom is more than a mere entrance, regardless of the glory of that entrance. It is reward for faithfulness added to entrance into that kingdom. Both calling and election are wholly within the sovereignty of God. To these undertakings man can add nothing. Yet, within the sphere of a testimony that is consistent and especially as a demonstration in outward life of that which is eternally wrought within, the believer may add the element of certainty which a holy life provides.

Dr. John Dick has written the following:

Election, being the purpose which God purposed in himself, an intrinsic act of the Divine mind, remains unknown till it be manifested in its execution. No man can read his own name, or that of another, in the Book of life. It is a sealed book, which no mortal can open. We are assured that there is such a decree, by the express testimony of Scripture; but of the persons included in it, nothing is known or can be conjectured, till evidence be exhibited in their personal character and conduct. An Apostle points out the only means by which this important point can be ascertained, when he exhorts Christians to "give all diligence to make their calling and election sure." To make sure, signifies in this place to ascertain, to render a thing certain to the mind. Now, the order of procedure is, first to make our calling certain, or to ascertain that we have been converted to God, and thus our election will be sure, or manifest to ourselves. It is the same kind of reasoning which we employ, in tracing out the cause by the effect. The operation of divine grace in the regeneration of the soul, is a proof that the man in whom this change is wrought, was an object of the divine favour from eternity.—*Lectures on Theology*, p. 190

One qualifying condition arises in connection with this theme which Dr. Dick has not mentioned, which is, that a believer overtaken by sin will not exhibit the experience which is normal, but he will exhibit other evidence of his regeneration that becomes manifest under such circumstances—such as a burden over his sin which no unregenerate person ever knows (cf. 1 John 3:4–10; Ps. 32:3–5). It is therefore designed of God that, even in the state of unconfessed sin, the believer will have clear evidence—if perchance he knows his own heart at all—that he is saved and that evidence will, to him at least, demonstrate that his calling and election are sure.

1 John 3:10. "In this the children of God are manifest, and the children of the devil: whosoever doeth not righteousness is not of God, neither he that loveth not his brother."

Here, again, the whole context (vss. 4–10) is involved. The sin of a true Christian is not a *lawless* sin—as that term is used in this Scripture. Because of the presence of the indwelling Spirit, the believer cannot sin and remain indifferent to it. The grieving of the Spirit is an experimental reality, and is well illustrated in the case of David as recorded in Psalm 32:3–4. Over against this, the unsaved are able to sin without self-condemnation beyond that which may arise from an accusing conscience. Verse 9 of this context declares that those born of God cannot sin lawlessly, and verse 10 asserts that this personal reaction of the heart to sin is a final test between those who are saved and those who are not. The conclusion is that whosoever sins lawlessly, or without self-reproach, is not of God. It is not said that a Christian who sins is not of God, else would all Scripture bearing on the fact of the Christian's sin and its specific cure through confession be rendered a contradiction. Other Scriptures to be included in this classification are: Matthew 5:13; 6:23; 7:16, 18–19, which passages might as well be listed as those dispensationally misapplied; 2 Timothy 2:12, in which the element of divine recognition with respect to reigning with Christ is in view, and not salvation or the believer's place in Christ Jesus; 2 Peter 3:17, where a danger of falling from steadfastness is suggested, yet often confused by Arminians as equivalent to falling from salvation itself; Acts 13:43; 14:22, where a true salvation will be demonstrated by continuing in *the* faith—not personal faith, but continuing true to the body of distinctively Christian doctrine; 1 Timothy 2:14–15, which is another specific warning that only that endures which is genuine. Note, also, 1 Thessalonians 3:5 and 1 Timothy 1:19 (cf. 1 John 2:19).

5. WARNINGS TO THE JEWS. Three important passages are grouped under this head; and, while the truth they convey is addressed primarily to Israel, there is, in two of them, a secondary application to all Gentiles.

Matthew 25:1–13. The entire Olivet Discourse, in which this portion appears, is Christ's farewell word to Israel. Having told them of their tribulation which is to be ended by His glorious appearing, they are warned by all the context from 24:36 to 25:13 to be watching for the return of their Messiah. That return is not imminent now, but will be at the end of their own age which is terminated by the tribulation. In 25:1–13 the Jews are especially warned that when their King returns with His Bride (cf. Luke 12:35–36) they will be judged and separated, and only a portion will enter their kingdom. This oncoming judgment for Israel is the message of the parable of the virgins (cf. Ps. 45:14–15). Five virgins being excluded from the earthly kingdom is in accord with much Old Testament Scripture (cf. Ezek. 20:33–44), but has no reference to a supposed insecurity of those from all nations who are in Christ.

Hebrews 6:4–9. "For it is impossible for those who were once enlightened, and have tasted of the heavenly gift, and were made partakers of the Holy Ghost, and have tasted the good word of God, and the powers of the world to come, if they shall fall away, to renew them again unto repentance; seeing they crucify to themselves the Son of God afresh, and put him to an open shame. For the earth which drinketh in the rain that cometh oft upon it, and bringeth forth herbs meet for them by whom it is dressed, receiveth blessings from God: but that which beareth thorns and briers is rejected, and is nigh unto cursing; whose end is to be burned. But, beloved, we are persuaded better things of you, and things that accompany salvation, though we thus speak."

Dr. C. I. Scofield in a note on this passage in his *Reference Bible* declares: "Heb. 6:4–8 presents the case of Jewish professed believers who halt short of faith in Christ after advancing to the very threshold of salvation, even 'going along with' the Holy Spirit in His work of enlightenment and conviction (John 16:8–10). It is not said that they had faith. This supposed person is like the spies at Kadesh-barnea (Deut. 1:19–26) who saw the land and had the very fruit of it in their hands, and yet turned back."

It has been assumed that the five items which appear in verses 4 and 5 are a description of a saved person and therefore it is possible for a Christian to "fall away." Doubtless these five things are true of a child of God, but so much more is true than is indicated here that these five things are seen to be wholly inadequate to describe the true child of God. As compared to those "once enlightened," the believer is "light in the Lord," and is a child of the light (Eph. 5:8). Compared to "tasting the heavenly gift," the Christian has *received* eternal life and to him righteousness has been imputed. As compared to being made a partaker of the Holy Spirit as an unsaved person does when enlightened with respect to sin, righteousness, and judgment (John 16:8–11), the Christian is born of the Spirit, baptized of the Spirit, indwelt, and sealed by the Spirit. As compared with those who may have "tasted the good word of God," the child of God has believed the Word unto salvation. As compared to those who merely taste the powers of the world to come, the believer experiences that transforming power which wrought in Christ to raise Him from the dead (Eph. 1:19). The illustration which follows in verses 7 and 8 is clarifying. Sunshine and shower on soil which brings forth herbs is nigh unto blessing, while sunshine and shower on soil which brings forth briers and thorns is nigh unto cursing. In like manner the appeal to the Jews addressed may, or may not, result in salvation. The controversy over this passage is determined in verse 9. "But, beloved [a term used only of Christians], we are persuaded better things of you, and things that accompany salvation." Evidently, then, the preceding five things were not intended by the writer to refer to those who are saved. It may be added that the impossibility of repentance is not due to a withdrawal on the part of God of the offer of salvation, but is due to the unsaved person's rejection of the one and only way that is open to him. If at any time he accepts the way set before him, he will be saved; for "whosoever will may come."

Hebrews 10:26–29. "For if we sin wilfully after that we have received the knowledge of the truth, there remaineth no more sacrifice for sins, but a certain fearful looking for of judgment and fiery indignation, which shall devour the adversaries. He that despised Moses' law died without mercy under two or three witnesses: of how much sorer punishment, suppose ye, shall he be thought worthy, who hath trodden under foot the Son of God, and hath counted the blood of the covenant, wherewith he was sanctified, an unholy thing, and hath done despite unto the Spirit of grace?"

The peculiar character of the hortatory passages in the Hebrews Epistle is evident in this context. The writer is concerned about conditions then obtaining—little appreciated today. This plight was well described by James when he said to Paul as Paul returned to Jerusalem from years of Gentile ministry: "Thou seest, brother, how many thousands [μυριάδες, literally, *myriads*—cf. Heb. 12:22; Rev. 5:11] of Jews there are which believe; and they are all zealous of the law" (Acts 21:20). The writer to the Hebrews is addressing Jews who are interested in Christ and have, in a sense, believed; but not to the extent of receiving the death of Christ as the fulfillment and termination of Jewish sacrifices. The confusion of law and grace is always distressing, but no such situation as this has ever existed before or since. These circumstances account for these exhortations which were addressed to Jews who, whatever their religious experience might have been, were yet unsaved. There are seven "if's" in this epistle which condition this type of Jews. The writer, of course, being a Jew, employs, as a recognition of Jewish unity, the pronoun *we*. These conditional passages are: "How shall we escape, if we neglect so great salvation?" (2:3); "Whose house are we, if we hold fast the confidence and the rejoicing of the hope firm unto the end" (3:6); "We are made partakers of Christ, if we hold the beginning of our confidence stedfast unto the end" (3:14); "This will we do, if God permit. For it is impossible for those who were once enlightened, . . . if they shall fall away, to renew them again unto repentance" (6:3–4, 6); "If we sin wilfully after that we have received the knowledge of the truth, there remaineth no more sacrifice for sins" (10:26); "If any man draw back, my soul shall have no pleasure in him" (10:38); "Much more shall not we escape, if we turn away from him that speaketh from heaven" (12:25).

This particular passage (Heb. 10:26–29) is parenthetical. It is not a continuation of the theme set forth in the preceding verse. Those enjoined in verse 25 are believers, while those addressed in this text are hesitating Jews who demur concerning a right relation to Christ. Sinning wilfully means that form of sin which is recognized in the Old Testament as not being a sin of ignorance. Wilful sin calls for divine forgiveness based on sacrificial blood. This warning reminds the Jew of the new situation in which the Mosaic sacrifices no longer avail, and it is therefore a choice between Christ's sacrifice or judgment. To sin now, after Christ has died, is more serious. Sin is no longer an insult to the character and government of God alone, but it becomes also a direct rejection of Christ. In so far as Christ has died for men, they are classified, or set apart, as those for whom He died, which is sanctification according to its true meaning. No New Testament Scripture describes more clearly the sinfulness of sin in this age than this; but it is not a warning to Christians, nor does it imply their insecurity. Dr. James H. Brookes has written this description of the related passage (6:4–6):

Perhaps there is no passage in the Sacred Scriptures that has caused greater distress to real Christians than this startling declaration. They are ready to ask themselves, is it possible after all that our salvation is an uncertain thing? May we fall away at last, and finally be lost? Do all the assurances of present and perfect safety, do all the promises of everlasting life, addressed to the believer, go for nothing? Does not the living Lord say He gives to His sheep eternal life, and they shall never perish, neither shall any pluck them out of His hand? How then is it here represented that there is danger of their destruction? To the tender conscience and anxious heart of the true child of God the warning of the apostle sounds like the voice of doom; and yet such an one is not the person to whom the faithful admonition is sent. It must be remembered that the epistle was written to Hebrew professors of the Christian walk, and to Hebrews who had become "entangled again with the yoke of bondage."—*The Truth*, XIII, 27

It will be recalled that there is a peculiar blindness upon Israel respecting the gospel. Of this blindness Christ said: "For judgment I am come into this world, that they which see not might see; and that they which see might be made blind" (John 9:39), and this blindness was predicted by Isaiah: "And he said, Go, and tell this people, Hear ye indeed, but understand not; and see ye indeed, but perceive not. Make the heart of this people fat, and make their ears heavy, and shut their eyes; lest they see with their eyes, and hear with their ears, and understand with their heart, and convert, and be healed" (Isa. 6:9–10). The Apostle refers to this again in 2 Corinthians 3:14–16. It is not strange, therefore, that there should be difficulty and hesitation on the part of unregenerate Jews.

6. WARNINGS TO ALL MEN. These warnings include two general themes:

Revelation 22:19. "And if any man shall take away from the words of the book of this prophecy, God shall take away his part out of the book of life, and out of the holy city, and from the things which are written in this book."

Next only to John 15:6 is this passage of importance in the Arminian contention. The precise meaning of the passage should be determined.

In the first place, the warning is of one sin only and that of adding to, or taking from, the prophecy of this book—evincing a peculiar divine protection over this book. The warning proves nothing with regard to the possibility of a Christian being lost because of any other sin. Again, it is evident, since the book remains unchanged, that no one has ever committed that sin. That a sovereign God would have power to destroy a creature could not be denied, but not when He has entered into covenant with His Son concerning those whom He has given to His Son that they shall be with Him where He is and behold His glory; nor could God break His covenant with the believers as outlined in Romans 8:30. God may not withdraw this terrible warning, but He can and has, in the light of His covenants, permitted no believer to commit this sin or to merit this punishment. Such a specific protection is a guarantee to security.

1 John 5:4–5. "For whatsoever is born of God overcometh the world: and this is the victory that overcometh the world, even our faith. Who is he that overcometh the world, but he that believeth that Jesus is the Son of God?"

The real meaning of this passage is hidden by the failure in the A.V. translation to put the last part of verse 4 in the past tense. It should read, "And this is the victory that overcame the world, even our faith." In other words, everyone, without exception if born of God, does, by that birth overcome the world—being saved out of it. By believing one becomes an overcomer, for an overcomer means simply the same general distinction that is in view when the term *Christian* is employed. There is an overcoming in daily life as described in Revelation 12:11; but the larger use of this specific term is found in the seven letters to the seven churches in Asia (cf. Rev. 2:7, 11, 17, 26; 3:5, 12, 21). If the thought of "those that are saved" is read into each of these letters, the meaning is made clear.

7. GENTILES MAY BE BROKEN OFF CORPORATELY. But one passage appears in this classification:

Romans 11:21. "For if God spared not the natural branches, take heed lest he also spare not thee."

As God set the nation Israel aside who are the "natural branches," that the door might be opened for Gentiles to hear the gospel in this age, in like manner He will set aside the Gentiles when their day of grace is over. The breaking off of either Jews or Gentiles in the corporate sense provides not the slightest ground for assuming that God will break off a Christian from his position in Christ Jesus.

8. BELIEVERS MAY LOSE THEIR REWARDS AND BE DISAPPROVED. Reference has been made previously to the doctrine of rewards. However, two major passages call for consideration and deserve extended exposition:

Colossians 1:21-23. "And you, that were sometime alienated and enemies in your mind by wicked works, yet now hath he reconciled in the body of his flesh through death, to present you holy and unblameable and unreproveable in his sight: if ye continue in the faith grounded and settled, and be not moved away from the hope of the gospel, which ye have heard, and which was preached to every creature which is under heaven; whereof I Paul am made a minister."

Two issues appear in this context: that of God's work for man and that of man's work for God. In fact, the contrast between divine responsibility and human responsibility appears many times in the Colossian Epistle. No end of doctrinal disorder has been engendered by the disarrangement of these so widely different ideas. A worthy student will not rest until he can trace his way through, and separate, these two lines of truth. Arminianism has continued very largely by its failure to recognize the far-flung difference between God's work for man, by which man is saved, empowered, kept, and presented faultless before God in glory —undertakings which are far beyond the range of human resources even to aid—and man's work for God, by which man renders devotion, service to God, and experiences the exercise of spiritual gifts—all of which, though divinely credited to man and bearing the promise of rewards, can be wrought by man only as he is enabled by the Holy Spirit.

The Apostle declares that he would have the believers to whom he wrote appear before God "holy and unblameable and unreproveable in his sight" (vs. 22). Though the Christian is enabled by the Spirit in all that he does, yet these are words which imply human responsibility and faithfulness. It naturally follows that, in the light of this responsibility, all depends upon those believers. This feature of the context is augmented by the further declaration: "if ye continue in the faith [Christian doctrine] grounded and settled, and be not moved away from the hope of the gospel, which ye have heard" (vs. 23). Over against this statement of human responsibility, this context begins with a reference to the work of God for men—"And you, that were sometime alienated and enemies in your mind by wicked works, yet now hath he reconciled in the body of his flesh through death" (vss. 21-22).

Because of a misleading punctuation which introduces only a comma after the word *death,* the two lines of thought have been not only connected, but the work of God for man has been supposed to depend on man's work for God. That would be acceptable Arminian interpretation or doctrine, but it is not the meaning of the passage. With no punctuation in the original text, it is allowable to place a full stop after the word *death* (vs. 22) and to begin a new part of the sentence with the next word *to*. This arrangement, without changing any words, divides properly between the two aspects of truth which are wholly unrelated in the sense that they are not interdependent. Thus the text is rescued from implying what it does not, that the work of God depends on the work of man. Such an idea would constitute a complete contradiction of all New Testament teaching respecting salvation through the grace of God alone. No more complete statement of God's work for man will be found than Colossians 2:10: "And ye are complete in him, which is the head of all principality and power."

1 Corinthians 9:27. "But I keep under my body, and bring it into subjection: lest that by any means, when I have preached to others, I myself should be a castaway."

Again the distinction between rewards for Christian service and salvation is in view. The subject is introduced, so far as this context is concerned, with the Apostle's question, "What is my reward then?" (vs. 18). And this question is preceded and followed by an extended testimony on the Apostle's part relative to his own faithful service. Already in 3:9–15 he has distinguished between salvation and rewards; but in this passage he considers only his reward. In this testimony, he likens the Christian's service to a race in which all believers are participating and in relation to which they must strive lawfully, and be temperate in all things. This reference to service as a race is followed by the Apostle's closing testimony in which he declares that he brings his body into subjection "lest that by any means, when I have preached to others, I myself should be a castaway." The rendering of ἀδόκιμος by the word *castaway* is not sustained by all. This Greek word is only the negative form of δόκιμος, which certainly means to be *approved* or *accepted*. As for his standing before God the believer is already accepted (Eph. 1:6) and justified (Rom. 5:1). As for his service, or that which man may do for God, he must yet appear before the judgment seat of Christ, where rewards are to be bestowed and failure in service will be burned (cf. 2 Cor. 5:9–10; 1 Cor. 3:15). The precise meaning of δόκιμος is seen in 2 Timothy 2:15, "Study to shew thyself approved unto God, a workman that needeth not to be ashamed, rightly dividing the word of truth." This injunction does not imply that salvation depends on faithful study;

it rather asserts that those who are saved should study lest they be disapproved and that is precisely the Apostle's meaning in the text under discussion. The Apostle's desire to be free from the trifling, irresolute, half-hearted manner of preaching which His Lord could never condone is worthy of a great servant of God, and may well be taken to heart by all who are called to preach the Word of God. There is no note of insecurity here. How could the man who wrote the eighth chapter of Romans be fearful lest he be cast away from God? Or how could the Holy Spirit who had said "They shall never perish" now imply that they might perish?

Other Scriptures belonging in this classification are Romans 8:17; Revelation 2:10; and all references to rewards throughout the New Testament.

9. BELIEVERS MAY EXPERIENCE LOSS OF FELLOWSHIP. This question has to do with the present, as rewards have to do with the future, in the believer's experience. Some vital passages are involved at this point.

John 13:8. "If I wash thee not, thou hast no part with me."

These are the words of Christ to Peter when Peter objected to the intent of Christ to bathe his feet. The word *wash* (νίπτω) represents a partial bathing and is in contrast here to *washed* (λούω) as used in verse 10, where the meaning is a full bath. All is symbolical of spiritual cleansing. There is a complete bathing (vs. 10) which corresponds to the once-for-all "washing of regeneration," and a partial bathing such as is promised in 1 John 1:9. The partial bathing is as oft repeated in the believer's life as he confesses his sin. Christ said Peter would have "no part" with Him unless Peter was partially bathed. The word "no part" (μέρος) suggests not a full part; that is, Peter would be lacking full fellowship with Christ unless he was cleansed. This is equally true of every Christian. It is after confession of sin that there is cleansing and fellowship; but the question of security with respect to salvation is not involved in this doctrine.

John 15:2. "Every branch in me that beareth not fruit, he taketh it away" (R.V.).

As before indicated, this is of a branch in Christ that is fruitless, and the taking away is evidently removal from this life. That God reserves the right to remove an unfruitful branch need not be questioned; but the removal is not from salvation, as a superficial Arminian interpretation would imply. The same conditions which govern fruit bearing gove n fellowship with Christ.

f Corinthians 11:29–32. "For he that eateth and drinketh unworthily, eateth and drinketh damnation to himself, not discerning the Lord's body. For this cause many are weak and sickly among you, and many sleep. For if we would judge ourselves, we should not be judged. But when we are judged, we are chastened of the Lord, that we should not be condemned with the world."

It is fitting that this passage which ends the carnality section of this Epistle should present both the effect and cure of carnality. Certain sins are specified in this passage as leading on to physical sickness and physical death. However, it is the direction of all sin that it leads to physical death (Rom. 8:6, 13), but this is far removed from spiritual death. The cure, as in 1 John 1:3–9, is self-judgment; but, if the sinning Christian does not judge himself, he is subject to chastisement and that to the end that he shall never be condemned with the world. Though this discipline might assume the extreme form of "sleep" or removal from this world, there is no basis for the thought that it means spiritual death.

1 John 5:16. "If any man see his brother sin a sin which is not unto death, he shall ask, and he shall give him life for them that sin not unto death. There is a sin unto death: I do not say that he shall pray for it."

This text is explicit. It refers to a "brother," which term is never used of the unregenerate, and declares definitely that a Christian may sin in such a way that the chastisement of death may fall upon him. If the sin were not unto death, prayer might avail for him. Again, there is no evidence that the "brother" ceases to be what he is in his relation to God, or that this death is spiritual death which leads on to the second death. The possibility of chastisement is also seen in John 5:14.

10. CHRISTIANS MAY FALL FROM GRACE. By popular usage the idea of falling from grace, though mentioned but once in the Bible, has been made to include all who, as is supposed, are lost after they have been saved.

Galatians 5:4. "Christ is become of no effect unto you, whosoever of you are justified by the law; ye are fallen from grace."

Christians may fall from grace, but it is not accomplished by sinning. They will have fallen from grace when they, having been delivered from the law with its merit system, turn back to the merit system again. It is safe to say that no person who has gained even a slight understanding of what it means to be perfected in Christ beyond the need of any human works to complete that perfection, has ever turned back to the law. People who trust Christ as Savior are perfected in Him whether they realize it or not, and it is those who do not realize it who may be influenced by legalists to turn to the merit system from which they have been delivered. Again, the context of the passage is the guide to the right interpretation of the passage in question. In the Galatian Epistle, the Apostle declares two important truths, namely, (1) that the law system is not a means to salvation, and (2) that the law system does not provide the rule of life for those who are saved by the grace of God. The law by its very nature supposes that the one to whom it is addressed needs to establish personal merit before God. It could have, therefore, no application to the one who, being in Christ, has the perfect merit of the Son of God. The liberty to which the Apostle refers and for which he exhorts the Christian to stand fast (Gal. 5:1) is this very freedom from an unbearable yoke of merit obligation. To turn from the blessing of the grace provision to the assumption that merit must be secured by human works, is to fall from grace. Christ becomes of no effect, to the extent that His perfect merit which grace provides is ignorantly abandoned for that which is a bondage to an intolerable merit system. God may be praised that it is impossible for a true believer to depart actually from grace. His departure from grace is only in the sphere of his own contemplation of his responsibility as a saved person. He may thus sacrifice his joy and peace, but there is no intimation that his salvation is sacrificed. If, perchance, men do not know what the position of a believer in grace is—and Arminians evince no such understanding—there is little hope that they would be able to comprehend what is involved in a fall from grace.

11. MISCELLANEOUS PASSAGES. Several texts which are not easily classified with others should be mentioned if this list is to be at all exhaustive: 1 Timothy 5:8, where *the* faith again is mentioned and the truth that to fail to care for one's household is a denial of the faith and constitutes a wrong which unbelievers are careful to avoid; 1 Timothy 5:12, where young widows are condemned for breaking a pledge (cf. R.V.); 1 Timothy 6:10, where *the* faith is mentioned again, and not personal faith. 2 Timothy 2:18 asserts that the faith of some respecting the specific doctrine of the resurrection was overthrown. In Revelation 21:8, 27, certain persons identified as *liars* it is said will be excluded from heaven. In this connection, it may be observed that a child of God who has told a lie is not a liar in the sense in which that word is used to classify the unbelievers—a Christian who has lied is not, from the Biblical viewpoint, the same as an unregenerate liar. This distinction applies equally to other sins by which the unsaved are identified, and to assert this does not even suggest that a sin is any less so when com-

mitted by a Christian. The whole intrusion of works of merit into the sphere of grace is the ground of misinterpretation of various passages: Philippians 2:12, for instance, where the believer is to work *out*, not work *for*, his salvation. He is to give expression outwardly of that which God is working *in*. Similarly, in a few instances the gospel is presented as something to *obey*—observe Acts 5:32; Hebrews 5:8–9. There is no intimation that men are saved by being obedient in their daily lives; it is a matter of obedience to the divine appeal which the gospel of grace presents.

CONCLUSION

Before turning to the consideration of the Calvinistic doctrine of safekeeping, a restatement is made that neither in the sphere of sovereign election, nor in the sphere of sovereign grace, nor in the sphere of human experience, nor in the sphere of Biblical interpretation have the Arminian advocates established their claims, and the insufficiency of their position will be disclosed further as this discussion turns from the negative to the positive. It may well be pointed out that Arminians have not taken up the security passages with candor and with an attempt to reconcile these to their insecurity contention. However, the major feature of this thesis is concerned with the constructive side of the question and it is now to have an extended examination.

Chapter XVI

THE CALVINISTIC DOCTRINE OF SECURITY

UNAVOIDABLY, much that enters into the Calvinistic doctrine of security has been alluded to by way of contrast or comparison in the foregoing analysis of the Arminian position. Perhaps enough has been presented respecting the Calvinistic view on the doctrines of original sin, efficacious calling, decrees, the fact and character of the fall, divine omniscience, divine sovereignty, and sovereign grace, though it may safely be re-stated that what is termed Calvinism—largely for want of a more comprehensive cognomen—is, so far as devout men have been able to comprehend it, the essential Pauline theology, especially in its soteriological aspects. After all, Systematic Theology is the attempt on the part of men to state in orderly arrangement what God has revealed in the Bible. The Word of God is consistent with itself and it is regrettable that good men do not agree among themselves about the interpretation. In seeking a reason, or reasons, for this lack of unity, certain suggestions may be advanced. First, it has pleased God so to embed the truth in the Sacred Text that only those who study unceasingly and who are qualified for the task by educational background, all of this coupled with true spiritual insight, are able to discern with some degree of accuracy its revelation in its length and breadth, its height and depth. Men with little or no conformity to these educational requirements have rendered superficial opinions, which are based on mere human reason and claim to be final. This shallow dogmatism has swept multitudes who think but little into cults and sporadic religious movements. It has long been recognized that the man who is least qualified to speak with authority will be, very often, the most dogmatic. A second explanation of disagreement in Bible interpretation is slavish conformity to human leaders. This tendency can easily beset the best of interpreters. Each sect feels called upon to maintain its theological schools and to pursue its peculiar point of view. Their theology is published and defended by those who are run in their specific molds. In the light of the fact that there is but one body of revealed truth setting forth but one system, that which God has given, the disagreement which obtains between sincere and educationally disciplined men may be accounted for on the basis of this tendency to cleave to the human authorities identified with a given sect. The creed of the denomination is more to be defended than the Word of God itself. In the present day, there is but little resentment when the Scriptures are discredited, but there is strong opposition experienced when the position occupied by the denomination is questioned. Men seldom change their preconceived views whether good or bad. Their early training and theological discipline serve as a mold from which the individual will seldom be extricated. Such a slavish bondage to human leaders and creeds may impede Calvinists as well as Arminians. It will be recognized by all, however, that Calvinists as a body, judging from their writings, are more concerned to be conformed to the Bible than any other group that is held together by common theological beliefs. Ignorance, intolerance, unteachableness, and slavish devotion to human leaders are the roots of doctrinal confusion with the attending evils which that confusion engenders. The names *Calvinism* and *Arminianism* may well be dismissed if only a clear understanding of the Word of God may be gained. However, these appellations do represent, in the main, two conflicting schools of theological thought, and it is the purpose of this thesis to defend the Word of God and Calvinism is favored only because it, in turn, favors the Scriptures of Truth. The Calvinistic interpretations, especially respecting security, are unstrained and show an amenableness to the Word of God. The great doctrines of Scripture bearing on security—universal depravity, effectual calling, decrees, the fall, omniscience, divine sovereignty, and sovereign grace—are taken by the Calvinists in the plain and natural meaning which may be drawn from the Sacred Text. It is not claimed that there are no truths which are too deep for human understanding; but these, when received in the natural sense of the language of the Scriptures, if not fully understood, are found to be harmonious with the revealed plan and purpose of God. It has been demonstrated in the previous chapter of this thesis that the Scriptures upon which the Arminian depends, for such Biblical appeal respecting insecurity as he chooses to make, are none of them in any final sense a support for his contention. His interpretation of these portions of the Word of God is well described by the text: "as also in all his epistles, speaking in them of these things; in which are some things hard to be understood, which they that are unlearned and unstable wrest, as they do also the other scriptures, unto their own destruction." Over against these passages to which the Arminians resort, is the positive, constructive, and consistent declaration of uncounted New Testament passages which in unqualified terms assert that the believer is secure. Added to these positive assertions of the Word of God are those deductions to be drawn from every doctrine which is at all related to a complete soteriology. No Arminian undertakes to demonstrate that the positive passages are uncertain in their meaning. Their only recourse is to claim that human responsibility must be read into these passages in order to make them harmonize with the interpretation they have placed on so-called insecurity texts. John 5:24 must read, "He that heareth My word, and believeth on Him that sent Me, hath everlasting life, and shall not come into condemnation—that is, *if he holds out to the end.*" Romans 8:30 must read, "Moreover whom He did predestinate by foreknowing their faith and works, them He also called provided they are willing to be called: and whom He called, them He also justified provided they do not sin: and whom He justified, them He also glorified provided they do not fall from their own steadfastness." It is no small responsibility to add to, or take from, the Word of God (Rev. 22:18–19), or to handle that Word deceitfully (2 Cor. 4:2).

Having previously discussed the Calvinistic beliefs respecting the great soteriological doctrines, it remains now to consider the direct and positive unfolding of eternal security as presented in the New Testament.

While there are unnumbered secondary declarations and inferences respecting the security of the true Christian, this chapter will present twelve major reasons, declared in the New Testament, why the believer once saved can never be lost. Liberty is to be claimed in connection with each of these reasons to point out what the rationalistic denial of the truth in question involves. These twelve reasons, it will be found, are equally divided in their relation to the three Persons of the Godhead— four are the responsibility of the Father, four are the responsibility of the Son, and four are the responsibility of the Spirit. This threefold fact at once lifts this theme to the level of a major doctrine of Soteriology. Of these twelve reasons it may be said that any one of them is in itself a final and sufficient basis for confidence that the child of God will be preserved unto heaven's glory. When twelve reasons, each complete and conclusive in itself, are contemplated, the evidence is overwhelming. In general, the New Testament presents the Father as purposing, calling, justifying, and glorifying those who believe on Christ; the Son is presented as becoming incarnate that He might be a Kinsman-Redeemer, as dying a substitutionary and efficacious death, as rising to be a living Savior both as Advocate and Intercessor, and as Head over all things to the

Church; the Holy Spirit is presented as administering and executing the purpose of the Father and the redemption which the Son has wrought. It is reasonable, then, that all three Persons of the Godhead should have their individual share in preserving to fruition that which God has determined.

I. THE REASONS WHICH DEPEND ON GOD THE FATHER

The four reasons for security which are assigned to the Father are: (1) the sovereign purpose of God, (2) the Father's infinite power set free, (3) the infinite love of God, and (4) the influence on the Father of the prayer of His Son.

1. THE SOVEREIGN PURPOSE OF GOD. By no process of worthy reasoning and certainly by no word of revelation can it be concluded that He who created all things according to His sovereign purpose—which purpose extends on into eternity to come and comprehends every minute detail that will ever come to pass—will be defeated in the realization of all His intention; nor should there be failure to accept the truth that the bringing of redeemed men into heaven's glory is a major divine purpose behind all His creative undertaking. The assumption is unfounded and vain which declares that the saving of souls and the outcalling of the Church is but a minor detail which, if unsuccessful, would, on account of its insignificance, have no important bearing on the main divine objective. It is true that, on the human side, man exercises his will in that he acts according to his desires and best judgment. It is also true and of greater importance that God molds those desires and enlightens that human judgment. It is natural for men to conclude that since in the range of their own experience their acceptance of Christ is optional, the salvation of a soul and its attaining to heaven's glory is a matter of indifference or uncertainty in the mind of God. The failure of one soul to be saved and to reach glory whom God has ordained to that end means the disruption of the whole actuality of divine sovereignty. If God could fail in one feature, be it ever so small, He could fail in all. If He could fail in anything, He ceases to be God and the universe is drifting to a destiny about which God Himself could know nothing. None would doubt that the incarnation and death of Christ were major features in the purpose of God; but all this, it is revealed, is for the purpose of bringing many sons into glory. It is written: "But we see Jesus, who was made a little lower than the angels for the suffering of death, crowned with glory and honour; that he by the grace of

God should taste death for every man. For it became him, for whom are all things, and by whom are all things, in bringing many sons unto glory, to make the captain of their salvation perfect through sufferings" (Heb. 2:9–10). God did not give His Son as a fortuitous venture, with uncertainty about whether a remnant of His purpose would be realized. Every devout mind would be shocked by the recital of such God-dishonoring insinuations; yet every feature of this impious sequence is unavoidably admitted if it be allowed that God could fail in the realization of His purpose in the instance of one soul. Ephesians 1:11–12 is a proper declaration in respect to the divine purpose: "In whom also we have obtained an inheritance, being predestinated according to the purpose of him who worketh all things after the counsel of his own will: that we should be to the praise of his glory, who first trusted in Christ." And, though often referred to previously, Romans 8:28–30 proclaims the same immutable divine intention, with plenary assurance that the sovereign purpose of God will be realized. The passage reads: "And we know that all things work together for good to them that love God, to them who are the called according to his purpose. For whom he did foreknow, he also did predestinate to be conformed to the image of his Son, that he might be the firstborn among many brethren. Moreover whom he did predestinate, them he also called: and whom he called, them he also justified: and whom he justified, them he also glorified." The primary pronouncement of this passage is that "all things work together for good to them that love God [a reference to those who are saved], to them who are the called according to his purpose." This entire program centers in His *purpose,* which began with predestination and foreknowledge acting in their combined effectiveness. That this intent which was foreseen and predetermined might be achieved, He calls, He justifies, and He glorifies. This purpose is for each individual who is saved. If it is inquired whether the individual must believe by the action of his own will, it will be remembered that the divine call consists in the moving of the human will—not by coercion, but by persuasion—and that, by so much, the only human responsibility—believing, which is of measureless importance—is guaranteed. All that God has purposed in behalf of those who are saved He has promised in unconditional covenant and His covenant cannot be broken, else the holy character of God is defamed. Would any pious individual assert that God might promise and not fulfill? Yet He has, by the very revelation of His sovereign intent, promised complete preservation of those who are saved at all. He does not hesitate to include the element of human faith in this great undertaking. When it is thus included, it is not the introduction of an uncertainty, as is easily supposed. There is no uncertainty whatever where He is the Author of faith. When God says He will save those who believe, it is understood from other Scriptures that His elect, under the persuasion which cannot fail, will believe. God's ability to make unconditional covenants in the outworking of His sovereign purpose is demonstrated in the covenants made with Abraham and David. The only responsibility in either of these covenants is contained in the sovereign "I will" of Jehovah. Both covenants reach on for their fulfillment to future ages. Because of their duration, if for no other reason, these covenants could not rest on the faithfulness of either of the men involved. The span of their lives scarcely marked the beginning of the realization of all that God promised in these covenants. It is of peculiar interest to note that, in the case of David—and what may be perplexing to Arminians—God declared that the sins of David's sons, through whom the covenant was to be perpetuated, would not in any case abrogate the covenant; though, it should also be observed, Jehovah reserved the right to chastise those in David's line who offended (2 Sam. 7:8–16; Ps. 89:20–37).

The word *promise* as employed by the Apostle Paul (cf. Rom. 4:13–14, 16, 20; Gal. 3:17–19, 22, 29; 4:23, 28), though much neglected in doctrinal study, represents precisely the form of unconditional promise which God made to Abraham—not the promise of the same thing, but that which in each case is unconditional and therefore an expression of divine sovereignty. The promise made to the believer of this age is not only concerning different objectives, but reaches out to realms unrevealed to Abraham. God did not covenant with Abraham that He would present Abraham faultless before the presence of His glory (Jude 1:24); nor did He promise that Abraham would be accepted in the Beloved (Eph. 1:6). Under present relationships, the word *promise* represents all that God in sovereign grace designs for the believer. Abraham is the divinely determined pattern of salvation by promise (Gen. 15:6; Rom. 4:3, 20–25); but the scope of the promise now is widely different in the case of the believer as compared to that which was addressed to Abraham. The force of this divinely arrayed principle to make a sovereign covenant of promise and to execute it apart from every human condition is seen in Romans 4:16, where it is written: "It is of faith [nothing on man's part], that it might be by grace [everything on God's part], to the end the promise might be sure." If the end in view depended at any point on human resources or factors, the promise could not be *sure;* but, being an unconditional, sovereign work of God, the result is as sure as the existence of the eternal God. Similarly, in Galatians 3:22 it is written that "the scripture hath concluded all [Jew and Gentile alike] under sin," which means that God accepts no merit from man which might be credited to his account in his salvation. This is so in order that "the promise," which is realized by faith in Jesus Christ, "might be given to them that believe"—meaning, who do no more than to believe. The Apostle is careful to point out that, in the case of Abraham, he was declared righteous by believing. It could not be because of law observance since the law was not given until five hundred years later; nor could it have been merited by circumcision, since Abraham was not then circumcised (Rom. 4:9–16). Thus the grace-promise with all it includes is addressed to the believer apart from the merit system which the law would impose, and apart from all ceremonials. It is the sovereign purpose of the sovereign God, which is accomplished to infinite perfection through sovereign grace on the sole condition of faith in Christ as Savior.

The Arminian insists that human merit is essential for safekeeping and by so much he denies that the eternal purpose in salvation is to be accomplished by unconditional sovereign grace. To him the promise is not sure, and he denies that God has concluded all under sin for the very intent that the human element should be dismissed forever. This Arminian misrepresentation is not an insignificant matter. The gospel he preaches is perilously near being "another gospel," that which merits the unrevoked anathema of Galatians 1:8–9.

The unconditional divine covenant of promise is the substance of a vast body of Scripture. It enters into every passage in which salvation and safekeeping are made to depend upon faith in Christ. The following texts will serve as illustration: "For God so loved the world, that he gave his only begotten Son, that whosoever believeth in him should not perish, but have everlasting life" (John 3:16); "Verily, verily, I say unto you, He that heareth my word, and believeth on him that sent me, hath everlasting life, and shall not come into condemnation; but is passed from death unto life" (John 5:24); "All that the Father giveth me shall come to me; and him that cometh to me I will in no wise cast out" (John 6:37); "And I give unto them eternal life; and they shall never perish, neither shall any man pluck them out of my hand" (John 10:28); "Moreover whom he did predestinate, them he also called: and whom he called, them he also justified: and whom he justified, them he also glorified" (Rom. 8:30).

2. THE FATHER'S INFINITE POWER SET FREE. The problem related to the exercise of divine power in the safekeeping of the believer is more complex than it would be were there no moral features involved. Granting that God is omnipotent, and to this all pious souls will agree, it would not be difficult to imagine a situation in which God could preserve an individual Christian by His arbitrary domination, or a situation in which He could surround the believer with influences which would safeguard him throughout his days; but Christians sin and are imperfect, which fact introduces a moral problem when their safekeeping is considered. Without doubt, it is this moral problem which is the formidable obstacle to security in the Arminian's mind. This issue will be discussed more fully in Chapter XVIII. The Arminian readily discloses his mind when asked the direct question, What would serve to unsave the Christian? His answer, of course, is *sin*—but not minor sins, such as all believers commit, else no Christian would endure at all and they evidently do endure; even Christians of the Arminian faith endure to some extent, and some do reach heaven at last. No Arminian would contend that those of their number who reach heaven do so on the basis of a sinless life. The contention is, rather, that those thus favored did not commit sins sufficiently wicked to unsave them. By so much, as all will admit, a rationalistic and unscriptural claim is introduced which distinguishes between big sins and little sins. Yet even more daring in its unbelief is the obvious confession involved, which asserts that sin may unsave after Christ has borne it. The Scriptures declare that Christ by His death became the propitiation for *our* sins (1 John 2:2), which certainly means that the believer's sins, in contrast to "the sins of the whole world," have had their specific and perfect judgment wrought out by Christ in His death—a judgment so perfect that the Father is rendered infinitely propitious by it. It would seem unnecessary to state here the qualifying truth that, though the Christian's sin does not surpass the propitiation which is originated to disannul its power, it does carry with it other penalties, and not the least of these is chastisement by the Father should the sinning Christian continue to sin without repentance and confession (1 Cor. 11:31–32).

The special point which this division of this theme aims to establish is that God the Father not only is able because of omnipotence to keep His own, but that He is set *free* through the death of His Son to keep them, in spite of the moral problem which the imperfection of each Christian engenders. The New Testament bears abundant testimony to the unrestrained ability of God to keep those whom He has saved through Christ. It is written: "My Father, which gave them me, is greater than all; and no man is able to pluck them out of my Father's hand" (John 10:29); "and being fully persuaded that, what he had promised, he was able also to perform" (Rom. 4:21); "What shall we then say to these things? If God be for us, who can be against us? . . . For I am persuaded, that neither death, nor life, nor angels, nor principalities, nor powers, nor things present, nor things to come, nor height, nor depth, nor any other creature, shall be able to separate us from the love of God, which is in Christ Jesus our Lord" (Rom. 8:31, 38–39); "Who art thou that judgest another man's servant? to his own master he standeth or falleth. Yea, he shall be holden up: for God is able to make him stand" (Rom. 14:4); "Now unto him that is able to do exceeding abundantly above all that we ask or think, according to the power that worketh in us" (Eph. 3:20); "who shall change our vile body, that it may be fashioned like unto his glorious body, according to the working whereby he is able even to subdue all things unto himself" (Phil. 3:21); "For the which cause I also suffer these things: nevertheless I am not ashamed: for I know whom I have believed, and am persuaded that he is able to keep that which I have committed unto him against that day" (2 Tim. 1:12); "Wherefore he is able also to save them to the uttermost that come unto God by him, seeing he ever liveth to make intercession for them" (Heb. 7:25); "Now unto him that is able to keep you from falling, and to present you faultless before the presence of his glory with exceeding joy" (Jude 1:24). To all this may be added the specific disclosure of Ephesians 1:19–21, wherein it is revealed that the very power which wrought in Christ to raise Him from the dead— the supreme power—is "to us-ward." Who, indeed, is able to estimate the advantage to the child of God of that immeasurable power?

To maintain his position, the Arminian must insert his own unwarranted qualifications into each of these divine declarations and must deny that God's power is free to act in the preservation of believers. The Arminian denial of the revelation that God is propitious toward the believer's sins is equivalent to the denial of all that enters into the doctrine of sovereign grace.

3. THE INFINITE LOVE OF GOD. That which actuated God from all eternity in His elective choice of those whom He would bring into glory was His love for them. If, as many scholars believe, the words *in love,* which in the Authorized Version are at the end of Ephesians 1:4, are to be made the opening words of that which follows, a flood of light falls on this important revelation respecting the motive of God. Under this

arrangement, the passage would read and probably should read, "in love having predestinated us." Love is one of the attributes of God. "God is love," which means that He has never acquired love, He does not maintain it by any effort whatsoever, nor does His love depend upon conditions; for He is the Author of all conditions. God loved before any being was created, and at a time—if time it be—when there was no other than His own triune Being. He loved Himself supremely, but upon a plane far above that of mere self-complacency. His love is as eternal and unchangeable as His own existence, and it was in that incomprehensible past that He also loved the beings He would yet create. Though expressed supremely by the death of Christ at a moment in time, and though seen in the preservation of, and providence over, His redeemed, His is a love of the dateless past and its continuation is as immutable as the predestination it devises. Yes, predestination is, so far from being a hard and awful predetermination of God, in reality, the supreme undertaking and satisfaction of His infinite compassion.

At an earlier point in this thesis, attention has been called to the truth that salvation springs not from the misery of men which God in mercy might choose to relieve, but it springs from the love God has for His creatures, which love can be satisfied by nothing short of their conformity to Christ in His eternal presence. It is this unchangeable endearment that the student of doctrine must contemplate and in the light of it he must form his conclusions. In this contemplation, it will not do to invest the divine compassion with the fitfulness and capriciousness which characterize human love, as though God loved His creatures when they were good, but withdrew His love when they were wrong. The fact is, though incomprehensible, that God loved men enough to give His Son to die for them even when they were enemies and sinners (Rom. 5:7–10). He was not merely shocked by their unworthiness enough to provide some relief; He actually died for them in the Person of His Son. It is in this connection—and at Romans 5—that the words "much more" occur twice and when contrasting the outworking of the love of God for the unsaved with the outworking of the love of God for the saved. It is not implied that He loves more, though the individual saved by His grace is more lovable than when unregenerate; it is rather that the opportunity has been made, through salvation, for His love to have a much more manifestation in those who are saved. "Much more then, being now justified by his blood, we shall be saved from wrath through him. For if, when we were enemies, we were reconciled to God by the death of his Son, much more, being reconciled, we shall be saved by his life" (Rom. 5:9–10). The preservation declared in the end of this passage is not due to the indwelling Christ, which is eternal life (Col. 1:27), but is due to the essential fact of Christ's own life and all that He, the resurrected Son of God, is to the believer.

If this truth respecting the immeasurable and immutable love of God for believers is recognized, it will be seen that, because of this unalterable motive, God will conclude perfectly what He has begun—that which He predestinated with infinite certainty. Love removed every barrier that sin erected and love will keep, by a much more manifestation even than that exhibited at Calvary, all whom He hath chosen in Christ before the foundation of the world.

Little place, indeed, does the Arminian make in his system for this unalterable, undefeatable love of God for those whom He has saved. To deny this love its full manifestation and satisfaction, as it is disclosed by God Himself, is to attempt to impair, if not to deny, the essential reality of one of God's most glorious attributes.

4. THE INFLUENCE ON THE FATHER OF THE PRAYER OF HIS SON. Many cognomens are used in the New Testament to designate those from among Jews and Gentiles who are saved—Christians, believers, brethren, children of God, the household of faith, the family of God, "my sheep," a kingdom of priests, His Body, saints—and each of these, to which others might be added, carries a specific meaning and suggests a peculiar relationship. There is, however, one title which, because of the One who used it and the circumstances under which it was employed, surpasses in hallowed exaltation all other appellations combined. The Lord Himself used it exclusively in that supreme hour when He was leaving this world and was returning to the Father—an hour when He was accounting to the Father respecting the completion of His incomparable mission to this world. The time and circumstances thus marked the climax of all that He had wrought while here in the world. Whatever term the Savior might employ at any time would be of the greatest significance, but above all and exalted to the highest heaven is that designation which He employs when He is in holy and familiar converse with His Father in heaven. At once the devout mind is aroused to its supreme attention to catch the terminology which is current in the intercourse between the Father and the Son. It is then in His High Priestly prayer that the Savior seven times refers to those who are saved as "those whom thou hast given me" (John 17:2, 6, 9, 11–12, 24). This so exalted company includes all that believe on Him throughout the age (John 17:20). This title at once suggests an event of measureless im-

port in past ages concerning which but little may be known. It is reasonable to believe that each individual ever to be saved by the grace of God through the Savior, Jesus Christ, was in the ages past individually presented as a particular love gift from the Father to the Son; that each individual represents a thought that could never be duplicated; and that if one of these jewels should be missing from the whole company, the Lord would be deprived as only infinity could be injured by imperfections.

While referring to believers as "those whom thou hast given me," the Son asks the Father this definite petition: "Holy Father, keep through thine own name those whom thou hast given me, that they may be one, as we are" (John 17:11). The prayer that they may be *one* no doubt refers to the organic unity of all believers, which is illustrated by the figure of a body and in its relation to its head. The implication is that no member shall be absent. But, more to the point, is the fact and force of the direct prayer to the Father by the Son, in which He makes request that the Father keep through His name those whom He has given to the Son. Naturally, the question arises whether this prayer of the Son will be answered. The Arminians hesitate to believe that it will be answered in the case of every believer, while the Calvinists assert that the prayer will be answered and point to the fact that no prayer by Christ has ever been unanswered, nor could it be. The request itself which this prayer presents should not be overlooked. The Son asks the Father to keep those saved whom the Father has given to the Son. If it could be demonstrated—which it cannot—that the Father has no interest of His own in these elect people, it must be observed that He, for the Son's sake, to whom nothing is denied, must employ His infinite resources to accomplish precisely what the Son has requested. It is thus that the prayer of the Son of God to the Father becomes one of the major factors in the believer's security. To deny the safekeeping of the believer is to imply that the prayer of the Son of God will not be answered.

II. THE REASONS WHICH DEPEND ON GOD THE SON

While the four reasons for the Christian's security which depend on God the Son are discussed separately in various places in the New Testament, they all appear together in one verse and as a fourfold answer to a challenging inquiry whether the child of God is secure. The passage reads: "Who is he that condemneth? It is Christ that died, yea rather, that is risen again, who is even at the right hand of God, who also maketh intercession for us" (Rom. 8:34).

The question with which this passage opens is preceded by a similar inquiry—"Who shall lay anything to the charge of God's elect?"—which question draws out the assuring answer, "It is God that justifieth." The argument is that if God has already justified, which is the case with everyone who believes in Jesus (cf. Rom. 3:26; 8:30), how can He lay anything to the charge of His justified one? It is in no wise the common problem of one person discovering imperfections or sin in another person. In such an undertaking, God, above all others, could identify the Christian's failures. He has never shut His eyes to those failures, nor does He fail to give righteous consideration to them. The believer's justification is secured on the ground of the imputed merit of the Son of God and it is legally his, being, as he is, in Christ Jesus. There could never be such a thing as a justification before God which is based upon human worthiness. On the other hand, a justification which is not subject to human merit could hardly be subject to human demerit. As in human relationships where there are ways by which an earthly father may correct his erring son without disrupting either sonship or family standing, in like manner God as Father maintains the perfect standing —even complete and eternal justification—of His child at the very moment it is necessary for Him to correct that child. The truth therefore stands that God, having justified the ungodly (Rom. 4:5), will not and cannot contradict Himself by charging them with evil, which charge amounts to the reversing of their justification. Bearing on this truth, Dean Alford quotes Chrysostom as saying: "He saith not, 'God who remitteth sins,' but which is much more, 'God who justifieth.' For when the vote of the judge himself acquits, and of such a Judge, of what weight is the accuser?" (*N.T. for English Readers,* new ed., on Rom. 8:34). The absolute equity of this arrangement must be comprehended, else the student will never understand that type of salvation which is wrought by sovereign grace and which he is appointed to preach.

The second question and the one which draws out the fourfold answer now under consideration—"Who is he that condemneth?"—is quite similar to the one which precedes it, though a different body of truth is summoned to serve as the answer. Here, as throughout the New Testament, the inquiry whether the believer is unconditionally safe forever through the provisions of infinite grace is answered in the affirmative. Concerning the complete answer to this second question, De Wette remarks: "All the great points of our redemption are ranged together, from the death of Christ to His still enduring intercession, as reasons for negativing the question above" (Alford, *loc. cit.*).

A sincere attention to this question and its fourfold answer is demanded, to the end that there may be a worthy understanding of the truth embraced in this particular theme which occupies so great a place in Soteriology. This interrogation whether the true believer will ever be condemned is both propounded and answered by the Holy Spirit. These are the words of God and not the words of a man alone. It is as though the divine Author anticipated the doctrinal confusion that was to arise and, with that in view, caused these momentous questions to be recorded with their unequivocal answers. Nevertheless, such direct questions and conclusive answers have not deterred a form of rationalistic unbelief, which poses as pious and sound, from denying the entire revelation.

The four answers to the question "Who is he that condemneth?" are here taken up separately and in their order, since they constitute the four reasons for the believer's security which belong, for their achievement, to the Son of God. These answers are: (1) Christ has died, (2) Christ is risen, (3) Christ advocates, and (4) Christ intercedes.

1. CHRIST HAS DIED. The first answer to the question "Who is he that condemneth?" is a citation of the fact that Christ has died, and properly so, since that death is a major ground for the assurance that the believer cannot be condemned. To a degree that is complete and final, Christ has Himself borne the condemnation which otherwise would fall on the Christian who has sinned. No new principle is thus introduced. It was on the basis of the efficacy of Christ's death for his sins that the believer was saved in the first place and apart from all penalty or punishment, a holy God being thus set free to pardon righteously every sin that ever was or ever will be, with respect to its power to condemn (Rom. 8:1, R.V.). It is the same divine freedom, based on the fact that Christ died for the Christian's sins (1 John 2:2), which creates the freedom of God to forgive righteously the sin—now within the sphere of fellowship with God—of the believer who confesses that sin (1 John 1:9). The solution of the problem of the salvation of the unregenerate person and of the preservation of those who are saved is identical. This divinely wrought solution is not only equitable and legal, but it is practical and reasonable. Though Satan-blinded minds do not see this truth until they are enlightened, the fact that the Substitute has borne the penalty is the simplest of methods by which a problem,

otherwise impossible of solution, may be wholly solved. Though God reserves the right to correct and chasten His child, He has never allowed an intimation to go forth by His authority, that His child would be condemned. In defense of his theological position, the Arminian must either deny that the death of Christ is a sufficient divine dealing with sin and, therefore, the believer may be disowned for the very sins which Christ bore, or he must abandon the testimony of the Bible outright and conclude that Christ did not die efficaciously for anyone. Such conclusions are the inescapable deductions from the Arminian position respecting the doctrine of substitution. Naturally, there is no intermediate ground. Either the believer must be condemned for each and every sin—which is the logical contention of Arminianism—or his sins are in no way a ground of judgment, the judgment of them having been borne by Another. There is no question about what the Bible teaches on these two propositions, nor about which one it favors.

2. CHRIST IS RISEN. The glorious truth of the resurrection of Christ becomes at once the ground on which two conclusive reasons for the security of the child of God are found to rest: (a) that the believer has partaken of the resurrection life of the Son of God, and (b) that the believer is a part of the New Creation over which the resurrected Christ is the all-sufficient Head. The latter of these two reasons will be discussed under those features of security which are the responsibility of the Holy Spirit. The former, now to be considered, is that the child of God partakes of the resurrection life of the Son of God. An exceedingly important statement of truth appears in Colossians 2 and 3. It is to the effect that the Christian is already in the sphere of resurrection by virtue of the fact that he is in the resurrected Christ. In chapter 2, the Apostle asserts directly that the Christian is raised with Christ (vs. 12). This reality is not a mere symbolism or figure; it is as real as Christ's own resurrection, in which it shares. To be "quickened" is to be made alive by the receiving of the resurrection life of Christ. The Christian has been, and is said to be even now, raised up and seated with Christ in the heavenlies (Eph. 2:6). To be in the resurrected Christ and to have the resurrected Christ within, constitutes a spiritual resurrection which, as to the believer's whole being, will be completed in due time by the resurrection of the body or by its transformation in translation. With this spiritual reality in mind, the Apostle writes in Colossians 3:1–4 and in respect to the believer's daily life, "If ye then be risen with Christ, seek those things which are above, where Christ sitteth on the right hand of God. Set your affection on things above, not on things

on the earth. For ye are dead, and your life is hid with Christ in God. When Christ, who is our life, shall appear, then shall ye also appear with him in glory."

The life which the believer receives in regeneration is the life of Christ in resurrection. That life cannot decrease or perish. It is the common claim of Arminians that, whatever eternal life may be, it can, and in many instances does, depart. Some have said that it is eternal, resurrection life while it is possessed, but that the Christian may become dispossessed of it. But that life is not a detached something which may come or go. It is a nature secured by divine generation and, like any nature which is possessed, it cannot be detached and dismissed. There seems to be a peculiar bond of relationship between two realities—"eternal life" and "shall not perish"—as these are twice used together by Christ (John 3:16; 10:28).

The denial of eternal security for the child of God—one who has received the resurrection life of Christ as an imparted nature—is to deny either the reality of this life or to deny its imperishable and abiding character.

3. CHRIST ADVOCATES. In 1 John 1:1—2:2, two important questions are answered, namely, what the effect of the Christian's sin is upon himself and what its cure, and what the effect of the Christian's sin is upon God and what its cure. In a previous section of this work this specific ministry of Christ has had a more complete consideration. At this point, however, the issue is crucial in its bearing on the security of those who are saved. Turning for the moment to the effect of the Christian's sin upon himself, it will be seen that in 1 John alone there are at least seven damaging consequences which result from that sin; yet it is not once intimated that the believer will be lost again. One of these penalties is that of the loss of communion with God the Father and the Son, and the cure—far removed, indeed, from being a re-regeneration—is a simple confession of the sin to God from a penitent heart (1 John 1:3–9). Attention has been called in Chapter XIII to thirty-three divine undertakings which together constitute the salvation of a soul. Among them is the truth that all sin is forgiven. Not one of these thirty-three transformations could be claimed alone or separated from the whole, nor could thirty-two be selected with the intentional omission of one. They constitute one indivisible whole; nor is one of these subject to a second experience of reception. Even the forgiveness of sin—which is unto union with Christ and into a state where there is no condemnation—is never repeated. The Christian's forgiveness in the

household and return to fellowship with the Father and the Son is quite another thing; yet it, too, is based on the same substitutionary death of Christ. The removal of the effect upon himself of the Christian's sin is, through divine grace, perfect and complete when the requisite confession is made. The provision is specific and sufficient whereby the sin is forgiven and the sinner cleansed (1 John 1:9).

On the other hand, the effect of the Christian's sin upon his holy God is most serious indeed. It is asserted with all possible emphasis that the least sin—such as believers habitually commit, as omissions and commissions—has the power in itself to hurl the believer down from his exalted position into perdition, were it not for that which Christ has wrought. It is here that the form of rationalism which characterizes Arminianism asserts itself. Apart from revelation, it is natural to conclude that God cannot get along with one who is sinning, even though that one is His own child by regeneration; but if it is discovered that God does get on with those who are imperfect, then the problem of the security of the believer is solved in so far as the Christian's sin affects God.

The central passage, 1 John 2:1, opens with the address, "My little children," which is complete evidence that this declaration—as is true of this entire Epistle—is addressed to those who are born of God (John 1:12–13). "The things" of which the Apostle writes are doubtless the particular doctrine of forgiveness and cleansing for the Christian as revealed in chapter 1, and that, also, which immediately follows in this verse, wherein the divine way of dealing with the Christian's sin is disclosed. The effect of these truths upon the believer—quite contrary to the claims of Arminians—is to deter him from sinning. The "natural" or unregenerate man who delights to sin will embrace a doctrine which lifts the penalty of sin; and at this point Arminians seem able to comprehend no more than the view of the natural man. That there are greater incentives to purity, holiness, and faithfulness than the mere dread of punishment, they fail to recognize. At least in their writings they make no mention of those higher motives. All this is largely due to the fact that they cannot, because of the very beliefs they profess, look upon themselves as accepted and sealed in Christ. Were they to see themselves in such a relation to God, reason as well as revelation would remind them of the corresponding obligation to live as an accepted and sealed person should live. So to live is the greatest motive that can actuate a human life. It far transcends in its effectiveness the mere fear of a law or punishment which, after all, everyone on every hand is disre-

garding. On the antinomian charge against the Calvinists which the
Arminians universally enter, Dr. Charles Hodge writes:

> Antinomianism has never had any hold in the churches of the Reformation.
> There is no logical connection between the neglect of moral duties, and the sys-
> tem which teaches that Christ is a Saviour as well from the power as from the
> penalty of sin; that faith is the act by which the soul receives and rests on Him
> for sanctification as well as for justification; and that such is the nature of the
> union with Christ by faith and indwelling of the Spirit, that no one is, or can
> be partaker of the benefit of his death, who is not also partaker of the power
> of his life; which holds to the divine authority of the Scripture which declares
> that without holiness no man shall see the Lord (Heb. xii.14); and which, in
> the language of the great advocate of salvation by grace, warns all who call
> themselves Christians: "Be not deceived: neither fornicators, nor idolaters, nor
> adulterers, nor effeminate, nor abusers of themselves with mankind, nor thieves,
> nor covetous, nor drunkards, nor revilers, nor extortioners shall inherit the
> kingdom of God." (1 Cor. vi.9, 10.) It is not the system which regards sin as
> so great an evil that it requires the blood of the Son of God for its expiation,
> and the law as so immutable that it requires the perfect righteousness of Christ
> for the sinner's justification, which leads to loose views of moral obligation;
> these are reached by the system which teaches that the demands of the law
> have been lowered, that they can be more than met by the imperfect obedience
> of fallen men, and that sin can be pardoned by priestly intervention. This is
> what logic and history alike teach.—*Systematic Theology*, III, 241

Evidently the Apostle John anticipates that the power of the truth he
is disclosing will tend to a separation from sin. This is the force of the
words, "that ye sin not." The phrase which follows, "if any man sin,"
refers to Christians exclusively. It could not include the unsaved along
with the saved. It is *any man* within the Christian fellowship. A similar
usage, among several in the New Testament, is found in 1 Corinthians
3:12–15 where the restricted classification is equally evident. The term
any man corresponds numerically to the pronoun "we" which follows
here immediately. The sufficient provision for the sinning Christian is
indicated by the words, "We have an advocate with the Father." The
scene is set in the high court of heaven with the Father as Judge upon
the throne (incidentally, it should be noted that, though the child of
God has sinned, God is still his Father). A prosecuting agent is present
also. The record of his activity as prosecutor is found in Revelation
12:10, which reads: "And I heard a loud voice saying in heaven, Now is
come salvation, and strength, and the kingdom of our God, and the
power of his Christ: for the accuser of our brethren is cast down, which
accused them before our God day and night." If any accusing voice were
needed, that need Satan himself supplies. The question "Who is he that

condemneth?" easily includes in the sphere of its possibilities vastly more than the charges which one human being might prefer against another. But even the prosecution by Satan cannot avail, for there is an Advocate, a Defender. What this means every hour to the believer will never be known in this life. The truth respecting the advocacy of Christ is in view in these declarations: "who is even at the right hand of God" (Rom. 8:34) and "now to appear in the presence of God for us" (Heb. 9:24).

If inquiry be made concerning what influence the Advocate brings to bear on the Father by which the believer is cleared from condemnation, some might venture the opinion that He is making excuses; but there are no excuses. Another might suggest that He pleads with the Father for leniency; but the Father, being holy, cannot be, and therefore is not, lenient with sin. Still another might propose that this Attorney, or Advocate, is a shrewd lawyer who is able to make out a case where no case exists; but—and great is the force of it—at this very point and in connection with the specific work of delivering the sinning Christian from condemnation, the Advocate wins an exalted title which He gains for no other service, namely, *Jesus Christ the Righteous*. The claim to this unique appellation is probably twofold: (1) He presents the evidence of His own sacrifice for the sin in question—the truth that He bore it fully on the cross. Thus when the Father withholds condemnation, His ground for doing so is *just,* since the Savior has died. It is in direct line with this aspect of the Advocate's work that this very context goes on to say: "And he is the propitiation for our sins." By the death of His Son for the Christian's sin, the Father is rendered propitious. (2) Christ is made unto the believer *righteousness* (1 Cor. 1:30; 2 Cor. 5:21), and He, as the Source of this imputed righteousness, is the One by whom the Christian is saved and in whom he stands forever.

It is evident then, that, while paternal discipline will be exercised by the Father over His erring child according to His good pleasure (Heb. 12:3–15), that child will not be condemned, since Christ who bore the Christian's sin appears in heaven for him and Christ is the very righteousness in which the Christian is accepted before God.

4. CHRIST INTERCEDES. Among the neglected doctrines—and there are many—is that which brings into view the present intercession of Christ in behalf of all that are saved. The very fact that He thus intercedes implies the danger which besets the believer in this the enemy's land, and the necessity of Christ's prayer in his behalf. The strange inattention which obtains with regard to this ministry of Christ may be

due to various causes and none, it is probable, more than the influence and power of Satan, who would rob the believer of the advantage and comfort which this intercession secures. As a practical experience, believers are without the knowledge of this intercession in their behalf and therefore deprived of the help and strength which this knowledge affords. The neglect cannot be attributed to the lack of revelation, for it stands out with more than usual clearness on the Sacred Page. Four major passages appear, and these should be given careful attention. It will be seen that the divine purpose in Christ's intercession, as exhibited in these passages, is the security of all those for whom He intercedes.

John 17:1–26. A quotation, or reproduction, of the text of this supreme chapter is uncalled for. The passage embodies the prayer of Christ and the reasonable conclusion is that it is the norm or pattern of that prayer which Christ continues to pray in heaven. If it were fitting for Him to intercede for His own who were then in the *cosmos* world, it is fitting that He shall pray for those who are now in the *cosmos* world. In this prayer His solicitude for all who are in the *cosmos* world is most apparent, so, also, His dependence upon the Father to keep them from the evil one. As before indicated, the request of the Son in behalf of the safekeeping of those who are saved, can be refused by the Father only on the supposition that Christ's prayer might not be answered; or that it is beyond the power of Infinity, even though the Father is released from all moral restraint by the death of Christ for sin. The latter position—that to preserve the believer is beyond the power of God even when the sin question is eliminated—Arminians have not hesitated to assume. Nevertheless, the Savior ceases not to intercede in behalf of those He has saved and to the end that they may be preserved forever.

Romans 8:34. "Who is he that condemneth? It is Christ that died, yea rather, that is risen again, who is even at the right hand of God, who also maketh intercession for us."

In this Scripture it is declared that there is no condemnation for the child of God because of the truth, among others already considered, that the Savior "maketh intercession for us." On the divine side of the problem of the eternal security of the Christian, there is evidently a definite dependence upon the prayer of the Son of God.

Luke 22:31–34. "And the Lord said, Simon, Simon, behold, Satan hath desired to have you, that he may sift you as wheat: but I have prayed for thee, that thy faith fail not: and when thou art converted, strengthen thy brethren. And he said unto him, Lord, I am ready to go with thee, both into prison, and to death. And he said, I tell thee, Peter, the cock shall not crow this day, before that thou shalt thrice deny that thou knowest me."

While this is the record of Christ's prayer for but one man and that man the one who was to deny his Lord, it is reasonable to assume that Christ sustains this same solicitude and care over each individual believer. Doubtless He could say to every believer many times in the day, "I have prayed for thee." The petition which Christ presented for Peter was secured. He prayed that Peter's faith should not fail, and it did not fail, though through all this experience Peter manifested the traits of a believer who is out of communion with his Lord. There is no intimation that Peter became unsaved, or that he was saved a second time. The doctrine respecting the believer's restoration to fellowship with God—confused by Arminians with salvation—is that which Peter illustrates. And finally,

Hebrews 7:23–25. "And they truly were many priests, because they were not suffered to continue by reason of death: but this man, because he continueth ever, hath an unchangeable priesthood. Wherefore he is able also to save them to the uttermost that come unto God by him, seeing he ever liveth to make intercession for them."

No more direct and unqualified declaration respecting the eternal security of the believer than this is recorded in the New Testament, and that security is here made to depend wholly on the intercession of Christ; that is, the believer is said to be secure in the most absolute sense because Christ prays for him—else language ceases to be a dependable medium for the conveying of thought.

In His priesthood over believers, Christ differs widely from the priests of the old order and in the one particular especially: that as they were subject to death and by death their ministry was interrupted, Christ's priesthood is interminable. He hath an immutable, or unchangeable, priesthood, and that corresponds to the equally important truth that He liveth forever. "Wherefore?" Because He liveth forever and, on that account, His ministry as Priest has no end. He is able to save the Christian—some say "to completeness" and others say "evermore" or "eternally" (ϵis τo $\pi a \nu \tau \epsilon \lambda \acute{\epsilon} s$ will sustain both conceptions; for that which is saved unto completeness is saved without end—all those that come unto God by Him; that is, those that trust in the Savior). This certitude is based on the enduring Savior's interminable ability as Priest to bring to pass eternal security. The assertion is unqualified and the unequivocal divine guarantee is made to depend directly and only, so far as this passage is concerned, upon the prevailing power of Christ's intercession. Such is efficacious power and the infinite reality of it cannot be comprehended by the mind of man; and to deny its supreme potency, as all do who disbelieve in the absolute security of the child of God, is to enter the sphere of unwarranted assumption.

The intercession of Christ, it is well to observe, is more than the mere exercise of prayer. Christ is a Shepherd and Bishop to those whom He saves. He guides His own away from the pitfalls and snares of Satan. The Christian could never know in this life what he owes to the interceding Shepherd who sustains him every hour of his life. David caught the same assuring confidence concerning his own relation to Jehovah when he said, "The LORD is my shepherd; I shall not want" (Ps. 23:1). David did not testify merely that he had not wanted anything up to that moment, but he boldly declares that his future is as certain as the Shepherdhood of Jehovah could make it.

Returning for the moment to the one text (Rom. 8:34) into which all four reasons for the believer's security which depend on God the Son are compressed, it may be restated that, by His substitutionary death, Christ provides the Father with righteous freedom to undertake eternal blessedness for those who believe. By His resurrection Christ provides the Christian with imperishable resurrection life. By His advocacy He meets the condemning effect of the believer's every sin as that sin is seen by God in heaven. And by His intercession He engages the infinite power of God—including His own Shepherdhood—in behalf of those who believe. Every step in this incomprehensible service of the Savior is in itself wholly sufficient to achieve the end in view; yet every step is challenged and disowned by Arminian rationalism.

What the Savior undertakes—especially as Advocate and Intercessor—is at His own appointment. He saves and keeps simply because of the truth that His salvation is by its very nature eternal. It follows, then, that He should never be implored to advocate or intercede, though unceasing thanksgiving should ascend to Him for these accomplishments.

III. RESPONSIBILITIES BELONGING TO GOD THE HOLY SPIRIT

Much, indeed, is directly undertaken by the Holy Spirit to the end that the child of God shall be safe forever. Under the present divine arrangement, He is the Executor of very much that the Godhead undertakes; however, as in the case of the Father and the Son, four distinctive achievements are wrought by the Third Person and these demand recognition.

1. THE HOLY SPIRIT REGENERATES. The widespread Arminian emphasis upon human merit has tended to obscure one of the primary realities of a true Christian, which reality is secured, not by merit, but by divine grace, in answer to saving belief in Christ. That reality is that the believer is regenerated and thus is introduced into a new estate, a new existence, a new relationship which is well defined as a new creation. In 2 Corinthians 5:17 it is written: "Therefore if any man be in Christ, he is a new creature: old things are passed away; behold, all things are become new." The Apostle likewise declares that "we are his workmanship, created in Christ Jesus" (Eph. 2:10). This passage reveals the truth that, as a result of the divine workmanship, the Christian is no less than a divine creation—a form of being which did not exist before. That new being is said to partake of the "divine nature," which implies that it is as enduring as the eternal God. Similarly, the same Apostle writes: "For in Christ Jesus neither circumcision availeth any thing, nor uncircumcision, but a new creature" (Gal. 6:15). Upon this specific aspect of the truth the Lord placed the greatest emphasis when speaking to Nicodemus. It is significant that, when declaring the necessity of the birth from above, Christ did not select a dissolute character, but He chose one who ranked highest in Judaism and whose character was beyond reproach. It was a personal message when He said to Nicodemus, "Ye must be born again," and the universally acknowledged mystery of it must not be suffered to detract from either the reality or the necessity of that divine regeneration. In the instance of human generation, a being originates who did not exist before and who will go on forever. Likewise, in spiritual regeneration a being originates which was not identified as such before and this being will go on forever. By what law of reasoning can it be assured that eternal existence belongs to a form of existence which outwardly seems to be temporal, and not to that form of existence which because of its source and essential character is not temporal but is eternal? An earthly parent imparts a nature to his child by human generation, and that nature is immutable. Thus, and to a degree which is far more exalted, the Holy Spirit forms a new creation which is immutable. An earthly father might disinherit and utterly abandon his son, but he cannot stop the son from resembling himself, and the reason is obvious.

The Arminian's difficulty is initial. To him salvation itself is no more than a state of mind, a good intention, a resolution, or an outward manner of life. Such passing or transient verities as these are far removed from that inviolable, divine creation which Christ pressed upon Nicodemus and that which is presented in every New Testament reference to this theme. It may be safely asserted that regeneration, as presented in the Scriptures, is an enduring actuality and the one who questions the eternal continuation of the child of God, questions the process (and its result) by which he becomes a child of God. When God is declared to be the Father of all who believe, reference is not made to a faint moral resemblance which a good life might suggest; it is a reference to legitimate Fatherhood and legitimate sonship grounded on an actual regeneration by the Holy Spirit.

2. THE HOLY SPIRIT INDWELLS. Closely akin to the truth respecting the regenerating work of the Holy Spirit is the fact that He indwells every true child of God. Besides, there is a distinct and extended testimony of the Scriptures to the specific truth of the Spirit's indwelling. The more complete induction bearing on this theme will appear under Pneumatology. Out of a formidable list of passages bearing on this particular theme, one declares specifically that the Spirit who indwells abides forever. This passage records the words of Christ and reports His prayer respecting the coming of the Holy Spirit into the world. These are the words of the Savior, "And I will pray the Father, and he shall give you another Comforter, that he may abide with you for ever; even the Spirit of truth; whom the world cannot receive, because it seeth him not, neither knoweth him: but ye know him; for he dwelleth with you, and shall be in you" (John 14:16-17). Thus the assurance is given that the Holy Spirit indwells the believer and that His presence is abiding. He may be grieved; but He will not be grieved away. He may be quenched—which carries the thought of resisting—but He cannot be extinguished. He never leaves the Christian, else the word of Christ is untrue and His prayer is unanswered. The Apostle writes, "Now if any man have not the Spirit of Christ, he is none of his" (Rom. 8:9). This great declaration is not a warning to the believer that he might lose the Spirit and be unsaved again; it is a direct statement to the effect that, if the Spirit is not present in the heart, that one has never been saved. The Apostle John points out (1 John 2:27) that the Spirit is identified, among other characteristics of His presence within, as the One who *abides*. This determining Scripture reads: "But the anointing which ye have received of him abideth in you, and ye need not that any man teach

you: but as the same anointing teacheth you of all things, and is truth, and is no lie, and even as it hath taught you, ye shall abide in him."

Again, the Arminian position can be sustained only by a denial of the truth set forth in those notable Scriptures which not only aver that the Spirit indwells each believer, but that He abides forever.

3. THE HOLY SPIRIT BAPTIZES. Not many New Testament doctrines are more misunderstood than that of the Spirit's baptism; and few misunderstandings could be more misleading than this, for on the right apprehension of that which is involved in this divine undertaking the believer's discernment of his possessions and positions depends, and the knowledge of these constitutes the true incentive for a God-honoring daily life. The fuller meaning of this ministry of the Spirit and its importance as the foundation of other doctrines must be reserved for a later volume (VI). As a ground upon which the certainty of eternal security rests, the baptism of the Spirit should be recognized as that operation by which the individual believer is brought into organic union with Christ. By the Spirit's regeneration Christ is resident in the believer, and by the Spirit's baptism the believer is thus in Christ. This union is illustrated in the Word of God by various figures—notably the members of a body in their relation to the head. This union is also said to be a New Creation humanity in its relation to the new and unfallen Last Adam, Christ Jesus. It would be enough to point out here that the glorious Body of Christ will not be marred or maimed because of amputated members, and that there will be no fall in the Last Adam; but the members of Christ's Body are constituted what they are on the sole basis of the truth that the merit of Christ is their standing, which merit is neither withdrawn nor does it fail in its potentiality. Likewise, the New Creation Headship guarantees the same perfect standing. Were it not for the fact that minds seem to be darkened on this point, it would be unnecessary to restate the obvious truth that God undertakes, along wholly different and adequate grounds, to govern in the matter of irregularities which appear in the Christian's life, and quite apart from holding over them the threat that an impossible separation from the New Creation Headship will follow should so much as one sin be committed. It would be simple, indeed, to devise a scheme by which sinless, unfallen human beings may reach heaven on the basis of their own worthiness; but God is undertaking to bring sinful, fallen beings into glory, and the plan He has devised, of necessity, can take no account either of human merit or demerit. Immeasurable grace is manifested in the provision of a righteous way by which fallen men may be translated

from a ruined estate to a new creation; but, after one is translated, there is no passing back and forth from one estate to the other as changing merit or demerit might seem to require.

Let it be restated that, by that baptism which the Spirit accomplishes, the believer is vitally joined to the Lord. Being in Christ, he is a partaker of the righteousness of God which Christ is. He is thus perfected to that point which satisfies infinite holiness, and on that ground and on no other God declares him justified in His own sight. Though He may discipline the justified one, God, having justified, cannot consistently lay anything to the charge of His elect (Rom. 8:33).

To the Arminian, salvation is no more than an indefinite divine blessing upon a life that is worthy of it, which blessing endures as long as personal worthiness continues. To the Calvinist, salvation is a divine achievement which is unrelated to human merit, which secures the forgiveness of sin, the gift of eternal life, imputed righteousness, justification, acceptance and standing in Christ, and final conformity to Christ in eternal glory.

4. THE HOLY SPIRIT SEALS. The last of the twelve reasons why the believer is secure, to be named in this connection, is that he is sealed by the Holy Spirit. The Spirit indwelling as an anointing is Himself the Seal. His presence in the Christian indicates a finished transaction, divine ownership, and eternal security. The believer is a temple of the Holy Spirit (1 Cor. 6:19); and, though woefully unrecognized and unappreciated by the best of men, that fact of indwelling is, apparently, a most distinguishing reality in the reckoning of God. It is an age-characterizing fact (Rom. 7:6; 2 Cor. 3:6). Three references to the Spirit's sealing are found in the New Testament. (1) *2 Corinthians 1:21–22:* "Now he which stablisheth us with you in Christ, and hath anointed us, is God; who hath also sealed us, and given the earnest of the Spirit in our hearts." Every one of the four parts in this passage speaks of security, and the truth is asserted that the presence of the Spirit in the believer's heart is a foretaste of the knowledge-surpassing experience of divine blessing yet to be enjoyed in glory. The passage breathes no intimation of uncertainty either about present blessings or about a future consummation. (2) *Ephesians 1:13–14:* "in whom ye also trusted, after that ye heard the word of truth, the gospel of your salvation: in whom also after that ye believed, ye were sealed with that holy Spirit of promise, which is the earnest of our inheritance until the redemption of the purchased possession, unto the praise of his glory." More correctly the passage begins, "upon believing, ye were

sealed," etc. (cf. R.V.). Here, again, the thought of the earnest, which the presence of the Spirit is, appears and it is made clear that the blessings which the present relation to the Spirit secures are but an indication of the glory yet to be. As the Spirit is an earnest of the future inheritance, He is also the "firstfruits" of it (Rom. 8:23). (3) *Ephesians 4:30:* "And grieve not the holy Spirit of God, whereby ye are sealed unto the day of redemption." This signal passage declares that the believer is sealed unto the day of redemption. The redemption to which reference is made is its final aspect when the body is changed so as to become like unto the body of Christ (Rom. 8:23), and the sealed one is complete forever—even conformed to the image of Christ in glory. Like every other declaration respecting security, this one presents no human condition, but is set forth as a work of God, and on a basis so righteous and so independent of human cooperation that no human responsibility could be included as a factor in this sublime out-working of grace through Christ.

In concluding this division of this treatment of the doctrine of security, it may be restated that of these twelve major reasons why the true believer is safe, any one of them alone would suffice to end all doubt and terminate all controversy for the individual who gives unprejudiced attention to the Word of God. These reasons cover an incomprehensible range of truth Arminianism does not enter; for that system, if consistent with itself, must deny every one of these twelve reasons, or else vitiate them by writing into them the human element which God, of necessity and for His own glory, has left out. Some among the Arminians may not comprehend this body of immeasurable truth; others may prefer to avoid assuming an attitude of bold rejection of these portions of the New Testament. At any rate and for whatever reason, the Arminian does not attempt even a feeble exposition of what are well classed as security passages.

CHAPTER XVII

THE CONSUMMATING SCRIPTURE

As THE LETTER to the Romans is designed to give the plan and scope of salvation by and through the grace of God made possible through the death of Christ, it is to be expected that that Letter will present the essential truth that the one who is saved is safe for all eternity. This Epistle is divided into three parts, namely, (1) salvation, chapters 1–8; (2) dispensation, chapters 9–11; and (3) exhortation, chapters 12–16. The first section, on salvation, may be divided into three parts. Having declared the lost estate of man in its peculiar form in the present age, the Apostle sets forth: (1) salvation for the unregenerate person which is consummated in justification (3:21—5:21); (2) salvation for the believer from the power of sin, or unto sanctification (6:1—8:17); and (3) security for those who are saved (8:1–39). From this outline, it will be seen that the portion 8:1–17 serves a double purpose, as it appears in two of these divisions. The present thesis is concerned with the security portion (8:1–39), which is built on the entire salvation revelation and consummates it with an argument for security which is both clear and conclusive. This argument closes with the Apostle's confession of his own belief respecting the safety of those who are saved. In this respect, as in many others, Arminianism cannot claim to be Pauline. The student will recognize that, after having set forth the essential character of salvation in its two major aspects, the Apostle must answer the pertinent question whether such a salvation, which is unrelated to human merit, will endure.

This great chapter—second in significance only to John 17—opens with an all but incredible proclamation which serves as a primary statement, the truth of which is proved by seven major arguments and these occupy the text of the chapter. This amazing, unqualified, divine assertion which it has pleased God to record and to fortify with infallible proofs is as follows: "There is therefore now no condemnation to them which are in Christ Jesus." The added words, "who walk not after the flesh, but after the Spirit," found in the A.V., are not, as recognized by all devout scholars (see R.V.), a part of this text in its original form, but have been added, perhaps by those who could not suffer to stand a statement so clear and assuring. This intended element of human worthiness is not only foreign to the original text, but is a contradiction of all the truth previously set forth in this Epistle and of that which follows. In like manner, this intrusion tends to disrupt every revelation respecting salvation by grace which is found in the New Testament. This added phrase—"who walk not after the flesh, but after the Spirit"—does belong properly in verse 4 where the believer's responsibility is in view. When challenged with the unqualified statement, "There is therefore now no condemnation to them which are in Christ Jesus," the reader is faced with the question whether this is literally and irrevocably true. If it is true, it guarantees a state of blessedness as expanded as heaven itself and as extended as the eternity which it includes. What greater ground of peace could be presented than that a fallen being, cursed with sin and its ruin, should enter a sphere of relationship with God wherein there is no condemnation now, or in eternity to come. If the answer be made that the promise is for the present and not the future, it will be seen that the Apostle, when arguing in the following context concerning this wonderful primary statement, treats it in every instance as of eternal duration; that is, by his own interpretation it reaches on forever. Though some restatement be involved, attention must be called to the truth that this blessedness is not made, in this declaration, to depend upon human worthiness, but upon the fact that the one thus blessed is in Christ Jesus. It will be recalled that, on the righteous ground provided by Christ in the sweet savor aspect of His death, and on the ground of the fact that the believer is translated into the new Headship wherein he partakes of all that Christ is—even the righteousness of God—there remains no longer any vestige of the legal, merit system which would cast its shadow of doubt over the perfection of God's manifestation of His sovereign grace. Acceptance with God is sealed forever, and on a basis which is righteous in every respect to the end that God Himself is declared to be just, and not merely merciful, when He justifies eternally the ungodly who do no more than to "believe in Jesus" (Rom. 3:26; 4:5). It becomes, therefore, an uncomplicated accomplishment on the part of God. Arminians are wont to make no other reply to this revelation than that "It is too good to be true," and that they would like to believe it if they could. Nevertheless, this wonderful revelation is the very heart of the New Testament message respecting sovereign grace and these great declarations yield to no other interpretation. It is not a mere pity for man's wretchedness, which actuates God in so vast an undertaking; He proposes to exercise and demonstrate His attribute of grace as that which can be manifested in no other way. This entire body of truth relative to the believer's position in Christ and through sovereign grace, lies back of the words, "There is therefore now no condemnation to them which are in Christ Jesus," and the one who is bold enough to challenge the full measure of truthfulness which this text asserts is, by inexorable logic, compelled to deny every factor which enters into the doctrine of sovereign grace. The Arminian contention that the salvation of a sinner is a cooperative affair with some responsibility resting upon God and some upon the sinner—an important contention if the dignity of the sinner is to be preserved—is not only foreign to the divine revelation, but is a contradiction of the very principle which that revelation sets forth. Men are either perfectly lost in the first Adam, or perfectly saved in the Last Adam, and by so much there could be no middle ground or compromise; therefore all modifications of the doctrine of sovereign grace are ruled out forever. Passing from one Adam to the Other is no human undertaking. God alone can do such a thing, and the sinner's relation to it could be no more than to believe on Him to do it in His own way, in and through Christ Jesus. In this no man may boast (Eph. 2:9).

Of supreme importance in the consideration of the eighth chapter of Romans are the indisputable facts that this is the divinely ordained book for the setting forth of the whole plan and scope of salvation by grace, and that the eighth chapter serves as the consummation of the doctrinal structure of this Epistle.

Since the opening statement of the eighth chapter of Romans is so unequivocal, the Apostle proceeds to offer seven proofs of its truthfulness. In approaching these, unavoidably some repetition of that line of argument already presented must be allowed.

I. DELIVERED FROM THE LAW

"For the law of the Spirit of life in Christ Jesus hath made me free from the law of sin and death. For what the law could not do, in that it was weak through the flesh, God sending his own Son in the likeness of sinful flesh, and for sin, condemned sin in the flesh: that the righteousness of the law might be fulfilled in us, who walk not after the flesh, but after the Spirit. For they that are after the flesh do mind the things of the flesh; but they that are after the Spirit the things of the Spirit.

For to be carnally minded is death; but to be spiritually minded is life and peace. Because the carnal mind is enmity against God: for it is not subject to the law of God, neither indeed can be. So then they that are in the flesh cannot please God" (vss. 2–8).

In this context, the law stands as the representation of the merit system—that divine arrangement which, according to the New Testament, is held as the antipodes of God's plan of salvation by grace. Beyond the one truth that both systems are ordained of God for application in such ages as He may elect, they set up contrasts at every point. The fact that, under the new order, the law principle is done away as having nothing to contribute to the outworking of the principle of grace (cf. Rom. 11:6; 4:4–5; Gal. 5:4), should not create the impression that the law did not originate with God; that it is not holy, just, and good; or that it has not had His sanction. On this point the Apostle is most emphatic. When arguing the power of the law as designed by God, he said, "What shall we say then? Is the law sin? God forbid" (Rom. 7:7); "Wherefore the law is holy, and the commandment holy, and just, and good. . . . For we know that the law is spiritual: but I am carnal, sold under sin" (Rom. 7:12, 14); "Wherefore then serveth the law? It was added because of transgressions, till the seed should come to whom the promise was made; and it was ordained by angels in the hand of a mediator" (Gal. 3:19). Though holy, just, and good, the law undertook no more than to serve as a rule of life for people already rightly related to God by His covenants with them. However, as for its holy demands, it is in no way to be compared with that manner of life which is set before the Christian under grace. Over against this, the heaven-high system of conduct under grace, while demanding a supernatural manner of life (cf. John 13:34; 2 Cor. 10:3–5; Eph. 4:30), does provide divine enablement; that is, by the presence of the indwelling Spirit the believer is able to do that which these high standards demand. Therefore, this truth is to be observed that, while requiring far less, the law system failed; yet, while presenting that heaven-high requirement in daily life which belongs to the grace relationship, there is expectation that these standards will be realized.

It is well to contemplate the glorious truth that, so far as the believer's standing in Christ is concerned, the heavenly ideals are reached to infinite perfection. Only in the sphere of the believer's daily conflicts is the grace ideal at times unrealized. It is too often supposed that the outworking of grace is restricted to the Christian's walk and conversation, and the real triumph of grace—the perfecting of the child of God forever—is unrecognized. No matter how disproportionate these issues become under Arminian influence, it must be remembered that to walk worthy of the heavenly calling—though of great importance—is not to be compared for a moment with the heavenly calling itself. The believer may often fail in his conflict with the world, the flesh, and the devil; but this should not blind one to those immeasurable, divine achievements which have already united the believer to Christ and thereby constituted him as perfect in the sight of God as his Savior. It is this faultless standing in Christ which conditions the believer's walk; never does the believer's walk condition his standing. Just here is where, more than elsewhere, the essential difference between Arminianism and Calvinism is demonstrated. The upholders of the Arminian system have never evinced ability to comprehend the truth regarding a perfect standing in Christ which is as enduring as the Son of God. To the Arminian, standing before God is just what a feeble believer makes it by his daily life. Under those conditions the Christian may fail and be lost again. For the moment it seems to be forgotten that every believer sustains an imperfect daily life and therefore, on that basis, all must be lost forever. The New Testament teaches that those who believe are saved from the merit system by having all its demands satisfied in Christ, and thus the believer endures forever. In the Arminian system God becomes a colossal failure, unable to realize His purposes in grace; in the Calvinistic system God never fails even to the slightest degree.

The all-important phrase in the context now under consideration (Rom. 8:2–4), so far as the present phase of truth is concerned, is, "for what the law could not do, in that it was weak through the flesh." By these words the Apostle is accounting for the failure of the law system (cf. Rom. 9:30–32). He does not imply that the law was, or is, weak in itself; it was powerless because the flesh to which it was addressed and on which it depended for response, was too weak to comply with its commandments. It follows that, if God would bring perfected beings into glory out of the midst of this weakness, He must adopt another and more efficacious plan than that which the merit system represents. The new plan adopted does, as seen in earlier chapters of Romans, secure a triumph of divine grace, even the justifying forever of the one who believes on Christ. Therefore, the discussion for the moment centers on the problem of the daily life of the justified one. This problem is greatly increased by the fact of "sin in the flesh," or the Adamic nature. This context asserts that the Adamic nature has been "condemned"—that is, *judged*—and to the end that the Holy Spirit may be free righteously to control that nature. The aim of all this divine provision concerning daily life is that "the law"—meaning the entire will of God for every moment of the believer's life—"might be fulfilled in us." The crucial word here is ἐν, which in this instance is furthest removed from the idea that the will of God is fulfilled *by* the believer. The contrast set up is between what the Spirit may do in the believer as compared to that which the believer, under a merit system, may do for God. However, that he may avail himself of the power of the Spirit in the daily-life problem, the Christian is told that he must "walk not after the flesh, but after the Spirit." The conclusion of the matter is that "there is therefore now no condemnation to them which are in Christ Jesus" because of the fact that they are delivered from the law, or merit, system.

II. THE FACT OF THE PRESENCE OF THE DIVINE NATURE

"But ye are not in the flesh, but in the Spirit, if so be that the Spirit of God dwell in you. Now if any man have not the Spirit of Christ, he is none of his. And if Christ be in you, the body is dead because of sin; but the Spirit is life because of righteousness. But if the Spirit of him that raised up Jesus from the dead dwell in you, he that raised up Christ from the dead shall also quicken your mortal bodies by his Spirit that dwelleth in you" (vss. 9–13).

Having pointed out that the flesh is opposed to God and that the walk of the flesh is in the way of spiritual death as the walk in the Spirit is in the way of life and peace, the Apostle declares that the Christian— with reference to position—is not in the flesh, though the flesh is in the Christian. The Christian is "in the Spirit." However, the Spirit is also in the Christian; for he states, "Now if any man have not the Spirit of Christ [the Holy Spirit], he is none of his." This indwelling reality is again asserted by the words, "if Christ be in you," and, "if the Spirit of him that raised up Jesus from the dead dwell in you." That indwelling One shall quicken the mortal body of the one in whom He dwells. This is not a reference to the present energizing of the body by the Spirit, but rather to the fact that the Spirit will quicken that body in resurrection from the dead. The presence of the indwelling Spirit guarantees the endurance of the believer—even his mortal body is under the divine covenant which assures its presence in glory. No Arminian uncertainty is admitted in this unalterable declaration. However, the Apostle does refer again to the believer's daily life and asserts anew the warning that to walk after the flesh is in the way of spiritual death, and to walk after the Spirit is in the way of life and peace. Having received the divine nature "There is therefore [with full consideration of an imperfect walk] now no condemnation to them which are in Christ Jesus."

III. THE CHRISTIAN A SON AND HEIR OF GOD

"For as many as are led by the Spirit of God, they are the sons of God. For ye have not received the spirit of bondage again to fear; but ye have received the Spirit of adoption, whereby we cry, Abba, Father. The Spirit itself beareth witness with our spirit, that we are the children of God: and if children, then heirs; heirs of God, and joint-heirs with Christ; if so be that we suffer with him, that we may be also glorified together" (vss. 14–17).

It is certain that "the foundation of God standeth sure, having this seal, The Lord knoweth them that are his" (2 Tim. 2:19); and it is impossible, unthinkable, and—what is more important—unscriptural, that God should lose one He has begotten into actual sonship. Some may "go out from us, but they are not of us" (1 John 2:19); the implication is that those "who are of us" never go out. God reserves the right to chasten an erring child, as He did the sons of David (cf. 2 Sam. 7:14; Ps. 89:30–33), but the chastisement of the child of God has for its supreme purpose, "that we should not be condemned with the world" (1 Cor. 11:31–32). "That which is born of God," the Apostle declares, endures; for "his seed remaineth in him" (1 John 3:9).

Likewise, to be a son of God is to be an heir of God, even "a joint-heir with Christ." Here all the riches of God are in view. Christ said "All things that the Father hath are mine" (John 16:15). The purpose of a will being made out to specified heirs is that they may receive that benefit without fail. None would contend that there is danger that all that the Father bequeathed to Christ will not be delivered; nor should it be intimated that a "joint-heir" will fail of his portion. The revealed truth that God bequeaths His riches to His "joint-heirs with Christ" means that they are to receive this benefit, else God has failed. As Christ said, "I will that they also, whom thou hast given me, be with me where I am" (John 17:24), in like manner the Father has willed to His heirs all His riches in glory; and to claim that they will not receive their portion is to assume that God is defeated. There is a common sharing of interest between the Father and the Son. This is indicated by the words of Christ, "All mine are thine, and thine are mine" (John 17:10). It is thus demonstrated that, because of the truth that believers are sons and heirs of God, "There is therefore now no condemnation to them which are in Christ Jesus."

IV. THE DIVINE PURPOSE

"And we know that all things work together for good to them that love God, to them who are the called according to his purpose. For whom he did foreknow, he also did predestinate to be conformed to the image of his Son, that he might be the firstborn among many brethren" (vss. 28–29).

Nothing could be more fundamental or more determining in this universe than the purpose of God. Comparable to the above passage is Ephesians 1:4–12. In that context such decisive statements as the following are found: "chosen in him" (vs. 4); "having predestinated us" (vs. 5); "according to the good pleasure of his will" (vs. 5); "the mystery of his will, according to his good pleasure which he hath purposed in himself" (vs. 9); "being predestinated according to the purpose of him who worketh all things after the counsel of his own will" (vs. 11); the divine objective is said to be, "that we should be holy and without blame before him" (vs. 4); "to the praise of the glory of his grace" (vs. 6); "that in the dispensation of the fulness of times he might gather together in one all things in Christ, both which are in heaven, and which are on earth; even in him" (vs. 10); and, "that we should be to the praise of his glory" (vs. 12).

From these declarations, a devout person will rightfully conclude that back of all secondary causes which may be divinely arranged to co-operate in the realization of the purpose of God, there is a sovereign intention—that which actuated God in creation and continues to actuate Him in providence and preservation—and when man has divested himself of self-centered prejudice, and is moved by common reason, he will conclude that this universe belongs to God by absolute title and that He therefore has inherent rights and indisputable freedom to execute things after the counsel of His own will. In this recognition of divine authority it is also acknowledged that man is but a creature and that his highest destiny will be realized, not in opposition to God, but in complete conformity to God.

The text cited—Romans 8:28–29—states that there are those who are "called according to his purpose" (they are said to "love God" and this implies that He has revealed Himself to them), and that for them He is so undertaking that all things are working together for good in their behalf. It is the usual idea that the "all things" here mentioned are to be observed in the minute details of a believer's experience in life. Such divine care is an actuality and should be acknowledged; but the major issues which are itemized in this context lift the specific "all things" into the highest realms of divine achievement. The saved one has been foreknown, predestinated, called, justified, and glorified. Such a sequence of blessings is rightfully classed as that which is "good."

There is no real occasion for reopening at this point the discussion of the relation that exists between divine foreknowledge and divine predestination. The Arminian contends that God predestinates only what He foreknows; the Calvinist contends that God foreknows because He predestinates, that is, the Calvinist believes that nothing could be foreknown as certain unless God had made it certain by predestination or foreordination. Attempts to arrange these great divine operations into a sequence are doomed to fail, since they are not independent but interdependent actions of the divine will. God could neither foreknow what He had not predetermined, nor could He predetermine what He did not foreknow.

This portion of Scripture points out the truth that certain persons are called according to the purpose of God and are the objects of both His foreknowledge and predestination. Upon this foundation the context goes on to declare that those thus designated will reach the destiny divinely purposed. God is causing everything to work together to that end. Should they fail to reach this end, on the human side the issue would be comparatively small; but on the divine side the issue would be as great as the failure of God the Creator. It will not do to conclude, as Arminians do, that God has left the whole matter of His sovereign purpose, as it applies to an elect company, to their own determination. He needs no alibi in case of failure, since there will be no failure. Pious men have never challenged Deity more violently than when they have implied that the realization of His sovereign purpose must be conditioned by secondary causes. God thus degraded and dishonored becomes, in the mind of men, no God at all. It still stands true, though all men stagger in unbelief (Rom. 4:20), that "there is therefore now no condemnation to them which are in Christ Jesus."

V. THE EXECUTION OF THE DIVINE PURPOSE

"Moreover whom he did predestinate, them he also called: and whom he called, them he also justified: and whom he justified, them he also glorified. What shall we then say to these things? If God be for us, who can be against us? He that spared not his own Son, but delivered him up for us all, how shall he not with him also freely give us all things? Who shall lay anything to the charge of God's elect? It is God that justifieth" (vss. 30–33).

It is certain that, in the vast range of creation, God has manifold purposes and there will be no question raised about whether His will is done in other spheres. It is only within the restricted realm of certain human beings that doubt is engendered relative to the sovereignty of God; and it is significant that such doubt springs from men and not from God. His Word may be taken as the declaration of what He deems to be true, and He asserts His own sovereignty with no condition or qualification. After all, the opinions of men, who are steeped in self-exalting prejudice and afflicted with satanic independence of God, are of no actual value. The entire theme of predestination is outside the human horizon. In the verses cited above, the Holy Spirit, the divine Author, asserts that precisely what God purposes He brings to glorious fruition. By specific steps and by wholly adequate means God realizes what He purposes. Whom He predestinates, He calls; whom He calls, He justifies; and whom He justifies, He glorifies. These are among the things which "work together for good" to those who are the called according to His purpose. Much has been written earlier regarding the divine call, which call not only invites with a gospel appeal, but inclines the mind and heart of the one called to accept divine grace. Here the human will—a secondary cause—is recognized. The will of man is guided by what he knows and what he desires. The divine method of reaching the will is by increasing man's knowledge and by stimulating his desires, while on the divine side of this method there remains not the shadow of possible failure. The end is as certain as any eternal reality in God. On the human side, man is conscious of doing only what he actually does: he chooses as an act of his own volition to receive the grace God offers in Christ Jesus. It is a problem to the mind of man how God can predetermine and realize the eternal salvation of a precise number which no human being has ever counted, and guarantee that not one will fail, and yet each one of that company is allowed the free exercise of his own will, and could, if he so determined, reject every offer of divine grace. By persuasion and enlightenment God realizes His purpose to the point of infinite completeness; yet no human will has been coerced, nor will one ever be. God's call is *efficacious,* for all who are called are justified and glorified.

All that enters into the problem of qualifying a sinner for heaven's holy associations is perfected in justification, it being the consummation of all that enters into salvation both as a dealing with demerit and as a provision of infinite merit before God—the very merit of Christ. As a divine undertaking, justification, which is secured without reference to any human cause (Rom. 3:24), incorporates, as essential to it, not only the value of the death and resurrection of Christ, but every step that enters into divine salvation by grace. Indeed, it is the very scope of that which justification incorporates that leads the Apostle to declare, as he does in verses 31 and 32, that God is "for us." This is a marvelous truth and His attitude of love is demonstrated by the fact that He did not spare the supreme gift of His Son, but delivered Him up for us all. Having given the supreme Gift, all else will easily and naturally be included. God gives unqualified assurance that He justifies all whom He predestinates and He bases that justification on the death and resurrection of Christ, which basis renders it at once a divine act altogether righteous in itself—even to the point of infinity. Little wonder that the Spirit's answer to His own question "Who shall lay anything to the charge of God's elect?" is, "It is God that justifieth." That is, the very thing which would serve as a charge against the believer has been so dealt with already, that there can be no charge recognized. From the standpoint of infinite holiness, it is no slight achievement for God to justify eternally an ungodly enemy who himself does no more than to believe in Jesus, and to do this in such a manner as to shield the One who justifies from every complication which mere leniency with sin and unworthiness would engender. This is not a human disagreement where one believer is charging another with evil; it is an issue of far greater proportions. It is God who is challenged to take account of the sin of His elect. The Arminian contends that God must judge and condemn the one He has saved if there is ought to charge against him. Over against this notion, which notion seems never to have comprehended the workings of divine grace, is the clear assertion that God has already justified the one who has given full proof of his election by believing on Christ, and this in spite of not just one evil alone being charged against him, but in spite of every sin—past, present, and future.

It remains true—regardless of human doubt, misunderstanding, and blindness—that the purpose of God for His elect is executed on a basis so righteous and reaching to such a degree of infinite perfection, that "there is therefore now no condemnation to them which are in Christ Jesus."

VI. CHRIST'S OWN ACHIEVEMENT

"Who is he that condemneth? It is Christ that died, yea rather, that is risen again, who is even at the right hand of God, who also maketh intercession for us" (vs. 34).

Since extended treatment of the four aspects of Christ's undertaking in behalf of the believer, as set forth in this verse, has been essayed in the previous chapter, the truth which the text presents need only be referred to here. By His substitutionary death, Christ has borne the condemnation of the sin of those to whom the value of His death has been applied in response to saving faith. Because of the value of His death having been applied, no condemnation can return upon that one. The resurrection of Christ has provided the gift of eternal, resurrection life that cannot die. The appearing of Christ as Advocate in the court of heaven in behalf of the sinning Christian guarantees that the very place where insecurity might find entrance the Lord Himself so advocates before the Father, by presenting the fact of His own sufficient sacrifice for that sin, as to preserve the one who sins on a basis so indisputable that the Advocate wins the title, "Jesus Christ the righteous." And, lastly, the Savior intercedes and by His intercession is able to save to completion all that come unto God by Himself (Heb. 7:25).

Any one of these four achievements of the Son of God is sufficient to answer the Arminian contention and, as set forth in the New Testament, they are intended to serve as a ground for the believer's safekeeping for all eternity. It therefore follows that the primary declaration of the eighth chapter of Romans, "There is therefore now no condemnation to them which are in Christ Jesus," is altogether true and is completely provided for by the Savior Himself.

VII. THE INCOMPETENCY OF CELESTIAL AND MUNDANE THINGS

"Who shall separate us from the love of Christ? shall tribulation, or distress, or persecution, or famine, or nakedness, or peril, or sword? As it is written, For thy sake we are killed all the day long; we are accounted as sheep for the slaughter. Nay, in all these things we are more than conquerors through him that loved us. For I am persuaded, that neither death, nor life, nor angels, nor principalities, nor powers, nor things present, nor things to come, nor height, nor depth, nor any other creature, shall be able to separate us from the love of God, which is in Christ Jesus our Lord" (vss. 35–39).

Thus far, arguments sustaining the doctrine of eternal security, as drawn from the Scriptures, have been based on those infinite resources which the Persons of the Godhead guarantee. This, the closing portion of Romans 8, approaches the fact of security from the negative side— setting aside that which other forces, both heavenly and mundane, effect. As for the first category, which enumerates mundane things (vs. 35), they are ordained for the believer's experience in the world and over them, by divine enablement, he is to be victor. By the authority of God, the believer is to recognize the force of these things and to prevail in spite of them. As for the second category, which is of celestial realities (vss. 38–39), the Apostle can say, "I am persuaded" that these shall not "be able to separate us from the love of God, which is in Christ Jesus our Lord." This phrase, "I am persuaded," is distinctive, being used but twice by the Apostle Paul, and but three times in the Sacred Text (A.V.); and in two of these instances—Romans 8:38; 2 Timothy 1:12—reference is made directly to the security of the child of God. In the present instance—Romans 8:38—he includes all believers; in the second—2 Timothy 1:12—he gives a personal testimony, and in these words: "For the which cause I also suffer these things: nevertheless I am not ashamed: for I know whom I have believed, and am persuaded that he is able to keep that which I have committed unto him against that day." It is no small distinction and encouragement to the one who believes that the true child of God is eternally safe, that he, in this particular, is in complete harmony with the great Apostle; especially is this true in the light of the fact that the Apostle's statement is given by inspiration. On the other hand, it is no small discredit and delinquency on the part of the one who denies the doctrine of eternal security that he, in attempting to maintain his contention, must impugn the inspired testimony of the one who above all men has been selected of God to receive and to transmit this very gospel of divine grace. Regardless of avowed sincerity, Arminians are not Pauline in their essential theology. To them the doctrinal hesitations of one leading Arminian are more worthy of adoption and promotion than are the unqualified, inspired teachings of the Apostle Paul. This attitude of unbelief is exhibited by the Arminians in their treatment—usually a dire neglect—of all unqualified New Testament declarations on the truth respecting security, and none more commonly than their treatment of Christ's words as recorded in John 10:28–29. In this context the Savior declares, "And I give unto them eternal life; and they shall never perish, neither shall any man pluck them out of my hand. My Father, which gave them me, is greater than all; and no man is able to pluck them out of my Father's hand." It is the Arminian gloss or evasion to say that no power can "pluck" the believer out of the hand of Christ or of the Father, except the believer himself, who, it is asserted, is able, because of the sovereignty of the human will, to remove himself from that security. The Lord seemed to anticipate such evidence of distress on the part of those who would "wrest the Scriptures unto their own destruction," and purposely inserted one phrase, namely, "and they shall never perish," which Arminians fail to receive at its face value.

It is to be observed that of all things celestial and mundane which the Apostle enumerates as forces which are potent in their spheres, yet impotent to cast as much as a shadow of doubt over the great truth of the believer's security, no mention is made of two subjects—the human will and human sin—which are the points of danger according to Arminian theology. With no consideration of the scope of the argument of this great chapter, the Arminian may suppose, contrary to fact, that the two features—the will and sin—are omitted from these categories because the Apostle believed that they do have power to separate the Christian from Christ. It will be discovered, rather, that these two factors are omitted because of the truth that they have been accounted for in earlier portions of this context. The human will has been brought into harmony with the divine purpose by the effectual call (vs. 30), and the Son of God by His intercession guards the believer from pitfalls and by His advocacy preserves from condemnation in case of actual evil. So, also, the Christian's sin has been judged by Christ in His substitutionary death and thus, like the issue of the will, having been disposed of earlier in the argument of the chapter, these subjects are not included in this closing category.

It therefore stands that the unqualified assertion that "there is therefore now no condemnation to them which are in Christ Jesus" is true, being sustained by at least seven major proofs, and the proof which concludes the seven is to the effect that all potent forces celestial or terrestrial are not able to separate the child of God from "the love of

God, which is in Christ Jesus our Lord"—a love set eternally free to realize its every desire toward meritless sinners, and on the ground of the redemption which is in Christ.

CONCLUSION

It is here dogmatically asserted, and on the basis of proofs from the Word of God which have been presented in this volume, that there is no Scripture which, when rightly interpreted, will even intimate that a Christian might be lost; that there is no salvation now offered to the unsaved which is not eternal in its nature; that no soul once saved has ever been lost again; and that the New Testament declares in terms both multiplied and unqualified that the believer, though he may be subject to correction and chastisement, is eternally safe from all condemnation.

"Being confident of this very thing, that he which hath begun a good work in you will perform it until the day of Jesus Christ" (Phil. 1:6).

"Blessed be the God and Father of our Lord Jesus Christ, which according to his abundant mercy hath begotten us again unto a lively hope by the resurrection of Jesus Christ from the dead, to an inheritance incorruptible, and undefiled, and that fadeth not away, reserved in heaven for you, who are kept by the power of God through faith unto salvation ready to be revealed in the last time" (1 Pet. 1:3–5).

Chapter XVIII

DELIVERANCE FROM THE REIGNING POWER
OF SIN AND HUMAN LIMITATIONS

I. DELIVERANCE FROM THE POWER OF SIN

CONTINUING THE CONTEMPLATION of the seven aspects of salvation, this, the fifth, has to do with God's provisions for the believer's triumph in his daily conflict with the world, the flesh, and the devil. Some anticipation of this general theme has been incorporated into earlier discussions which enter into this book, and the theme must reappear for a more exhaustive treatment both in Ecclesiology and in Pneumatology. Though practically unknown to courses and works dealing with Systematic Theology, that part of salvation which secures deliverance from the threefold source of evil—assigned to the present chapter— and that part of salvation which secures ability to rise to a God-honoring state of mind and heart and to the realization of every divinely appointed good work—assigned to the latter half of this same chapter—are requisite to any complete comprehension of all that God accomplishes in His sovereign purpose to "bring many sons unto glory." The problem of the daily life of the believer is vital from various points of consideration, and none more important than that which relates it to the security of the believer. The shallow appraisal which the Arminian system places on that which constitutes salvation leads its advocates to estimate a saved person, though forgiven the sins committed before he was saved, to be himself in no way changed into a new creation, indwelt by the Holy Spirit, or subject to new ideals by which he may live to the glory of God. Were these great provisions recognized and incorporated into that system, its promoters could evince a more comprehensive understanding of all that enters into the relation which the believer's daily life and conduct sustain to his perfect salvation and eternal security in Christ. It is well to remember that God foreknows every situation that will arise in any believer's life. No sin is a surprise to God, and yet He does not hesitate to save those He knows will not be perfect in their walk before Him. Foreseeing what will beset the Christian, He provides not only that he shall not be condemned be-

355

cause of sin, but that he may claim supernatural power through the indwelling Spirit to defeat every foe. This provision of power means much as an undergirding to the doctrine of security, and as assurance that God does not condone sin, nor does He fail in any plan or purpose. The greatest importance must be assigned to the fact that God undertakes for the Christian in the sphere of his state, or daily life, as He undertakes for the Christian in the sphere of his standing, or perfect acceptance, forever in Christ.

Having secured for the believer a perfect union with Christ, a perfect standing, and a perfect acceptance in Christ, and on a ground of such infinite equity that God remains just when He justifies the ungodly, there remains only the problem of communion, fellowship, and a walk which is well-pleasing to God. As a son may be in fellowship or out of fellowship with his earthly father without affecting the immutable fact of sonship, in like manner the child of God may be in fellowship and communion or out of fellowship and communion with his heavenly Father without disturbing the immutable fact of a sonship relation to God. Sonship does not stand alone in the field of immutable realities which are brought into existence by the power of God and based on the merit of Christ. All these, based on the merit of Christ, are independent of the issues which enter into a believer's daily life, as important as that life may be in its own sphere. As before stated, any normal person might devise a plan by which sinlessly perfect individuals might go to heaven, and, in such a plan, there would be no need for Christ to die. It is a far different thing to get fallen men with all their sinfulness into heaven. Only God can devise such an arrangement. This He has done, and in that arrangement which God has devised He has provided a perfect sacrifice for sin and a perfect standing for the one who believes. Having accomplished all this to a degree that answers the demands of His own holiness, it becomes no vain assumption on His part when He declares the Christian to be saved and safe in Christ forever. The Calvinist recognizes this truth, believes it, and proclaims it with all due consideration of the wholly different and independent plan of God by which the believer may be enabled to walk worthy of his perfect standing in Christ. On the other hand, Arminians have always evinced a reprehensible blindness—not unlike that of unregenerate men—concerning these so vital distinctions. Arminianism's misleading error in the field of Soteriology is that it persists in attempting to build the believer's standing upon his feeble and faltering daily life, rather than on the sufficient and immutable merit of Christ. The Arminian Soteriology becomes little more than a system of human conduct; for, though the idea of regeneration is incorporated, it is, in the Arminian idea of it, of no abiding value, being supported only by a supposed human virtue.

In attempting to present at this point the issues of the Christian's daily life, it is with the understanding that these issues, however weighty and consequential they are deemed to be, are divinely dealt with upon a separate basis which is wholly independent of that perfect arrangement by which the believer is both saved by Christ and eternally safe in Christ.

It is generally recognized that the Christian faces three opposing forces which are sources of evil—the *cosmos* world, the flesh, and the devil—and that, when he was in his unregenerate state, these forces were in no way arrayed against him; for he was then a part of the *cosmos* world, restricted in his being to the flesh, and under the dominion of Satan. Conscience and social ideals may have made their feeble demands upon him, but he knew little, if anything, of the unceasing conflict which besets the child of God. In other words, the believer in his problem of daily life, because of new foes and new standards of holy living which rightfully impose their claim upon him, is far less able to live the life set before him than he was able to live with more or less virtue in the sphere of the unregenerate man. It follows, then, that if the believer must sustain his salvation by a correct manner of life, as the Arminian contends, he, because of impossible heavenly demands and because of supernatural foes, is unconditionally defeated before ever he begins. The Arminian's preaching of his ideals has been tolerated only because of an inability, if not an unwillingness on his part, to face the stupendous issues involved. It sounds practical, simple, and it ministers to the inherent conceit of man, to propose a salvation which endures on the basis of human merit. In such a scheme there is little need of the sustaining grace of God. He may be called in to forgive wherein man has failed in his self-saving program. As water seeks its level, Arminianism, in its modern form, has departed from its original claim to orthodox truth and for the reason, among others, that the defenders of that system have never relied upon supernatural forces in the realization of their soteriological scheme.

Since the Christian's three foes—the world, the flesh, and the devil—have been considered at length in Volume II of this work and are yet to reappear on later pages, only a brief mention of these foes will be entered here. However, their true character must not be suppressed else the understanding of the true character of divine salvation from these foes, which salvation is the immediate objective in the present volume, will have no sufficient background of reality.

1. THE WORLD. Of the four Greek roots—αἰών, οἰκουμένη, γῆ, and κόσμος—which in the Authorized Version are translated *world,* only the last-named is set forth as in conflict with the believer. A study of the 187 uses of this word in the New Testament, as already pointed out, discloses the truth that the *cosmos* is a vast system and order over which Satan is the prince (John 12:31; 14:30; 16:11), and into which all unregenerate humanity is federated with its educational and entertainment programs, its governments, its jealousies, its armaments, and its warfare. Out of this *world* the believer when saved is rescued (Col. 1:13; John 15:19; 1 John 5:19), and from it he is to be preserved, though he, as a witness to it, must remain in it. Its standardization of human life to its own ideals, its allurements, its control of the necessities of life, the protection it affords in its governments, its ridicule of true piety, and its misconceptions constitute the *cosmos* a most complex, subtle, and formidable foe of the child of God. He can maintain his twofold relation to the *cosmos*—a dweller in it and a witness to it—only by supernatural power. The word of Christ, "In the world [*cosmos*] ye shall have tribulation: but be of good cheer; I have overcome the world" (*cosmos*—John 16:33), is freighted with deep meaning—too deep, indeed, for human comprehension. Since Christ by His death has overcome the *cosmos,* it is declared of the believer that he, too, has overcome the *cosmos.* In 1 John 5:4–5 it is written, "For whatsoever is born of God overcometh the world: and this is the victory that overcometh the world, even our faith. Who is he that overcometh the world, but he that believeth that Jesus is the Son of God?" Too often this passage has been taken as an exhortation to the Christian to overcome the *cosmos;* but, plainly, it is here declared that, having believed, the child of God has, by his new relation to Christ, overcome the *cosmos.* In a primary sense, the believer partakes of all that Christ is and of what He has done. It would be impossible to be in Christ and not be outside the *cosmos.* Nevertheless, while all this is true with reference to position, yet the Christian must claim an experimental victory in his daily life over the appeal which the *cosmos* is ever making to him. Of surpassing import, however, is the truth that, in the reckoning of the Spirit on whom the believer must depend for his daily deliverance, the *cosmos* is judicially overcome already. The truth that Christ has overcome the *cosmos* and that the believer partakes of that reality from the moment he is saved is the sufficient legal ground upon which the believer may,

by the Spirit, be preserved from the *cosmos* though remaining here as a witness to it.

2. THE FLESH. When approaching this theme, distinction must be drawn between σῶμα and σάρξ. The former represents the physical body while the latter, though sometimes used of the physical body, represents a living reality which includes in it a fallen nature with all its inherent forces and relationships—a fallen nature which knows no eradication, but continues with the believer as long as he is in the world and which is overcome only by a ceaseless appropriation of the power of the indwelling Spirit. It is written that, if in dependence upon the Spirit the believer is walking, he will not fulfill the lust of the flesh (Gal. 5:16). Nevertheless, there must be a legal ground upon which the Holy Spirit may control the flesh with its Adamic nature. It is written that, to this end, Christ died as a judgment of the old nature (Rom. 6:1–10) and the flesh (Rom. 8:3). This judgment of the flesh by Christ did not put the flesh to death; it rather provided a legal, righteous ground upon which the Spirit of God serves as Deliverer. This, again, the truth that the believer may be saved from the reigning power of sin on the principle of faith, is emphasized. God is thus undertaking for the believer in his daily life, and none can doubt that God has a definite purpose to capacitate in the sphere of his walk that one He has saved with an eternal salvation. No manner of walk, however perfect, will even tend to preserve the child of God. He is secure by another provision altogether, namely, his place in the resurrected Christ. In the matter of a consistent life, which glorifies the One who saves him, the believer may claim all the supernatural power of the indwelling Spirit.

3. THE DEVIL. The Christian's conflict with Satan and his need of supernatural deliverance from that foe is widely published in the New Testament. The student who is pursuing these pages in order, will have read many previous pages on this specific theme. That which calls for restatement in the present chapter is the twofold fact that Satan was judged by Christ in His death, and that there is deliverance from Satan's power which is made possible by the indwelling Spirit. That there is a conflict with Satan need not be argued. One passage out of many will serve to recognize this truth: "For our wrestling is not against flesh and blood, but against the principalities, against the powers, against the world-rulers of this darkness, against the spiritual hosts of wickedness in the heavenly places" (Eph. 6:12, R.V.). The judgment of Satan is announced in various portions of the New Testament. It is written: "Of judgment, because the prince of this world is judged" (John 16:11);

"Blotting out the handwriting of ordinances that was against us, which was contrary to us, and took it out of the way, nailing it to his cross; and having spoiled principalities and powers, he made a shew of them openly, triumphing over them in it" (Col. 2:14–15). Like a criminal who has been sentenced to die and awaits the day of his execution, so Satan is already judged and awaits the day of the administration of his sentence. The truth that there is complete deliverance from Satan's power is taught in the clearest terms: "Finally, my brethren, be strong in the Lord, and in the power of his might. Put on the whole armour of God, that ye may be able to stand against the wiles of the devil" (Eph. 6:10–11); "Ye are of God, little children, and have overcome them: because greater is he that is in you, than he that is in the world" (1 John 4:4). This order of truth must not be overlooked, namely, that it is possible for the Holy Spirit to defend the believer and deliver him from Satan's power on the ground of the fact that Satan has been judged by Christ in His death. Though judged, Satan is a living, mighty power and is to be resisted by the believer's steadfast faith (1 Pet. 5:8–9).

CONCLUSION

Thus it is disclosed that with respect to every sin or disposition which is contrary to God, the believer is directed to find deliverance or salvation from it by the power of the indwelling Spirit, who acts in perfect freedom because of the specific judgments wrought by Christ on the cross against the world, the flesh, and the devil. Such a deliverance is a form of salvation and takes its place in the entire saving work of God.

The truth respecting the consequence of the Christian's sin is yet again declared. It is to be noted that God anticipates sin in the believer. This fact does not make Him the author of it; it only reveals that His own plan does not contemplate and expect sinless perfection on the part of those whom He saves and keeps. The marvel never lessens in the mind of devout believers, that God's plan incorporates a way whereby imperfect saints are to be taken into heaven's glory. The divine anticipation of the Christian's sin is seen in the provision for it. It is written in 1 John 1:6–9 that the believer's sin may be cured, in its effect upon himself, by the confession of it to God. This is not another regeneration. The child of God is still in union, though not in communion, with God when he sins. The unsaved are saved by believing and the saved are forgiven and cleansed by confessing. In neither case is there any penal judgment laid on the one who has sinned. It could not be, since it has been laid upon the Substitute.

It therefore remains true that God not only provides a way whereby the believer may be kept from sinning, but He also provides a way whereby the believer may be preserved as His child and returned to fellowship with Himself when he has sinned.

II. SALVATION FROM HUMAN LIMITATIONS

To be delivered from evil to the end that God may be honored, who is the Savior of those who believe, is not the complete realization of the divine ideal. Added to such deliverance is the necessity for the child of God to become *empowered* unto every good work, such as is foreordained (Eph. 2:10), and such as becomes those who are saved and appointed to the high task of representing God in this *cosmos* world. As has been amplified thus far in the chapter, Christians are enjoined to avoid evil and, should it intrude, must be saved from it. As it is written: "For the grace of God that bringeth salvation hath appeared to all men, teaching us that, denying ungodliness and worldly lusts, we should live soberly, righteously, and godly, in this present world; looking for that blessed hope, and the glorious appearing of the great God and our Saviour Jesus Christ; who gave himself for us, that he might redeem us from all iniquity, and purify unto himself a peculiar people, zealous of good works" (Titus 2:11–14). Salvation which is of God's grace is "not of works." It could never be brought into being by human works. It is a work of God; yet it is "unto good works," and these are possible only as one is created anew in Christ Jesus and provided with supernatural efficacy. The extensive body of truth which sets forth the Spirit's energizing ministry unto a God-honoring life and service will be traced but briefly at this point.

1. THE SPIRIT PRODUCES CHRISTIAN CHARACTER. The *cosmos* world has its scheme of "character building." Too often this is not character at all, but only reputation. It is always the product of human effort and, naturally, results in human glory. Over against this is the divine plan for Christian character which consists in those realities which are wrought in the heart by the indwelling Spirit. Such a character is best described by nine words which represent the "fruit of the Spirit." "But the fruit of the Spirit is love, joy, peace, longsuffering, gentleness, goodness, faith [faithfulness], meekness, temperance" (self-control—Gal.

5:22–23; cf. R.V.). These nine graces are not only declared to be the direct production of the Spirit in and through the believer, but they are held, in this context, to be over against, or in contrast to, the works of the flesh. These fleshly works are enumerated in verses 19–21. Every word in the list which represents the fruit of the Spirit indicates a divine characteristic which is generated directly by the indwelling Spirit. This exhibit of the Spirit is the normal experience of the child of God, and will be his portion unless impediments are allowed to assert themselves in the believer's way of life before God.

2. The Spirit Empowers unto Christian Service. This aspect of the Spirit's work in the Christian introduces at once the doctrine of gifts energized by the Spirit. A gift in the New Testament sense of the word is something which the Spirit does, and uses the believer to do it. It is not at all a human effort aided by the Spirit. It is said to be a "manifestation of the Spirit" (1 Cor. 12:7). So, also, to every believer some gift is appointed; that is, he is appointed to a specific task and empowered to accomplish it. If this divine provision is not realized, it is due, again, to some want of adjustment. It is also said that there are diversities of gifts, though, in every instance, they are wrought by the selfsame Spirit. The important Scripture bearing on this theme is as follows: "Now there are diversities of gifts, but the same Spirit. And there are differences of administrations, but the same Lord. And there are diversities of operations, but it is the same God which worketh all in all. But the manifestation of the Spirit is given to every man to profit withal. For to one is given by the Spirit the word of wisdom; to another the word of knowledge by the same Spirit; to another faith by the same Spirit; to another the gifts of healing by the same Spirit; to another the working of miracles; to another prophecy; to another discerning of spirits; to another divers kinds of tongues; to another the interpretation of tongues: but all these worketh that one and the selfsame Spirit, dividing to every man severally as he will" (1 Cor. 12:4–11; cf. Rom. 12:3–8; Eph. 4:11; 1 Pet. 4:10–11).

To these realities which are generated in the believer's life by the Spirit—the fruit of the Spirit and gifts by the Spirit—may be added the revelation that the Spirit teaches the Word of God to the believer (John 16:12–15; 1 Cor. 2:9—3:1; 1 John 2:27); He inspires praise and thanksgiving (Eph. 5:19–20); He leads the child of God (Rom. 8:14; Gal. 5:18); He actuates what has been taken by faith (Rom. 8:16); and He makes intercession in and for the Christian (Rom. 8:26–27).

CONCLUSION

By this greatly restricted treatment of the Spirit's work in empowering the child of God unto a holy character and service, which becomes the one who is perfected in Christ, it is again seen that God does undertake in the sphere of the believer's daily life, and, apart from the notion that these exhibitions of the Spirit will add anything to the believer's perfect standing in Christ, it is observable that it is the divine intent that the saved one shall be delivered from weakness and limitations, which dishonor God and cause the Christian to fail to adorn the doctrine which he professes.

CHAPTER XIX

THE BELIEVER PRESENTED FAULTLESS

THE CONSUMMATING EXPERIENCE for the sinner whom God saves is his presentation in glory. Of this the Apostle writes: "Now unto him that is able to keep you from falling, and to present you faultless before the presence of his glory with exceeding joy" (Jude 1:24). In this passage, the word "falling" is better translated "stumbling" (R.V.), and it should be observed that the "exceeding joy" is that of the One who conceives, constructs, and consummates the whole undertaking. The entire enterprise is strictly His own. Similarly, when writing to the Corinthian believers, the Apostle Paul declared what is true of all believers—the Body and Bride of Christ—"For I am jealous over you with godly jealousy: for I have espoused you to one husband, that I may present *you as* a chaste virgin to Christ" (2 Cor. 11:2). Here again the force of the text is discovered when the italicized words "you as" are omitted; for the Apostle did not desire merely to present believers *as* a chaste virgin, but his purpose was rather to present a chaste virgin to Christ. In like manner, it was the supreme desire of Christ in His sacrificial death, that He might claim a perfected Bride. Of this it is revealed: "Husbands, love your wives, even as Christ also loved the church, and gave himself for it; that he might sanctify and cleanse it with the washing of water by the word, that he might present it to himself a glorious church, not having spot, or wrinkle, or any such thing; but that it should be holy and without blemish" (Eph. 5:25–27).

The truth that the believer will be presented faultless before the presence of God's glory is unfolded in the New Testament with magnificent detail. The changes to be wrought are incomprehensible; but, in all, they indicate that the transformation, so extended, is calculated to obliterate almost every vestige of those elements which together constitute humanity in its present existence. To be reconstructed until completely adapted to, and meet for, the celestial sphere, is an exalted distinction which is guaranteed by infinite competency and sustained by sovereign intention. This is the portion of every believer, not varied according to degrees of human merit; for it is the standardized divine achievement in behalf of all who believe.

Some of the changes which enter into this immeasurable transformation, a portion of which is already incorporated into the believer's present estate, are listed here:

I. HEAVENLY CITIZENSHIP

The fact that heavenly citizenship begins in this life and at the moment one believes does not alter the abiding character of it, though so great a development from the present order to that which is to follow must ensue. Though that citizenship is now possessed with respect to the right and title, it is, nevertheless, unoccupied and therefore unexperienced. Immeasurable advantage and ascendency await tenure of that exalted estate.

II. A NEW FRATERNITY

This feature of coming felicity comprehends a vast field of eternal realities. It begins with the new birth into actual and legitimate sonship to God, which, in turn, engenders the whole compass of the family and household relationship. Not only sonship to God is wrought, but noble kinship to all the saints of all the ages, and, apparently, to all the unfallen heavenly hosts. These ties are perfectly established while in this world, yet the larger, joyous experience of them awaits the gathering together of all who are Christ's with Him in glory.

III. A STANDING PERFECTED FOREVER

A perfect standing in Christ is not only begun in this life, but its incalculable value is to be demonstrated and experienced throughout eternity. Little can the human mind grasp the oncoming restfulness and blessedness of the consciousness that the standing is secured, and qualities instituted and divinely approved which are properly required in the sphere of infinite holiness and purity. As conceived by the poet Thomas Binney (1826):

> Eternal Light! Eternal Light!
> How pure the soul must be,
> When placed within Thy searching sight,
> It shrinks not, but, with calm delight,
> Can live, and look on Thee!

O! how shall I, whose native sphere
   Is dark, whose mind is dim,
Before the Ineffable appear,
And on my naked spirit bear
   That uncreated beam?

There is a way for man to rise
   To that sublime abode:—
An offering and a sacrifice,
A Holy Spirit's energies,
   An Advocate with God:—

These, these prepare us for the sight
   Of Holiness above:
The sons of ignorance and night
May dwell in the Eternal Light,
   Through the eternal Love!

IV. A RENEWED BODY

But little can be anticipated of the coming zest, satisfaction, and comfort of a renewed body which will be fashioned like unto Christ's glorious body (Phil. 3:21). A wide distinction is to be observed between the *possession* of eternal life and the experience of it which is yet to be. The present experience of human life in a death-doomed body is little to be compared to the experience of eternal life in a renewed body that corresponds to Christ's resurrection body—that which, to the point of infinity, is suited to the eternal needs of the Second Person of the Godhead. In describing this stupendous change, the Apostle declares (1 Cor. 15:42–57) that this body of corruption will put on incorruption, this body of mortality will put on immortality, this body of "dishonour" will put on glory, this body of weakness will put on inconceivable power, this body which is "natural"—adapted to the soul—will become a spiritual body—adapted to the spirit.

V. FREEDOM FROM THE SIN NATURE

Again all human powers of anticipation are wholly inadequate. So embedded in the very structure of the present existence is the sin nature with all its unholy demands and its contrariness to the indwelling Spirit (Gal. 5:17), that no imagination can forecast the hour of release to describe it.

VI. TO BE LIKE CHRIST

If the believer's destiny were not so clearly asserted, it could not be believed by any in this world. The testimony of the Scriptures, however, cannot be diminished: "And we know that all things work together for good to them that love God, to them who are the called according to his purpose" (Rom. 8:28); "And as we have borne the image of the earthy, we shall also bear the image of the heavenly" (1 Cor. 15:49); "Beloved, now are we the sons of God, and it doth not yet appear what we shall be: but we know that, when he shall appear, we shall be like him; for we shall see him as he is" (1 John 3:2). Though these statements seem to reach far beyond the range of possible things, this exalted destiny comports with that which is required in the very purpose of God. It will be remembered that salvation is wrought to the end that the grace of God may be revealed. God's grace is infinite and therefore requires that the undertakings which measure that grace shall extend into infinite realms. Likewise, salvation is wrought to satisfy the infinite love of God, and, in the satisfying of that love, God must do His utmost for the objects of His affection—for whom He is free to act at all. Conformity to the image of Christ is the supreme reality in the universe, and divine love can be content with nothing less as the measure of its achievement. In general, the likeness to Christ includes all other features indicated in this listing of heavenly realities.

VII. TO SHARE IN CHRIST'S GLORY

Precisely what Christ comprehended when He prayed, "Father, I will that they also, whom thou hast given me, be with me where I am; that they may behold my glory, which thou hast given me" (John 17:24), finite minds could not know in this world. So, likewise, the title deed recorded in John 17:22, "And the glory which thou gavest me I have given them," cannot be broken. Consequently, it is written: "But we all, with open face beholding as in a glass the glory of the Lord, are changed into the same image from glory to glory, even as by the Spirit of the Lord" (2 Cor. 3:18); "For our light affliction, which is but for a moment, worketh for us a far more exceeding and eternal weight of glory" (4:17); "It is sown in dishonour; it is raised in glory: it is sown in weakness; it is raised in power" (1 Cor. 15:43); "When Christ, who is our life, shall appear, then shall ye also appear with him in glory" (Col. 3:4); "For it became him, for whom are all things, and by whom are all things, in bringing many sons unto glory, to make the captain of their salvation perfect through sufferings" (Heb. 2:10); "But the God of all grace, who hath called us unto his eternal glory by Christ Jesus, after that ye have suffered a while, make you perfect, stablish, strengthen, settle you" (1 Pet. 5:10). Added to this is the glory which is the result of cosuffering with Christ—the reward for the burden the believer may experience for lost souls: "For I reckon that the sufferings of this present time are not worthy to be compared with the glory which shall be revealed in us" (Rom. 8:18); "If we suffer, we shall also reign with him" (2 Tim. 2:12).

By all this it will be seen that the salvation of a soul, as purposed by God, contemplates the fruition of that purpose. Whom He predestinates, He glorifies, and "He which hath begun a good work in you will perform it until the day of Jesus Christ" (Phil. 1:6). Failure is impossible with God. Because of this, the New Testament writers are exceedingly bold in declaring the certainty of coming glory for everyone who believes. That no intimation of possible failure is mentioned, is due to the truth that the end is as certain as the ability of infinity to achieve it. Arminians are casting doubts upon God's supreme ability to bring to pass that which He has determined, and upon the truthfulness and dependable character of the words which record the divine purpose and competency; but such efforts to weaken the testimony of God respecting Himself cannot avail. Note the words of Balaam respecting Israel—the people of God's earthly election: "God is not a man, that he should lie; neither the son of man, that he should repent: hath he said, and shall he not do it? or hath he spoken, and shall he not make it good? Behold, I have received commandment to bless: and he hath blessed; and I cannot reverse it. He hath not beheld iniquity in Jacob, neither hath he seen perverseness in Israel: the LORD his God is with him, and the shout of a king is among them. God brought them out of Egypt; he hath as it were the strength of an unicorn. Surely there is no enchantment against Jacob, neither is there any divination against Israel: according to this time it shall be said of Jacob and of Israel, What hath God wrought!" (Num. 23:19–23). Of Jehovah's attitude toward this elect people it is said: "For the gifts and calling of God are without repentance" (Rom. 11:29). If it is possible that, because of sovereign election, God will never change His purpose toward the earthly people and see no "iniquity in Jacob" nor any "perverseness in Israel," if He will never repent regarding any gift or calling of that nation, is it deemed an impossibility that He is able to preserve the Body and Bride of His Son for whom it is said that Christ died in a most specific sense (Eph. 5:25–27)?

CONCLUSION

In reviewing this extended thesis which has aimed to present the seven aspects of the saving work of God, it will be seen that salvation is of Jehovah, whether it be in the sphere of the finished work, the enlightening work, the saving work, the keeping work, or the presenting work. In every respect and in every step of its majestic progress it is a work of God alone—a work which is wrought in spite of the sin of those whom He saves and in spite of any hazard which the will of man might engender. God is sovereign over all and is both free and able to realize all that He has purposed to do.

As before observed, the salvation of a sinner is, so far as revelation discloses, the sole exercise of one of God's most conspicuous attributes, namely, His grace. Not only must salvation provide an adequate scope for the exercise of this attribute—measuring its amplitude completely— but it must satisfy God to an infinite degree. As for the amplitude, the divine undertaking begins with that which is perfectly lost. On this subject, humanity could have no worthy opinions. To them, at worst, man is in need of much divine consideration. They cannot approach in thought the unfathomable reality of the lost and doomed estate of man. Such words as are written down in Romans 3:9–19 are seldom accepted by men at their intended meaning. To be lost is to be utterly condemned of God, to be joined to Satan, and to be consigned along with Satan to the lake of fire. Such a judgment is not pronounced over some trivial failure of men. The very fact that the uttermost judgment must be meted out upon him discloses in unmistakable terms the depth of meaning which God assigns to man's lost estate. Over against this, salvation lifts the saved one to the heights of heaven—with reference to eternal abode —and transforms that one into the image of Christ. To have made any being like Christ is the most consequential undertaking in the universe. It represents the limit to which even infinity may go. It is this distance between the abysmal depths of the lost estate and conformity to Christ in heaven, which not only exercises the divine attribute of grace, but measures it completely. As for the divine satisfaction, reason alone dictates that, since God cannot fail of any purpose, His measurements of His grace in the salvation of a soul will satisfy Him to infinity. So completely is the demonstration of grace set forth in each saved individual that, were but one saved thus by grace, that one would answer entirely the divine expectation and serve as a conclusive display before all intelligences of the exceeding, superabounding grace of God; not of works, lest any man should boast.

It were enough for God to disclose the fact that He intends to bring many sons into glory; but He is not satisfied with a limited revelation. He, rather, honors men by spreading before them for their wonder and delight the steps which He takes and the righteous ground upon which all that He undertakes is accomplished. It is in the sphere of eternal realities to be wrought by unrestrained, infinite ability; and the devout mind, having taken cognizance of these facts, may well hesitate to deny to God the authority, power, and the freedom through Christ, to do all His adorable and holy will. The prayer of the Apostle is in order: "That the God of our Lord Jesus Christ, the Father of glory, may give unto you the spirit of wisdom and revelation in the knowledge of him: the eyes of your understanding being enlightened; that ye may know what is the hope of his calling, and what the riches of the glory of his inheritance in the saints, and what is the exceeding greatness of his power to us-ward who believe, according to the working of his mighty power, which he wrought in Christ, when he raised him from the dead, and set him at his own right hand in the heavenly places, far above all principality, and power, and might, and dominion, and every name that is named, not only in this world, but also in that which is to come" (Eph. 1:17–21).

> My hope is built on nothing less
> Than Jesus' blood and righteousness;
> I dare not trust the sweetest frame,
> But wholly lean on Jesus' Name.
> On Christ, the solid Rock, I stand;
> All other ground is sinking sand.

CHAPTER XX

THE TERMS OF SALVATION

OUTSIDE THE DOCTRINES related to the Person and work of Christ, there is no truth more far-reaching in its implications and no fact more to be defended than that salvation in all its limitless magnitude is secured, so far as human responsibility is concerned, by believing on Christ as Savior. To this one requirement no other obligation may be added without violence to the Scriptures and total disruption of the essential doctrine of salvation by grace alone. Only ignorance or reprehensible inattention to the structure of a right Soteriology will attempt to intrude some form of human works with its supposed merit into that which, if done at all, must, by the very nature of the case, be wrought by God alone and on the principle of sovereign grace. But few, indeed, seem ever to comprehend the doctrine of sovereign grace, and it is charitable, at least, to revert to this fact as the explanation of the all-but-universal disposition to confuse the vital issues involved. It is the purpose of this section to demonstrate that the eternal glories which are wrought in sovereign grace are conditioned, on the human side, by faith alone. The practical bearing of this truth must of necessity make drastic claims upon the preacher and become a qualifying influence in the soul-winning methods which are employed. The student would do well to bring his message and his methods into complete agreement with the workings of divine grace, rather than to attempt to conform this unalterable truth to human ideals.

Salvation which is by faith begins with those mighty transformations which together constitute a Christian what he is; it guarantees the safekeeping of the Christian, and brings him home to heaven conformed to the image of Christ. The preacher or soul-winner who is able to trace through these limitless realities and to preserve them from being made to depend to any degree upon human responsibility other than saving faith in Christ, merits the high title of "a good minister of Jesus Christ, nourished up in the words of faith and of good doctrine" (1 Tim. 4:6). A moment's attention to the transforming divine undertakings which enter into salvation of the lost will bring one to the realization of the truth that every feature involved presents a task which is superhuman, and, therefore, if to be accomplished at all, must be wrought by God alone. Such a discovery will prepare the mind for the reception of the truth, that the only relation man can sustain to this great undertaking is to depend utterly upon God to do it. That is the simplicity of faith. However, since moral issues are involved which have been divinely solved by Christ in His death, He has become the only qualified Savior, and saving faith is thus directed toward Him. "Whosoever believeth in him" shall not perish, but have everlasting life. But even when the supernatural character of salvation is recognized, it is possible to encumber the human responsibility with various complications, thus to render the whole grace undertaking ineffectual to a large degree. These assertions lead naturally to a detailed consideration of the more common features of human responsibility which are too often erroneously added to the one requirement of *faith* or *belief*.

I. REPENT AND BELIEVE

Since repentance—conceived of as a separate act—is almost universally added to believing as a requirement on the human side for salvation, a consideration of the Biblical meaning of repentance is essential. This consideration may be traced as follows: (1) the meaning of the word, (2) the relation of repentance to believing, (3) the relation of repentance to covenant people, (4) the absence of the demand for repentance from salvation Scriptures, and (5) the significance of repentance in specific passages.

1. THE MEANING OF THE WORD. The word μετάνοια is in every instance translated *repentance*. The word means *a change of mind*. The common practice of reading into this word the thought of sorrow and heart-anguish is responsible for much confusion in the field of Soteriology. There is no reason why sorrow should not accompany repentance or lead on to repentance, but the sorrow, whatever it may be, is not repentance. In 2 Corinthians 7:10, it is said that "godly sorrow worketh repentance," that is, it leads on to repentance; but the sorrow is not to be mistaken for the change of mind which it may serve to produce. The son cited by Christ as reported in Matthew 21:28–29 who first said "I will not go," and afterward repented and went, is a true example of the precise meaning of the word. The New Testament call to repentance is not an urge to self-condemnation, but is a call to a change of mind which promotes a change in the course being pursued.

This definition of this word as it is used in the New Testament is fundamental. Little or no progress can be made in a right induction of the Word of God on this theme, unless the true and accurate meaning of the word is discovered and defended throughout.

2. THE RELATION OF REPENTANCE TO BELIEVING. Too often, when it is asserted—as it is here—that repentance is not to be added to belief as a separate requirement for salvation, it is assumed that by so much the claim has been set up that repentance is *not* necessary to salvation. Therefore, it is as dogmatically stated as language can declare, that repentance is essential to salvation and that none could be saved apart from repentance, but it is included in believing and could not be separated from it. The discussion is restricted at this point to the problem which the salvation of unregenerate persons develops; and it is safe to say that few errors have caused so much hindrance to the salvation of the lost than the practice of demanding of them an anguish of soul before faith in Christ can be exercised. Since such emotions cannot be produced at will, the way of salvation has thus been made impossible for all who do not experience the required anguish. This error results in another serious misdirection of the unsaved, namely, one in which they are encouraged to look inward at themselves and not away to Christ as Savior. Salvation is made to be conditioned on feelings and not on faith. Likewise, people are led by this error to measure the validity of their salvation by the intensity of anguish which preceded or accompanied it. It is in this manner that sorrow of heart becomes a most subtle form of meritorious work and to that extent a contradiction of grace. Underlying all this supposition that tears and anguish are necessary is the most serious notion that God is *not* propitious, but that He must be softened to pity by penitent grief. The Bible declares that God *is* propitious because of Christ's death for the very sin which causes human sorrow. There is no occasion to melt or temper the heart of God. His attitude toward sin and the sinner is a matter of revelation. To imply, as preachers have done so generally, that God must be mollified and lenified by human agony is a desperate form of unbelief. The unsaved have a gospel of good news to *believe*, which certainly is not the mere notion that God must be coaxed into a saving attitude of mind; it is that Christ *has* died and grace is extended from One who is propitious to the point of infinity. The human heart is prone to imagine that there is some form of atonement for sin through being sorry for it. Whatever may be the place of sorrow for sin in the restoration of a Christian who has transgressed, it cannot be determined with too much

emphasis that for the unsaved—Jew or Gentile—there is no occasion to propitiate God or to provide any form of satisfaction by misery or distress of soul. With glaring inconsistency, those who have preached that the unsaved must experience mental suffering before they can be saved, have completely failed to inform their hearers about how such required torture may be secured. It should be restated that, since genuine grief of mind cannot be produced at will and since many natures are void of depression of spirit, to demand that a self-produced affliction of mind shall precede salvation by faith becomes a form of fatalism and is responsible for having driven uncounted multitudes to despair. However, it is true that, from the Arminian point of view, no greater heresy could be advanced than this contention that the supposed merit of human suffering because of personal sins should be excluded from the terms on which a soul may be saved.

As before stated, repentance, which is a change of mind, is included in believing. No individual can turn to Christ from some other confidence without a change of mind, and that, it should be noted, is all the repentance a spiritually dead individual can ever effect. That change of mind is the work of the Spirit (Eph. 2:8). It will be considered, too, by those who are amenable to the Word of God, that the essential preparation of heart which the Holy Spirit accomplishes in the unsaved to prepare them for an intelligent and voluntary acceptance of Christ as Savior—as defined in John 16:8–11—is not a sorrow for sin. The unsaved who come under this divine influence are illuminated—given a clear understanding—concerning but *one* sin, namely, that "they believe not on me."

To believe on Christ is one act, regardless of the manifold results which it secures. It is not turning from something to something; but rather turning to something from something. If this terminology seems a mere play on words, it will be discovered, by more careful investigation, that this is a vital distinction. To turn from evil may easily be a complete act in itself, since the action can be terminated at that point. To turn to Christ is a solitary act, also, and the joining of these two separate acts corresponds to the notion that two acts—repentance and faith—are required for salvation. On the other hand, turning to Christ from all other confidences is one act, and in that one act repentance, which is a change of mind, is included. The Apostle stresses this distinction in accurate terms when he says to the Thessalonians, "Ye turned to God from idols to serve the living and true God" (1 Thess. 1:9). This text provides no comfort for those who contend that people must first, in real contrition, turn from idols—which might terminate at that point—and afterwards, as a second and separate act, turn to God. The text recognizes but one act—"Ye turned to God from idols"—and that is an act of faith alone.

Those who stress repentance as a second requirement along with believing, inadvertently disclose that, in their conception, the problem of personal sin is all that enters into salvation. The sin nature must also be dealt with; yet that is not a legitimate subject of repentance. Salvation contemplates many vast issues and the adjustment of the issue of personal sin, though included, is but a small portion of the whole. Acts 26:18, sometimes drafted in proof of the idea that the unsaved must do various things in order to be saved, rather enumerates various things which are wrought for him in the saving power of God.

3. THE RELATION OF REPENTANCE TO COVENANT PEOPLE. The term *covenant people* is broad in its application. It includes Israel, who are under Jehovah's unalterable covenants and yet are to be objects of another, new covenant (Jer. 31:31–34), and the Church, composed of all believers of the present age, who are also now the objects of that new covenant made in Christ's blood (Matt. 26:28; 1 Cor. 11:25). A covenant implies relationship because it secures a right relation to God in matters belonging within the bounds of the covenant. A covenant that is unconditional, as the above-named covenants are, is not affected by any human elements, nor is it changeable even by God Himself. However, the *fact* of a covenant and the experience of its blessings are two different things. It is possible to be under the provisions of an unconditional covenant and to fail for the time being to enjoy its blessings because of sin. When sin has cast a limitation upon the enjoyment of a covenant and the covenant, being unchangeable, still abides, the issue becomes, not the remaking of the covenant, but the one issue of the sin which mars the relationship. It therefore follows that, for covenant people, there is a need of a divine dealing with the specific sin and a separate and unrelated repentance respecting it. This repentance is expressed by confession to God. Having confessed his sin, David did not pray for his salvation to be restored; he rather prayed for the restoration of "the joy" of his salvation (Ps. 51:12). In like manner, it is joy and fellowship which confession restores for the believer (1 John 1:3–9). When Christ came offering Himself to Israel as their Messiah and announcing their kingdom as at hand, He, with John and the apostles, called on that people to repent in preparation for the proffered kingdom. There was no appeal concerning salvation or the formation

of covenants; it was restoration of the people by a change of mind which would lead them to forsake their sins (Matt. 10:6 ff.). The application of these appeals made to covenant Jews concerning their adjustments within their covenants to individual unregenerate Gentiles, who are "strangers from the covenants" (Eph. 2:12), is a serious error indeed. In like manner, a Christian may repent as a separate act (2 Cor. 7:8–10). The conclusion of the matter is that, while covenant people are appointed to national or personal adjustment to God by repentance as a separate act, there is no basis either in reason or revelation for the demand to be made that an unregenerate person in this age must add a covenant person's repentance to faith in order to be saved.

4. THE ABSENCE OF THE DEMAND FOR REPENTANCE FROM SALVATION SCRIPTURES. Upwards of 115 New Testament passages condition salvation on *believing,* and fully 35 passages condition salvation on *faith,* which latter word in this use of it is an exact synonym of the former. These portions of Scripture, totaling about 150 in all, include practically all that the New Testament declares on the matter of the human responsibility in salvation; yet each one of these texts omits any reference to repentance as a separate act. This fact, easily verified, cannot but bear enormous weight with any candid mind. In like manner, the Gospel by John, which is written to present Christ as the object of faith unto eternal life, does not once employ the word *repentance.* Similarly, the Epistle to the Romans, which is the complete analysis of all that enters into the whole plan of salvation by grace, does not use the word *repentance* in connection with the saving of a soul, except in 2:4 where repentance is equivalent to salvation itself. When the Apostle Paul and his companion, Silas, made reply to the jailer concerning what he should do to be saved, they said, "Believe on the Lord Jesus Christ, and thou shalt be saved" (Acts 16:31). This reply, it is evident, fails to recognize the necessity of repentance in addition to believing. From this overwhelming mass of irrefutable evidence, it is clear that the New Testament does not impose repentance upon the unsaved as a condition of salvation. The Gospel by John with its direct words from the lips of Christ, the Epistle to the Romans with its exhaustive treatment of the theme in question, the Apostle Paul, and the whole array of 150 New Testament passages which are the total of the divine instruction, are incomplete and misleading if repentance must be accorded a place separate from, and independent of, believing. No thoughtful person would attempt to defend such a notion against such odds, and those who have thus undertaken doubtless have done so without weighing

the evidence or considering the untenable position which they assume.

5. THE SIGNIFICANCE OF REPENTANCE IN SPECIFIC PASSAGES. When entering upon this phase of this study, it is first necessary to eliminate all portions of the New Testament which introduce the word *repentance* in its relation to covenant people. There are, likewise, passages which employ the word *repentance* as a synonym of believing (cf. Acts 17:30; Rom. 2:4; 2 Tim. 2:25; 2 Pet. 3:9). Also, there are passages which refer to a change of mind (Acts 8:22; 11:18; Heb. 6:1, 6; 12:17; Rev. 9:20, etc.). Yet, again, consideration must be accorded three passages related to Israel which are often misapplied (Acts 2:38; 3:19; 5:31). There are references to John's baptism, which was unto repentance, that are outside the Synoptics (Acts 13:24; 19:4).

Four passages deserve more extended consideration, namely:

Luke 24:47. "And that repentance and remission of sins should be preached in his name among all nations, beginning at Jerusalem."

It will be seen that repentance is not in itself equivalent to believing or faith, though, being included in believing, is used here as a synonym of the word *believe*. Likewise, it is to be recognized that "remission of sins" is not all that is proffered in salvation, though the phrase may serve that purpose in this instance. Above all, the passage does not require human obligations with respect to salvation. Repentance, which here represents believing, leads to remission of sin.

Acts 11:18. "When they heard these things, they held their peace, and glorified God, saying, Then hath God also to the Gentiles granted repentance unto life."

Again repentance, which is included in believing, serves as a synonym for the word *belief*. The Gentiles, as always, attain to spiritual life by faith, the all-important and essential change of mind. It is also true that the passage does not prescribe two things which are necessary to salvation (cf. vs. 17).

Acts 20:21. "Testifying both to the Jews, and also to the Greeks, repentance toward God, and faith toward our Lord Jesus Christ."

First, though unrelated to the course of this argument, it is important to note that the Apostle here places Jews on the same level with Gentiles, and both are objects of divine grace. The Jew with his incomparable background or the Gentile with his heathen ignorance, each, must undergo a change of mind respecting God. Until they are aware of God's gracious purpose, there can be no reception of the idea of saving faith. It is quite possible to recognize God's purpose, as many do, and not receive Christ as Savior. In other words, repentance toward God could not itself constitute, in this case, the equivalent of "faith toward our Lord Jesus Christ," though it may prepare for that faith. The introduction of the two Persons of the Godhead is significant, and that Christ is the sole object of faith is also most vital. Those who would insist that there are here two human obligations unto salvation are reminded again of the 150 portions in which such a twofold requirement is omitted.

Acts 26:20. "But shewed first unto them of Damascus, and at Jerusalem, and throughout all the coasts of Judaea, and then to the Gentiles, that they should repent and turn to God, and do works meet for repentance."

Again, both Jews and Gentiles are addressed as on the same footing before God. Two obligations are named here, in order that spiritual results may be secured—those to "repent and turn to God." The passage would sustain the Arminian view if repentance were, as they assert, a sorrow for sin; but if the word is given its correct meaning, namely, *a change of mind*, there is no difficulty. The call is for a change of mind which turns to God. This passage, also, has its equivalent in 1 Thessalonians 1:9, "Ye turned to God from idols."

CONCLUSION

In the foregoing, an attempt has been made to demonstrate that the Biblical doctrine of repentance offers no objection to the truth that salvation is by grace through faith apart from every suggestion of human works or merit. It is asserted that repentance, which is a change of mind, enters of necessity into the very act of believing on Christ, since one cannot turn to Christ from other objects of confidence without that change of mind. Upwards of 150 texts—including all of the greatest gospel invitations—limit the human responsibility in salvation to believing or to faith. To this simple requirement nothing could be added if the glories of grace are to be preserved.

II. BELIEVE AND CONFESS CHRIST

The ambition to secure apparent results and the sincere desire to make decisions for Christ to be definite have prompted preachers in their general appeals to insist upon a public confession of Christ on the part of those who would be saved. To all practical purposes and in the majority of instances these confessions are, in the minds of the unsaved, coupled with saving faith and seem, as presented, to be of equal importance with that faith. This demand upon the unsaved is justified, if justified at all, upon two texts of Scripture which should have consideration:

1. SCRIPTURE BEARING ON CONFESSION OF CHRIST. *Matthew 10:32.* "Whosoever therefore shall confess me before men, him will I confess also before my Father which is in heaven."

This verse, which occurs in the midst of Christ's kingdom teachings and as a part of His instructions to His disciples whom He is sending forth with a restricted message to Israel (cf. vss. 5–7) and which was to be accompanied by stupendous miracles (cf. vs. 8) such as were never committed to preachers in the present age, applies, primarily, to these disciples themselves in respect to their faithful delivery of this kingdom proclamation, and could be extended in its appeal only to the Israelites to whom they were sent. The carelessness which assumes that this Scripture presents a condition of salvation for a Jew or Gentile in the present age is deplorable indeed.

Romans 10:9–10. "That if thou shalt confess with thy mouth the Lord Jesus, and shalt believe in thine heart that God hath raised him from the dead, thou shalt be saved. For with the heart man believeth unto righteousness; and with the mouth confession is made unto salvation."

This message, falling as it does within the specific teachings which belong primarily to the way of salvation by grace, is worthy of more consideration. The force of the positive statement in verse 9, "If thou shalt confess with thy mouth the Lord Jesus, and shalt believe in thine heart that God hath raised him from the dead, thou shalt be saved," is explained in verse 10: "For with the heart man believeth unto righteousness; and with the mouth confession is made unto salvation." In the latter verse the true meaning and use of the word "confess" is suggested. Of this word in this same passage the late Dr. Arthur T. Pierson wrote: "That word means to speak out of a like nature to one another. I believe and receive the love of God. In receiving His love I receive His life, in receiving His life I receive His nature, and His nature in me naturally expresses itself according to His will. That is confession. Alexander Maclaren has said: 'Men do not light a candle and put it under a bushel, because the candle would either go out or burn the bushel.' You must have vent for life, light, and love, or how can they abide? And a confession of Christ Jesus as Lord is the answer of the new life of God received. In receiving love, you are born of God, and, being born of God, you cry, 'Abba, Father,' which is but the Aramaic word for 'Papa'—syllables which can be pronounced before there are any teeth, because they are made with the gums and lips—the first word of a new-born soul, born of God, knowing God, and out of a like nature with God speaking in the language of a child."

The two activities named in these verses are each expanded with respect to their meaning in the immediate context which follows. Of believing it is said: "For the scripture saith, Whosoever believeth on him shall not be ashamed. For there is no difference between the Jew and the Greek" (vss. 11–12). Salvation is promised to both Jew and Greek (though in his case a Gentile) on the one condition that they believe. Such, indeed, shall not be ashamed. Of confession it is said: "For the same Lord over all is rich unto all that call upon him. For whosoever shall call upon the name of the Lord shall be saved" (vss. 12–13). It cannot be unobserved that the confession of verses 9 and 10 is declared to be a calling on the name of the Lord. In other words, this confession is that unavoidable acknowledgment to God on the part of the one who is exercising saving faith, that he accepts Christ as his Savior. As Abraham *amened* the promise of God—not a mere unresponsive believing (Gen. 15:6; Rom. 4:3), so the trusting soul responds to the promise which God proffers of salvation through Christ.

2. Two CONCLUSIVE REASONS. There are two convincing reasons why the Scripture under consideration does not present two human responsibilities in relation to salvation by grace.

a. To claim that a public confession of Christ as Savior is required in addition to believing on Christ, is to contend that 150 passages in which believing alone appears are incomplete and to that extent misleading. A certain type of mind, however, seems able to construct all its confidence on an erroneous interpretation of one passage and to be uninfluenced by the overwhelming body of Scripture which contradicts that interpretation.

b. To require a public confession of Christ as a prerequisite to salvation by grace is to discredit the salvation of an innumerable company who have been saved under circumstances which precluded any public action.

CONCLUSION

Confession of Christ is a Christian's privilege and duty and may be undertaken at the moment one is saved, but it is not a condition of salvation by grace, else works of merit intrude where only the work of God reigns.

III. BELIEVE AND BE BAPTIZED

In any discussion respecting the word βαπτίζω it must be recognized that this term is used in the New Testament to represent two different things—a real baptism by the Spirit of God by which the believer is joined in union to Christ and is in Christ, and a ritual baptism with water. John distinguished these when he said, "I indeed baptize you with water unto repentance: but he that cometh after me is mightier than I, whose shoes I am not worthy to bear; he shall baptize you with the Holy Ghost, and with fire" (Matt. 3:11). Though this word sustains a primary and secondary meaning and these are closely related ideas, the fact that the same identical word is used for both real and ritual baptism suggests an affiliation between the two ideas with which this word is associated. In fact, Ephesians 4:5 declares that there is but one baptism. The contemplation of these facts respecting this word is essential to a right understanding of the theme under discussion. The question naturally arises when it is asserted that one must believe and be baptized, whether a real or a ritual baptism is in view. There are two passages demanding attention:

Mark 16:15–16. "And he said unto them, Go ye into all the world, and preach the gospel to every creature. He that believeth and is baptized shall be saved; but he that believeth not shall be damned."

A strange inattention to the evidence which serves as proof that reference is made in this text to real baptism by the Spirit, has characterized the interpretation of the passage. This evidence should at least be weighed for all that it is. Should it prove upon examination that reference is made to real baptism by the Spirit, which baptism is essential to salvation, the difficulty of a supposed regenerating baptism is immediately dismissed. Dr. James W. Dale, in his *Christic and Patristic Baptism* (pp. 392–94), has discussed this vital issue in an extended argument. He writes:

All, so far as I am aware, who interpret the language of the Evangelist as indicating a ritual baptism, do so without having examined the question—"May not this be the *real* baptism by the Holy Spirit and not *ritual* baptism with water?" This vital issue has been assumed without investigation, and determined against the real baptism of the Scriptures, without a hearing. Such assumption is neither grounded in necessity, nor in the warrant of Scripture; whether regarded in its general teaching or in that of this particular passage. That there is no necessity for limiting the baptism of this passage to a rite is obvious, because the Scriptures furnish us with a real baptism by the Spirit, as well as with its symbol ritual baptism, from which to choose. There is no scriptural warrant in the general teaching of the Bible for identifying a *rite* with salvation; nor can such warrant be assumed in this particular passage (which does identify *baptism* and salvation), because there is no evidence on the face of the passage to show, that the baptism is ritual with water, rather than real by the Spirit. These points must be universally admitted: 1. The passage does not declare a ritual baptism by express statement; 2. It contains no statement which involves a ritual baptism as a necessary inference; 3. The Scriptures present a real and a ritual baptism, by the one or the other of which to meet the exigencies of any elliptically stated baptism; 4. That baptism which meets, in its scripturally defined nature and power, the requirements of any particular passage, must be the baptism designed by such passage. We reject ritual baptism from all direct connection with this passage, in general, because, the passage treats of salvation and its conditions (belief and baptism). All out of the Papal church admit, that ritual baptism has not the same breadth with belief as a condition of salvation, and are, therefore, compelled to introduce exceptions for which no provision is made in the terms of this passage. We accept the real baptism by the Holy Spirit as the sole baptism directly contemplated by this passage, in general, because, it meets in the most absolute and unlimited manner *as a condition of salvation* the obvious requirement on the face of the passage, having the same breadth with belief, and universally present in every case of salvation. We accept this view in particular: Because it makes the use of "baptized" harmonious with the associate terms, "believeth" and "saved." The use of these terms, as well as "baptized," is elliptical. "Believe" has in the New Testament a double usage; the one limited to the action of the intellect, as, "the devils believe and tremble"; the other embraces and controls the affections of the heart, as, "with the heart we believe unto righteousness." It is the higher form of "belief" that is universally recognized as belonging to this passage. "Saved," also, is used in the New Testament, with a double application; as of the body, "all hope that we should be saved was taken away"; and of the soul, "He shall save his people from their sins." Again it is this higher salvation that is accepted without question. So, "baptized" is used in a lower and a higher meaning; applied in the one case to the body, as "I baptize you with water"; and in the other case applied to the soul, as "He shall baptize you with the Holy Ghost." By what just reasoning, now, can "believeth," and "saved," be taken in the highest sense, and "baptized," in the same sentence and in the same construction, be brought down to the lowest? We object to such diversity of interpretation as unnatural and without any just support. The only tenable supply of the ellipsis must be, "He that believeth" (with the heart upon Christ), "and is baptized" (by the Holy Ghost into Christ) "shall be saved" (by the redemption of Christ). The construction allows and the case requires, that a relation of dependence and unity subsist between "believeth" and "baptized." There is evidently some *vinculum* binding these words and the ideas which they represent, together. MIDDLETON (Greek article, *in loco*) says: "In the *Complutens*. edit. the second participle has the article, which would materially alter the sense. It would imply, that he who believeth. as well as he who is baptized, shall be saved; whereas the reading of the MSS. insists on the fulfilment of both conditions in every individual." This is true; but it is not all the truth. This faith and this baptism must not only not be disjoined by being assigned to different persons, but they must not be disjoined by being assigned to different spheres, the one spiritual and the other physical; and being conjoined, in like spiritual nature, and meeting together in the same person, the whole truth requires, that they shall be recognized not as two distinct things existing harmoniously together, but as bearing to each other the intimate and essential relation of cause and effect, that is to say, the baptism is a consequence proceeding from the belief.

Believing has the influence over the soul, through the power of God in accordance with His promise in the gospel, of bringing the one who believes into the estate of salvation with all its values which are received from Christ. The new relation to Christ of being in Him is wrought by the Holy Spirit's baptism, and it could not be absent in the case of any true salvation. On the other hand, all who have been saved have been saved quite apart from ritual baptism. The form of speech which this text presents is common in the Bible, namely, that of passing from the main subject to one of the features belonging to that subject, as, "Thou shalt be dumb, and not able to speak" (Luke 1:20). The word *dumb* is amplified by the words *not able to speak*. In the text in question, the word *believeth* is amplified by the words *and is baptized*, and with reference to real baptism which is an integral part of salvation.

Acts 2:38. "Then Peter said unto them, Repent, and be baptized every one of you in the name of Jesus Christ for the remission of sins, and ye shall receive the gift of the Holy Ghost."

A very general impression obtains among informed students of the Sacred Text that the translation of this passage is injured by the rendering of two prepositions ἐπί and εἰς by the words *in* and *for*. That ἐπί is better translated *upon*, and εἰς is better rendered *into* would hardly be contested. To this may be added the demand of some worthy scholars that the word *believing* should be supplied, which would give the following rendering: "Repent, and be baptized every one of you, [believing] upon the name of Jesus Christ into the remission of sins." By so much the passage harmonizes with all other Scripture, which, from the interpreter's standpoint, is imperative (2 Pet. 1:20); and the remission of sins—here equivalent to personal salvation—is made to depend not upon repentance or baptism.

Dr. J. W. Dale is convinced that it is real baptism by the Spirit which is referred to here and also in verse 41. He proposes that the same arguments which he advanced to prove that Mark 16:15–16 refers to real baptism by the Spirit serve as valid evidence in Acts 2:38, 41. He

feels a particular relief that there is no need, according to this interpretation, of defending the idea that 3,000 people were baptized by
ritual baptism in what could have been but slightly more than half a
day and as a surprise necessity for which preparations could not have
been made either by the candidates or administrators, whereas, Dr.
Dale contends, to reckon this baptism to have been real and that which
unavoidably does enter into the salvation of every soul and does not
follow after as a mere testimony, is to encounter no insuperable difficulty whatever. Most of all, he points out, by this interpretation this
passage is rescued from the misinterpretation which exalts ritual baptism to the point of being all but essential to salvation.

It is significant that the Apostle Peter follows this exhortation contained in Acts 2:38 with a promise respecting the reception of the Holy
Spirit. In the disproportionate emphasis which has been placed on
ritual baptism—doubtless stimulated by disagreement on its mode—
the great undertaking of the Spirit in real baptism which conditions the
believer's standing before God and engenders the true motive for Christian character and service, has been slighted to the point that many
apparently are unaware of its existence. Such a situation is not without
precedent. At Ephesus the Apostle Paul found certain men who were
resting their confidence in "John's baptism," who confessed "We have
not so much as heard whether there be any Holy Ghost" (Acts 19:1–3).
In other words, the student would do well to note that the truth regarding the baptism with the Spirit is itself more important than the Christian public, led by sectarian teachers, supposes it to be.

CONCLUSION

The above examination of two passages, on which the idea of baptismal regeneration is made to rest, has sought to demonstrate that
ritual baptism, however administered, is not a condition which is to be
added to believing as a necessary step in salvation.

IV. BELIEVE AND SURRENDER TO GOD

On account of its subtlety due to its pious character, no confusing
intrusion into the doctrine that salvation is conditioned alone upon believing is more effective than the added demand that the unsaved must
dedicate themselves to do God's will in their daily life, as well as to
believe upon Christ. The desirability of a dedication to God on the part

of every believer is obvious, and is so stressed in the Sacred Text that many sincere people who are inattentive to doctrine are easily led to suppose that this same dedication, which is *voluntary* in the case of the believer, is *imperative* in the case of the unsaved. This aspect of this general theme may be approached under three considerations of it: (1) the incapacity of the unsaved, (2) what is involved, and (3) the preacher's responsibility.

1. THE INCAPACITY OF THE UNSAVED. The Arminian notion that through the reception of a so-called common grace anyone is competent to accept Christ as Savior if he will, is a mild assumption compared with the idea that the unregenerate person, with no common or uncommon grace proffered, is able to dedicate his life to God. Much has been written on previous pages regarding the overwhelming testimony of the Bible to the utter inability and spiritual death of the unsaved. They are shut up to the one message that Christ is their Savior; and they cannot accept Him, the Word of God declares, unless illuminated to that end by the Holy Spirit. Saving faith is not a possession of all men but is imparted specifically to those who do believe (Eph. 2:8). As all this is true, it follows that to impose a need to surrender the life to God as an added condition of salvation is most unreasonable. God's call to the unsaved is never said to be unto the Lordship of Christ; it is unto His saving grace. With the reception of the divine nature through the regenerating work of the Spirit, a new understanding and a new capacity to respond to the authority of Christ are gained. Those attending upon these issues in practical ways are aware that a self-dedication taxes the limit of ability even of the most devout believer. The error of imposing Christ's Lordship upon the unsaved is disastrous even though they are not able intelligently to resent it or to remind the preacher of the fact that he, in calling upon them to dedicate their lives, is demanding of them what they have no ability to produce. A destructive heresy is abroad under the name The Oxford Movement, which specializes in this blasting error, except that the promoters of the Movement omit altogether the idea of believing on Christ for salvation and promote exclusively the obligation to surrender to God. They substitute consecration for conversion, faithfulness for faith, and beauty of daily life for believing unto eternal life. As is easily seen, the plan of this movement is to ignore the need of Christ's death as the ground of regeneration and forgiveness, and to promote the wretched heresy that it matters nothing what one believes respecting the Saviorhood of Christ if only the daily life is dedicated to God's service. A pseudo self-dedication to God

is a rare bit of religion with which the unsaved may conjure. The tragedy is that out of such a delusion those who embrace it are likely never to be delivered by a true faith in Christ as Savior. No more complete example could be found today of "the blind leading the blind" than what this Movement presents.

2. WHAT IS INVOLVED. The most subtle, self-satisfying form of works of merit is, after all, found to be an engaging feature in this practice of applying to unbelievers the Lordship of Christ. What more could God expect than that the creatures of His hand should by supposed surrender be attempting to be obedient to Him? In such idealism the darkened mind of the unsaved, no doubt, sees dimly some possible advantage in submitting their lives to the guidance of a Supreme Being—of whom they really know nothing. Such notions are only human adjustments to God and resemble in no way the terms of divine adjustment, which first condemns man and rejects all his supposed merit, and then offers a perfect and eternal salvation to the helpless sinner on no other terms than that he believe on Christ as his Savior.

If the real issue in self-dedication to God is stated in its legitimate though extreme form, the possibility of martyrdom is first in evidence. One who is faithful unto God is enjoined to be faithful unto death (Rev. 2:10). Such, indeed, is a glorious challenge to the devout believer and millions have accepted the challenge and suffered a martyr's death; but would any zealous advocate of the idea that the Lordship of Christ must be applied to the unsaved as a condition of salvation, dare to propose to the unsaved that they must not only believe on Christ but be willing to die a martyr's death? The very proposal of such a question serves only to demonstrate the unwisdom and disregard for revealed truth which this error exhibits.

The unregenerate person, because of his condition in spiritual death, has no ability to desire the things of God (1 Cor. 2:14), or to anticipate what his outlook on life will be after he is saved. It is therefore an error of the first magnitude to divert that feeble ability of the unsaved to exercise a God-given faith for salvation into the unknown and complex spheres of self-dedication, which dedication is the Christian's greatest problem.

3. THE PREACHER'S RESPONSIBILITY. It is the preacher's responsibility, not only to preserve his message to the unsaved from being distorted by issues other than that of simple faith in Christ, but, when speaking to Christians in the presence of the unsaved regarding the issues of Christian character, conduct, and service, to declare plainly

that the truth presented has no application to those who are unsaved. Such a reminder, oft repeated, will not only preserve the unregenerate individuals who are present from the deadly supposition that God is seeking to improve their manner of life rather than to accomplish the salvation of their souls, but will also create in their minds the so important impression that they are, in the sight of God, hopelessly condemned apart from Christ as Savior. God alone can deal with a situation wherein a large percentage of the members of the church are unsaved, and yet are habitually addressed as though they were saved and on no other basis than that they belong to the church. It is surprising, indeed, that any unsaved person ever gains any right impression respecting his actual relation to God, when he is allowed to believe that he is included in all the appeals which are made to Christians regarding their daily life. If the importance of attention to this wide difference between the saved and the unsaved is not appreciated and respected by the preacher, the fault is nearly unpardonable since the results may easily hinder the salvation of many souls. Next to sound doctrine itself, no more important obligation rests on the preacher than that of preaching the Lordship of Christ to Christians exclusively, and the Saviorhood of Christ to those who are unsaved.

CONCLUSION

A suggestion born of this theme is that in all gospel preaching every reference to the life to be lived beyond regeneration should be avoided as far as possible. To attend to this is not a deception nor a withholding of the truth from those to whom it applies. It is the simple adjustment to the limitation and actual condition of those to whom the gospel is addressed. To such among the unsaved who, because of the weakness and inability which they observe in themselves, are fearful lest they would not "hold out" as Christians, it is desirable to remind them that, in the new relation to Christ which will exist after they receive Him, new abilities will be possessed by which they can live to the glory of God. Such proffered assurance is far removed from the practice of introducing obligations which are exclusively Christian in character and as something to which they must consent in order to be saved. Multitudes of unsaved people have been diverted from the one question of their acceptance of Christ as Savior to other questions regarding amusements and unchristian ways of living. As an unsaved person has no motive or spiritual light by which to face such problems, that person can only be bewildered by these issues. His problem is not one of giving up what in his unsaved state seems normal to him; it is a problem of receiving the Savior with all His salvation.

V. BELIEVE AND CONFESS SIN OR MAKE RESTITUTION

But a moment need be devoted to this error which prevails among certain groups of zealous people. The Scripture employed by advocates of this error is that which applies only to Christians. The passage reads: "If we confess our sins, he is faithful and just to forgive us our sins, and to cleanse us from all unrighteousness" (1 John 1:9). This declaration, as has been seen, is addressed to believers who have sinned and presents the ground on which such may be restored to fellowship with God. The notion that restitution must be made before one can be saved is based on the God-dishonoring theory that salvation is only for good people, and that the sinner must divest himself of that which is evil before he can be saved. In other words, God is not propitious respecting sin; He is propitious toward those only who have prepared themselves for His presence and fellowship. Over against this, the truth is ignored that the unregenerate person cannot improve his fallen condition and, if he could, he would be bringing merit to God where merit is wholly excluded to the end that grace may abound and be magnified through all eternity. The preacher must ever be on his guard to discourage the tendency of the natural man to move along lines of reformation rather than regeneration. Those who are serious regarding their lost estate are best helped by that body of truth which declares that God, through Christ, must save and will save from all sin; that He must and will deal with the very nature which sins; and that He must and will rescue men from their estate under sin. There are various ways by which the natural man proposes to be saved and yet retain his dignity and supposed worthiness, and one of these is the contention that sin must be confessed and restitution made as a human requirement in salvation. It is God who justifies the ungodly (Rom. 4:5); it is while men are "enemies, sinners, and without strength" that Christ died for them (Rom. 5:6–10); and all their unworthiness is accounted for by Christ in His death. There is a duty belonging only to Christians—to set things right after they are saved—and there should be no neglect of that responsibility. It therefore remains true that those who are saved are saved on the one condition of believing upon Christ.

VI. BELIEVE AND IMPLORE GOD TO SAVE

None of the errors being considered seems more reasonable than this, and none strikes a more deadly blow at the foundation of divine grace. The error includes the claim that the sinner must "seek the Lord," or that he must plead with God to be merciful. These two conceptions, though nearly identical, should be considered separately.

1. "SEEK YE THE LORD." This phrase, quoted from Isaiah 55:6, represents Jehovah's invitation to His covenant people, Israel, who have wandered from their place of rightful blessings under His covenants, to return to Him. It was appointed to that people to "seek the LORD while he may be found" and to "call upon him while he is near"; but the gospel of the grace of God in the present age declares to Jew and Gentile alike that "there is none that seeketh after God" (Rom. 3:11), and that "the Son of man is come to seek and to save that which was lost" (Luke 19:10). This declaration that in this age there are none who seek the Lord, accords with the testimony of the New Testament relative to the incapacity of those who are lost to turn to God. Apart from the new birth, the unsaved "cannot see the kingdom of God" (John 3:3), their minds are blinded by Satan (2 Cor. 4:3–4), and they can exercise faith toward God only as they are enabled to do so by the Holy Spirit (Eph. 2:8). In the light of these revelations, there is little ground for the hope that the unsaved will "seek the Lord," and, what is far more essential to the right understanding of the way of salvation by grace, the unsaved are not asked to seek the Lord. If this is true, the unsaved should never be placed in the position of those who must discover God or prevail upon Him to be gracious.

2. BELIEVE AND PRAY. The question which arises at this point is one of whether God is propitious. If He is propitious, there remains no occasion for the unsaved to try to find Him, to wait until He is on "the giving hand," or to implore Him to save. He is propitious to an infinite degree and the problem confronting the mind of man is one of adjustment to that revelation. The transforming effect of the truth that God is propitious penetrates every phase of Soteriology. His flood tide of blessing—all that is impelled by infinite love—awaits, not the imploring, prevailing appeal that might move one to be gracious, but rather it awaits the simple willingness on the part of men to *receive* what He has already provided and is free to bestow in and through His Son, the Savior.

Attention has been called in an earlier discussion to the fact that salvation begins in the heart of God and is precisely what His infinite love demands and ordains. Its whole scope and extent is the reflection of that immeasurable love. It embraces all that infinity can produce. The sinner's plight is serious indeed and the benefits he receives in saving grace cannot be estimated; but all this together is secondary compared with the satisfaction which God's great love demands. As before stated, but two obstacles could hinder the satisfaction of divine love—the sin of the creature He loves and the will of that creature. As the Creator of all things, even these obstacles take their place in the divine decree which ordained all things that exist. Nevertheless, He has, as the only One who could do it, met by the sacrifice of His Son the obstacle which sin imposed, and He, too, secures the glad cooperation of the human will. The effect of the death of His Son is to render God righteously free to act for those whom He loves, and that freedom for love to act is propitiation. Therefore, it must be again asserted that God is propitious. It is infinite love that now invites the sinner to eternal glories, and it is infinite love that awaits the sinner's response to that invitation.

With this marvelous revelation in view, there is no place left for the idea that the sinner must "seek the Lord," or that the sinner must plead with God to be merciful and kind. No burden rests on the unsaved to persuade God to be good; the challenge of the gospel is for the unsaved to believe that God is good. Since these great truths are revealed only in the Word of God, the unsaved are enjoined to believe God's Word, and the Scriptures hold a large share in the divine undertaking of bringing men to salvation (John 3:5). It is common, however, for some who, with great passion of soul, attempt to preach the gospel, so to fail in the apprehension of the divine propitiation that they imply that salvation is secured by entreating God, and by so much the value of Christ's mediation in behalf of the sinner is nullified.

The example of the prayer of the publican is usually cited as the best of reasons for urging the unsaved to plead with God for His mercy and salvation. What, it is asked, could be more appropriate than that the unsaved should pray as did the publican, "God be merciful to me a sinner" (Luke 18:13)? The appeal on the part of the publican is assumed to be the norm for all sinners, though, in reality, it contradicts the very truth of the gospel of divine grace. The incident must be examined carefully. It is essential to note that the publican—a Jew of the Old Testament order and praying in the temple according to the re-

quirements of a Jew in the temple—did not use the word *merciful*—
which word is properly associated with the idea of kindness, bighearted-
ness, leniency, and generosity. According to the original text, which in
the Authorized Version is too freely translated, the publican said, "God
be propitiated to me the sinner." The word ἱλάσκομαι, which means
"to make propitiation," appears in the text. There is a wide difference
between the word *merciful* with all its implications and the word
propitiation. By the use of the word *merciful* the impression is conveyed
that the publican pleaded with God to be magnanimous. By the use of
the word *propitiation*—if comprehended at all—the impression is conveyed that the publican asked God to cover his sins in such a way as to
dispose of them, yet, at the same time, to do this in a way that would
protect His own holiness from complicity with his sins. If the publican
did as Jews were accustomed to do in his day when they went into the
temple to pray, he left a sacrifice at the altar. It is probable that he
could see the smoke of that sacrifice ascending as he prayed. What he
prayed was strictly proper for a Jew of his time to pray under those
circumstances. However, his prayer would be most unfitting on this side
of the cross of Christ. With reference to the word *merciful*, it was not
in the publican's prayer nor would it be a proper word for a penitent to
use, on either side of the cross. God cannot be merciful to sin in the
sense that He treats it lightly, whether it be in one age or another. But
with reference to the word *propitiation* and its implications, that word
was justified in the age before Christ died and when sin was covered
by sacrifices which the sinner provided. It was suitable for the publican,
having provided his own sacrifice, to ask that his sacrifice be accepted
and himself absolved. However, on this side of the cross when Christ
has died and secured propitiation and it is established perfectly forever,
nothing could be more an outraging of that priceless truth upon which
the gospel rests than to implore God to be propitious. Such prayers may
be enjoined through ignorance, but the wrong is immeasurable. When
this prayer is made, even for God to be propitious, there is a direct assumption expressed that God is *not* propitious, and to that extent the
petitioner is asking God to do something more effective than the thing
He has done in giving His Son as a sacrifice for sin. A moment's consideration would disclose the immeasurable wrong that is committed when
God is asked to be propitious, when, at the infinite cost of the death of
His Son, He is propitious. The truth that God is propitious constitutes
the very heart of the gospel of divine grace, and the one who does not
recognize this and sees no impropriety in the use of the publican's prayer

today has yet to comprehend what is the first principle in the plan of salvation through Christ. Men are not saved by asking God to be good, or merciful, or propitious; they are saved when they believe God has been good and merciful enough to provide a propitiating Savior. The sinner is saved, not because he prevails on God to withhold from him the blow of judgment that is due him for his sin, but because he believes that that blow has fallen on his Substitute. If it is thought that all this is but a mere theological distinction and that after all God is love and the sinner will be treated in love, consideration should be given to the fact that it was for the very purpose of providing a righteous ground for salvation of sinners that the Son of God became incarnate, that He died, and that He arose from the dead. To imply that all this—and there is no salvation apart from it—is only a theological speculation, is to reject the whole plan of salvation through a Savior and to assume to stand before God, who is Consuming Fire, without shelter, shield, or surety.

In consummating this section on the human terms which condition the salvation of a soul, it may be restated:

a. Every feature of man's salvation from the divine election in past ages and on through successive steps—the sacrifice of the Savior, the enlightenment by the Spirit, the immediate saving work of God in its manifold achievements, the keeping work of the Father, the Son, and the Spirit, the delivering work of the Spirit, the empowering work of the Spirit, and the final perfecting and presenting in glory—is all a work so supernatural that God alone can effect it, and, therefore, the only relation which man can sustain to it is to trust God to do it. Such a dependence is not only reasonable, but is all and only that which God requires on the human side for the eternal salvation of a soul. That human trust acknowledges that, according to revelation, God can deal righteously with sinners on the ground of the death of His Son for them. The sinner thus trusts in the Saviorhood of Christ.

b. It has been asserted that the primary divine purpose in saving a soul is the satisfying of infinite divine love for that soul and the exercise of the attribute of sovereign grace. Should the slightest human work of merit be allowed to intrude into this great divine undertaking, the purpose of manifesting divine grace would be shattered. It therefore follows that, of necessity, men are saved by believing apart from every form of human worthiness.

c. In the preceding pages it is also pointed out that the New Testament declares directly and without complication in at least 150 passages that men are saved upon the sole principle of faith; and, in this connection, it has been demonstrated that it is not a matter of believing and repenting, of believing and confessing Christ, of believing and being baptized, of believing and surrender to God, of believing and confessing sin, or of believing and pleading with God for salvation, but it is believing alone. Such belief is apart from works (Rom. 4:5), it is a committal of one's self to Christ (2 Tim. 1:12), and it is a definite turning—an act of the will—to God from every other confidence (1 Thess. 1:9).

"Believe on the Lord Jesus Christ, and thou shalt be saved."

EPILOGUE

MUCH HAS BEEN required and much has been undertaken in this analysis of that which enters into the provision, plan, and purpose of the triune God for the salvation of fallen men. The entire Word of God makes its contribution to this vast theme; yet it has pleased God to compress into one terse saying the whole divine revelation respecting Soteriology. This saying is the message of the most familiar text in the Bible and is universally recognized as transcendent by people of every nation and tongue to whom the Word of God has gone. Such a universal appraisement of one Biblical utterance becomes decisive evidence that this Scripture answers more completely and perfectly than any other the deepest needs and desires of the human heart.

It is written:

> For God so loved the world,
> That he gave his only begotten Son,
> That whosoever believeth in him
> Should not perish,
> But have everlasting life.

It will be observed that every major feature of Soteriology is present in this incomparable text and that it is properly marshaled as a proof text in behalf of each of these doctrines.

(a) "God so loved the world." At once and with sublime propriety the whole enterprise of saving men is declared to arise in the love of God. Indeed, it is the ruined *cosmos* world which He loves; but this truth only enhances the lofty, yet gracious, character of that love. This is not a love for an elect company alone—as though the title, *The Cosmos World,* could ever be applied to the elect company who are saved out of it and whom the *cosmos* hates (John 15:18)—but it is a love for the *cosmos* which *hates,* which is *lost,* and which *needs* to be saved (cf. 1 Tim. 2:4; 2 Pet. 3:9). What, indeed, would be the present wretchedness and the future despair of all men were it not for the supreme revelation that "God is love"?

(b) "That he gave his only begotten Son." Here in seven words is found the "unspeakable gift" of the Father, the immeasurable sacrifice of the Son through the eternal Spirit, and the boundless benefit to the sinner. Compressed into this phrase is the whole story of the substitutionary death—both with regard to merit and demerit—and all other achievements of the Savior in His sacrifice upon the cross. The phrase embraces His humiliation, His humanity, His death, His resurrection, and His eternal identification with the human family; so, also, it speaks of all the benefits He became to a lost world and to the redeemed.

(c) "That whosoever believeth in him." By this significant declaration, it is implied that not all will believe and that there is an elect company in view. It is likewise asserted that salvation is through Christ alone, and that it is secured, on the human side, by faith alone uncomplicated by any works of merit.

(d) "Should not perish." The estate of the lost is implied and there is no slight importance to be assigned to the fact that this implication, with all its assurance of eternal woe, fell from the lips of the Son of God into whose hand all future judgment is committed.

(e) "But have everlasting life." Here, as above, the character and the eternal extent of salvation are disclosed, and that eternal life, like every feature of divine grace, is a gift from God.

Thus it is revealed that in this incomparable text is enfolded at least nine of the great doctrines of Soteriology, namely, infinite love, infinite sacrifice for sinners, sovereign election, sovereign grace, unlimited redemption, salvation a work of God, salvation from perdition, eternal security, and salvation by grace through faith alone.

> O Christ, what burdens bowed Thy head!
> Our load was laid on Thee;
> Thou stoodest in the sinner's stead,
> Didst bear all ill for me.
> A Victim led, Thy blood was shed;
> Now there's no load for me.
>
> Death and the curse were in our cup—
> O Christ, 'twas full for Thee;
> But Thou hast drained the last dark drop—
> 'Tis empty now for me.
> That bitter cup—love drank it up;
> Now blessings' draught for me.
>
> Jehovah lifted up His rod—
> O Christ, it fell on Thee!
> Thou wast sore stricken of Thy God;
> There's not one stroke for me.
> Thy tears, Thy blood, beneath it flowed;
> Thy bruising healeth me.

The tempest's awful voice was heard—
   O Christ, it broke on Thee!
Thy open bosom was my ward,
   It braved the storm for me.
Thy form was scarred, Thy visage marred;
   Now cloudless peace for me.

Jehovah bade His sword awake—
   O Christ, it woke 'gainst Thee!
Thy blood the flaming blade must slake;
   Thy heart its sheath must be—
All for my sake, my peace to make;
   Now sleeps that sword for me.

For me, Lord Jesus, Thou hast died,
   And I have died in Thee;
Thou'rt risen: my bands are all untied,
   And now Thou liv'st in me.
When purified, made white, and tried,
   Thy GLORY then for me!